SOCIAL WORKERS

A Canadian Guide

THIRD EDITION

ELAINE J. VAYDA
M.S.W.
Associate Professor
York University
School of Social Work

MARY T. SATTERFIELD
M.S.W., LL.B.
of the Ontario Bar

CARSWELL
Thomson Professional Publishing

The paper used in this publication meets the minimum requirements of American National Standard for Information Sciences - Permanence of Paper for Printed Library Materials, ANSI Z39.48-1984.

Canadian Cataloguing in Publication Data

Vayda, Elaine J., 1927-
Law for social workers : a Canadian guide

3rd ed.
Includes bibliographical references and index.
ISBN 0-459-23884-1 (bound) ISBN 0-459-23878-7 (pbk.)

1. Law — Canada. 2. Social workers — Canada.
I. Satterfield, Mary T., 1930- . II. Title.

KE450.S6V39 1997 349.71'024362 C97-932511-0
KF390.S6V39 1997

Typesetting: Video Text Inc., Barrie, Ontario, Canada

CARSWELL
Thomson Professional Publishing

One Corporate Plaza, 2075 Kennedy Road, Scarborough, Ontario M1T 3V4
Customer Service:
Toronto 1-416-609-3800
Elsewhere in Canada/U.S. 1-800-387-5164
Fax 1-416-298-5094

Preface

Our decision to embark on a third edition of this book was influenced by more than the need to update cases and legislation. We wanted to reframe our definition of social law as a category which, unlike corporate or commercial law, cannot be contained easily within the traditional legal subject classifications. Social law, which deals with human social activity, follows the human developmental life cycle, both individual and family, and acts to define, limit, protect, remedy, and punish, both at the time of normal transitional life events and unanticipated, critical events. The former include birth, school entry, marriage, retirement and planning for aging, death, while the latter include separation, divorce, loss of employment or shelter, need for financial and social assistance, involvement in criminal activity, and physical and mental illness and incapacity.

Law is, by definition, objective and specific in its application as well as reflective of fixed time beliefs, perceptions, and normative standards. It cannot adjust easily to complexities embedded in culture, gender, age, physical or emotional dysfunction. Nor can it always adjust to include situational circumstances in making decisions that balance communal and individual social needs.

It is our intent in this edition to highlight the uneasy fit of legal process to human diversity. We want to inform and challenge human service workers. The adversarial approach to the search for justice is seen to be too blunt to serve well either specific persons or the wellbeing of the social community. Alternate approaches such as dispute resolution, mediation and arbitration have proven to be effective substitutions for traditional courtroom confrontations.

New questions have emerged to vex us, for example, how to define the family in the determination of rights, privileges, and exclusions and how to select those factors that should be given weight in accessing the best interests of children. Other current dilemmas include deciding whether and in what circumstances adoptions should be open, how to cope with new reproductive technology, how to define and deal with young offenders, determining what rights people have in regard to anticipating how they wish to be treated if they should fall ill and lose the ability to participate in decision-making, and defining the boundaries of the right of persons with mental illness to refuse treatment.

In order to focus on these issues, to adopt a developmental perspective and structure, and to highlight the strain between social complexities and legal process, we have added new material, rearranged and redefined sections, and cited new case law and legislation.

Finally, we hope to foster a critical analysis of both law and social work theory and practice. Postmodernists would argue that laws and theories can be deconstructed to reveal presuppositions or a world view that is biased to favour the privileged in any society. Those who are more marginal to a society, frequently children or persons less privileged by reason of race, gender, ethnicity, social class, or physical or mental disability can be at risk from those same laws or practices. Equity, justice, and mutual caring are requisites for a healthy society. To achieve these goals, society requires ongoing challenge from those who work at the interface between social work and law. Both social workers and lawyers are advocates for achieving justice and fair treatment amid competing and colliding interests and perceptions. Both professions have a responsibility to practice within a critical framework, to use advocacy to redress inequity and to promote general awareness of inequity. We will attempt to address these questions throughout the book.

A unifying aspect of both social work and legal education is the use of a case approach to clients' problems and remedies. Whenever possible, cases will be used for illustration. It is assumed the reader is aware of the psycho-social issues which need attention. The legal issues arising from the situation will be emphasized, rather than the social work perspective.

The legal cases presented throughout this book are included to give the reader a sense of how decisions are reached. The details in the cases will be similar in some respects to situations affecting the reader's clients. Published legal cases identify by name the parties to the dispute, a practice which may cause discomfort to social workers who are required to protect the identity of clients.

Our intent is not to suggest that social workers can replace legal counsel. Rather, our hope is to encourage social workers to help clients identify their rights and responsibilities, to help them to decide when legal assistance should be sought, to help them to locate appropriate assistance and to provide informed support for clients involved in legal proceedings.

Acknowledgments

We were encouraged always by the responses of colleagues across the country who urged us to complete this second edition. Questions, concerns and issues expressed by colleagues and students kept us involved in and mindful of our primary purpose in updating material and developing legal and social issues that have become relevant since the first edition.

We are grateful to Yvonne McInnis who typed pages of scrawled additions and insertions and to our editors at Carswell for all their assistance.

Finally, to our spouses, Gene and Peter, who gave encouragement and did not complain about weekends and evenings surrendered to the book.

Table of Contents

Part IV Criminal Law

PART I

FUNDAMENTALS

1

Social Work and Law: The Life Cycle of the Family

> The young lawyer in the community legal clinic wrinkled her nose in an expression of mild disdain at the suggestion that social workers and lawyers ought to work together. She pointed out with some vehemence that her clients needed assurance that their interests would be protected to the best of her ability. She argued that social workers represent societal authority and that they serve agency bureaucracy rather than the client's wishes. In an adversarial system, a social worker may often be her client's adversary; therefore, to her, a social worker as advocate was a contradiction in terms.
>
> The social worker, a youth services counsellor, looked worried as he remarked that his 17-year-old client faced a court appearance on a first offence charge of theft. The boy had told him that he could not find a lawyer who would represent him since he had no money and legal aid had turned him down. The social worker said he was fed up with lawyers who are only interested in fees and not in people, especially people who are poor and powerless.

In the last two decades, concern has mounted that the problems of many clients, especially of the poor, have not been well served by either law or social work. For the legal profession, access to legal assistance was recognized as problematic for the disadvantaged. Some lawyers are also aware of the inadequacy of single-issue remedies for complex socio-legal problems. It has been observed that, "No phenomena are absolutely 'legal'; even 'hard law' subjects such as Land Law exist only because a mechanism is needed to achieve certain social ends; they cannot be divorced from the social world in which they operate.[1] Recent casebooks in both law and social work focus on juvenile rights, discrimination in housing and employment, and reflect an interest in welfare, mental health, and divorce and separation mediation. In addition, there is a growing literature on alternatives to adjudicative solutions for individual, family and public interest disputes.[2]

Social work practitioners and educators have recognized that traditional delivery of service has not created significant change in the lives of many recipients. A new generation of social workers is not content to rely on the assessment and treatment of individual and family psychopathology. They have argued for a holistic approach, one in which assessment of a problem demands an ecological scan that not only includes individual and family systems but also a structural analysis of the influence of societal institutions on the definition of problems. For example, institutionalized racism, sexism, and power inequities may be reflected in laws. A biased interpretation of regulations can adversely affect clients' lives. The client's reaction may be powerlessness flowing from these structural defects. This enlarged view requires a broad range of knowledge and strategies for service that can be undertaken with the fullest possible participation of the client. Change in attitude and behaviour of clients may depend upon a perception that internal and external resources are interrelated.[3]

In the last decade, thousands of people from diverse countries and cultures have emigrated to Canada, many fleeing harsh economic and political upheaval. New languages, customs and world views have demanded new services, both legal and social, capable of accommodating language and cultural barriers.

Social work has embraced systems theory for more than a decade and social workers are expected to act as advocate for and with individuals confronting hostile systems as well as advocate on behalf of persons sharing similar life situations. More recent social work theory has suggested other models that focus on social justice, on identification and utilization of client strengths rather than pathology, and on methods of enabling clients to develop empowerment strategies. Another model works with individual or family narratives or life stories that encourages these stories to be perceived differently by acknowledging the authenticity of specific systemic inequities in order that persons may choose to act for appropriate social change.[4]

Knowledge of law is essential for social work practice defined in this way. Phillips has specified four areas about which social workers must be informed. His view is that they need a knowledge of legal aid plans and procedures for fixing eligibility, and the names of specific lawyers who are perceived as sympathetic and interested. They need up-to-date knowledge of welfare entitlements in order to be able to question or challenge a board's decision. They need to understand their roles in court, where they may become involved as witness, as plaintiff, as impartial reporter or *in loco parentis*. Finally, they need to be knowledgeable about the mandate and practice of their agency in regard to rules that are set internally and rules that are statutory and whether and through what procedures rules can be challenged.[5]

Lawyers, whose practices are not devoted primarily to corporate matters, are aware that the need for legal assistance comes at crisis points in the human life cycle. Crises include divorce or separation, death, physical or mental abuse, injury, illness, incapacity to make decisions, threat of eviction, wrongful dismissal, arrest, trial, and incarceration. These critical events may cause temporary decompensation in individual coping ability as well as in emotional control. Persons in these situations may urgently need emergency planning and special resources. At these times, both lawyers and social workers become engaged in the practice of social law. Each requires the assistance and expertise of the other in order to function optimally in the service of the client's best interest. Critical situations where law and social need intersect define the terrain of social law.[6]

It is not only in the response to problems of poverty, human rights, and the environment that the two professions have begun to depart from traditional practice. There has been a growing recognition that the problems of family breakup cannot be left to the judiciary or to the marital therapists for resolution. The social and emotional costs to all concerned far outweigh the considerable legal costs of adversarial resolutions to questions of custody, access, and support. The courtroom may become the last resort for resolution with mediation and pre-trial negotiation the preferred method of dispute resolution between the parties. It has been noted by responsible members of the legal profession that in family law matters the adversary system does not function to the benefit of anyone except perhaps to inflate legal fees, and that the conflict has destructive consequences.[7] In a working paper, the Law Reform Commission observed that " . . . in general the adversary approach promotes a ritualistic and unrealistic approach to family problems."[8] Mediation has become an effective instrument to help families through the crisis of separation and divorce with the least damage to children, parents, and extended family members. Conciliation is a natural climate for lawyers and social workers to develop a working relationship based on mutual respect for each other's expertise.

An obstacle to co-operation between social work and law resides in the distorted and stereotyped views each profession has maintained about the other. It is tempting to disclaim simplistic thinking, but elements of exaggeration are manifest in the respective attitudes of lawyers and social workers. Lawyers have been seen by social workers as rigid, technical, precise, interested in logic and facts but uncomfortable when confronted with human ambiguity.[9] Because many social workers are employed by agencies, lawyers are unwilling to accept them as professionals with a direct accountability to their clients. Social workers are believed to be emotional and imprecise, relying too much on subjective impressions. The difference in attitude of the social worker and lawyer can be demonstrated by looking at the language each uses. Social work language is one using ambiguous words which convey care and welfare; legal language is concerned with proof, precision, and unambiguity. The lawyer is retained to use the law to obtain the client's expressed wishes, while the social worker feels obliged to work for the client's needs as perceived by the worker. These distinctions are often more apparent than real.[10]

It is true that social work agencies for the most part tend to depersonalize their workers. A client is discouraged from requesting the services of a particular worker and instead may receive an appointment with an intake worker before being assigned to an ongoing worker. This practice is viewed by many lawyers as an indication that social work is charity and not a skilled discipline practised through the establishment of a professional relationship requested by the client. To be fair, is legal practice so different? In a large firm which represents clients possessing a Legal Aid Certificate, a client would be just as unlikely to see the lawyer requested and would probably be given an appointment with the most junior associate or articling student. To the general public, however, legal assistance is still identified with individual legal practitioners whereas social work is generally identified with a social agency.

The fact that lawyers and social workers conceptualize in different ways may be demonstrated by speculating on how each might regard a familiar situation.

> Mrs. S. was served notice that she would have to vacate her apartment because the building was to be demolished to make way for an office development. She ignored the notice and refused to communicate with anyone about her plans for moving. A public health nurse gained access and reported that Mrs. S. appeared unkempt, confused and was living in two rooms cluttered with newspapers, cardboard boxes and cartons. Mrs. S. shouted at the nurse that she would not leave her home and ordered her to leave. The nurse noticed a shotgun in a corner of the room and hastily departed. The nurse told the neighbourhood community worker that she feared that Mrs. S. may pose a danger to herself or to others, that she was probably incompetent and may need to be committed to a mental health facility. Mr. P., the community worker, agreed to try to visit Mrs. S. to evaluate the situation. Talking to her through her unopened door, he told her that he was there to help her under-

stand her rights in regard to her desire to remain in her home. Mrs. S. opened the door a crack and Mr. P. gave her his card and told her about the community centre. He noted the shotgun and was told by Mrs. S. that it had belonged to her husband who had died seven years ago. She had lived alone since then. She said she only went out to buy food, and to go to the bank. She used to do her laundry in the basement but now she was afraid of drug dealers who use the building. Mr. P. said he could understand her fear, he thought the building was not a safe place; he asked if he could come in so that they could talk where they would both feel safer. Mr. P. had noticed the unsafe condition of the nearly abandoned building. Mrs. S. let him come in but told him that she had made up her mind that she would stay in her home until she died. Mr. P. said he would arrange for her to talk with the lawyer at the community centre who would explain to her what her rights were in regard to her remaining in her apartment. He offered to come to take her to the community centre. He told her that if it turned out that she would have to leave her home, he would be able to plan with her about where she might live, and he noted that she had managed well on her own for seven years and that with a little help he thought she might be able to continue to care for herself. Mrs. S. agreed with this plan.

Both the community worker and the lawyer could begin to work cooperatively to serve the needs of this client. If the client's mental capacity should be in question, however, the responsibilities of the social worker and the lawyer might diverge. If the social worker is employed in a public agency whose mandate includes protecting the public and the lawyer has a duty to represent her client's wishes in so far as possible, if the situation should come to trial, the lawyer may feel that the social worker's testimony may contain information gained from the client in confidence and may not represent the client's interests.[11]

There are similarities between the two professions. Both use a case-by-case approach to situations, both place a high value on the dignity of the individual, and both are committed to helping. Differences persist that must be seen as tendencies in order to avoid over-simplification. In general, social workers view human behaviour as relative to circumstances while lawyers take a more absolutist view in which human behaviour is defined by the law as legal or illegal. Social workers choose collaboration and conciliation in most instances while lawyers may more often choose confrontation and opposition as more appropriate approaches. As our case example demonstrated, interdisciplinary collaboration between social workers and lawyers can work to enhance clients' options. Interdisciplinary education is a reality in many universities and can serve as a bridge between the two professions.[12]

The curriculum thrust in many schools of social work is to encourage students to work with clients at various levels of intervention to promote substantive changes in access to resources through empowerment to press for those resources. This means that social workers not only engage with clients as individuals and within families but seek to unite clients who share common concerns wherever possible and to mobilize others who may be able to interpret regulations, provide new resources or amend or initiate relevant legislation that will have far-reaching effects. The aim is to provide advocacy for individuals, to encourage groups to participate as advocates and to exert pressure and influence to seek broader change through the formulation of policy.

The problems are most evident when the social worker works with an agency which exercises authority over a client based on a statutory mandate such as child welfare, which duty also includes protection of the public and the censure of the client. When a social worker has a duty to investigate, the legal position the social worker adopts may appear to the lawyer to have been gained from the client in confidence, or derived from a social policy followed by the agency and then "used against" the client. This situation is anathema to a lawyer as this would be contrary to solicitor-client privilege. Legal training demands that a fundamental duty of the lawyer is to

> . . . act fearlessly to raise every issue, advance every argument, and ask every question, however distasteful, which he thinks will help his client's case and to endeavour to obtain for his client the benefit of any and every remedy and defense which is authorized by law.[13]

It is this narrow but intense focus on the individual which is at the root of the social worker-lawyer conflict. The social worker is trained to take a systemic view of a situation and to promote action which will advance the well-being of more than one participant in the proceedings. These differences do not represent irreconcilable polarities. Lawyering is not strictly adversarial. The lawyer is in fact quite familiar with regulatory authority which allows for investigation in confidence and then taking a position to prosecute where indicated. Such is the nature of regulatory authority. The lawyer himself is accordingly regulated by the Law Society.

During legal proceedings the social worker loses effective control. When the case is heard in court, the social worker can only be a witness and only if called as a witness. His professional judgment is not conclusive and this threatens his sense of professional status. The consequence may be hostility toward the lawyer whose intervention is seen as a negation of social work expertise. The lawyer, however, may feel it is his duty to protect the rights of this client.

A British lawyer, writing on law addressed to social workers observed that: "In general, rights, duties, and remedies characterize legal thinking while social workers may think first of needs and relationships.[14] The difference in approach is established in the training focus for each profession. For example, a man, terminally ill, is living with a woman, but is legally married to another woman from whom he has been separated for many years. A social worker might not introduce the subject of his will or suggest that he may want to get legal advice on this matter because the focus of concern would be on the psychological aspects of the situation. In another instance, a social worker may be working toward the rehabilitation of an accident victim, helping that person to accept the residual physical disability and adjust to an altered life, but that worker may never bring up the question of adequate financial compensation which legal intervention may be able to secure. The goal of counselling through the establishment of a therapeutic, helping relationship can obscure the concrete needs of clients that should be pursued concurrently through legal channels.[15]

There are other aspects of law that are viewed with impatience and apprehension by both lawyers and social workers. Law can be seen as repressive, especially for the disadvantaged or minority groups. Law can be seen to be applied blindly without concern for situational differences or circumstances, a theme expressed so eloquently by Shakespeare through Portia's appeal to the jury in "The Merchant of Venice". Paradoxically, the same law can be seen to protect and ensure the rights of all groups and individuals against capricious or discriminatory actions. Law and social work are human endeavours shaped by prevailing notions of social relationships and behaviour. Law is constantly evolving through judicial interpretation and ongoing legislation. Change is a slow process and can lag far behind the relentless movement of social reality and the immediate needs of individuals. A case in point is the interest in public sector law and in government intervention, regulation, and control of aspects of the private sector in order to protect the health and welfare of the public at large.[16]

There are attempts to reconcile or rationalize legal and social work thought within a common framework. A modern critique of legal thought seeks to import into legal reasoning a moral reasoning similar to social work thought. Gilligan demonstrates that the "logic of justice" approach, typical of lawyers' and judges' reasoning, solves dilemmas by a choice of principles such as "life is more important than property". An "ethic of care" approach, more characteristic of social workers, sees dilemmas rooted in persons and situations and seeks to find resolutions to partially satisfy both needs. Both are problem solving approaches which may frequently produce the same result.[17] Both legal and social work approaches are essentially remedial and libertarian in nature.

Endnotes

1. A. Phillips, "Social Work and the Delivery of Legal Services" (1979), 42 Modern Law Review 29.
2. See (1981), 1 Windsor Yearb. Access Justice. The statements are even more true today.
3. For a detailed discussion of social work practice informed by systems theory, see C.R. Germain and A. Gitterman, *The Life Model of Social Work Practice* (New York: Columbia University Press, 1980); Carol H. Meyer, *Assessment in Social Work Practice* (New York: Columbia University Press, 1993).
4. See Saleeby, D. (ed.), *The Strengths Perspective in Social Work Practice*. New York, Longman, 1990. While, M. and D. Epstein, *Narrative Means to Therapeutic Ends*, New York: Norton, 1990. Leonard, Peter, "Knowledge/Power and Postmodernism: Implications for the Practice of a Critical Social Work Education.", *Canadian Social Work Review*, Vol. 11, Number 1, Winter, 1994.
5. Note 1 above, at 36.
6. See D.J.D. Katkin, "Law and Social Work: A Proposal for Interdisciplinary Education", *Journal of Legal Education*, Vol. 26, 296. See also E.J. Vayda, "Educating for Radical Practice", *Canadian Journal for Social Work Education* (1980) 6:1 at 101-106.
7. In Great Britain, the Central Council for Education and Training in Social Work (CCETSW) published "Legal Studies in Social Work Education" August 1974. It recommended that these studies focus on four kinds of law:
    1. Professional law which explores the legal authority of certain agencies to act to protect children or to determine eligibility for benefits.
    2. Law and society which considers the general function of law to regulate human interchange.
    3. The administration of law through organization and procedure: *i.e.*, courts, tribunals.
    4. General law which canvasses laws affecting the day to day life of the client as citizen, tenant, accident victim, consumer, recipient of welfare benefits.
8. Law Reform Commission of Canada, *The Family Court* (Working Paper No. 1) (Ottawa, 1977) at 11.
9. H. Irving, *Divorce Mediation: The Rational Alternative* (Toronto: Personal Library Publishers, 1980) at 38.
10. For a study of lawyers and social workers' perceptions of themselves

and each other, see A. Smith, "The Social Worker in the Legal Aid Setting: A Study of Interprofessional Relationships" *Social Service Review*, June 1970, 44:2.

11. Adapted from a case presented in contemporary Group Work, 2nd ed., Charles Garvin, Prentice-Hall, Englewood Cliffs, N.J., 1987.
12. M. Weil, "Research on Issues in Collaboration Between Social Workers", *Social Service Review* 56 (1982), pp. 393-405.
13. "Rule 8, Commentary 1", Rules of Professional Conduct, Law Society of Upper Canada.
14. Note 1 above, at 38.
15. J.D. McClean, *The Legal Context of Social Work* (Toronto: Butterworths, 1975) at 2.
16. H.N. Janisch, "Administrative Tribunals in the 80's: Rights of Access by Groups and Individuals" (1981), 1 Windsor Yearb. Access Justice 303. Also consider current prosecutions by governments of the tobacco industry.
17. See a discussion of C. Gilligan's, "In a Different Voice: Psychological Theory and Women's Development" (1982) in C. Menkel-Meadow, "Portia In a Different Voice: Speculations on a Woman's Lawyering Process" (1985), Berkeley Women's Law Journal 39.

Bibliography

Chambers, D., Social Policy and Social Programs (New York: MacMillan, 1993).

Coughlan, Steven G. "The Adversary System: Rhetoric or Reality" (Fall, 1993) 8 Canadian Journal of Law & Society 139-170.

Ginsberg, Leon. Understanding Social Problems, Policies, and Programs. (1994) Columbia; University of South Carolina Press.

Lee, J.A.B., The Empowerment Approach to Social Work Practice (New York: Columbia University Press, 1994).

Lockyer, James E. "The Roles and Responsibilities of the Legal Profession in Furthering Access to Justice" (1992) 12 Windsor Yearb. Access to Justice 356-374.

Menkel-Meadow, C. "Portia in a Different Voice: Speculations on a Woman's Lawyering Process" (1985) Berkeley Women's Law Journal 39.

Miller, G. & Holstein, J., Constructionist Controversies: Issues in Social Problem Theory (New York: Aldine de Gruyter, 1993).

Mohr, J.W. "The Future of the Family, the Law and the State" (1984) 4 Canadian Journal of Family Law 261.

Saleeby, D., The Strengths Perspective in Social Work Practice (White Plains, N.Y.: Longmaer, 1992).

Weil, M. "Research on Issues in Collaboration Between Social Workers and Lawyers." (1982) 56:3 Social Service Review 393-405.

Whitner, Gary E. "The Development of Forensic Social Work." (May-June, 1983) 28 Soc. Work.

Zemans, F.H. "The Non-Lawyer as a Means of Providing Legal Services" and John Quinn, "Multidisciplinary Legal Services and Preventive Regulation" in R.G. Evans and M.J. Trebilcock, eds. *Lawyers and the Consumer Interest* (Toronto: Butterworths, 1983).

2

A Primer of Law for Social Workers

We have learned in working with students over the years the folly of presuming prior knowledge. What follows is a very basic overview of the foundation of lawmaking in Canada. A review of these basic elements will permit a more informed understanding of the material that will be presented.

Both social work and law deal in words as the primary instrument of their professions. Words are ambiguous and exact meaning is difficult to convey. Social workers are not distressed unduly by the imprecisions of language which they accept as a fact of human discourse. The law, however, must be concerned with exactness of meaning, particularly with the language used in the construction of statutes. The framers of statutes are not always successful in achieving clarity, and, consequently, revisions and amendments are often required. Legal writing is often an irritation for social workers, lawyers, and the general public. There seems to be a preoccupation with form and ritual, with repetition, ponderous phrases and qualifying clauses. All this is true, but careful legal drafting provides safeguards against ambiguity of content and limits what is included or excluded by that particular statute or document. There are instances, however, where the statutory language is purposively ambiguous, in order to permit some interpretive variation. Most likely, however, it is unintentional.[1]

Anyone wishing to gain some confidence in comprehending statutory language must, of course, confront the statute itself. This seems self-evident, but it is not unusual for social workers to be so intimidated by the form and wording of a statute that they rely on a summary of the provisions of an Act provided by the media, or their agency or the government.

They also may not know that the statute itself is readily available at government bookstores. To non-lawyers, the legal language of documents such as wills and contracts is unintelligible at first reading, and seems filled with unnecessary words which are designed to obscure their intent. There is reason, beyond mere custom, for the precise form required, which is to ensure a proper legal document which fulfils its specific purpose.

HOW LAW IS DEFINED

Many definitions of the law exist which have been stated with elegance and precision. The following definition bears remarkable similarity to some definitions of social work. S. M. Waddams states that "the law in any society is the society's attempt to resolve the most basic of human tensions, that between the needs of man as an individual, and his needs as a member of a community".[2] Law is a system for conflict resolution and rests on a structure of rules and procedures which facilitate this task. Change is possible, but it is a slow process of legislative and judicial accommodation to prevailing notions of social relationships.

Black's Law Dictionary defines law in this way:

> Law in its generic sense is a body of rules of action or conduct prescribed by controlling authority, and having binding legal force. . . . The term is also used in opposition to "fact." Thus questions of law are to be decided by the court, while it is the province of the jury [or judge where there is no jury] to resolve questions of fact.[3]

The late Mr. Justice Willard Estey, as he then was, has called the development of the concept of trial by jury a cunning approach

> . . . whereby the court assigned the risky task of finding the truth to the members of the community itself. The court instructed the jury on the law, and the jury applied that law to the facts which it had found in order to arrive at a judgment resolving the issue. The result we call the judgment of the court.[4]

Black's definition, in referring to the origins of law, states that law is derived either from individual precedents, from legislation, or from custom.[5]

This definition is positivistic; that is, it describes the law from a functional point of view. There are some who feel that there are overriding moral values which would make some laws unjust and that such laws should be opposed.[6] The danger here is obvious, for who is to determine which moral values shall prevail? Critics of social work theory and practice have identified a similar dilemma by pointing out that social welfare policies, services, and practices are not neutral but based on moral and political bias. The constant tension between the functional, positivistic definition and a search for a definition approaching a concept of universal justice provides some guarantee against complacency, both for law and for social work. The final word on definition is the claim that "law is what the courts declare to be the law".[7]

THE RULE OF LAW

The concept of the rule of law originated early in the 17th century when the British Chief Justice held that even the King could not interfere with the processes of justice. Under our modern parliamentary system, the government itself cannot make law outside of those powers given to it by law. The rule of law is an attempt to protect society from personal whims or the politics of the moment. We, as a people, submit to decisions made impartially within the four corners of rational, general principles which have been accepted as binding. The rule of law is an ideal of western democratic thought, never totally achieved.

NATURE OF THE ADVERSARIAL PROCESS

The adversarial system sets two opposing parties against one another to contend for a result favourable to one of them. The rationale of this system is that the rigour and zeal of each side to present the most compelling case in its favour and the most damaging case against the opposition will ensure that the truth of any given situation will be revealed in the balance. In such a system, the judge is constrained to act impartially rather than as a prosecutor. The rules of natural justice will provide a procedure to ensure that both parties receive a fair hearing. It should be noted that in working with clients who come from countries where a different model of law is practised, a simple explanation of the adversarial process may help to reassure clients who feel attacked by a process they do not understand.[8]

NATURAL JUSTICE

In all courts of law, natural justice requires that a judge be impartial, or at least not obviously biased. It requires that each party to a dispute be able to present his or her case fully, that each party has a right to be notified of a hearing, to rebut the evidence which is produced, to have the right to cross-examine witnesses, the right to legal representation if that is desired, the right to have the proceedings open to public scrutiny, and the right to appeal unless a statute specifically prohibits it.

In hearings before administrative tribunals, full rights to natural justice are afforded if the statute so provides. At the very least, where no such provision is made, natural justice requires that a person be informed of the case that is to be met and be afforded an opportunity to tell his or her side. There are instances, particularly in administrative tribunal hearings, where some or all of the rights of natural justice may be considered not applicable either for reasons of expediency or policy underlying the task of the tribunal.

COMMON LAW

Common law is a system of law based on judge-made decisions in contrast with a system of codified law, such as Roman law. The Province of Quebec, the state of Louisiana and many countries in the world function under a civil code based on Roman law. The remaining Canadian provinces, all other American states, England, Australia, and New Zealand are common law jurisdictions. Recent immigrants may therefore find our laws incomprehensible. In defining common law, Jowitt states:

> It is sometimes used in contradistinction to statute law, and then denotes the unwritten law, whether legal or equitable in its origin, which does not derive its authority from any express declaration of the will of the legislature. This unwritten law has the same force and effect as the statute law. It depends for its authority upon the recognition given by the courts to principles, customs and rules of conduct previously existing among the people. This recognition was formerly enshrined in the memory of legal practitioners and suitors in the courts; it is now recorded in the law reports which embody the decisions of the judges together with the reasons which they assigned for their decisions.[9]

The pattern of laws called the common law has evolved over 1,000 years of English history. Mr. Justice Estey referred to the three-fold magic of the common law as:

> (a) The judgment in the settlement of each dispute arising in the community itself becomes part of our principles or concepts for the legal governance of the community.
> (b) Because the body of concepts is thus ever growing and because the concepts arise out of actual differences within the community, the law, as the body of concept is called, is flexible and adaptable to the changing community.
> (c) As the principles or concepts are those visibly evolving from the life of the community itself, the body of the law so produced is accepted by the inhabitants as their own and not resisted as the imposed will of others.[10]

THE CONCEPT OF EQUITY

Equity incorporates the concept of justice into the law, so that a remedy is not denied because of a legal technicality. Equity also applies to the power of courts to control their own processes so that justice is done to the person before the court, unless he has misconducted himself so that the equitable treatment is undeserved.

For example, an exemplary parent who absconds with a child in the face of a custody order to the other parent is likely to be denied continuing custody because of her misconduct. A direct application from the same parent, supported by evidence would, on the other hand, be more likely to succeed.

THE MEANING OF PRECEDENT

In reaching decisions, courts rely on decided cases based on the principle of *stare decisis* which means "to stand by what has been decided". In so far as possible, similar cases must be decided similarly. Since it is unlikely that the facts of any two situations will match in all respects, courts look for the principle behind a decision, or the reason called *ratio decidendi*, in any given case. This reason may then make it possible to generalize from any one case to others that are similar. A court rendering a decision is expected to identify the reason or principle cited in a previous decision or similar case which was reached by the highest court in that particular provincial jurisdiction as the precedent for the current decision on the case at hand.

Judicial opinions about the law which are not necessary to decide the issues in a particular case are called *obiter dicta* or that which is said "by the way". Until recently, only *obiter* statements of the Supreme Court of Canada were considered to be binding on all other courts. Recently, an Ontario case[11] held that *obiter* opinions of the Ontario Court of Appeal are likewise binding on all lower courts.

Throughout this book you will find citations of relevant cases. Legal argument and judicial decisions are built upon the search for relevant cases. Two judges considering the same set of facts and relevant cases may reach different conclusions using equally compelling and persuasive reasons as the basis for their findings. The value of reading these decisions lies in the realization that law is not hardened but remains flexible and is always subject to the limitations of human understanding.

Judges may also take note of decisions made in co-ordinate or higher courts, or common law jurisdictions such as the United States or Commonwealth countries, for their persuasive value, but are bound only by the decision of the highest court in their own province. All courts in Canada are bound by the Supreme Court of Canada. The process just described could be rigid and confining if precedents were always binding, but the courts have utilized various methods to provide for flexibility. Judges are free to engage in a process of distinguishing the facts of the precedent case from the facts of the case under consideration. It is not within the purpose of this book to explore the problems of the judiciary, but it can be seen that the spectrum of possibilities in reaching decisions may extend from rather rigid reliance on precedent on the one hand to judicial law-making on the other hand, with various weightings of the use of precedents along the curve. In common law a judicial decision will resolve the specific dispute before the court and may also establish a general principle, which may be used as a precedent by a judge in a future case.[12]

STATUTORY LAW

Statutory law encompasses those laws which are enacted by an elected legislative body either at a federal or provincial level. Social workers are familiar with statutes such as the Child and Family Services Act, the Young Offenders Act, and the Family Law Act.[13] The primary remedy for a defect in the common law is through the enactment of legislation. It is interesting to note, however, that when the ultimate court of appeal overrules a line of cases in the lower courts and enunciates a rule that was never enunciated before, this is not looked upon as a change in the law. According to common law theory, the law was always as it is now revealed to us and we were in error, prior to the latest decision, in thinking that it was something else.[14]

Statutory legislation begins with definitions of terms, identifies the parties to whom the statute is addressed, the references to related legislation, the conditions that make the statute operative, the conduct explicitly included or excluded, the mandatory or discretionary provisions, the penalties, and the general purpose of the statute. Statutes should be read slowly; line by line with attention to punctuation and qualifications.[15]

When judges attempt to ascertain the intent of legislation, they usually assume that a particular statute has been enacted for a remedial reason, that is, in order to correct a defect in the existing common law. There are three major rules for statutory interpretation, or how the statute is to be construed. They are the "literal rule", the "golden rule", and the "mischief rule". The literal rule speaks to the fact that words are to be understood in their literal or ordinary sense. The golden rule means that the courts must reach a conclusion in interpretation that will avoid an absurdity. The mischief rule requires the court to consider the evil or defect the law was meant to remedy and to see that the decision reached reinforces the remedy and does not compound the mischief.[16]

To understand a judicial opinion, it is instructive to read or brief an actual case report. In order to identify the essential elements of an opinion, one should look to answer the following questions:

- Who are the parties to the dispute? What does each want?
- What are the facts as the court describes them? Is this an appeal from a lower court finding?
- What is the legal issue or question that the court is being asked to decide?
- What cases does the court canvass, the precedents that are cited as considerations in reaching a decision?
- What is the court's decision or holding; the decision will include a phrase such as "Held that . . .". This states the conclusion of law reached by the court as to the facts decided.
- Is there a dissenting or concurring opinion and how does it differ from the majority opinion?
- To what extent does the decision follow from the cited precedents? What guidance will the opinion offer future courts? Does this decision set a precedent? An annotated case report will be helpful in this endeavour.[17]

SUBORDINATE LEGISLATION

There is a distinction between primary legislation which is enacted by Parliament and the Legislatures of the provinces and subordinate legislation which is enacted under the authority of a statute, by a person, body or tribunal that is subordinate to a sovereign legislative body. Examples of subordinate legislation are bylaws, regulations and rules, ordinances, statutory instruments, and orders in council.[18] All municipal enactments are subordinate legislation, made under the authority of a provincial statute. Municipalities and their councils are creatures of provincial legislation and their power to enact bylaws derives entirely from provincial enabling legislation.

Because of the proliferation of statutory enactments in the last decade, both the federal and provincial governments have enacted enabling legislation delegating power to an inferior body, ministry, board, commission, or tribunal to make regulations relating to a particular statute without further legislation. It has been argued that there are dangers inherent in this process because regulations when passed have the force of the statute itself. Waddams points out that this practice makes it possible to withdraw difficult issues from public scrutiny by drafting universal rules to which exceptions are then made by regulations. He cites the extreme example of the War Measures Act which empowers the government to make by Order in Council (with no parliamentary debate or approval) any laws it deems necessary for security.[19] Similar allegations have been made about rules under the authority of the Income Tax Act, the Immigration Act, and the Unemployment Insurance Act.

PARAMOUNTCY

There are laws which are within the power of both the federal Parliament and a provincial Legislature. There must be a way to resolve the inevitable conflicts and inconsistencies which will occur when both laws are held to be valid. The rule which has been adopted by the courts is that of federal paramountcy, which upholds the federal law in those situations where conflict occurs and the issue is within federal power. Where the power is exclusively provincial, however, federal paramountcy must give way to provincial jurisdiction.[20]

PROCEDURAL LAW

Procedural law is the process which must be followed when government, courts, or legal bodies intervene. These procedures determine what will happen, what steps must be included, what steps cannot be omitted, and in what order and in what time frame these steps must occur. Procedural rights are, of course, enshrined in the concept of natural justice. Procedural rights guarantee only a fair hearing and not necessarily that the outcome will be just. For example, a person who appeals a decision of a court or tribunal may receive a full and fair hearing but the outcome allowed by the governing statute may be considered inadequate or unfair.

There are many instances where procedural rights which are enshrined as rules of natural justice can serve to overturn an unjust ruling. Such an instance occurred in a case heard in the New Brunswick Court of Queen's Bench.[21]

> A judge of the Provincial Court, Family Division, committed a juvenile to the charge of the Director of Child Welfare after conviction for possession of marijuana and recommended that the juvenile be moved out of his school and out of the district since home supervision was improper. A social worker for the Director of Child Welfare permitted the juvenile to stay overnight with his father. The next day the judge, upon learning where the boy spent the night, and

angered by the action of the social worker, issued warrants for the arrest of the juvenile, his father, a man living in the father's home, the school principal, and the social workers involved to ensure their attendance at a summary hearing of the matter that afternoon. The judge conducted the hearing himself, including the examination and cross-examination of witnesses.

The social worker applied to quash the order of the judge. The New Brunswick Court of Queen's Bench, Trial Division, allowed the application and quashed the order. The Trial Division held that the order was invalid because the arrest warrants were illegal, the judge held the hearing without notice to the parties which was required to found his jurisdiction and the hearing was conducted in breach of the rules of natural justice.

In his decision, Meldrum J. observed that the judge had a right to pursue the best interests of the child. The questions were whether there had been a fair hearing with full disclosure, adequate opportunity to examine and cross-examine witnesses and to present any other relevant evidence. In addition, he held that the judge must remain open to rational argument on the issue of transfer. He felt the judge erred on all counts.

The appeal judge fortunately put a stop to what appeared to be a general roundup of social workers. Procedural safeguards are there to remedy precipitous action and to ensure uniform protection to all who stand before the court.

STANDING

Standing is a procedural right granted after a review of a person's substantive rights. Ordinarily in private legal actions a person must have an interest, that is something to be gained, lost, or otherwise directly affected, in order to gain status or "standing" as a party to a proceeding. Rules of civil procedure require all persons whose presence is necessary to enable the court to adjudicate effectively and completely on the issues be joined as a party. Powers exist to add those who do not consent voluntarily.[22] The Attorney-General's power to sue is, in fact, discretionary. A person who would like, for example, to see a certain law enforced or the charge dropped has no power to compel action;[23] nor can he pursue the matter in court as a private person.[24] The Supreme Court of Canada became convinced that a person might have sufficient interest to sue where he had no standing and developed a line of authority which grants the private person standing to sue for a declaration that a statute is invalid.

Where, in a matter, the Attorney-General has not or is not likely to speak to the public interest and where a serious issue is raised and no other party can proceed, standing may be granted with judicial discretion.[25] The Supreme Court has expanded the ground to non-constitutional matters, in a case of interest to social workers. A welfare recipient challenged the validity of continued transfer payments by Canada to Manitoba when the Province had failed to comply with the financial assistance required under the empowering legislation.[26]

Standing may also be afforded to a party to intervene in a matter to enable the court to hear all relevant issues. For example, in a Charter challenge that the witness protection laws in a sexual assault trial prevent the accused from obtaining a fair hearing, the Women's Legal Action Fund was granted status as an intervenor.[27] They argued for the right to maintain confidentiality of treatment records of the victim.

JURISDICTIONAL POWERS

The central fact which determines the distinction of governmental power is that of confederation. In a federal state, the power of government is distributed between a central or national authority and regional or provincial authority. The United Kingdom and New Zealand are examples of a unitary state. The laws of the provincial legislature are considered "co-ordinate" in their relationship to Parliament. Co-ordination recognizes that there are two levels of government each with respective powers. In contrast, local or municipal governments are subordinate to the provincial authority. Though the balance of powers between the federal and provincial governments has shifted from time to time, the basis of this balancing act is the legal guarantee of co-ordinate power.[28] The topic of jurisdictional powers or federal-provincial relations is a highly complex issue which occupies a central position in Canadian political affairs. The debate over federal-provincial power is beyond the scope of this book.

The Constitution Act, formerly the British North America Act, which forms a part of our Constitution gives these powers, among others, to the federal government.

1. Power to regulate trade and commerce.
2. Power to regulate banking.
3. Matters of marriage and divorce.
4. Criminal law and penitentiaries (sentences over two years).
5. Power to levy indirect as well as direct taxes.
6. Indians, and lands reserved for Indians.
7. Immigration and naturalization.

The federal government also has the power to appoint judges of the superior and district courts of each province.

Among the powers of the provincial legislatures under the Con-stitution Act are the following:

1. Management of prisons in the province (sentences under two years);
2. Establishment, maintenance, and management of hospitals and charities in the province other than marine hospitals;
3. Solemnization of marriage in the province (formality of marriage);
4. Property and civil rights in the province;
5. Maintenance of provincial courts of both criminal and civil jurisdiction;
6. Making laws in regard to education in the province.

The reader will note that marriage is both a federal and provincial matter but divorce is exclusively under federal jurisdiction. Property, however, is exclusively a provincial matter. Because the division of powers spelled out by the Constitution Act is expressed in general terms, significant questions of interpretation have arisen. The Supreme Court of Canada, the ultimate court of appeal, is vested with the right to review the validity of legislation enacted by both federal and provincial legislative bodies.[29]

HOW A BILL IS PASSED

A bill is passed into law when it has been approved by the provincial legislature or the federal Parliament. The government introduces a bill through a "First Reading". It is then printed and released for public reaction. It may then be moved for a "Second Reading", followed by a full debate. If the bill passes the Second Reading, it is considered passed in principle. The bill is then referred to an appropriate committee for detailed study and recommendations for amendments. It is then read a third time, amendments are debated and, if approved and passed, it then goes to the Lieutenant Governor of the province or the Governor General of Canada for royal assent. In the case of federal bills the process is repeated in the Senate. The bill is then considered law, but it may contain a provision that it is not to come into effect until the government wishes to proclaim it law. Social workers anxious for legislative change need to be aware of the laborious process from idea to enactment. For example, the Young Offenders Act was 15 years in the making.

Provincial statutes are published annually, federal statutes after completion of a session which may go on in excess of one year. Modern statutes may have a short title which appears in the text of the statute itself.

Every 10 to 15 years a set of revised statutes is issued which consolidates all the amendments.

THE CONSTITUTION ACT, 1982

A fundamental change in our legal system was brought about by the proclamation of the Constitution Act, 1982. The effect of this constitutional document was to provide Canada, for the first time, with a written Constitution which terminated the authority of the United Kingdom Parliament over the Dominion of Canada. This was accomplished by the incorporation of the British North America Act, 1867 (renamed the Constitution Act, 1867) and all subsequent amendments to it became the Canadian Constitution.[30] As a result, the Constitution may be amended in Canada without recourse to the British Parliament. The Act declares that the Constitution is the supreme law of Canada, and any law that is inconsistent with it is, to the extent of the inconsistency, of no force and effect.[31]

A further significant feature of the Constitution Act was the entrenchment of qualified judicial supremacy.[32] The judiciary is empowered to determine which laws are inconsistent with the Constitution. The ultimate effect shifts Canada from the British model of parliamentary sovereignty toward the American model of judicial supremacy, at least to the extent that the judiciary is empowered to define the scope of the rights and freedoms set out in the Charter of Rights. The Charter is a remarkable reflection of the Canadian art of compromise. Neither the judiciary nor Parliament is absolutely supreme; the power of each is qualified by the authority of the other.[33]

The Honourable Pierre Elliott Trudeau stated:

> . . .Thus, our Supreme Court, when it acts in constitutional matters, is of necessity participating in the governance of Canada. This is not a new development, somehow made necessary by the adoption of the Charter of Rights, and which — as some critics wrongly alleged — would tend to "Americanize" us. The Supreme Court of Canada, and before it the Judicial Committee of the Privy Council, have been engaged in law-making or in adjudicating power for Canada, its people, and its provinces since the first constitutional decision rendered after the adoption of the BNA Act.[34]

Amendments to the Constitution

Any change in the Charter provisions, or in any other aspect of the Constitution requires resolutions by both the Senate and the House of Commons, together with resolutions by legislative assemblies of at least two thirds of the provinces that have at least fifty per cent of the population.[35] Given this complex arrangement, changes will be rare indeed. Both the Meech Lake Accord and the subsequent Charlottetown Accord, which would have changed the amending formula, were rejected and failed to become law.

The role of the federal government has been to initiate as well as to expand on regulated social programmes for all Canadians. Of special interest is the limitation to the federal spending power whereby provinces could opt out of federal cost-sharing programmes but seek federal compensation for their own programmes which are compatible with undefined "national objectives". For example, the federal medicare was imposed on provinces initially reluctant to embrace this legislation. It is questionable whether federal legislation empowering universal day care could now be imposed.

Charter of Rights and Freedoms

The Canadian Charter is exceptional in permitting the courts to balance private rights against the public interest. This fundamental ideological conflict is at the root of many Charter appeals.[36] The Constitution entrenches a number of rights and freedoms in the Charter[37] which apply to all Canadians in relation to their dealings with government at both the federal and provincial levels. The Charter does not affect relationships between private individuals.[38] All Canadians are specifically guaranteed these rights, regardless of age, sex, or place of residence in Canada. Indeed non-Canadians benefit from some rights, including refugee claimants[39] and anyone charged with an offence in Canada.[40] This "bundle of rights" includes democratic rights, certain fundamental freedoms, legal rights, equality rights, mobility rights, official language and minority language educational rights, affirmation of Canada's multicultural heritage and existing aboriginal rights. The late Mr. Justice Walter Tarnopolsky pointed out that the Charter was drafted to be applicable to all rights, those existing at the time of enactment and those that may arise in the future. This contrasts with a "frozen concepts" interpretation of the Canadian Bill of Rights, which applies only to rights existing at the fixed time of its enactment in 1960.[41]

Qualifications to Rights and Freedoms

All sections of the Charter must be read in the context of section 1, which declares that all the rights and freedoms set out in it are guaranteed, "subject only to such reasonable limits prescribed by law as can be demonstrably justified in a free and democratic society" The first effect of this provision is to import the common law concept of "reasonableness" as it applies to all forms of law, whether it is statutory, regulatory, or judge-made law. Therefore, the rights and freedoms set out are not absolute, but are subject to reasonable limits which are justifiable in a "free and democratic society" This last phrase appears to contemplate limits on Charter rights which may be imposed by Parliament or a legislature and also by the judiciary, which are all part of such a society. As a result, laws which limit a freedom, for example, freedom of association, where it is "reasonably justifiable" for the benefit of society, could be enacted or held to be valid. For example, where the War Measures Act curtails certain liberties guaranteed by the Charter, these limitations might be held to be valid under the section 1 qualification. Determination whether or not a law is in conflict with the Charter of Rights is given to the judiciary.[42]

The second qualification to rights and freedoms was the delay in the applicability of equality rights, which came into force in April, 1985, in order to permit governments to make the necessary revisions to existing laws.[43]

The third qualification is the "opting out" clause, which permits provincial governments to pass legislation which conflicts with the Charter and restricts a right or freedom embodied in the Charter. Conceptually, it permits regional diversity for a limited period. Rights which may be restricted include the fundamental freedoms, legal rights and equality rights. Any such conflicting legislation will remain in force for five years only, unless it is renewed by that government. The result may be that certain rights will not be uniformly applicable throughout the country.

The opting out provision has been used most frequently in Quebec in regard to language and human rights legislation.[44] Quebec invoked the notwithstanding clause in order to impose a law requiring commercial signs to be in French. The Supreme Court struck down this law as being in violation of section 2 of the Charter which contains the guarantee of fundamental freedoms. To circumvent this decision and protect language law, the Quebec government invoked section 33 of the Charter. This section declares that Parliament or the legislature of a province may expressly state that an act or a provision of an act shall operate notwithstanding a provision included in section 2 or sections 7-15 of the Charter. The notwithstanding clause has also been invoked by Saskatchewan in order to make its labour laws affecting public servants not subject to section 2 of the Charter. Thus they could retain provincial law prohibiting strikes for public servants engaged in essential services.

Since the advent of the Charter, its impact is now evident. Members of the legal profession have noted a pervasive "sense of civil rights that has swept the nation" in popular thought. Some aspect of the Charter is an issue in a large number of cases before the courts and governments must consider the Charter when new laws are drafted.[45]

Charter Rights

Fundamental freedoms guaranteed by the Charter are the freedom of conscience and religion, freedom of thought, belief and expression (which includes freedom of the press and the media), freedom of peaceful assembly and freedom of association.[46]

Democratic rights guaranteed to all Canadians are the right to vote in federal and provincial elections, and the right to stand for office. For example, the Ontario government extended the right to vote to mental hospital in-patients and these rights have also been extended to prisoners and others nationwide.[47]

Both Parliament and the legislatures must sit at least annually and must not continue for more than five years without a general election, thereby guaranteeing parliamentary governments.[48] No right to vote in municipal elections is guaranteed.

The *legal rights* entrenched in the Charter had the most immediate impact upon the average Canadian resident. These rights now include the right to life, liberty and security of the person and the right not to be deprived of them except in accordance with the principles of fundamental justice. Section 7 has been given a wide and liberal meaning by our highest court. The Supreme Court has ruled that "fundamental justice" means more than mere procedural fairness. It means substantive guarantees of the rights and freedoms of the Charter. Therefore, a person may not be subject, under provincial regulatory laws such as the Highway Traffic Acts, to penalties without the protections afforded by criminal procedures.[49] Criminal legislation which prohibited the performance of abortions without approval by a committee of doctors was found to have interfered with a woman's right to security of the person.[50] Cabinet decisions, formerly regarded as not reviewable by courts of law, may be reviewed if sufficient evidence is presented that a cabinet decision to test cruise missiles threatens the life, liberty and security of the person.[51]

The protection against unreasonable search and seizure means that an investigative authority, with the power to prosecute, must obtain a warrant from an impartial court or justice of the peace, whenever possible, before any person is searched, before any private business or dwelling is entered, and before anything is seized. To obtain a warrant there must be reasonable and probable grounds to believe that an offence has been committed and that evidence exists at the place.[52] A search or seizure made without a warrant *may* be acceptable if a court finds it was not unreasonable in all the circumstances. Some exceptions to the rule are, therefore, search for and seizure of weapons or any evidence of criminal activity pursuant to a lawful arrest with a warrant. A police officer may, for example, search a person arrested for selling drugs, although an overly intrusive search might be unreasonable if it is merely done as a matter of routine. In arrests without a warrant, circumstances may permit lawful seizure of evidence. Hot pursuit of a criminal into a place, or a search of the person before evidence can be destroyed are examples. The seizure of evidence of criminal activity lying in plain view when police are in attendance on another matter is another exception. A person may also consent to a search, thereby rendering an illegal search legal.[53]

Protection against arbitrary detention or imprisonment is guaranteed. The right not to be arbitrarily detained or imprisoned applies only if a person has been detained. A "detention" likely means "some form of compulsory restraint" and not a consent to police questioning.[54] At a minimum, an unlawful detention may mean detention where no grounds for an arrest are present.[55]

The right to retain, instruct and be represented by counsel applies on arrest or detention. Under the common law a person must be told the reasons for his arrest. The Charter does expand his rights to obtain counsel. He must, upon arrest, be given a real opportunity to speak to a lawyer in confidence.[56] The Young Offenders Act spells out procedures to be followed in taking a statement from a youth prior to and subsequent to an arrest, affording even more protection than that given by the Charter.[57] Other guaranteed rights include the right to legal representation, to trial within a reasonable time, to trial by jury for offences punishable by more than five years, the right to be presumed innocent until found guilty in a fair and public trial, and the right not to be denied bail without just cause.

The Charter rights respecting the trial and pre-trial procedures for persons charged with an offence have been the subject of the most voluminous litigation. The presumption of innocence, partially codified in section 11(*d*) is the thread which weaves through the nine subsections. It is the foundation for the duty of fairness in pre-trial procedures, in a fair hearing, and in restrictions against further punishments. For example, enumerated principles include:

1. A corporation can be a "person" charged with an offence.[58]
2. The court will consider the impairment of the accused's interests from the time he is charged in deciding whether there has been unreasonable delay.[59]
3. Amendments to the Justices of the Peace Act now ensure that Justices of the Peace are independent.[60]

4. The "reverse onus" procedure, whereby a person charged with possession of a narcotic for the purpose of trafficking was required to establish that he was not trafficking has been struck as unconstitutional.[61]
5. A police officer disciplined by regulatory authority is not "charged with an offence". Therefore, professionals subject to regulatory authority by their professional associations may likely be precluded from the section 11 protections. But if the consequences are severe, section 11 will likely apply.[62]

The Charter establishes the right against self-incrimination, which many Canadians erroneously believed they already possessed as a result of watching American television. If convicted, the right not to be subjected to cruel and unusual punishment, or if acquitted, not to be tried again for the same offence are also guaranteed by the Charter,[63] unless the acquittal is set aside on appeal.

Equality rights protect persons from discrimination by governments by providing that every individual is equal before the law and is entitled to equal benefit of the law without discrimination based on race, national or ethnic origin, colour, religion, sex, age, or mental or physical disability. However, equality rights do not preclude governments from initiating special programmes to improve the circumstances of disadvantaged individuals or groups. Such special programmes might include "affirmative action" for women or special provisions for the blind or physically disabled.[64]

There is no universally accepted definition of equality in Canada. Read as a whole, the equality guarantee is best understood as a requirement that persons who are equal, or similarly situated,[65] be treated equally. Where distinctions exist, persons should be treated unequally only in proportion to their inequality.[66] While this is by no means a settled approach, the courts have asked: what is an unfair distinction?

1. The distinctions between individuals apply only to individuals. Where a group of persons asserts collective rights section 15 may not be available to them.[67]
2. Girls may not be denied the right to play hockey with a Minor Hockey Association on the basis of gender. Discrimination on the basis of sex if also prohibited by section 28.[68]
3. Different quality of education between school districts is not discrimination based on geography.[69]
4. The insanity of accused persons who are therefore subject to indeterminate detention on a Lieutenant Governor's Warrant is not discrimination.[70]
5. New grounds of discrimination need not be similar to other grounds. Marital status is a prohibited ground of discrimination.[71]

6. Welfare recipients are entitled to equal benefit of the law, even though the amounts paid to them are discretionary, because the discretion is controlled by Regulations which *are* subject to the equality guarantee.[72]
7. Community college teachers on strike are not similarly situated with other teachers in the province because they bargain individually with a multiplicity of employers.[73]

Mobility rights guarantee that everyone may enter and leave Canada, move freely from one province to another, and live or seek employment anywhere in the country. Where a province has an employment rate below the national average, that province may initiate special programmes for people who are socially or economically disadvantaged in that province.[74] Otherwise, persons may enter and leave and move freely subject to laws passed under section 1.

The Supreme Court has ruled that these guarantees are indeed about mobility and do not create a separate right to work such that a non-citizen resident could in fact be excluded from a professional association on the basis of citizenship. The subsections are to be read together, not separately.[75]

Official language and minority language education rights establish the use of either English or French in all matters which deal with federal institutions or services and with the federal government. French and English are the official languages and have equal status in federal matters. Only New Brunswick, Quebec and Manitoba have the right to use either language in the legislature, courts, and official documents and only New Brunswick provides all citizens with the right to communicate with any provincial government office in either language and makes both languages official in the province.[76] While Ontario has many bilingual services, the provincial government has avoided introducing entrenching legislation.

Language education rights entitle any citizen educated in English in Canada to have his children educated in English in Quebec, and to continue to have his children educated in English if he moves to Quebec. The reverse applies to the children of French-speaking citizens elsewhere in Canada. If their primary language is French, their children must be provided with the opportunity to be educated in French when their numbers are sufficient to warrant it. In all cases the education is to be provided from public funds.[77]

The judiciary has demonstrated a certain discomfort with enforcing Charter rights to obtain funding for educational services. The Ontario Court of Appeal pointedly said, "[l]egislative action in the important and complex field of education is much to be preferred to judicial intervention".[78] Nonetheless, the court has recognized that facilities must be provided to give effect to the right to French language education in the province.[79]

Aboriginal rights of Indians, Métis and Innuit which existed at the time the Constitution Act was proclaimed are affirmed by the Charter. They include all existing treaty rights and freedoms and land claims settlements in existence in 1982. They cannot be diminished by subsequent legislatures, but aboriginal rights are *not* expanded or otherwise entrenched by the Charter.[80] Native issues such as the different status of men and women under treaty and unresolved land claims are neither settled nor advanced by the Charter.

Interpretation of the Charter must be carried out in a manner which is consistent with Canada's multicultural heritage and does not deny or negate other rights and freedoms already in existence.[81] However, the scope of existing rights and the legal meaning of "multicultural heritage" remain unclear.

Broad Interpretation of Charter Rights and Freedoms

The Supreme Court has taken many steps to define its approach to the Charter and has boldly grasped the task of analyzing a statute in light of the guarantees of the Charter as reflected in this statement:

> The task of expounding a constitution is crucially different from that of construing a statute. A statute defines present rights and obligations. It is easily enacted and is easily repealed. A constitution, by contrast, is drafted with an eye to the future. Its function is to provide a continuing framework for the legitimate exercise of governmental power and, when joined by a Bill or a Charter of Rights, for the unremitting protection of individual rights and liberties. Once enacted, its provisions cannot easily be repealed or amended. It must, therefore, be capable of growth and development over time to meet new social, political and historical realities often unimagined by its framers. The judiciary is the guardian of the constitution and must, in interpreting its provisions, bear these considerations in mind.[82]

The court will also look at the purpose and content of the statute and will analyze the charter guarantee in light of the interests it was meant to protect. When a statute titled "The Lord's Day Act", which prohibited Sunday shopping was defended with reference to the Christian belief of resting on the seventh day, the court ruled that to force a religious practice on all people violated the fundamental freedom of conscience and religion. If the legislature seeks to defend the prohibition on Sunday shopping, it must make its purpose inoffensive to a Charter right.[83] For example, such a law might be called "An Act to Secure All Workers a Day Off". Rights protected by the Charter are given a higher priority than any other interest.[84]

Several Charter cases demonstrate judicial interpretation of Charter principles. In *Singh v. Canada*, the court decided that an immigration inquiry tribunal makes no error in deciding to proceed with the inquiry prior to receiving evidence on and considering constitutional arguments as to the tribunal's jurisdiction. Procedural decisions are entirely within the discretion of the tribunal since constitutional issues cannot be decided in a vacuum.[85] In a ruling on an Act to Amend the Education Act (Ontario) (1987), the court stated that it was never intended that the Charter could be used to invalidate other provisions of the Constitution. Therefore, the provincial power pursuant to section 93 of the Constitution to enact legislation in relation to denominational separate schools remains unimpaired by the Charter.[86] In *R. v. Blake*, the balance between individual rights and those of the collectivity are perceived as a fundamental difference between U.S. and Canadian values. The court comments that individual rights must be seen in the context of collective rights which enhance the participation of individuals and groups in society and therefore, freedoms guaranteed in the Charter will not always be supreme.[87] In response to a Canadian Civil Liberty Association Charter challenge, the court concluded that guiding children toward the development of proper moral standards is not rationally connected to Christian religious indoctrination and that such indoctrination infringes upon Charter freedoms. The court added that the development of proper moral standards could be encouraged without resort to religious indoctrination in public schools.[88]

Charter litigation has not, however, made the courts more accessible. The extra costs for research alone are prohibitive. If an important issue is brought to the higher courts with inadequate evidence or insufficiently presented arguments, we could be saddled with a bad precedent for several years. Those who can afford to litigate are the best protected, and even when the government funds a challenge through legal aid or special grants, the government still exercises control over the allocation of funds.

Enforcement

The enforcement provisions permit anyone whose rights and freedoms under the Charter have been infringed or denied to apply to a court for the appropriate remedy.[89] For example, a person who claims he was unreasonably denied bail and is detained in custody may now apply to a court to be released from custody until trial on the ground that a Charter right has been violated. In hearings where a violation of the Charter is alleged, the judge has the power to exclude evidence which was obtained in violation of the person's rights, if admission of the evidence would bring the administration of justice into disrepute,[90] even if the evidence is relevant. For example, an accused may now claim that an incriminating statement made by him to police was obtained by the use of undue force, in violation of his right to security of his person. The judge has the power to exclude this evidence, even if it is relevant to his guilt, if admission of the statement would bring the administration of justice into disrepute. The significance of this provision lies in the judge's power to exclude evidence in these circumstances.

In all matters dealing with the Charter, the assistance of a lawyer is imperative. No one should attempt to sail these uncharted waters without expert legal assistance.

Privacy of Individuals and Access to Information

The Access to Information Act and the Privacy Act[91] gives the right of access to information held by the federal government. In Ontario, the Freedom of Information and Protection of Individual Privacy Act, 1987,[92] consolidates the two functions into one Act. It gives a right of access to personal information and to information held in the ministries, provincial boards, agencies, commissions and Crown corporations. Manuals used by public servants, for example, must be made available to the public. As well, academics, journalists, policy analysts, and other interested parties have applied to obtain certain records of practices and decisions. The Acts governing personal information also set out codes for the collection, disclosure, use, management, and accountability of information about individuals.

Each Act provides for registers of what information is available, where to get it, how to apply, time limits on response, and exemptions such as cabinet documents and security sensitive material. All personal information generally requires the consent of the person about whom it is made. In most instances the onus is on the government office to provide a reason for withholding information, which decision may be reviewed by a Commissioner and thereafter appealed to the court. Each government has an office to administer the Acts and within every government institution there is an information co-ordinator to facilitate access to the information requested.

Endnotes

1. G.L. Gall, *The Canadian Legal System*, 3rd ed., Carswell, 1990, p. 314.
2. S.M. Waddams, *Introduction to the Study of Law* (Toronto: Carswell Co., 1979) at 2.

3. Black's Law Dictionary, 5th ed. (St. Paul, Minnesota: West Publishing Co., 1979) at 795-6.
4. W.E. Estey, "Who Needs Courts?" (1981), 1 Windsor Yearb. Access Justice 263 at 265.
5. Note 3 above, at 796.
6. Note 1 above, at 10-11.
7. D.P. Derham, F.K.H. Maher, and Waller, "What Then is Law?" in *An Introduction to Law*. (Wellington: Sweet & Maxwell, 1968) at 81. Quoted in Gall, note 1 above at 13.
8. The information in this chapter is discussed in greater detail in Waddams, note 2 above, and in Gall, note 1 above.
9. J. Burke, ed., *Jowitt's Dictionary of English Law*, 2nd ed. (London: Sweet & Maxwell) Vol. 1 at 391.
10. Note 4 above, at 264.
11. *Re R. and McKibbon* (1981), 34 O.R. (2d) 185, 61 C.C.C. (2d) 126. Affirmed 35 O.R. (2d) 124, 64 C.C.C. (2d) 441 (C.A.). Affirmed [1984] 1 S.C.R. 131.
12. J. Miller, "Teaching Law and Legal Skills to Social Workers", 16 Journal of Education for Social Workers, Fall, 1980 at 87-95.
13. The statutes of each province and of the federal government can be found in consolidated form in any law library. They are called the revised statutes of the jurisdiction, for example, R.S.O. (Revised Statutes of Ontario) and R.S.C. (Revised Statutes of Canada). Child and Family Services Act, S.O. 1984, c. 55; Young Offenders Act, S.O. 1984, c. 19; Family Law Act, S.O. 1986, c. 4.
14. F.W. Maitland, *The Constitutional History of England* (Cambridge: The University Press, 1908) at 23.
15. W. Statsky, *Case Analysis and Fundamentals of Legal Writing*. (St. Paul, Minnesota: West Publishing Co., 1984) at 43.
16. See E.A. Driedger, "Statutes: The Mischievous Literal Golden Rule" (1981), 59 Can. Bar Rev. 780; and M. Zander, *The Law Making Process* (London: Butler & Tanner Ltd., 1980).
17. R. Albert, *Law and Social Work Practice*. Springer Publishing Co., New York, 1986, at 19-20. Cited from *Black's Law Dictionary* (St. Paul, Minnesota: West Publishing Co., 1968).
18. Gall, note 1 above, at 24.
19. Waddams, note 2 above, at 145.
20. The Constitution Act, 1982, being Schedule B of the Canada Act 1982 (U.K.), 1982, c. 11, ss. 91, 92.
21. *Re Theriault* (1980), 29 N.B.R. (2d) 42, 66 A.P.R. 42 (Q.B.).
22. Rules of Civil Procedure, O.Reg. 560/84, r. 5.03.
23. *Danson v. Ont. (A.G.)* (1985), 2 C.P.C. (2d) 109, 51 O.R. (2d) 405, 18

C.R.R. 278, 20 D.L.R. (4th) 288 (H.C.). Affirmed (1986), 9 C.P.C. (2d) 1, 55 O.R. (2d) 1, 27 D.L.R. (4th) 758, 16 O.A.C. 246 (Div. Ct.). Reversed (1987), 19 C.P.C. (2d) 249, 22 O.A.C. 38, 60 O.R. (2d) 676, 41 D.L.R. (4th) 129. Leave to appeal to S.C.C. granted (1988), 65 O.R. (2d) x (note), 29 C.P.C. (2d) xlv (note).

24. *R. v. Century 21 Ramos Realty Inc.* (1987), 32 C.C.C. (3d) 353, 87 D.T.C. 5158, 19 O.A.C. 25, 58 O.R. (2d) 737, 37 D.L.R. (4th) 649, 29 C.R.R. 320, 56 C.R. (3d) 150 (C.A.). Leave to appeal refused (1987), 38 C.C.C. (3d) vi, 56 C.R. (3d) xxviii (note), 44 D.L.R. (4th) vii (note), 62 O.R. (2d) ix (note), 22 O.A.C. 319 (note).
25. *Min. of Justice, Can. v. Borowski*, [1981] 2 S.C.R. 575, [1982] 1 W.W.R. 97, 24 C.R. (3d) 352, 24 C.P.C. 62, 12 Sask. R. 420, 39 N.R. 331, 64 C.C.C. (2d) 97, 130 D.L.R. (3d) 588.
26. *Finlay v. Min. of Finance*, [1986] 2 S.C.R. 607, [1987] 1 W.W.R. 603, 23 Admin. L.R. 197, 17 C.P.C. (2d) 289, 71 N.R. 338, 33 D.L.R. (4th) 321.
27. *R. v. Seaboyer* (1987), 37 C.C.C. (3d) 53, 58 C.R. (3d) 289, 20 O.A.C. 345, 61 O.R. (2d) 290, 35 C.R.R. 300 (C.A.). Leave to appeal to S.C.C. granted (1988), 39 C.C.C. (3d) vi (note), 64 C.R. (3d) xxx (note), 63 O.R. (2d) x (note), 30 O.A.C. 80 (note), 89 N.R. 78 (note), 30 O.A.C. 160 (note), 90 N.R. 320 (note), 35 C.R.R. 300n.
28. P.W. Hogg, *Constitutional Law in Canada* (Toronto: Carswell Co., 1985) at 82-3.
29. *Ibid.* Note that the Privy Council was the final court of appeal after 1867. In 1949, the Canadian Supreme Court was given the ultimate decision-making authority with no further appeal to the Privy Council.
30. Constitution Act, note 20 above, s. 52(2).
31. *Ibid.*, s. 52(1).
32. See L.D. Barry, "Law, Policy and Statutory Interpretation under a Constitutionally Entrenched Canadian Charter of Rights and Freedoms." (1982), 60 Can. Bar Rev. 237.
33. Constitution Act, note 20 above, s. 52(1).
34. Trudeau, Pierre Elliott. Convocation Speech at the opening of the Bora Laskin Law Library, U. of T. Law Jr., 4, 1991, p. 296.
35. Canadian Charter of Rights and Freedoms, Part 1 of the Constitution Act, 1982, being Schedule B of the Canada Act 1982 (U.K.), c. 11, s. 38.
36. *Re Lavigne and Ont. Public Service Employees Union (No. 2)* (1987), 60 O.R. (2d) 486 (H.C.).
37. Canadian Charter of Rights and Freedoms, note 35 above, ss. 1-34.
38. *Ibid.*, s. 32(1) and E.G. Ewaschuk, "The Charter: An Overview and Remedies," (1982) 26 Crim. Rep. 54. Relations between private individuals are subject to Human Rights legislation.

39. *Singh v. Min. of Employment and Immigration*, [1985] 1 S.C.R. 177, 12 Admin. L.R. 137, 14 C.R.R. 13, 17 D.L.R. (4th) 422, 58 N.R. 1.
40. Charter, note 35 above, s. 11.
41. Tarnopolsky, W.S., and G.A. Beaudoin (eds.) *The Canadian Charter of Rights and Freedoms: Commentary* (Toronto, Carswell: 1982).
42. "Reasonable limit" has been held to mean "proportionate" to the social goal to which the law is directed. See *R. v. Oakes*, [1986] 1 S.C.R. 103, 53 O.R. (2d) 719 (headnote), 50 C.R. (3d) 1, 24 C.C.C. (3d) 321, 19 C.P.R. 308, 26 D.L.R. (4th) 200, 65 N.R. 87, 14 O.A.C. 335.
43. "The Canadian Constitution: Highlights" Government of Canada, 1982 at 3.
44. See *Ford v. A.G.*, Que., [1988] 2 S.C.R. 712, 54 D.L.R. (4th) 577, 10 C.H.R.R. D/5559, 19 Q.A.C. 69 (*sub nom. Chaussure Browns's Inc. v. Que. (P.G.)*), 90 N.R. 84.
45. *Ibid.*
46. Charter, note 35 above, s. 2.
47. Election Act, R.S.O. 1990, c. E.6.
48. Charter, note 35 above, ss. 3 and 4.
49. *Ref. re s. 94(2) of the Motor Vehicle Act (B.C.)*, [1985] 2 S.C.R. 486, 69 B.C.L.R. 145, 48 C.R. (3d) 289, 36 M.V.R. 240, [1986] 1 W.W.R. 481, 23 C.C.C. (3d) 289, 18 C.R.R. 30, 24 D.L.R. (4th) 536, 63 N.R. 266.
50. *R. v. Morgentaler, Smoling and Scott*, [1988] 1 S.C.R. 30, 63 O.R. (2d) 28, 62 C.R. (3d) 1, 37 C.C.C. (3d) 449, 31 C.R.R. 1, 44 D.L.R. (4th) 385, 82 N.R. 1, 26 O.A.C. 1.
51. *Operation Dismantle Inc. v. R.*, [1985] 1 S.C.R. 441, 12 Admin. L.R. 16, 13 C.R.R. 287, 18 D.L.R. (4th) 481, 59 N.R. 1.
52. *Hunter v. Southam*, [1984] 2 S.C.R. 145, 33 Alta. L.R. (2d) 193, 27 B.L.R. 297, 41 C.R. (3d) 97, [1984] 6 W.W.R. 577, 55 A.R. 291, 14 C.C.C. (3d) 97, 2 C.P.R. (3d) 1, 9 C.R.R. 355, 11 D.L.R. (4th) 641, 84 D.T.C. 6467, 55 N.R. 241.
53. M. Dambrot, "Search and Seizure" in *Criminal Procedure 1986-87* (Toronto: Law Society of Upper Canada, 1986) at 19.
54. P. Hogg, note 28 above at 756.
55. *R. v. Duguay, Murphy and Sevigny* (1985), 50 O.R. (2d) 375, 45 C.R. (3d) 140, 8 O.A.C. 31, 18 C.C.C. (3d) 289, 17 C.R.R. 203, 18 D.L.R. (4th) 32 (C.A.).
56. *R. v. Anderson* (1984), 45 O.R. (2d) 225, 39 C.R. (3d) 193, 2 O.A.C. 258, 10 C.C.C. (3d) 417, 7 D.L.R. (4th) 306 (C.A.).
57. Young Offenders Act, note 13 above, s. 56.
58. *R. v. Big M Drug Mart*, [1985] 1 S.C.R. 295, 37 Alta. L.R. (2d) 97,

[1985] 3 W.W.R. 481, 60 A.R. 161, 18 C.C.C. (3d) 385, 85 C.L.L.C. 14,023, 13 C.R.R. 64, 18 D.L.R. (4th) 321, 58 N.R. 81.

59. *Rahey v. R.*, [1987] 1 S.C.R. 588, 57 C.R. (3d) 289, 193 A.P.R. 183, 33 C.C.C. (3d) 289, 33 C.R.R. 275, 39 D.L.R. (4th) 481, 75 N.R. 81, 78 N.S.R. (2d) 183.
60. The prior legislation in Ontario allowed police officers to select the Justice of the Peace who laid charges. These justices were employed on a fee for service basis which raise serious questions of partiality. See *Ref. re Justices of the Peace Act; Re Currie and Niagara Escarpment Commission* (1984), 48 O.R. (2d) 609, 16 C.C.C. (3d) 193, 14 D.L.R. (4th) 651, 6 O.A.C. 203 (C.A.).
61. *R. v. Oakes*, note 42 above.
62. *Trumbley v. Metro Police Force*, [1987] 2 S.C.R. 582 (*sub nom. Trimm v. Durham Regional Police*), 29 Admin. L.R. 106, 37 C.C.C. (3d) 120, 32 C.R.R. 244, 45 D.L.R. (4th) 276, 81 N.R. 197, 24 O.A.C. 357; *R. v. Wigglesworth*, [1987] 2 S.C.R. 541, 28 Admin. L.R. 294, 60 C.R. (3d) 193, [1988] 1 W.W.R. 193, 37 C.C.C. (3d) 385, 32 C.R.R. 219, 45 D.L.R. (4th) 235, 81 N.R. 161, 24 O.A.C. 321, 61 Sask. R. 105.
63. Charter, note 35 above, ss. 7-14. See also *The Canadian Charter of Rights, Annotated* (Toronto: Canada Law Book, 1982) for the explosion of cases dealing with issues raised by the Charter.
64. Canadian Charter of Rights and Freedoms, Part 1 of the Constitution Act, 1982, being Schedule B of the Canada Act 1982 (U.K.), c. 11, s. 15.
65. *Addy v. Canada*, [1985] 2 F.C. 452, 8 C.C.E.L. 13, 5 C.P.C. (2d) 127, 19 C.R.R. 193, 22 D.L.R. (4th) 52 (Fed. T.D.).
66. A.F. Bayefsky and M. Eberts, eds., *Equality Rights and the Canadian Charter of Rights and Freedoms* (Toronto: Carswell, 1985) at 2.
67. *Ref. re An Act to Amend the Education Act* (1986), 53 O.R. (2d) 513, 23 C.R.R. 193, 25 D.L.R. (4th) 1, 13 O.A.C. 241. Affirmed [1987] 1 S.C.R. 1148, 40 D.L.R. (4th) 18, 77 N.R. 241, 22 O.A.C. 321.
68. *Blainey v. Ont. Hockey Assoc.* (1986), 54 O.R. (2d) 513, 10 C.P.R. (3d) 450, 21 C.R.R. 44, 26 D.L.R. (4th) 728, 14 O.A.C. 194 (C.A.). Leave to appeal to S.C.C. refused (1986), 58 O.R. (2d) 274 (headnote), 10 C.P.R. (3d) 450n, 21 C.R.R. 44n, 72 N.R. 76 (note), 17 O.A.C. 399 (note) (S.C.C.); *Re Family Benefits Act* (1986), 186 A.P.R. 338, 26 C.R.R. 336, 75 N.S.R. (2d) 338 (C.A.).
69. *Weinstein v. Min. of Education for B.C.*, 65 B.C.L.R. 46, [1985] 5 W.W.R. 724, 20 D.L.R. (4th) 609 (S.C.).
70. *R. v. Swain* (1986), 53 O.R. (2d) 609, 50 C.R. (3d) 97, 24 C.C.C. (3d) 385, 18 C.R.R. 209, 13 O.A.C. 161 (C.A.). Leave to appeal to S.C.C.

granted (1987), 59 O.R. (2d) 463 (headnote), 55 C.R. (3d) xxxii (note), 27 C.R.R. 296, 75 N.R. 400 (note), 21 O.A.C. 320 (note) (S.C.C.).

71. *Re MacVicar and Supt. of Family and Children's Services*, 10 B.C.L.R. (2d) 234, [1987] 3 W.W.R. 176 (*sub mon. M. (N.) v. B.C. (Supt. of Family and Child Services)*), 29 C.R.R. 37, 34 D.L.R. (4th) 488 (S.C.).
72. *Silano v. B.C.*, 29 Admin. L.R. 125, 16 B.C.L.R. (2d) 113, [1987] 5 W.W.R. 739, 33 C.R.R. 331, 42 D.L.R. (4th) 407 (S.C.).
73. *Re Lavigne and Ont. Public Service Employees Unions (No. 2)* (1987), 60 O.R. (2d) 486 (H.C.).
74. Charter, note 64 above, s. 6.
75. *Law Society of Upper Canada v. Skapinker*, [1984] S.C.R. 357, 20 Admin. L.R. 1, 11 C.C.C. (3d) 481, 8 C.R.R. 193, 9 D.L.R. (4th) 161, 53 N.R. 169, 3 O.A.C. 321.
76. Charter, note 64 above, s. 16.
77. Charter, note 64 above, s. 23.
78. *Ref. re Education Act of Ont. and Minority Language Rights* (1984), 47 O.R. (2d) 1 (C.A.) at 57.
79. *Marchand v. Simcoe County Bd. of Education (No. 2)* (1987), 61 O.R. (2d) 651, 33 C.R.R. 189, 44 D.L.R. (4th) 171 (H.C.).
80. Charter, note 64 above, s. 25 and the Constitution Act, 1982, being schedule B of the Canada Act 1982 (U.K.), 1982, c. 11, s. 35.
81. Charter, note 64 above, ss. 26 and 27.
82. *Hunter v. Southam*, [1984] 2 S.C.R. 145, 33 Alta. L.R. (2d) 193, 27 B.L.R. 297, 41 C.R. (3d) 97, [1984] 6 W.W.R. 577, 55 A.R. 291, 14 C.C.C. (3d) 97, 2 C.P.R. (3d) 1, 9 C.R.R. 355, 11 D.L.R. (4th) 641, 84 D.T.C. 6467, 55 N.R. 241 at S.C.R. 155.
83. *R. v. Big M Drug Mart*, note 58 above.
84. *Ref. re s. 94(2) of the Motor Vehicle Act (B.C.)*, [1985] 2 S.C.R. 486, 69 B.C.L.R. 145, 48 C.R. (3d) 289, 36 M.V.R. 240, [1986] 1 W.W.R. 481, 23 C.C.C. (3d) 289, 18 C.P.R. 30, 24 D.L.R. (4th) 536, 63 N.R. 266.
85. *Singh v. Canada (Minister of Employment and Immigration)*, [1992] 1 F.C. 332, 14 Immigration Law Review (2d) 126 (T.D.).
86. *Ref. re An Act to Amend the Education Act (Ontario)* (1987), 40 D.L.R. (4th) 18, [1987] 1 S.C.R. 1148, 77 N.R. 241.
87. *R. v. Blake* (1988), 42 C.C.C. (3d) 271 (Man. Prov. Ct.).
88. *Canadian Civil Liberties Association v. Ontario (Minister of Education)* (1990), 65 D.C.R. (4th) 1, 71 O.R. (2d) 341 (C.A.).
89. Charter, note 64 above, s. 24(1).
90. Charter, note 64 above, s. 24(2).

91. Access to Information Act and the Privacy Act, R.S.C. 1985, c. A-1.
92. Freedom of Information and Protection of Individual Privacy Act, R.S.O. 1990, c. F.31.

Bibliography

Banks, Margaret A., *Using a Law Library*, 3rd ed (Toronto: Carswell Co., 1980).

Borovoy, Alan, *When Freedoms Collide* (Toronto: Lester & Orpen Dennys, 1989).

Fitzgerald, Patrick, *This Law is Ours* (Toronto: Prentice-Hall, 1977). *A Handbook of Canadian Legal Terminology* (Toronto: General, 1977).

Flynn, William J., *A Handbook of Canadian Legal Terminology* (Toronto: General, 1977).

Gall, Gerald L., *The Canadian Legal System* (Toronto: Carswell Co., 1990).

Guy, James. J., *How We Are Governed: The Basics of Canadian Politics and Government* (Toronto: Harcourt Brace & Company Canada, 1994).

Hogg, Peter W., *Constitutional Law of Canada* (Toronto: Carswell Co., 1985), for a superb discussion of the Constitution Act.

Hogg, Peter, "*The Difficulty of Amending the Constitution of Canada*" (Spring, 1993) 31 Osgoode Hall Law School., p. 41-61.

McConnell, W.H., "*A Half Century of Constitutional Turbulence*" (1993) 57 Sask. L. Review, 105-205.

Romney, Paul, "*Constitutional Inadequacy*"(Spring, 1995) 8 Can J.L. & Soc. 183-196.

3

Human Rights

Human rights legislation exists in each of the provinces in addition to the federal Human Rights Code which applies to federal employees, railway, airline, and interprovincial employees.[1]

In general, such legislation, particularly prior to the enactment of the Charter of Rights, gave Canadians some legal assurance that fundamental rights of access to jobs, housing, and public facilities would not be denied capriciously on prohibited grounds of discrimination either by institutions or by individuals. The Charter is designed to protect individual rights against the state; human rights legislation is designed to protect individuals rights against the acts of other individuals.

HUMAN RIGHTS CODE

The Ontario Human Rights Code[2] was built on the precedents established by the first Ontario Human Rights Code in 1962, but the new Code includes more prohibited grounds of discrimination and is potentially more effective.[3] Enforcement procedures have been given greater emphasis. This Code prohibits discrimination on the basis of race, ancestry, place of origin, colour, ethnic origin, citizenship, creed, sex, age, marital status, family status, or handicap in contracts, employment, access to accommodation and membership in vocational organizations. There is a provision which states that "no person shall infringe or do, directly or indirectly, anything that infringes a right under this Part".[4]

It also contains definition clauses, that is, it sets out specific actions and specific exceptions pertaining to rights. In addition, it imposes a condition on contracts made with the provincial government so that a finding of discrimination may compel the government to cancel a contract or withhold a grant.[5] The Ontario Human Rights Commission sets in place a race relations division of the Commission[6] which has the authority to investigate complaints, to intervene in community problems arising from discrimination, to recommend affirmative action programmes, and to mediate a situation arising out of a complaint. Community education and preventive services remain as functions of the Commission.

REPRESENTATIONS OF PARTIES IN A BOARD OF INQUIRY PROCEEDING

A party to a board of inquiry proceeding may be represented by counsel or an agent. A tribunal may exclude from a hearing anyone, other than a lawyer qualified to practise in Ontario.

ENFORCEMENT OF AN ORDER

An order of the board of inquiry may be enforced in the same manner as a judgment of the court.[7] If an order of a board of inquiry is ignored, a prosecution may be launched and if the person is convicted of non-compliance with an order, he or she may be subject to a fine of up to $25,000.

APPEALS

Any party may appeal a decision or order of a board of inquiry to the Divisional Court.[8] The appeal may be launched on the basis of law or fact or both and the court may affirm or reverse the decision of the board.[9]

The following cases are examples of human rights code. Louis Blatt was hired by the Catholic Children's Aid Society of Metropolitan Toronto to be a child care worker in a boys residence and was discharged on the same day as he was hired. He was thought to be well qualified for the job. But in giving information for pay and benefit purposes, he disclosed that he lived with his fiancee in what he referred to as a "common law" relationship. According to the Director of Foster Care Resources for the Society who made both hiring and firing decisions, these living arrangements were unacceptable because of a conflict with the therapeutic milieu of the Society's programme for the boys and also a conflict with the Society's position toward family life.

Mr. Blatt launched a complaint with the Ontario Human Rights Commission which looked at whether there was a breach of the section of the Code which prohibits discrimination on the basis of marital status. The decision was that the Society's objection related to a moral judgment about

Blatt's life style rather than to marital status. The Code, it found, was silent on morality and so the employee was dismissed.[10]

In another case, a 22-year-old single male telephoned in response to a newspaper advertisement for a two bedroom apartment and was invited to view the accommodation. He alleged that the rental agent asked his occupation and he replied that he was a university student. The agent stated that it was management's policy not to rent to single students. The complainant was not asked to produce any evidence of his financial status or a reference from his previous landlord. He filed a complaint with the Commission alleging discrimination in accommodation because of age and marital status, because he believed that a policy against renting to students adversely affected persons aged between 18 and 25.

The Commission contacted the owner of the building, who confirmed the existence of the policy. The respondent requested that conciliation negotiations be entered into immediately. In conciliation, the respondent agreed to inform all staff that the policy had been abolished, to invite the complainant to apply for the next available rental accommodation, and to compensate him in the amount of $150 for out-of-pocket expenses incurred as a result of discrimination. In addition, the respondent agreed to send the Commission written assurances of the company's policy of non-discrimination and to post Human Rights Code cards in all the apartment buildings.[11]

In the first case, the act of discrimination was not within the board's jurisdiction because Mr. Blatt's marital status was not at issue. The fact that he was living with a woman other than his wife was not a ground of discrimination prohibited by the Code. In the second case, the decision makes it clear that a landlord may not refuse housing to a young student solely on the basis of his student status.

HANDICAPPED PERSONS AND DISCRIMINATION

The Code defines handicap as:

> (i) any degree of physical disability, infirmity, malformation or disfigurement that is caused by bodily injury, birth defect or illness . . . including diabetes mellitus, epilepsy, any degree of paralysis, amputation, lack of physical coordination, blindness or visual impediment, deafness or hearing impediment, muteness or speech impediment, or physical reliance on a dog guide or on a wheelchair or other remedial appliance or device,
>
> (ii) a condition of mental retardation or impairment,
>
> (iii) a learning disability . . . , or
>
> (iv) a mental disorder.[12]

Though the Code offers protection against discrimination to all persons affected by these handicaps, there are significant limitations. For example, if a person does not have access to premises, services, goods, facilities, or accommodation because they are not appropriate for a person with a given handicap, the Code presumes no infringement. This is true only if the person is barred because of the physical nature of the facility. Discriminating attitudes on the part of owners or managers are seen as a breach of the Code.[13]

In employment issues, the test is whether the person is incapable of performing a *bona fide*, essential occupational requirement and not just an unessential duty or requirement.[14]

Compensation below the minimum wage paid for work performed in sheltered workshops is legal only if the operator of the workshop has obtained proper authorization. Other areas of discrimination permitted under the Code include:

1. special interest organizations may restrict membership or participation on the ground of handicap;[15]
2. residential accommodation can be denied or restricted on the ground of handicap where the occupants share bathroom or kitchen facilities with the owner or the owner's family;[16]
3. "special interest organizations" that serve handicapped persons may restrict employment, or give preference in employment, if the qualification is reasonable and *bona fide* given the nature of the employment;[17]
4. an individual may refuse to employ a person because of a handicap, where the primary duty is to attend to the medical needs of that individual or relative of that individual;[18]
5. where reasonable, certain employment benefit plans may discriminate on the ground of handicap. Employment may not be made conditional on qualification for such plans, and an excluded employee must be compensated.[19]

GENERAL HUMAN RIGHTS

Public Assistance Recipients

Those individuals who are receiving public assistance may not be denied accommodation for this reason or generally harassed. If a landlord can prove with reasonable evidence, however, that the person is habitually delinquent in paying the rent, then the Code is not deemed to have been infringed. Residential accommodation can be denied or restricted because the person is receiving public assistance, where the occupants share bathroom or kitchen facilities with the owner or the owner's family.

Discrimination against recipients of public assistance is a chronic concern of social workers. The rights of victims of AIDS and the rights of individuals regarding mandatory drug testing in the workplace remain controversial issues.

AIDS

Auto-immune disease syndrome is an alarming development because of the increasing incidence of the disease in all parts of the world, its inexorable course leading to agonizing debilitation and death and the lack of a reliable course of treatment or cure. Transmission occurs through sexual contact and through blood exchange.

Ethical issues have been generated as a consequence of establishing a system of reporting and recording those already infected, those testing positive to HIV antibodies and thus at potential risk of being carriers, and of informing those whose intimate sexual contact with these individuals may place them at considerable risk. There is the danger of creating social pariahs, of isolating those affected from essential social supports, of jeopardizing jobs and relationships, and of forcing people to avoid medical attention because of the potential economic and social consequences.

An old ethical dilemma reappears in responding to the current crisis. This dilemma is the weight to be placed on the individual's right to privacy as opposed to the rights of society collectively to act in its general best interests.

The experiences of social workers involved in work with AIDS patients should be shared with policy makers at all levels of government and non-government institutions in order to minimize the influence of public fear and ignorance in setting policy and procedures. Both social workers and lawyers need to act as advocates to provide guidance to services, to counteract misinformation and to work toward establishing an adequate support system composed of housing, medical facilities and resources, economic and emotional support, and legal protection.

Drug Testing in the Workplace

A "human rights" issue which is not specifically addressed by human rights legislation is the practice of routine or mandatory drug testing in the workplace. The most commonly used form of testing is urinalysis. By administrating an inexpensive test, traces of cannabis in urine can be detected.[20] There are other means used, but they are not as prevalent.

Employees in the public sector may be protected from routine blood testing by sections 7 and 8 of the Charter.[21] These sections guarantee security of the person in accordance with the principles of fundamental justice, and security against unreasonable search and seizure. In effect, intrusive procedures against a person are prohibited unless conducted in accordance with due process of law, or unless there are reasonable and probable grounds to believe that the person being tested is using prohibited drugs. A justification for routine or random drug testing may occur where public safety is at issue.

An American analysis of the most commonly used testing procedure, urinalysis, concluded that a blood test is a "search", bringing it within the American constitutional equivalent of the Charter's section 8 prohibition against unreasonable search and seizure.[22] A later case found that, although taking of a urine sample does not involve forced penetration of body tissues, such tests are entitled to the same scrutiny as blood tests because urine tests are in many respects more private than blood tests and may therefore infringe the right to security of the person guaranteed by section 7 of the Charter.[23] A similar analysis in another case concluded that the act of analyzing urine was as much an invasion of privacy as the actual taking of the sample.[24]

Section 7

The legality of drug testing will ultimately depend upon its method and impact. For example, if it is mandatory and is administered on a surprise or routine basis and is then taken to be conclusive proof of drug use leading to dismissal, it would almost certainly offend the Charter guarantee of due process by section 7.

Section 8

Whether drug testing by urinalysis is a reasonable search under section 8 of the Charter is also a relevant question. Canadian courts have provided some applicable principles, although in a different context. A threshold criterion has been set and it requires that the necessity for the search must be established on reasonable and probable grounds. Consequently a test which is routine for all or administered at random would not be based on reasonable and probable grounds and would offend the Charter. On the other hand, if such tests were administered on the basis of observed behaviour of specific individuals, they would likely meet the "reasonable and probable grounds" test. Routine tests of all persons who are employed where public safety is a major consideration, such as airline pilots or bus drivers, would also be likely to meet the test of reasonableness.

DNA TESTING

Testing of accused persons for their DNA (deoxi/ribonucleic acid), which might connect them to a crime, is a new and unsettled area of human rights law. When and under what circumstances can the person of an accused be examined to obtain DNA samples? Is the property of that person open to examination without consent? We have read a great deal about persons who were acquitted after many years because their DNA was held not to match evidence taken at the scene of the crime.[25] These and other questions and the legal boundaries are not yet established.

Remedies

If an employee's rights have been infringed and the Charter applies, the offended person can apply to a court for the appropriate remedy. For example, a person who lost employment could likely claim damages for the loss.

When the Charter is not applicable because the employment is in the private sector, the affected person may still apply to a court for a remedy and damages. The most likely claim would be for wrongful dismissal,[26] but could also include actions for intentional harm such as battery[27] or intimidation.[28]

Endnotes

1. See Table of Concordance — Human Rights.
2. Ontario Human Rights Code, R.S.O. 1990, c. H.19.
3. J. Keene, *Human Rights in Ontario* (Toronto: Carswell Co., 1983) at 1.
4. Note 2 above, s. 8.
5. *Ibid.*, s. 25(3).
6. *Ibid.*, s. 27.
7. Statutory Powers Procedure Act, R.S.O. 1980, c. 484, s. 19.
8. Note 2 above, s. 41(1).
9. *Ibid.*, s. 41(3).
10. *Blatt v. Metro. Toronto Catholic Children's Aid Society* (1980), 1 C.H.R.R. D/72 (Ont. Bd. of Inquiry).

11. Ontario Human Rights Commission, Annual Report, 1982-83, at 51-2.
12. Note 2 above, at s. 9(b).
13. *Ibid.*, s. 16(1). See also Keene, note 3 above, at 159ff.
14. Keene, note 3 above, at 162-3.
15. Note 2 above, s. 17.
16. *Ibid.*, s. 20(1).
17. *Ibid.*, s. 23(a).
18. *Ibid.*, s. 23(c).
19. *Ibid.*, s. 24(1), (3) and (4).
20. P. Hunter, "Your Urine or Your Job" (1986) 19 Loyola of L.A. Law R. 1451 at 1455.
21. Canadian Charter of Rights and Freedoms, Part 1 of the Constitution Act, 1982, being Schedule B of the Canada Act 1982 (U.K.), 1982, c. 11, ss. 7 and 8.
22. *Schmerber v. California* (1966), 384 U.S. 757.
23. *Storms v. Coughlin* (1984), 600 F.Supp. 1214.
24. *McDonnel v. Hunter* (1985), 612 F.Supp. 1122.
25. Notably *R. v. Morin* (1977), 6 C.R. (5th) 137 (C.A.), and *R. v. Milgaard*, [1992] 1 S.C.R. 866, 71 C.C.C. (3d) 260, both were acquitted, after conviction and long periods of incarceration, on DNA evidence.
27. D.J. Besharov, *"The Vulnerable Social Worker: Liability for Serving Children and Families* (Silverspring, Md.: National Assoc. of Social Workers, 1985).
27. A. Linden, *Canadian Tort Law*. (Toronto: Butterworths, 1983) at 38.
28. *Rookes v. Barnard*, [1964] 1 All E.R. 367, [1964] A.C. 1129, [1964] 2 W.L.R. 269 (H.L.); and *Central Can. Potash Co. v. A.G. Sask.*, [1978] 1 S.C.R. 42, 6 C.C.L.T. 265, [1978] 6 W.W.R. 400, 88 D.L.R. (3d) 609, 23 N.R. 481.

Bibliography

Bayefsky, Anne F. and Mary Eberts, eds., *Equality Rights and the Canadian Charter of Rights and Freedoms* (Toronto: Carswell, 1985).

Beckton, Claire F. "The Interpretation of the Equality Guarantees in the Charter." Ottawa Public Law Branch, Department of Justice May 1985.

Berger, Thomas R., *Fragile Freedoms, Human Rights and Dissent in Canada* (Toronto: Clarke, Irwin, 1982).

Bryden, Philip, Steven Davis, and John Russell, eds. Protecting Rights and

Freedoms: Essays on the Charter's Place in Canada's Political, Legal and Intellectual Life (Toronto: University of Toronto Press, 1994).

Carver, Peter. The Canadian Charter of Rights and Freedoms and Disabled Persons: A Research Report" (Vancouver: Public Interest Advocacy Centre, 1987).

Chotalia, Shirish. The Vriend decision: a case study in constitutional remedies in the human rights intext. (Case Comm.) *Vriend v. Alberta* (1994), 18 Alta. L.R. 825-839.

Howe, R. Brian. "The Reputations of Human Rights Commissions in Canada", (Fall, 1994) 9 Can.J.L.& Soc. Policy 1-20.

Hughes, Margaret. "Personal Guardianship and the Elderly in the Canadian Common Law Provinces: An Overview of the Law and Charter Implications" in *National Themes in Family Law*. M. Hughes and D. Pask, eds. (Toronto: Carswell, 1988).

Hunter, Patricia. "Your Urine or Your Job". (1986) 19 Loyola of L.A. Law R. 1451.

Law and the Physically Handicapped (Windsor: Community Law Programme, Faculty of Law, University of Windsor, 1981).

Law and the Visually Impaired (Windsor: Community Law Programme, Faculty of Law, University of Windsor, 1981).

Manfredi, Christopher P. "Appropriate and Just in the Circumstances" Public Policy and the Enforcement of Rights under the Canadian Charter of Rights and Freedoms. (September, 1994) 27 Can.J.Pol.Sc. 435-463.

4

Confronting the Courts

THE COURT SYSTEM

"All rise."

"Oyez! Oyez! All persons having business before this Honourable Court draw near and you shall be heard. God save the Queen.

"Be seated please."[1]

The black-robed crier shuffles papers on a raised dais. Behind him, above everyone else sits a solemn faced person in silken robes, dwarfed by an enormous Coat of Arms. Beside the crier sits yet another person, not robed, fidgeting with a flat grey box — a recording machine! Two black-robed people stand at either end of a long table at the foot of the dais, respectfully facing the silken robe.

In a typical courtroom, civility, ceremony and solemnity prevail. The judge is always addressed by a standing, bowing participant and is referred to as "Your Lordship" in the Court of Appeal and formerly in the Supreme Court or "Your Honour" in all other courts. Even a justice of the peace is called "Your Worship". The Zuber Commission recommended that all judicial officials, at all levels of court, be addressed as "Your Honour."[2] This has largely been adopted in Ontario, but old custom lingers. Lawyers at the long counsel table are referred to as "counsel" in court, opposing lawyers refer to one another as "my friend". The clerk of the court opens the court, calls cases and records decisions on court documents while the court reporter records all the evidence in trial — every word! Symbols of solemnity proclaims that this is where JUSTICE is done.

Every person appearing before a court must enter into a predetermined role. In effect, before any matter is tried, both the person and the issue are re-defined in legal terms.[3] The contrast with social work practice and training is marked. All social work training is directed to making people comfortable in an atmosphere of informality. The entire court process demands formality and assigns prescribed roles to all participants. The effect on clients is to increase, not lessen, their anxiety.

On many occasions, social workers are called upon to appear in court to give evidence in connection with their professional employment, or to assist clients who are summoned to appear as witnesses, or are themselves the subject of a court proceeding. On other occasions clients are required to appear before a board or tribunal to have a dispute settled. For most citizens outside the legal profession the experience is intimidating and confusing, affecting client and social worker alike.

The courts are society's formal means of dispute resolution. They are divided into courts of civil and criminal jurisdiction. Criminal law matters are always determined in the courts, while civil matters are determined both in courts and in decision-making boards and tribunals. Both criminal and civil courts are further divided into courts of superior and inferior jurisdiction. Tribunals are special bodies set up to decide many specific matters, including immigration, labour and income maintenance disputes, such as family allowance, welfare and unemployment insurance. The sole function of all courts is to decide disputes rationally and fairly according to established rules of procedure and evidence. Many boards and tribunals also have a decision-making function similar to that of the courts but their powers are much narrower in scope since their authority is entirely statutory.

A FIELD GUIDE TO THE PROPER COURT

Why a particular matter must be heard in a particular court is a mystery to the non-lawyer. Why can custody and access be decided either in a provincial family court or a superior court (Ontario Court — General Division), whereas family property matters must always be decided at the superior court level? Similarly, why can a charge of theft be tried in provincial criminal court, or the superior court of the province? In determining the appropriate court, it is not sufficient to be aware of the difference between civil and criminals matters. The issues to be addressed, the quantum or amount of money involved, the parties to the dispute, federal and provincial powers, and rules of procedure all combine to determine under what circumstance and in which court a case will be heard.[4]

To confound the confusion, the Province of Ontario, and other jurisdictions across Canada have been engaged in major revisions and consolidations. For example, there has been considerable progress in combining all family matters in Unified Family Courts which have authority to deal with all matters arising from family relationships, including all disputes, custody, support, property and child protection disputes. The monetary jurisdiction of provincial small claims court continues to expand, and in Ontario, they are now a part of the General Division, a superior court with federally appointed judges. Rules of the Court, which set out court procedure and the documents required to bring a claim before a judge, are also being subjected to major revisions.

A further initiative which is expected to settle a great many legal proceedings without the necessity of trial is the proposal requirement for mediation of all civil matters at an early stage. "Disclosure conferences" are now required in criminal proceedings as well as other initiatives to keep minor offences out of court entirely. The conclusion, therefore, is that anyone who has a court proceeding pending must check with the court, or a lawyer, to know where the matter should be commenced.

These changes are designed to avoid costly and lengthy court proceedings where possible, which should advantage all potential litigants. Non-adversarial methods of resolution are being encouraged, but formal court proceedings are available if necessary, or if other approaches fail.[5]

Federal Courts[6]

The Federal Court of Canada, Trial Division, tries cases that are purely federal in nature, as defined by the Constitution Act, such as civil claims against the federal government or any of its agencies, departments or federal Crown corporations. This is also the court which hears applications to review the decisions of federal boards and tribunals.[7] Although it is a superior court, there is no provision for trial by jury. Appeals from the Federal Court, Trial Division, are heard by the Appeal Division and further appeals may be heard by the Supreme Court of Canada.

The Supreme Court of Canada is the final court of appeal in both civil and criminal matters. Appeals may be taken on matters of law either with leave of the court or as a matter of right depending on the decision being appealed. The Supreme Court of Canada also has original jurisdiction in constitutional matters. For example, issues affecting mineral rights within provincial boundaries and off-shore oil rights have been referred to the Supreme Court because of the constitutional issue. Questions concerning the validity of legislation enacted by a province may also be referred to the Supreme Court. The further important feature of the Supreme Court of Canada lies in the fact that its decisions are binding on all other courts and must be followed by them.

Provincial Courts

Provincial small claims court

Provincially constituted courts have authority under the Constitution Act to decide all matters which are under the power of the provinces, such as property, civil rights of citizens of the province and the supervisory authority over children. They also have power to hear matters granted to them under federal laws which are made under the federal power. The most important of these is the authority to hear criminal matters under the Criminal Code of Canada.

Each district of a province has a small claims court to deal with money claims to small amounts. Increase will enable claimants to recover larger sums through a simple procedure. Parties frequently represent themselves or may be represented by counsel or an agent. Appeals may be taken to a single judge of the Superior Court (General Division). These courts deal with the greatest number of civil claims.

Provincial family court

Provincial Family courts deal with two broad areas of law — family matters such as custody, access, support, child protection, wardship, adoption and criminal matters involving children. The family court has concurrent jurisdiction with the provincial superior court in family law matters. Certain criminal proceedings involving family violence may also heard in the family court, most notably spousal assaults and failure to provide the necessaries of life for children. Interestingly, neglect of a child may be heard as a civil matter under child welfare legislation or as a criminal offence under the Criminal Code. Both may be heard by a provincially appointed judge. Under the Young Offenders Act,[8] family courts have jurisdiction to try criminal offences committed by children under the age of 16.

Provincial family courts are unique to the extent that they are often less formal, parties may be unrepresented and the judge may play a more active role in eliciting the evidence. Many of these courts have ancillary social services attached to them, which may include participation by social workers, psychologists and psychiatrists. Their function is to ascertain the social issues relevant to families or which affect children. Counselling may be provided to family members or to persons appearing before the court. Family courts are designed by statute to respond to human needs in a helping, rather than purely adversarial, way.[9] This dual role creates ethical conflicts for lawyers as well as social workers. Law is adversarial by nature, social work conciliatory. Both professions can feel compromised when they depart from their traditional approaches in an attempt to address the dilemmas of families and children under legal and emotional stress.[10]

Provincial criminal courts

Provincial criminal courts have power to try virtually all "true" crimes, including Criminal Code offences except murder,[11] and most other offences created by federal statute, most notably drug offences. They also have power to try offences created by provincial statute, although these are now customarily tried in provincial offences court or a summary offences court. Preliminary hearings of indictable offences and decisions about whether or not a case will proceed to trial in a higher court are also made here. Proceedings are conducted before a judge sitting without a jury. Once the trial commences, an expedited procedure may be followed, but the trial itself may be delayed for many months because of crowded court dockets and the unavailability of witnesses. Appeals are heard in the Superior Court, with the possibility of further appeal to the Court of Appeal for the province. Provincial courts try the great majority of criminal cases in Canada, over 90 per cent in any given year.[12]

Provincial offences court

The Provincial Offences Act of Ontario[13] applies to all provincial legislation which creates a penalty upon violation.[14] The purpose of the Act is to simplify the procedure for provincial offences and to distinguish between provincial offences or "quasi-crimes" and true criminal offences. As a result, a great range of violations can now be prosecuted in a provincial offences court, including landlord and tenant offences, employment violations, environmental offences and violations of municipal bylaws, as well as highway traffic and liquor offences. The procedure in provincial offences court is simple: parties can prosecute or defend themselves or appear by agent, and the court may be presided over by a justice of the peace or by a provincial court judge. Appeals are heard either in a provincial court or to a Superior Court.

Unified Family Court[15]

The tremendous increase in the number of divorce petitions, coupled with the realization that many divorcing couples have only modest assets to divide, created a need for a local, less costly procedure. Judges sitting in Unified Family Court have Superior Court powers vested in them including full powers to deal with all property, custody and support matters, as well as the authority to grant a divorce. An increasing number of family matters are now heard in these courts where they are established. Some of these courts have mediation services. Where there is no Unified Family Court, parties must proceed in the Superior Court.

Surrogate Court[16]

Where wills, trusts and estates of deceased persons are concerned, the surrogate court is the proper court. Under the former Infants Act[17] and Minors Act,[18] this court also had jurisdiction over the custody, right of access to and support of children. Social workers may encounter custody and access orders made under these former Acts which are valid unless superseded by a more recent order. These Acts have been replaced in Ontario by the Children's Law Reform Amendment Act.[19] In Ontario, the Surrogate Court is now part of the Ontario Court (General Division), a Superior Court.

Superior Court of the province

In civil matters, this court has power to hear all money claims, regardless of the amount, has concurrent jurisdiction with the provincial court in many family law matters and has exclusive jurisdiction to hear divorce petitions by virtue of the fact that its judges are federally appointed. This is also the court of residual jurisdiction, meaning that where a statute is silent about the proper court, the Superior Court of the province will hear it. Jury trials are available with some exceptions, but are infrequently selected by the parties in civil matters.

In criminal proceedings, the Superior Court has power to hear all indictable offences, although in practice only the most serious offences such as murder, manslaughter and sexual assault are tried there. Murder must be heard in the Superior Court, by judge and jury except in Alberta, where a judge alone may hear it.[20] Otherwise, at the election of the accused, cases may be tried with or without a jury. It is always the nature of the offence, as defined in the Criminal Code or other federal statute, which determines whether or not it is a Superior Court matter.

In some provinces, a divisional court is constituted as a division of the Superior Court, sitting as a panel of three judges. It has the important functions of hearing appeals from decisions of administrative tribunals, applications for judicial review of their decisions and exercising a judicial supervisory role over them.

Family law division

The family law division of the Ontario Court (General Division) was specifically established to hear and decide all matters relating to family law for much the same reason as the Unified Family Court. There is no monetary limit. Where there is no Unified Family Court, this is the proper court for divorce and property matters.

Court of Appeal

The Court of Appeal is the highest court of a province in both civil and criminal matters, with power to hear appeals of cases originating from every court of the province, unless an appeal is restricted by law. Its decisions are binding on all other courts of the province. The only further appeal, and only in certain circumstances, is to the Supreme Court of Canada.

REFORM OF ONTARIO COURTS

Historically, the need for reform of a legal system has arisen when the procedures then in effect no longer met the needs of the society at the time. The preamble to the Zuber Commission Inquiry cited an instance of court reform in the time of Moses.

> Court Reform in Ancient Times
>
> On the morrow Moses sat to judge the people, and the people stood about Moses from morning till evening. When Moses' father-in-law saw all that he was doing for the people, he said, "What is this that you are doing for the people? Why do you sit alone, and all the people stand about you from morning till evening?" And Moses said to his father-in-law, "Because the people come to me to inquire of God; when they have a dispute, they come to me and I decide between a man and his neighbours, and I make them know the statutes of God and his decisions." Moses' father-in-law said to him, "What you are doing is not good. You and the people with you will wear yourselves out, for the thing is too heavy for you; you are not able to perform it alone. Listen now to my voice; I will give you counsel, and God be with you! You shall represent the people before God, and bring their cases to God; and you shall teach them the statutes and the decisions, and make them know the way in which they must walk and what they must do.
>
> Moreover choose able men from all the people, such as fear God, men who are trustworthy and who hate a bribe; and place such men over the people as rulers of thousands, of hundreds, of fifties, and of tens. And let them judge the people at all times; every great matter they shall bring to you but any small matter they shall decide themselves; so it will be easier for you,

> and they will bear the burden with you. If you do this, and God so commands you, then you will be able to endure, and all this people also will go to their place in peace."
>
> So Moses gave heed to the voice of his father-in-law and did all that he had said. Moses chose able men out of all Israel, and made them heads over the people, rulers of thousands, of hundreds, of fifties, and of tens. And they judged the people at all times; hard cases they brought to Moses, but any small matter they decided themselves. Then Moses let his father-in-law depart, and he went his way to his own country.[21]

The need for reform in Ontario became increasingly apparent. The cost of justice had far exceeded the income of the average individual, accessibility to justice was unevenly distributed throughout the province, and the multitude of courts with overlapping jurisdiction were incomprehensible to most persons.

Mr. Justice Thomas Zuber of the Ontario Court of Appeal undertook a major inquiry into the Ontario courts and their physical accommodation, personnel, administrative structure, accessibility and cost. The result of his committee's inquiry and deliberations was a major report. Aside from cost considerations and physical aspects, the major recommendation was that Ontario courts be restructured, renamed and rationalized into a two-tiered system (as opposed to five) which would be economically, geographically and intellectually more accessible to the public. The two levels of trial courts would be comprised of local courts of limited jurisdiction and a superior court of general jurisdiction. In effect, the result would be a Provincial Court and a Superior Court for the Province. The Provincial Court should be recognized as a single local court with criminal, civil and family jurisdiction, including youth court and surrogate court powers, which would sit in both large and small communities throughout the province. The Superior Court would consolidate the Supreme Court and District Court into a single superior trial court for the province into a considerably enlarged court which would sit throughout the year in each designated region of the province. The Court of Appeal would be renamed as the Supreme Court of the Province so that the name will designate its importance as the court of last resort for Ontario. These recommendations have now largely been adopted, with some revisions.[22]

BOARDS, COMMISSIONS AND TRIBUNALS

In addition to the civil and criminal court systems, a number of special-purpose commissions, boards, and tribunals have been established under both federal and provincial legislation. Examples of federally established tribunals include the Immigration Appeal Board and the

Unemployment Insurance Commission Board of Referees. Provincially constituted boards include the Social Assistance Review Board, the Workers Compensation Board and the Criminal Injuries Compensation Board. Their purpose is to provide a simplified means of dispute resolution outside of the courts.

A case which illustrates the operation of a statutory tribunal in an appeal capacity follows:

> Mrs. W., a mother of two young children, was found to be eligible for mothers' allowance under the Family Benefits Act (Ontario) since she had no other means of support, had been separated from her husband more than three months and her husband was not making court-ordered support payments. Once found eligible by the Director, she became entitled to receive regular payments. After a six-week reconciliation with her husband, which she did not report because he was unemployed, she was found to be ineligible for a six-month period for which the money was already paid. The overpayment was deducted from her family benefits cheques. Mrs. W. appealed to the Social Assistance Review Board. The Board reduced the overpayment period to five months. On further appeal to the (then) Supreme Court of Ontario, the decision that she was ineligible during reconciliation was upheld, since there is no discretion in the statute to pay benefits for a period when a person is not eligible. As a result the payments were deducted from her monthly cheque.[23]

It is paradoxical that reconciliation is encouraged by statute, which enjoins counsel to advise clients seeking a divorce concerning reconciliation counselling,[24] but the family benefits legislation is so constructed that persons needing public assistance are at risk of losing benefits if they reconcile. If you have a client who faces this dilemma, it is possible to report the reconciliation and obtain welfare benefits which provide less money than mothers' allowance. If there is a delay of several weeks in reporting reconciliation, however, welfare payments are not retroactive and mothers' allowance overpayment must be repaid.

A person who has been refused unemployment insurance and feels the refusal is erroneous has a right of review by the Unemployment Insurance Commission Board of Referees. In some circumstances, a further appeal from the decision of a tribunal may be taken to a superior court.

Where the tribunal or board has the power to make recommendations only or is an internal review body, the decision is said to be "administrative". Its decisions may not be subject to review by the courts at all, depending on the terms of the governing act. Other tribunals have decision-making powers. An example is the Ontario Review Board,[25] which has power to review detention and to order or discharge with conditions, or continued detention with conditions of persons committed to mental hospitals under Lieutenant Governor's warrants.[26,27]

All tribunals have a number of common characteristics. Principally, they are entirely creatures of the statutes which create them; they possess only those powers granted in the governing Acts. The tribunal members may be drawn from members of the public at large or from those with special expertise, such as labour and management representatives on labour boards, or from lawyers who may comprise a majority or minority.

Hearings before tribunals are usually less formal than proceedings before the courts, in order to provide for a speedy, inexpensive determination of the issue. The simplified procedure permits parties to represent themselves. However, tribunals have built up their own precedent and procedure over the years, with the result that hearings before some tribunals have become increasingly complex and protracted, often requiring legal representation to protect the interests of the parties. In many instances, statutory boards and tribunals may permit parties to be represented by agents, including social workers. In such cases, representation by an agent is at the discretion of the chairman and is not necessarily a right.

The Statutory Powers Procedures Act[28]

The legal concepts of "natural justice" and "fairness" apply very specifically to the manner in which tribunals conduct their hearings and arrive at their decisions. Here, the distinction between tribunals with decision-making powers and those with a review function only becomes significant. Where the statute grants a power of decision to a board, the Statutory Powers Procedure Act requires a hearing, opportunity to make full answer and defence and right to representation by counsel. In effect, the full panoply of rights afforded by natural justice applies. Where the function of the board is advisory only, the full range of legal protections afforded by the Statutory Powers Procedure Act does not apply. However, the doctrine of fairness requires, as a minimum, that the person be advised of the allegations against him and be afforded an opportunity to reply on his own behalf. Fairness also appears to require a hearing, permitting the person to be present to make representations, particularly where a substantial consequence will flow from the recommendations of the board.[29]

Endnotes

1. The cry which opens every sitting of the General Sessions of the Peace in The Ontario Court (General Division) sitting in criminal matters.

2. Report of the Ontario Courts Inquiry, "The Zuber Commission Report." (Ontario Ministry of the Attorney-General, 1987).
3. Professor A. Grant, Osgoode Hall Law School, speaking in the Intensive Criminal Law Program.
4. See G. L. Gall, *The Canadian Legal System* (Toronto: Carswell Co., 1990), Chapters 5 and 6 for an excellent discussion of the Canadian court system.
5. Also see Chapter 5 "Alternatives to Litigation."
6. Constituted under federal statutes with judges federally appointed.
7. Federal Court Act, R.S.C. 1985, c. F-7.
8. The Young Offenders Act was proclaimed in force April 2, 1984.
9. See, for example, the Provincial Courts Act, R.S.O. 1980, c. 398, the Child and Family Services Act, S.O. 1984, c. 55 and the Young Offenders Act, S.C. 1981-82-83, c. 110.
10. For an interesting discussion, see R. Komar. "Enforcement of Judgments and Orders in the Ontario Provincial Courts (Family Division)". Paper presented to Young Lawyers Division, Canadian Bar Association, Nov./Dec. 1982.
11. See Criminal Code, R.S.C. 1985, c. C-46, s. 469, which excludes such offences as treason, piracy, and criminal acts against Parliament and the Sovereign from trial in provincial court.
12. *The Justice System in Ontario* Government Publication, p. 39.
13. R.S.O. 1980, c. 400.
14. *Ibid.*, s. 145. See also W.D. Drinkwalter and J. Douglas Ewart, *Ontario Provincial Offences Procedure*. Toronto: Carswell Co., 1980.
15. Courts of Justice Act, R.S.O. 1990, c. C-43, as amended.
16. *Ibid.*
17. R.S.O. 1970, c. 222.
18. R.S.O. 1980, c. 292 [rep. 1982, c. 20, s. 4].
19. R.S.O. 1990, c. C-12.
20. Criminal Code, note 11 above.
21. Exodus 18:13-27 as quoted in "The Zuber Commission Report", note 2 above.
22. Zuber Report, note 2 above.
23. *Willey v. Social Assistance Review Bd.*, Ont. H.C., July 3, 1981 (unreported).
24. Divorce Act, S.C. 1986, c. 3, s. 10.
25. Criminal Code, R.S.C. 1985, c. C-46, as amended.
26. Mental Health Act, R.S.O. 1980, c. 262, s. 24.
27. An example of an internal board is the National Parole Board, which is part of Correctional Services Canada and has power to release prisoners before their full sentence has expired. Neither their recommen-

dations nor decisions to release are reviewable by the courts as a matter of right.

28. R.S.O. 1980, c. 484.
29. *Nicholson v. Haldimand-Norfolk Bd. of Police Commrs.*, [1979] 1 S.C.R. 311, 88 D.L.R. (3d) 671, 78 C.L.L.C. 14,181, 23 N.R. 410; *Martineau v. Matsqui Institution Inmate Disciplinary Bd. (No. 2)*, [1980] 1 S.C.R. 602, 13 C.R. (3d) 1, 15 C.R. (3d) 315, 50 C.C.C. (2d) 353, 106 D.L.R. (3d) 385, 30 N.R. 119.

Bibliography

Bogart, W.A. *Courts and Country: The Limits of Litigation and the Social and Political Life of Canada* (Don Mills, Ontario. Oxford University Press, 1994).

Casey, Brian, "The Players at a Criminal Trial", in *From Crime to Punishment*, 3rd ed., (ed.) Joel E. Pink and Donald C. Perrier (Toronto: Carswell, 1997) at 173-179.

Embree, John D., "The Advisory System of Justice", in *From Crime to Punishment*, 3rd ed. (ed.) Joel E. Pink and Donald C. Perrier (Toronto: Carswell, 1977) at 187-196.

Fradsham, Allan A. *Alberta Rules of Court Annotated 1994* (Toronto: Carswell, 1993).

Fuerst, Michelle, "When Societal Interests Outweigh a Right to Confrontation: Charter Protection for Child Witnesses" (1996), in *The Charter's Impact on the Criminal Justice System*, ed. Jamie Cameron (Toronto: Carswell, 1996) at 161-179.

Gall, Gerald L. *The Canadian Legal System.* Toronto: Carswell Co., 1990.

How To Make Small Claims Court Work For You: A Step by Step Guide to Making or Responding to a Claim. Toronto: Ministry of the Attorney General, 1993.

Jones, David Phillip, "Discretionary Refusal of Judicial Review in Administrative Law". (1981), 19 Alta. L. Rev. 483.

McCormick, Peter J. *Canada's Courts*. Toronto, J. Lorimer, 1994.

Murray, Donald C. "The Jury Trial", in *From Crime to Punishment*, 3rd ed., (ed.) Joel E. Pink and Donald C. Perrier (Toronto: Carswell, 1997) at 239-263.

Stortini, R. "The Role of the Canadian Jury." (1982), 24 C.L.Q. 244.

Williston, Brian D. "Trial Proceedings", in *From Crime to Punishment*, 3rd ed., (ed.) Joel E. Pink and Donald C. Perrier (Toronto: Carswell, 1977) at 181-186.

5

The Trial Process

INTRODUCTION

The trial is a contest between two adversaries, with one party emerging victorious. Each party is pitted against the other and each in turn presents all the evidence to support its position. Matters are, therefore, said to be "tried". The trial process has characteristics which have developed to ensure not only a fair trial but the appearance of fairness, on the principle that "justice must not only be done but be seen to be done". Proceedings are open to the public except in special circumstances where they are held in camera. Any citizen may enter any court to observe a legal proceeding.

Civil law deals with private matters such as property, contracts, financial matters, matrimonial disputes, custody of children, private wrongs, civil rights, and some regulatory matters. Civil law is largely a provincial responsibility. Some civil matters which affect the whole nation, such as immigration and telecommunications, are federal.

Criminal law deals with prohibited acts which are "crimes" or offences against society at large and are punished by the state on behalf of all of society. Criminal law and criminal procedure are exclusively within federal jurisdiction. There are also large numbers of provincial statutes which are regulatory in nature, create penalties, and are dealt with as "quasi-criminal" offences. The same conduct may sometimes incur both civil damages and criminal penalties. For example, a person who is criminally convicted of wilfully damaging property may also be required to pay civil damages for the same act.

Our society has begun to recognize that the adversarial process, which "tries" disputes is not necessarily the best or most effective means of resolving disputes. The trial process has become very cumbersome, sometimes protracted and exceptionally costly to litigants. Neither can the trial process recognize the interlocking complexities of any dispute. An alternative dispute resolution system has developed which uses methods such as fact finding, early neutral evaluation, mediation or conciliation, or arbitration to achieve resolution. These processes provide for flexibility in selecting the appropriate procedure, and an innovative approach which permits the needs and interest of the disputants to be recognized.[1]

CIVIL ACTIONS

Civil actions are commenced by the issuance of either an application or claim by the court, which is then personally served upon the other person, commanding him to appear in court. A claim filed in a provincial or family court is called an Application. The claim sets out the claimant's version of the facts in the dispute. These documents are personally delivered to the person named in the claim. If this person disputes the claim, he is entitled to submit a Defence or Answer to the court. If this is not done, judgment or a court order may be awarded to the claimant by default.

The persons then exchange documents called Pleadings which set out the facts and law upon which each side will rely. Each party is entitled to examine documents which their opponent intends to produce in evidence at the trial. If the case comes to trial, the plaintiff must prove his or her case on a "balance of probabilities", which simply means that the claim made by the applicant, more probably than not, is true. It is worth noting that the majority of civil cases never come to trial, but are settled out of court. In divorce matters, a Petition is filed with the court and is personally served on the respondent.

Many civil matters are now "pre-tried" in order to reduce the number of issues in dispute. Pending disposition of the whole matter, a judge may make interim orders which may award interim custody of children or support or possession of the family home to one of the parties, or some other order which continues in effect until trial or final order.

CRIMINAL PROCEEDINGS

All offences created by the Criminal Code,[2] the Narcotics Control Act,[3] the Food and Drugs Act[4] and a few other federal statutes are true criminal offences.[5] The court in which the offence is tried is determined by the type of offence. There are three types of criminal offences under the Criminal Code — indictable, summary conviction, and "Crown election"

Indictable offences are generally the more serious, such as murder, sexual assault, arson, robbery, fraud, theft over $1000, and possession of a narcotic for the purpose of trafficking. Being more serious matters, the trial process is more complex and formal. The person charged, called the accused is entitled to a preliminary hearing before a provincial court judge in the criminal division of the provincial court. The judge is required to determine if there is sufficient evidence to commit the person to stand trial. The test for such a decision, based on the evidence presented at the preliminary hearing, is "whether a cautious jury, properly instructed could convict".[6]

If the accused is committed for trial, an Indictment or document specifying the charge is laid before a superior court judge. The accused is entitled to trial by jury, if he so elects. A jury is usually mandatory for murder trials.

Penalties upon conviction range from a fine or suspended sentence to life imprisonment, depending on the circumstances of each case and whether or not a minimum sentence is imposed by the Criminal Code or other statute. In a few circumstances, notably for second convictions for impaired driving,[7] the law requires a mandatory minimum sentence. There were also mandatory minimum sentences for importation of drugs. However, the effect of the Charter, in some cases,[8] has been to temper the length and seriousness of these sentences.

Summary conviction offences, as the name suggests, are prosecuted by a simpler and more expeditious procedure. They are initiated by an Information, the document which details the charge, and are tried by a provincial court judge without a jury. These are generally the less serious offences, such as causing a disturbance or wilful damage to property. The maximum penalty which can be imposed is a $2000 fine, six months imprisonment, or both. Agents may represent accused persons in these proceedings or the accused may represent himself.

"*Crown election*" means that the prosecutor has the right to proceed either by indictment or summarily. The procedure is determined by the election: if it is indictable, the longer, more formal procedure is followed, if summary, the simpler form. The penalty is determined both by the election and by the circumstances of the case. Examples of such offences are assault, possession of property with a value over $1000 obtained by crime, damage to property and impaired driving.

PRE-TRIAL DISCLOSURE

It is axiomatic that a fair and speedy trial is desirable in both civil and criminal proceedings and is now guaranteed by the Charter.[9] In particular this is the case where the fate of a child or an accused person in custody is in the balance. A child's developmental needs cannot await a decision about care. Similarly, the accused person is presumed to be innocent until found guilty, yet his detention in custody awaiting trial may totally disrupt his life and that of his family. To expedite the work of the court, pre-trial disclosure is now mandatory. In both civil and criminal matters, disclosure is an established practice so that only those issues in dispute need come to trial. The following judgment[10] emphasizes the interest of the court in compressing the trial process through preliminary work that does not jeopardize fairness. This case also addresses the issue of the role of the child's legal representative when the child is too young or immature to give instructions.

Counsel brought a motion for the child in a Crown wardship proceeding. He sought an order that the mother of his infant client submit to an oral examination under oath to disclose her plans for the child so that he could take a position at trial on behalf of the infant. The mother opposed the application for Crown wardship and wished to keep the child. The essential allegation of the Children's Aid Society was that the mother was incapable of caring for the infant because of her history as a chronic schizophrenic. The mother's counsel was opposed to such a preliminary examination on the grounds that it might prejudice her client's position and was an intrusion into her client's rights. The child's lawyer argued that he could not represent the child's best interests unless he knew the mother's plans since his client could give no instruction. The judge stated, "it is my opinion that a sensible use of pre-trial discoveries will increase settlements and lighten the demand for trial days."[11] He ordered the examination to proceed with the mother's counsel present, but not the Society counsel who would, however, have access to a transcript of the examination.

APPEALS

As a safeguard, the decisions of trial judges, justices and chairs of tribunals are subject to appeal or to judicial review where an error is alleged, unless specifically exempt by statute. Reasons for appeal or judicial review are classified as "errors in fact", "errors in law", "procedural errors", and "jurisdictional errors". Errors in fact are said to occur when it is alleged that the facts presented in evidence at the trial or hearing have been improperly interpreted by the judge or chairperson. Errors in law are said to occur where it is believed that the relevant law has been misapplied. When a procedural right has been denied or omitted, a procedural error is alleged, and where the power to hear the matter at all is challenged it is then described as a jurisdictional error.

If an appeal is contemplated, it is always advisable to consult a lawyer without delay or the opportunity may be lost. There are strict time limitations governing appeals in both civil and criminal matters.[12]

DRAMATIS PERSONAE

Judges

The function of all judges is to decide the matters brought before them impartially and fairly. In the course of a trial the judge makes rulings on trial procedure and on the admissibility of the evidence, but generally takes no initiative in the presentation of evidence. The exception may occur in family law matters, where a judge will sometimes play an active role, since a fully adversarial proceeding is not necessarily the appropriate means of resolving a family dispute. Despite their broad powers, judges must be governed by the relevant law in making their decisions.

Not all judges have equal powers. The Constitution Act gives both the federal government and the provinces certain powers. All superior court judges of a province are appointed by the federal government, as are Federal Court judges and judges of the Supreme Court of Canada.[13] Superior court judges sit in the superior court, and the Court of Appeal for the province. Provincial court judges are appointed by the province. The source of a judicial appointment and the court to which judges are appointed determines their jurisdiction to hear and determine a particular matter. Judges of superior courts have the broadest power to hear most matters. Matters which they are excluded from hearing are set out in the statutes, for example, the Young Offenders Act.[14] This statute, which is federal legislation, designates a "youth court", which is a provincial court, to hear and determine criminal offences committed by young persons.

Judicial power to hear a matter may have far-reaching social consequences. For example, in a case before the Supreme Court of Canada, one issue raised was whether a provincial court judge, appointed by the province, had the power to award custody of a child to a Children's Aid Society.[15] Custody matters are clearly within the provincial power,[16] but the superior courts, whose judges are federally appointed, have traditionally exercised the *parens patriae* function (literally, "father of the country"), whereby the superior courts exercise the power of guardianship over persons under disability (including children) in the name of the sovereign.[17] The Supreme Court of Canada held that provincial court judges do indeed have sufficient powers to award custody.

Impartiality of judges is preserved by their security of tenure, except in the most extreme circumstances. They are therefore independent of the government which appoints them. Nevertheless their conduct is restricted and they are obliged to maintain impartiality. To further emphasize the requirement for impartiality, criminal sanctions flow from any attempt by any person to influence the course of judicial decision-making outside the trial process.[18] Exceptions to this principle include procedures approved by the courts such as pre-trial conferences in both civil and criminal matters.

Masters

Masters are judicial officers of the provincial Superior Court who have authority to make *interim* orders in civil matters. The final decisions on these matters must be made by a judge.

Justices of the Peace

Justices of the peace may have a significant impact on the lives of social work clients since they have decision-making powers in limited circumstances in criminal and "quasi-criminal" matters. These are the persons who issue summonses to appear in court and warrants to apprehend upon failure to appear. They also preside over the swearing of charges under oath, the interviewing of guarantors of accused persons released on bail, and the administering of oaths, affirmations and statutory declarations,[19] which are all statements taken under oath. For example, as a witness to an accident, one may be required to swear under oath that his statement is true. Justices also have power to conduct trials of most provincial offences, including highway traffic offences, bylaw infractions, landlord and tenant disputes and liquor law violations.

Parties

Persons appearing before the court who are named in the initiating document are referred to as "parties". In civil matters in the superior courts they are called "plaintiff" and "defendant", but "petitioner" and "respondent" in divorce actions. Provincial civil courts, such as family courts, generally use the terms "applicant" and "respondent".

In criminal matters the parties are always the Crown, representing the state, and the accused person. The Crown is represented by a "Crown prosecutor". The accused person is referred to as the "defendant" or the "accused".

Lawyers

In serious civil actions or criminal proceedings, parties are usually represented by lawyers, who are referred to as "counsel" in the court. All lawyers practising in Canada are members of their provincial Law Society, which controls admission to the profession in the province, establishes rigorous rules of conduct and ensures their enforcement. In order to appear as counsel in superior court matters, whether civil or criminal, the lawyer must have been admitted to the Bar of the province. In all indictable criminal proceedings, both the Crown prosecutor and defence counsel must be members of the Bar. Only in certain provincial court matters may the party be represented by someone other than a lawyer, although a party is always able to speak on his or her own behalf.

Lawyers are officers of the court in which they appear, and therefore have a particular obligation to assist the court. At the same time, they are retained by one of the parties and have an overriding obligation to advance and defend the best interests of that client. As a result, actions which are seen as harsh or unreasonable from a social work perspective may be considered by the lawyer to be both appropriate and necessary to protect the client's best interests in an adversarial system.

Crown Attorneys

In criminal matters, the Attorney General or Solicitor General of a province or the Attorney General of Canada, as representative of the Crown, has responsibility for the prosecution of criminal offences. The duty is delegated to assistant Crown attorneys, who are agents of the Attorney General and conduct criminal prosecutions at all court levels. As part of the prosecutorial function, Crown attorneys advise the police with respect to the evidence required to sustain a criminal charge, decide whether a charge which has been laid should proceed, and make submissions to the court with respect to bail pending trial and to sentencing upon conviction.

Agents

Parties appearing in certain matters under provincial jurisdiction may be represented by agents who are not lawyers, which could include social workers or community legal workers in appropriate circumstances. The function of an agent is to assist a party in the proceeding, to marshall the evidence, and to lead it in a consistent and organized manner. There is, however, no absolute right to representation by an agent; permission to appear as agent is at the discretion of the court or tribunal. The agent must not hold himself out to be a lawyer or to be practising law, and must not charge a fee for any service provided as agent. This prohibition is strictly enforced.

Witnesses

All persons who appear before the court to give testimony under oath in a proceeding are referred to as witnesses for one of the parties. Generally, the witness is a person who has personal knowledge of the matter, or has specialized knowledge which will assist the court.

Juries

A jury is a group of citizens who are eligible for jury duty under the provincial Juries Act,[20] are selected at random and are summoned to attend superior court for a specified period. From the persons summoned, called the jury panel, the jury is selected in open court and is sworn to be impartial between the parties.[21] A civil jury has six members; a criminal jury has twelve.

The task of the jury is to assist the judge in decision-making, but each has separate functions. The judge is the arbiter of the law, instructs the jury on the relevant law, and rules on the admissibility of evidence in the trial. The jury decides on the facts in dispute, but must be guided by the law as stated by the judge in reaching a decision. The ultimate decision in both civil and criminal cases is determined by the jury. In civil cases, judgment for the plaintiff or defendant is "found" by the jury, including the amount of monetary damages awarded. A verdict of "conviction" or "acquittal" is reached in criminal cases, but where the jury convicts, the sentence imposed is at the discretion of the trial judge. Only where the conviction is for murder does the jury participate in sentencing, by recommending the minimum period of imprisonment before parole eligibility.

Endnotes

1. See Chapter 6 — Alternatives to Litigation.
2. R.S.C. 1985, c. C-46.
3. R.S.C. 1985, c. N-1.
4. R.S.C. 1985, c. F-27.
5. Constitution Act, 1982, being Schedule B of the Canada Act 1982 (U.K.), 1982, c. 11, s. 91.
6. See *U.S.A. v. Shepherd,* [1977] 2 S.C.R. 1067, 34 C.R.N.S. 207, 30 C.C.C. (2d) 424, 70 D.L.R. (3d) 136, 9 N.R. 215.

7. Criminal Code, note 2 above.
8. *Smith v. R.*, [1987] 1 S.C.R. 1045, 34 C.C.C. (3d) 97, 31 C.R.R. 193, 40 D.L.R. (4th) 435.
9. See *R. v. Askov*, 59 C.C.C. (3d) 449, [1990] 2 S.C.R. 1199, 79 C.R. (3d) 273.
10. *Re M.* (1982), 29 C.P.C. 44 (Ont. Fam. Ct.).
11. *Ibid.*, at 47.
12. The effect of a successful appeal is to vary the original order.
13. Constitution Act, note 5 above, s. 96.
14. Young Offenders Act, R.S.C. 1985, c. Y-1.
15. *Reference re s. 6 of the B.C. Family Relations Act*, [1982] 1 S.C.R. 62, [1982] 3 W.W.R. 1, 26 R.F.L. (2d) 113, 36 B.C.L.R. 1, 131 D.L.R. (3d) 257, 40 N.R. 206.
16. *Reference re Adoption Act, Children's Protection Act, Deserted Wives' and Children's Maintenance Act*, [1938] S.C.R. 398, 71 C.C.C. 110, [1938] 3 D.L.R. 497.
17. *Black's Law Dictionary*, 5th ed. (St. Paul, Minnesota: West Publishing Co., 1979) at 1003.
18. Criminal Code, note 2 above.
19. In *Currie v. Niagara Escarpment Comm.*, released June 20, 1984, the Supreme Court of Ontario held that justices of the peace are not impartial as required by the Charter because their actions are controlled and their tenure determined by the government which employs them. The Attorney General of Ontario stated his intention to appeal this decision.
20. For example, see Juries Act, R.S.O. 1990, c. J.3.
21. Prospective jurors are subject to rejection by either party to the proceedings, either for cause or without cause. In criminal matters, the Crown may "stand aside" up to 48 prospective jurors whereas the accused may reject only 12 without cause.

Bibliography

Doherty, David, "Jury Instructions: Effective Camouflage?" (Winter, 1996) 16 *Advocates Society Journal* 16-18.

Feldthusen, Bruce, "Access to the Private Therapeutic Records of Sexual Assault Complainants" (December, 1996), 75 Canadian Bar Review 537-563.

Gorman, Wayne, "Hearsay in Sexual Offense Prosecutions" (May, 1997) 39 Criminal Law Quarterly 443-512.

LaJoie, Karen, "Bringing Justice to the People" [Practice of Criminal Law in the Northwest Territories] 4 National No. 7 (October, 1995), 39-43.

MacKenzie, Gavin, "Breaking the Dichotomy Habit: The Adversary System and the Ethics of Professionalism (January, 1996) 9 Canadian Journal of Law and Jurisprudence 35-50.

MacLeish, John A., "Advocacy in Jury Trials" (Summer, 1996) 15 Advocates Society Journal, No. 1, pp. 5-23.

Pink, Joel E. and Donald C. Perrier (eds.) *From Crime to Punishment,* 3rd ed. (Toronto: Carswell, 1997).

Poelman, Glen H., "Discovery Procedure and Practice: Recent Developments" (February, 1996), 34 Alberta Law Review 352-373.

6

Alternatives to Litigation

There has been a growing recognition that the traditional adversarial system does not serve the complex emotional and social aspects of any dispute. In recognition of the inadequacy of the judicial process, there has been a proliferation of alternate forms of dispute resolution. These include negotiation, fact finding, early neutral evaluation, conciliation, mediation, co-mediation, mediation/arbitration and arbitration among the alternate processes. They can be viewed on a continuum of dispute resolution, from the least complex negotiation to the most structured, with litigation and the court process as the ultimate alternative. There is also growing recognition of the usefulness of these alternative processes, not only for family and labour disputes, but for all civil actions and possibly even for some criminal proceedings.

A definition of some of the terms may help to identify the different processes. These distinctions to some extent depend on the level of activity of the neutral third party. They include:

1. **Negotiation** — two or more parties enter into discussions between themselves with the intention of resolving issues in dispute without the assistance of an outside party;
2. **Conciliation** — an outside party acts as a go-between with two or more parties in order to help them to begin discussions, to re-establish a relationship and possibly to help them to reach a resolution to the issues in dispute. This process is sometimes called "shuttle diplomacy" and can be seen as a species of mediation or as part of the mediation process;
3. **Mediation** — an outside party provides a structured process to

assist two or more parties to resolve their dispute on their own terms. This outside party may recommend ways to resolve the dispute, but has no power to decide for the parties or bind them to any particular solution;

4. **Co-Mediation** - mediation undertaken by two outside parties who provide a structured process to assist in settlement, generally where there are many disputants or extremely complex issues to be settled;
5. **Arbitration** — an outside party hears and assesses opposing sides to a dispute and makes a decision as to how it is to be resolved. The decision may be advisory only or may be binding on the disputing parties;
6. **Litigation** — the parties to a dispute use the formal court process in which a judge hears both sides and makes a decision about the issues in dispute which is binding on all parties. Unlike mediation and arbitration, the parties have no say in the identity, skill, training or aptitude of the judge.

Schools of social work now include courses in family dispute resolution and divorce mediation in their curriculum courses. Faculties of law have also introduced courses in alternate dispute resolution, including those dealing with family matters. Additional spurs to the adoption of alternate dispute resolution are the escalating costs of legal services, especially protracted litigation, and the long delays before cases come to trial. Minor matters in disputes between neighbours and school children are the focus of new programs which train pupils, teachers and community members in conflict resolution.

Judges, lawyers, and social workers are showing increased interest in resolving conflicts at the point where a marriage or relationship has broken down. By appointing a neutral third party skilled in dispute negotiation, a lengthy court battle may be averted. Custody and access matters concerning children are particularly suited to social work mediation. Matters concerning property should be mediated exclusively by lawyers or financial experts who possess the necessary knowledge in property and tax matters.

It is a worn truism that parents know what is best for their children, more than any third party, whether that be a judge, lawyer, or counsellor. Voluntary settlements, which are worked out by both spouses on an emotional level as well as an intellectual one, are not only more humane than those forced by litigation, but also more practical. Mutual agreement means that neither party is the "loser" or has been taken advantage of, so there is less likelihood of revenge erupting later, leading to new and prolonged legal battles.[1]

Provisions found in the Divorce Act and Children's Law Reform Act have resulted in the development of training programmes for mediators[2] and arbitrators in alternate dispute resolution. It is essential that social workers who have an interest in mediation secure special training in mediation. Social work expertise is especially valuable because social workers would be aware of the many contradictions and balances to be considered when determining the arrangement which would best meet the interests of the participants to the dispute. In family matters, the total family's needs, both economic and psychological are interdependent and must be addressed in mediation.

Those interested in training programmes have recognized the need for standards in determining qualifications for those who would provide mediation or arbitration services. Presently, there does exist a *caveat emptor* market in the private sector, but codes of ethics have now been developed by professionl mediation organizations.[3] Training programmes now emphasize communication skills and recognition of the unique needs and interests of the parties as the basis for a mutually acceptable resolution.

ALTERNATIVE DISPUTE RESOLUTION IN THE SUPERIOR COURTS

Pre-trial Hearings and Case Conferences

These hearings are for the purpose of reducing and resolving the issues in dispute between the parties. Pre-trials or case conferences may occur at any stage of litigation, including the period before legal proceedings are formally initiated. They give the parties the opportunity to attempt to resolve contentious issues in a more informal atmosphere than that of a courtroom. Counsel and both parties are generally present and the judge may see counsel separately as well as each party separately. The judge enters the arena by making comments, asking questions and doing whatever seems necessary to focus the discussion, clarify issues and search for resolution. Pre-trial conferences are confidential and the parties and their respective lawyers are ensured that the proceedings are conducted "without prejudice", meaning that the pre-trial proceedings cannot be referred to at trial. The judge at a pre-trial cannot preside at trial regarding the same issue. Agreements that are reached on any of the issues in dispute are recorded by the respective lawyers as Minutes of Settlement, signed by the parties, and may form part of the judgment of the court.

Pre-trial conferences encompass aspects of both mediation and arbitration and often include an early neutral evaluation by the judge of the likely outcome if the issues go to trial. No resolution can be imposed on the parties, so the judge must use the skill of mediation to focus and isolate areas of common agreement and to control the destructive effects of anger. However, the use of authority which resides in the judge and his experience with family matters are powerful influences on the openness of the parties to resolve issues in dispute. The judge's comments can help the parties to assess their alternatives, which can promote settlement without trial. Approximately 50 per cent of all family law cases settle at pre-trial.

MEDIATION OR CONCILIATION

The purpose of mediation is not reconciliation of the couple. The function of the mediator is to facilitate communication between the parties in order to enable them to work out their own solutions. This process may be ordered by the court with the consent of the parties.[4]

Mediation services have been developed in many jurisdictions throughout the United States and Canada. They provide an informal forum, outside the courts, for couples to work out arrangements for custody, access, and support through negotiation rather than in the adversarial atmosphere of the courtroom. The purpose is to move on from the fact of marriage breakdown and to assist couples to arrive at decisions through mutual negotiations. Unlike the adversarial approach, no blame is attached to either party in an attempt to sort out realistic options and consequences and to make choices and compromises. Some characteristics of effective mediation services are that they be: crisis-oriented, short-term, and available when needed; voluntary, available to either partner to petition for help; integrated into the formal court system so that they have the availability and the authority and dignity of the court; conducted with the guarantee of complete confidentiality; and multidisciplinary in nature. In Ontario, family court mediation services are attached to many family courts.

Unfortunately, mediation services are not uniformly available and therefore are not universally accessible. There may also be long delays in obtaining services. The legal profession has been slow to recognize and to support the value of mediation, which has resulted in inadequate mediation services within the legal system.

THE MEDIATOR

The role of the mediator, as the word suggests, is to come between the warring parties, isolate issues, look for areas of agreement, and possible resolutions. The objective is to assist the parties to reach agreement on outstanding issues. However, in mediation, the two parties may be so antagonistic that the mediator may need to shuttle between the parties to attempt to find potential areas of agreement upon which to build decisions. This process may reduce the number of issues that must come before the court and may be the most appropriate approach where the parties are unable to communicate with one another.

In Ontario, the Children's Law Reform Act,[5] specifically provides for mediation as does the Divorce Act. Once an application for custody or access is made, at the request of the parties, the court may appoint a person to mediate any matter specified in the order. The mediator must consent to act in this capacity and agree to file a report with the court within the specified time about the matters in issue.

Mediation, unlike arbitration, does not result in a decision or award made by the mediator in regard to the issues in dispute. Mediation provides the parties with a neutral third party who will assist them to isolate those issues on which they can agree so that few if any issues need to come to court. If no agreement can be reached, the court route is available to the parties, without prejudice. The mediation process can be either confidential or open, as the parties select.

There has been an increase in recourse to mediation to resolve all aspects of family disputes. Across Canada and internationally there is a thrust toward the establishment of organizations directed toward encouraging a more extensive use of mediation services. In Ontario as in other provinces, there are provincial organizations such as the Ontario Association of Family Mediation, Family Mediation Canada is the national organization which provides and updates a national directory of mediators and mediation services. Internationally, the Association of Family and Conciliation Courts and the Academy of Family Mediators actively promote mediation resolution of family disputes outside the normal litigation process. However, there are no uniformly recognized standards for mediators, although these are being developed.

The ADR Pilot Project — Ontario

An innovative, mandatory mediation initiative was created by the Government of Ontario on a pilot basis. All civil actions in the General Division, except family and labour matters, were required to attend at mediation at an early stage. More than fifty percent of cases referred have settled, giving mediation as a means of resolving disputes enormous impetus. However, the future of this pilot project and mediation services under court auspices is uncertain.

ARBITRATION

Where neither negotiation nor mediation is possible or appropriate, the couple may submit to arbitration wherein the decision-making power is vested in the arbitrator by the parties.[6] The arbitrator sits as an adjudicator, who must make a decision about the issues and is empowered to do so by the parties. She must therefore remain impartial between the parties.

There are two levels of arbitration, advisory and binding. Advisory arbitration implies that the parties may accept or reject the arbitrator's recommendations. If they accept, the recommendations are binding on the parties. If they reject them, they may then resort to the courts. In this event, the couples will have been advised that the arbitrator's report will be made available to the judge. Binding arbitration requires agreement at the outset that the decision of the arbitrator will be binding upon the parties with the same force as a court order.

Arbitration provides the parties to a family dispute with another alternative to the courts. The arbitrator is one who is agreeable to both parties and who is an expert in family law. This knowledge of family law is essential in order to avoid the dangers of decisions informed mainly by the personal beliefs of the arbitrator.

The arbitration hearings are arranged by the parties rather than imposed by the court system. The parties select their own procedure; for example, they can choose whether there will be oral evidence, what documentary evidence will be introduced, whether witnesses will be called and experts relied on, and whether the hearing will be recorded. Issues which are in dispute between the parties may include property, the amount and form of equalization payments, spousal and child support, as well as custody and access concerning children. Issues arising from the terms of contracts or the rights and obligations deriving from common-law relationships may also be presented for consideration and resolution.

When custody and access issues are in dispute and the parents appear to be using the child to batter one another, the arbitrator may need to call for an independent assessment which will provide assistance in making recommendations in the best interest of the child. It may be appropriate to retain other experts to complex financial and business matters.

Whenever a domestic contract such as a marriage contract or a separation agreement is contemplated, a clause requiring future contractual disputes to be settled by mediation or arbitration is often included. Such a provision can deflect future litigation.

ALTERNATE DISPUTE RESOLUTION

A growing body of literature and an expanding experience in other forms of dispute resolution confirms their utility as alternatives to litigation. Programmes and services designed to provide for mediation of disputes have developed in many communities, both in Canada and the United States, sometimes in multi-service neighbourhood centres. As court systems become clogged with cases delayed or postponed for long periods of time, as the cost of legal services increases, people who are involved in disputes with family members, with neighbours or other persons in the community or with consumer complaints have begun to utilize these services. The mediators, frequently social workers, attempt to facilitate the negotiation of a voluntary resolution which is acceptable to disputing parties. The process is focused on the complaint, but is not a legal proceeding and is informal and voluntary. A written, signed agreement may be reached which has the same legal force as any other contract which is enforceable by the courts if the terms are violated by either party. If the attempt at resolution fails, legal recourse is always possible.

Endnotes

1. H. Irving and B. Schlesinger, "Child, Custody, Canada's Other Lottery," in *The Child and the Courts,* I.F.G. Baxter and M.A. Eberts, eds. (Toronto: Carswell, 1978) at 71.
2. Divorce Act, S.C. 1986, c. 4, s. 10; Children's Law Reform Act, R.S.O. 1980, c. 68, s. 31.
3. See, for example, The Codes of Ethics of Family Mediation Canada, The Society for Professionals in Dispute Resolution and the Arbitration and Mediation Institute (Canada).
4. H. Irving, *Divorce Mediation: The Rational Alternative* (Toronto Personal Library Publishers, 1980). Although Irving and others use the terms conciliation and mediation interchangeably, their origins are different and some authors feel they are distinct processes.
5. Children's Law Reform Act, note 2 above, s. 31.
6. See the Arbitration Act, R.S.O. 1990, c. A-24.

Bibliography

Adams, George W. and Naomi L. Bussin, "*Alternative Dispute Resolution and Canadian Courts: A Time for a Change*", (May, 1995) 17 *Advocates Quarterly*, 133-157.

Ashley, Daniel and Julia Menard, "A Community Response to Crime and Conflict", (Aug. 1996) 21 *Law Now*, No. 1, 42-43.

Byron, Jeanne, "Resolving Conflict Out of Court", (Dec. 1995) 20 *Law Now*, No. 3, 19-22.

Carter, Thomas, "When Dreams Die: Family Transition Mediation", (Oct. 1996), 21 *Law Now*, No. 2, 14-16.

"Court-Connected Family Mediation Programs in Canada", (Research Paper: No. 20), Edmonton, Alta., Alberta Law Reform Institute, 1994, Vol. 1.

Folberg, Jay and Ann Milne, *Divorce Mediation* (New York: Guilford Publications, Inc., 1988).

Frost, Joyce and William Wilmot. *Interpersonal Conflict* (Dubuque: William C. Brown, 1978).

Goldberg, Steven, Eric Green and Frank Sander, *Dispute Resolution* (Boston: Little, Brown and Co., 1985).

Goss, Joanne, "An Introduction to Alternative Dispute Resolution", 39 *Alberta Law Review* 1-33.

Guravich, Michael B., "Counselling and Mediation in the Family Courts of New Brunswick", (Winter, 1996) 12 *Solicitor's Journal* No. 2, 23-26.

Irving, Howard J. and Michael Benjamin, *Family Mediation: Theory and Practice of Dispute Resolution* (Toronto: Carswell, 1987).

Kressel, K.N. Jaffee, B. Tuchman, C. Watson and M. Deutsch, "A Typology of Divorcing Couples: Implications for Mediation and the Divorce Process." (1980) 19(2) *Family Process*, 101-116.

Landau, Barbara. "Mediation: An Option for Divorcing Families." (1988) 9 The Advocates Quarterly 1-21.

Leonoff, Arthur and Robert J. Montague, *Guide to Family Assessments* (Toronto: Carswell, 1996).

Marlow, I. and Sauber, S.R., *The Handbook of Divorce Mediation* (New York: Plenum Press, 1990).

McLeod, James G., *Family Dispute Resolution: Litigation and Its Alternatives* (Toronto: Carswell, 1987).

Menard, A. and A. Salins, (1990) "Judicial Response to Family Violence: The Importance of Message", *Mediation Quarterly*, 7(4) Summer, 293- 302.

Miller, Marla S., "Mediation in Divorce", (May, 1994), 18 *Law Now*, No. 8, 16-19.

Muggli, Tracy, "Abused Women in Jeopardy: The Case Against Divorce Mediation", *The Social Worker*, Vol. 64(3) Fall, 1996, 21-28.

Payne, Julien D. and Eileen Overend. "Divorce Mediation: An Overview of Process and Strategies" in *National Themes in Family Law*, M. Hughes and D. Pask, eds. (Toronto: Carswell, 1988).

Phegan, Ruth, "The Family Mediation System: An Art of Distributions", (March, 1995), 40 *McGill Law Journal*, 365-413.

Portlock, Peter, "Dispute Resolved Through Mediation", (May, 1994) 18 *Law Now*, No. 8, 9-12.

"*Resolving Community Disputes: An Annotated Bibliography about Community Justice Centres*", ed. by Catherine Morris, Victoria, University of Victoria Institute for Dispute Resolution, 1994.

Severson, Margaret M. and Tara V. Bankston, "Social Work and the Pursuit of Justice Through Mediation", *Social Work*, Sept. 1995, Vol. 40, No. 5, 683-689.

Shaffer, Martha. "Divorce Mediation: A Feminist Perspective." (1988) 46 Univ. of Toronto Faculty of Law Rev. 162-200.

Simpson, Stuart, "I Won't See You in Court (Alternate Dispute Resolution Choices)", (May, 1994) 18 *Law Now*, No. 8, 6-8.

7

The Social Worker and the Court: Evidentiary Issues

INTRODUCTION

It is possible that social workers can practise for many years without ever being called to appear in court in a professional capacity. Most, however, have had at least one experience as participants in a court hearing. Workers in agencies with a legal obligation to protect the welfare of children and those workers directly involved with correctional services are most likely to encounter the experience, but private practitioners, those in medical and mental health settings, and workers engaged as client advocates may also be required to appear and give evidence. The process is one that many clients will also encounter as a consequence of their lifestyles. Apprehension and intimidation are felt by both workers and clients as they anticipate their day in court. The uninformed worker can offer little assurance to the client. For this reason, social workers need information on the rules of evidence, guidelines for presenting evidence, withstanding cross-examination and surviving the entire ordeal.

OATHS AND AFFIRMATIONS

When a person is sworn in as a witness, he is required to promise to tell the truth, usually by placing a hand on the Bible. If a person chooses, he has the right to state that he wishes "to affirm" that he will tell the truth and the Bible is omitted. The significance of the oath, which is rooted in religious and social morality, lies in the solemn public declaration by the witness of his intention to tell the truth, because he is aware of the moral and criminal consequences which may befall him if he lies.

THE NATURE OF EVIDENCE

Only those statements, admissions, objects or things which are said or offered under oath in a proceeding are evidence. Once a person is before the court, the presiding judge is bound by the rules of evidence to consider only those facts which are legally relevant and admissible.

> Evidence of a fact is that which tends to prove it — something which may satisfy an enquirer of the fact's existence. Courts of law usually have to find that certain facts exist before pronouncing on the rights, duties and liabilities of the parties, and such evidence as they will receive in furtherance of the task is described as "judicial evidence".[1]

RELEVANCE

The relevance of a particular item of evidence is determined primarily by its direct relationship to the issue being tried, but also by rules which have developed to guide judges in accepting or rejecting evidence. As a result, a fact that may be socially relevant to the issue before the court is not necessarily legally relevant. For example, in a wardship application brought by a Children's Aid Society, neglect of the child by its parents would certainly be relevant to whether or not a wardship order should be made. But if the same parents were charged with assaulting another person's child, neglect of their own child would not likely be considered to be legally relevant to the issue of assault, even though it may point, in social terms, to irresponsible behaviour toward children. Under the rules of evidence, the general rule is that all evidence which is sufficiently relevant to an issue before the court is admissible and all that is irrelevant, or insufficiently relevant, should be excluded.[2]

Best Evidence Rule

A rule of law requires that the most persuasive evidence available must be used to prove the fact which is being put forward. For example, an original document, rather than a photocopy, must be produced if it is available.

QUESTIONS OF LAW

In determining the evidence which will be considered by the trial judge or any other trier of fact, there are always three considerations, namely: the procedure to be followed, the burden of proof and the standard of proof.

Procedure

The procedure is the framework which determines the parties and the rules for the conduct of the hearing, whether it be a trial before a judge (and sometimes a jury), a board or tribunal or an arbitrator. The procedure also determines what evidence will be admitted and under what conditions.

Burden of Proof

The complaining parties in a legal dispute, whether civil or criminal, can succeed only if they can prove their claims. The responsibility to prove a claim or allegation is called the "burden of proof". The proof consists of evidence presented at trial or hearing, with the onus or burden of proof residing with the complainant or the Crown. In criminal proceedings, the accused parties are presumed to be innocent. In a civil proceeding, the status quo is presumed to be correct unless upset by the evidence presented.

There are some situations where a reverse onus exists and the person against whom the claim has been made must show by evidence that the claim is untrue. For example, in bail hearings, a person who has failed to show up for hearing must convince the judge that he will appear for trial. In a child welfare proceeding, once a child has been found to be a child in need of protection, it is the parties, not the Society, who must persuade a judge that the child is no longer in need of protection.

Standard of Proof

The standard of proof will vary depending on whether the suit is civil or criminal. The standard of proof concept is defined as the standard which will be used to assess whether the evidence to be presented is sufficient to allow the court to conclude that what has been presented actually proves the assertions of the complaining party, who is then entitled to a legal remedy to redress the wrong. In other words, the standard of proof refers to how convincing the evidence must be to support the claim of the complaining party.

Criminal proceedings, instigated by the Crown to determine whether someone has violated a criminal law, require evidence that allows the court to conclude *beyond a reasonable doubt* that the accused is guilty as charged. These words are used in instructions to the jury in a criminal trial to indicate that innocence is to be presumed unless guilt is so clearly proved that the jury has no reasonable doubt as to the guilt of the person charged.

A relatively less demanding standard, based on a preponderance of the evidence or on a *balance of probability*, is required in civil cases. In effect, this standard weighs which set of facts seems more probable to the court. If the court is unconvinced, the suit will fail.

TYPES OF EVIDENCE

There are a number of ways of classifying evidence, but essentially it falls into four major groupings: testimonial, real, direct and circumstantial, with considerable overlap among them.[3]

Testimonial evidence is spoken evidence which includes statements and assertions by a witness, made for the purpose of establishing the truth of the statement. For example, a mother who gives evidence that her child was born on January 1, 1980 in Toronto does so to establish the date and place of birth. But testimonial evidence in this example is also direct evidence, since the mother speaks from her own knowledge of the birth.

Real evidence is an object, thing, or location which speaks for itself. The physical appearance of a person, his demeanour, an object, a view of the scene of a crime, tape-recordings, documents, papers, and agency records, are all real evidence.

Direct evidence is given when a witness states that he saw or perceived something with his own senses. For example, a witness to an automobile accident will give direct evidence of what he saw and heard. In the process, he will also be giving testimonial evidence.

Circumstantial evidence is the statement of a fact from which the existence of another fact may be inferred. For example, where money is missing and only one person had access to the place it was kept, access to the money is circumstantial evidence from which theft by that person may be inferred. But circumstantial evidence may be presented in testimonial, real or direct form.

Hearsay Evidence

Second-hand testimony is not good enough for the courtroom. What a witness "heard" someone who is not present "say" is not admissible in evidence, except in special circumstances. Evidence must be given by the person who heard, saw or sensed the event. The reason for the hearsay rule is rather sensible. Events become distorted and diluted in the retelling and are therefore less credible.

Child Welfare Exception

An important exception to the hearsay rule for social workers is contained in the Child and Family Services Act.[4] Evidence of a person's past conduct towards children, whether or not it is hearsay, must be considered by the judge before ordering that a child be placed in or returned to that person's care and custody. In effect, the right of a child to safe care takes precedence over the general rule against admissibility of hearsay.

Public Records Exception

Official records are excepted from the hearsay rule and allowed as evidence without further proof. Such records include: collections of data, birth and death records, a child abuse registry, daily logs, and investigative reports such as a social work log of contacts or reports.[5]

Opinion Evidence

Opinion evidence is a statement offering conclusions about the issue being tried by the court. The basic rule is that opinion evidence is not admissible, since witnesses who are giving evidence are only permitted to speak about those facts within their personal knowledge.[6] For example, a witness at a child abuse hearing can testify to hearing a child cry and parents shouting, but cannot conclude that the parents were abusing the child unless he actually witnessed the abuse. The problem, of course, is that all facts contain some opinion, reached by applying observation (or perception) to past experience or knowledge. The question is how much fact survives the opinion.

Expert Opinion Evidence

Generally, expert opinion evidence is considered to be an exception to the opinion evidence rule. The general rule in Canada has therefore developed that only persons who are qualified by some special skill, training or experience can be asked their opinion on a matter in issue.[7] The rationale for permitting expert evidence at all is twofold. First, it provides information to the court which is necessary to understand the technical or scientific issues in a case. Second, where the court is itself incapable of drawing the necessary inferences from the facts presented, an expert is permitted to state his opinions and conclusions.[8] Put another way,

> [T]he opinion of witnesses possessing peculiar skill is admissible whenever the subject matter of inquiry is such that inexperienced persons are unlikely

> to prove capable of forming correct judgment upon it without such assistance.[9]

With increasing frequency, social workers are being called as expert witnesses, especially in cases involving child protection, custody, access, adoptions, and in criminal behaviour such as domestic violence and abuse. The expert witness is primarily called to give evidence on matters which he or she has investigated in his professional capacity and about the conclusions he has drawn as a result of his professional inquiry. The distinction which permits the expert in a field to be qualified is his personal knowledge in a field and the expected application of a more precise and careful method of applying the observed or perceived data to his expert personal knowledge and experience.[10] It therefore follows that an expert may be qualified to give expert opinion evidence only in his field of expertise. Outside this field, the expert is treated like any other witness and opinion evidence outside the specific field of expertise is excluded.[11]

Even where a witness is qualified to give expert testimony, whether or not the testimony will be accepted is a question of law which must be decided by the trial judge. Once accepted, the judge must also decide whether the expert opinion evidence is believable.[12] Some statutes authorize the judge to receive evidence which he believes to be reasonable and credible,[13] providing somewhat greater latitude to the evidence he may admit.

EXPERT WITNESSES

Who may qualify as an expert witness

There is no specific formula to determine who is an expert. Neither practical experience nor academic training is the sole criterion. Rather, the court must be satisfied that the witness is skilled, but how the skill was acquired is immaterial. The test of expertness is skill alone, in the field in which the witness's opinion is sought.[14] A working definition of a skilled person is one who has, by dint of training and practice, acquired a good knowledge of the science or art concerning which his opinion is sought and the practical ability to use his judgment in that science.[15] Nevertheless, the way the expertise was acquired may affect the importance or weight given to the evidence by the trial judge. For example, a judge may give greater weight to the evidence of an experienced social worker than to that of a newly-graduated social worker.

Guidelines for an Expert Witness

The person seeking to be qualified as an expert witness should first prepare a current *curriculum vitae*. A written curriculum vitae is a great help to the judge or lawyer in qualifying a person to give expert testimony. Expert qualifications should include as many of the following as are pertinent:

1. employment history and relevant experience in the field;
2. relevant education;
3. special courses and training in the field;
4. supervisory experience;
5. special awards or citations;
6. speeches, articles, lectures, workshops in the relevant field, including groups to which they were addressed;
7. membership in professional associations;
8. previous court experience and whether qualified or not, including the level of court (provincial, district or supreme); and
9. work and training under recognized experts in the field.

How the expert is qualified

1. First present the *curriculum vitae* as the basis for qualification.
2. Settle precisely what area of expertise is expected and why counsel requires expert opinions. If possible, get this information in a written request from counsel. It will help in preparation and can minimize the risk of misunderstanding what is being asked of you.
3. Ascertain whether a written report of your investigation or assessment is required. Try to get as clear an understanding as possible of what questions to address in your report and respond to these succinctly and in clear language. Be certain to obtain consent and authorization for any interviews you conduct or any relevant material you may request.
4. Determine whether you will be required to be involved in any pre-trial meetings.
5. Find out if other experts are testifying and try to anticipate questions or challenges to your testimony.
6. Ascertain how much time will be required and whether you may specify times convenient to you.
7. Some persons may prefer to be formally ordered by the court to testify rather than appearing at the request of a party to the proceedings because it may minimize the appearance of bias and so raise the perception of objectivity which is expected of an expert witness.
8. Verify through written confirmation from counsel what liability pro-

tection the court provides in regard to breaches of confidentiality and potential breaches of professional codes of ethics.

9. Take with you to court only what has been required, your expert testimony or any files, documents, records, or notes that have been specified.
10. Review your file and be familiar with your information, facts, and relevant issues so that you can respond without undue hesitation.
11. Use plain language, avoid jargon and explain technical terms that you cannot avoid. Respond to questions asked but offer no gratuitous information. If necessary, acknowledge the fact that a second interpretation may be a possibility where appropriate. Do not attempt to answer questions about which you have no knowledge.
12. The main objections raised by counsel to expert testimony arise because of hearsay questions (the validity of what someone else told you) and whether there is a proper base for the opinions you expressed. After an objection is raised, the court rules on the objection and instructs counsel or the witness on how to proceed. Do not engage in this exchange.
13. After you have testified, find out whether you are excused and can leave or whether you are asked to remain or return. You may try to negotiate time favourable to you which the court may or may not accommodate.[16]

The process of qualifying a person as an expert witness is as follows. The party or his lawyer informs the court of his wish to have the person qualified as an expert witness and leads the witness through the qualifications and experience. The opposing party may then cross-examine to challenge whether the expertise is relevant to the particular issue. Only the judge has the authority to qualify or disqualify a person as an expert. Only after qualification may a witness give expert evidence, but it does not necessarily follow that the testimony will be accepted by the judge.

What disqualifies expert testimony

Expert testimony may be rejected where the judge finds that:

1. the testimony is not relevant to the issue before the court; or
2. the expert witness is indeed expert, but not in the relevant field; or
3. the state of knowledge in the expert's field is so unreliable that even a expert cannot speak with reasonable certainty. Expert testimony of psychiatrists or psychologists are examples of evidence which may be disqualified because of uncertainty or conflicting opinion. Most readers

have observed the testimony of two experts assessing the same person and reaching completely opposite conclusions.

PRIVILEGED COMMUNICATION

The ethical principle of confidentiality is converted, in law, to the concept of privilege. When testifying in court, no privilege attaches to communications made by a client to a social worker. Conversations with a social worker in a confidential client-worker relationship are not protected and may be ordered to be divulged in court. Similarly, records relating to worker-client interviews and involvement are subject to subpoena and must be produced if required by the court. Third parties, such as agency supervisors or therapy group co-members cannot claim privilege and may also be subject to subpoena in a court action. Where some possibility of an eventual court appearance exists, clients should be informed that the worker may be required to divulge the content of their interviews as well as their records to the court. Otherwise the client may feel that confidentiality has been betrayed.

Canadian law extends privilege only to communications made to a lawyer by his client and to communications between spouses during marriage. In the latter instance, only the spouse to whom the communication is made may claim the privilege except where an offence was directed against the life, health or liberty of the spouse or minor child in which case privilege does not attach.[17] Neither clergy nor medical practitioners are protected by privilege, although a court has declined to order disclosure of admissions made to a psychiatrist by a patient.[18] In at least one instance, a court has refused to order disclosure of communications made by a client to a marriage counsellor on the grounds that confidentiality was essential to the worker-client relationship, although no privilege is granted by statute.[19] Medical records, however, may be protected by statute,[20] but no similar provision applies to social work records, except for those protected under the adoption provisions of child welfare legislation. In practice, the judge may or may not require disclosure of confidential information, depending on the necessity to have the information before the court. The decision is in the judge's absolute discretion. If it is ordered, it must be disclosed for the records produced.[21] Without such an order, records and information must not be disclosed without the written consent of the client or clients, if more than one.

An American case, which is frequently cited as a landmark case, may be relevant to Canadian law. The complainants alleged that the therapist had a duty to warn them since the patient had confided to the therapist his intention to kill their daughter. The psychiatrist did warn the campus police but not the daughter or her family. The campus police did not detain the patient and shortly after his release he did kill the daughter. The court held that the parents should have been warned and stated that the welfare of the community overrides doctor- patient confidentiality. Most courts have taken the position that a therapist, who has been told during therapy of the intent to injure another party, has a responsibility to inform the victim or those who could warn the victim or the police. In Canada, American cases or precedents, while not binding, can be persuasive to the court.[22]

Privilege does not attach to confidential relationships when the benefits to be gained by silence do not outweigh the benefits of disclosing the truth in a court of justice. The Ontario Court of Appeal ruled that the need for confidential family counselling did not supersede the need to detect and prosecute child abuse.[23]

TESTIFYING IN COURT OR AT A HEARING

Examination-in-Chief

"Examination-in-chief" refers to the initial statements made by a witness in support of facts as he or she knows them. Once a person is sworn and identified for the record, he will be asked a series of questions by the lawyer who has requested his testimony. If no lawyer is present, the judge will usually question the witness. Answers should be in response to the questions. They may be either brief or lengthy, as the question requires, but they *must* be on topic. The witness should not ramble and should not volunteer information or opinions without being asked. If the answer is unknown or uncertain, the witness should say so and not guess. Even where a lawyer is present, the judge may intervene for clarification.

Where a social worker has been qualified as an expert witness, the lawyer will ask a series of questions about the worker's contact with the person or circumstances about which the expert evidence is being sought. The facts on which the opinion is based will be elicited. On the basis of these facts, the social worker will be asked his opinion about the issue in question. It is therefore particularly important that the social worker and lawyer review both the worker's qualifications and the nature of his evidence. This will increase the likelihood that his expert opinion will be accepted by the court.

Cross-Examination

The purposes of cross-examination are to test the reliability of a witness's testimony, and to elicit further information which the opposing lawyer hopes will be favourable to his client. Cross-examination may challenge the witness's perception, memory, sincerity, expertise and ability to answer questions directly. It is not a personal attack upon the witness, even if that is the way it feels to the person being cross-examined.[24] It is an attack on the evidence which has been presented and is very much a part of the adversarial process. Nevertheless, it is a very stressful experience, even for the most seasoned witness.

Special Rules Governing Testimony of Children

Children under twelve years must be examined on a voir dire by the trial judge to determine whether they understand the nature of an oath as a condition to being allowed to testify under oath. Literally "voir dire" means to speak the truth and such a hearing occurs when the court needs to make a determination before the trial can proceed. If a child fails such an examination, the evidence may be taken unsworn, if the judge feels the child does understand the duty to speak the truth. The child does not have to appreciate the consequences of lying but must be seen to understand that an oath or an affirmation is a promise to tell the truth.

Except in child abuse matters, no case can be decided on the unsworn evidence of a child alone; it must be corroborated by some other material evidence which may be a medical report, photograph or evidence of another person. If there is nothing more than uncorroborated evidence of a child "of tender years" the trial may be quashed at the outset. However, special rules have been developed to permit children to give evidence of abuse to them.

England has introduced legislation to allow the use of live video in child abuse cases and to permit a child to give evidence in a less intimidating setting.[25] In a widely publicized Ontario child protection hearing where sexual abuse, attempted murder and cannibalism were alleged, the judge permitted recorded videos of interviews with helping professionals to be introduced as evidence, with the weight placed on this evidence subject to legal argument. Counsel for one of the parties subsequently wished to withdraw his consent to the introduction of the videos and he sought to cross-examine the children. He was severely admonished by the court.[26]

Guidelines for Giving Testimony

The need to be concrete and specific when giving testimony is a point worth repeating and reinforcing. Shakespeare, who wrote without knowledge of psychiatric words would have provided testimony which was unassailable upon cross-examination because of his recording of observable facts.

Act V — Scene 1 — *Macbeth*

Doctor:	When was it she last walked?
Gent:	Since his majesty went into the field, I have seen her rise from her bed, throw her nightgown upon her, unlock her closet, take forth paper, fold it, write upon 't, read it, afterwards seal it, and again return to bed; yet all this while in a most fast sleep.
Doctor:	A great perturbation in nature, to receive at once the benefit of sleep, and do the effects of watching! In this slumbery agitation, besides her walking and other actual performances, what, at any time, have you heard her say?
Gent:	That, sir, which I will not report after her.
Doctor:	You may to me, and 'tis most meet you should.
Gent:	Neither to you or any one, having no witness to confirm my speech.

Enter Lady Macbeth, with a taper.

	Lo you, here she comes! This is her very guise; and, upon my life, fast asleep. Observe her; stand close.
Doctor:	How came she by that light?
Gent:	Why, it stood by her. She has light by her continually; 'tis her command.
Doctor:	You see, her eyes are open.
Gent:	Ay, but their sense is shut.
Doctor:	What is it she does now? Look, how she rubs her hands.
Gent:	It is an accustomed action with her, to seem thus washing her hands. I have known her continue in this a quarter of an hour.

States of depression, anxiety or hyperactivity are better described in terms of observed behaviour. Similarly, judgments as to the state of cleanliness, or neatness of a person or a dwelling should be reserved and only the observable elements described. If the witness cannot find words to describe what he has observed, then he should probably reconsider whether his generalized judgment has a basis in fact or is an impression which cannot be defended.

When testifying in court, the witness is bound by legal rules and must give evidence within these boundaries. The following guidelines should help:

Examination-in-Chief

1. Keep in mind the purpose of the hearing, for example, custody of a

child, delinquency of a minor, a criminal charge against an adult, or a landlord and tenant dispute.
2. Refresh your memory from the case file and your case notes but be prepared to produce the relevant parts of the file and your notes.
3. You must produce the file for the court if it is subpoenaed.
4. Be guided by the lawyer representing your client as to the type of questions he will ask, and the way you should answer them.
5. Listen carefully and answer the question asked, as concisely as possible. Do not ramble.
6. When giving expert testimony, state the relevant facts first, then your opinion based on those facts.
7. If you are giving testimony without a lawyer representing your client, or as an officer of the court (perhaps as a probation officer), state the facts as you know them, and then your conclusion based on the facts. Make a recommendation to the court only when you are asked to do so.

Cross-Examination

1. Listen carefully and answer *only* the question that is asked. Do not ramble or volunteer information.
2. Do not guess. If you do not know the answer, say so. Avoid comments such as "I don't remember". Either you know the answer or you do not.
3. Watch for catch questions, such as, "Did you discuss this case with anyone?" Of course you did, with the lawyer, your supervisor, and probably others, which is of course allowed. Answer honestly.
4. If you contradict an earlier statement, do not get flustered. For example, you may have testified that a person was calm at a given time and later in your testimony say that this same person appeared upset. When challenged, simply state which statement is correct.
5. Answer every question put to you, unless the lawyer for your client objects.
6. Keep calm. Remember it is your evidence which is being tested, not you as a person.
7. Admit your beliefs honestly if asked. For example:
   Q: Do you have a preference about what you would like to happen in this case?
   A: Yes, I do.
   Q: You want the Society to get custody of Mary so that she will not be living with her mother?
   A: Yes. I do think that would be best for Mary. But I have answered your questions truthfully.
8. If you are being paid, remember that it is acceptable that experts be paid

and that other witnesses receive a per diem allowance to appear in court.[27]

Preparing Clients to Give Evidence

This is often a frightening experience for a person who has not been in court before. Explanation to clients about the court process usually helps them to deal with their anxiety and to give their evidence more clearly. It is usually helpful to explain what a courtroom looks like, where the judge, court reporter, the parties and lawyers sit, and where the witness box is located. It also helps to describe how a trial is conducted, and what issue is to be tried.

Going over the client's story with him before trial helps to "set" the circumstances in his mind. But impress on the client that the lawyer and presiding judge will only want to hear that part of the story which is relevant to the issue before the court. The client is not likely to have the opportunity to tell his whole story, which may be frustrating to him. It is usually reassuring to a potential witness to know that judges hear many cases, understand the law, and are trying to assure that everyone has a fair hearing.

Guidelines for clients

In addition to the guidelines listed above, the following matters should be also impressed on the client.

1. If summoned or subpoenaed, the client must attend. There can be serious consequences to himself or others if he fails to appear.
2. He must tell the truth, even if it is painful. Lying under oath, called perjury, is a serious matter which can hurt both the witness and others.
3. A witness must always be respectful to the judge and cannot dispute what he says or argue in any way.
4. Neat and clean dress and appropriate behaviour always operates in a client's favour and makes it possible for his evidence to be considered on its own merits.[28]
5. Once an order is made, it is binding on the persons involved unless it is appealed successfully or expires according to its terms.

Preparing the Child Witness

The entire rationale for preparing clients to give testimony is, of course, to ensure that necessary evidence will be heard by the court. The child as witness requires a supportive guide. A specialized social worker may be an ideal person to help the child overcome the legal and psychological handicaps which impede the ability to testify.[29] A compelling illustration of sensitive social work preparation in a legal setting occurred in a Community Legal Clinic in Toronto serving young people involved in legal proceedings.

> The children, Billy, age 8, and Carol, age 5, had been sexually abused by their father. With the mother's full co-operation, the father had been charged and a trial date set. The only evidence against the father had to come from the children, who were frightened and confused about what was expected of them. Billy, in particular, said he was not going to say anything and no one could force him to say anything. He knew that his father could go to jail as a result of his testimony.
>
> The social worker established a relationship with Billy through drawings in which his fear and unhappiness could be identified and worked through. They drew a courtroom and all the participants in a trial, where they would sit or stand and what they would do. With the introduction of anatomically correct dolls, Billy's excitement and interest increased. He said he would show the worker what his father had done, and the worker supplied a vocabulary which enabled Billy to label and describe what had happened to him and to Carol. Billy also began to release some of his anger against his father by letting the boy doll hit the father doll.
>
> The children appeared at the trial and though the process was a painful one, were able to participate in the proceedings. Throughout the hurtful episode, they were supported by the worker. It is possible to speculate that the work of helping them prepare to give testimony also provided help in facing the reality of the abusing situation. This process may prevent the repression and distortion of these early traumatic events which might adversely affect their subsequent emotional and sexual development.[30]

Changes to the Criminal Code now permit the use of a screen or closed-circuit television in the courtroom when it is deemed necessary to obtain a full and candid account of the acts which have been alleged.[31] This arrangement is directed at protecting the child from having to confront the perpetrator of the alleged abuse as well as serving to protect the formality of the courtroom. There are generally two models which can be utilized; either one in which the child is isolated in a room apart from the courtroom but where there is television monitoring of the questions being put to the child or where the courtroom itself is child-centered in that only the judge, child and child's counsel are present and the accused and counsel for the accused are isolated in another room but can hear the child's testimony. Cross-examination may take place using the same arrangements. At issue is the need to assure fairness to the accused as well as to protect the child from the further trauma of re-experiencing assault through the court process itself. The Ontario Court of Appeal has ruled that the use of closed-circuit television for this purpose is not in itself prejudicial to the accused if the judge or jury are instructed not to draw adverse inferences from the procedure but rather to see it as necessary because of the age of the child.[32]

REPORTS TO THE COURT

Social workers are often required to provide reports to the court in both civil and criminal proceedings. These reports call upon the worker's expertise to provide information which may not otherwise be available to the court. The civil proceedings which most frequently accept such reports into evidence are those dealing with custody and adoption. In criminal proceedings, they are usually ordered after a finding of guilt, to assist the judge in making an appropriate disposition that is "fit" in all the circumstances.

In preparing these reports, the factors to be considered are their relevance to the matter before the court, their intelligibility to the judge and the parties, and their accuracy. Sources of information must be correctly acknowledged and opinions must have a basis in fact or observation.

Most reports and assessments which are to be presented to the court or to the lawyer will be divided into specific sub-headings. The most important part of the report, however, will be the summary statement, because frequently that is all a busy judge or lawyer will read. The summary therefore must convey a succinct and accurate response to the question which the social worker was asked to address in his investigation. The summary statement is more than a restatement of what was said previously; it is an integration of the information that reflects the worker's thinking about the matter.

A social worker charged with the task of preparing an assessment to be introduced in a custody hearing should be aware of the legal issues which are considered by the court. The *Report on Family Law* (1976), prepared by the Law Reform Commission of Canada, recommended that dispositions regarding custody should consider the kind of relationships the child has with the significant persons in his or her life, the personality, emotional, and physical needs of the child, the capacity for parenting of the disputing parties and the plans they present for the child's future, the preference of the child to the extent that this can be ascertained, and the financial resources and needs of each of the parents. Mr. Justice Bayda of the Saskatchewan Court of Appeal, expressed his frustration in a custody matter:

> No one bothered to bring forward much information in respect of the two individuals who of all the persons likely to be affected by these proceedings least deserve to be ignored — the children. We knew their names, sex and ages, but little else. Of what intelligence are they? What are their likes? Dislikes? Do they have any special inclinations (for the arts, sports or the like) that should be nurtured? Any handicaps? Do they show signs of anxiety? What are their personalities? Characters? What is the health of each? . . . Apart from the speculation that these children are "ordinary" (whatever that means) there is nothing on which to base a reasoned objective conclusion as to what must be done for *this* child and *that* child, as individuals and not as mere members of a general class, in order that the welfare and happiness of each may be ensured and enhanced.[33]

He further complained that the parents were not similarly differentiated so that he could see them as individuals rather than being presented only with evidence showing how badly each had treated the other.

If an assessment does not address these issues, the court has difficulty making an informed determination. The "best interests" criterion in the Children's Law Reform Act, discussed in a later chapter, should also be reviewed. Finally, anyone accepting a referral for an assessment from the court or from counsel should insist upon a detailed agreement regarding the specific service that is to be provided. All parties should be clear as to the questions to be answered, where the process will take place, who is to be present, what reports will be prepared, and who will have access to these reports.

Guidelines for Reports to the Court

1. Keep firmly in mind the reason for the proceeding and the purpose of the report. For example, the purpose of a report in a custody hearing is to provide information about a parent's capacity to care for that child, whereas in an adoption hearing the purpose is to determine the suitability of an adopting home for a particular child. Pre-sentence or Family History reports in criminal proceedings are ordered to provide the judge with social and behavioural information about the accused person before sentence is imposed.
2. Be as brief as possible. If there is a great deal of corroborating data, such as persons interviewed, an extensive school report or explanatory information, attach it to the report.
3. Reports should be written in clear language without the use of social work or psychological jargon. It is more helpful to say "There is little evidence of family cohesion or parental control" when describing family structure and function, than to say: "The parents and children have

weak familial identification patterns and the parents have insufficient ego strengths to assume parental authority."

4. State in summary form the facts which will support your conclusions. For example, rather than saying "It appears that Mr. B. does not take an active parenting role", it is more informative to say, "Mr. B. is seldom at home because of work and extensive outside interests and he does not take an active role in parenting the children."
5. When facts are equivocal, state the contradictions. Avoid social work "weasel words" such as "it appears that", "it seems that", "it is possible that", "one might conclude that". For example, an abusing parent may also be a concerned and loving parent at other times. If that is the case, say so.
6. Be careful about using words which may have legal significance, such as "remorse", "guilty", "restitution", or "insane".
7. State your opinion in summary form. It should reflect the facts, your own observations, and the conclusions you have reached, based on your knowledge and understanding of the person or family. In other words, your report should provide a clear picture.
8. Always date and sign the report to signify the time period referred to and the maker of the report.

A Generic Outline for Reports

Though situations and circumstances vary, the following outline focuses on information which may be required to assist the court. This outline should be used *selectively* depending upon the purpose for the report.

1. Identifying data (name, age, sex, marital status, family composition).
2. Precipitating events leading to the hearing.
3. Significant social circumstances.
   (a) Family structure and function.
   (b) Economic situation.
   (c) Housing adequacy.
   (d) Employment or educational status.
   (e) Health factors (physical, emotional, substance abuse).
   (f) Physical and intellectual capacity.
   (g) Peer group, friends and associates.
   (h) Interests and activities.

As well as describing these factors, include comments about their effect on the individual and the family; for example, a child's reading disability might have more significance in a family of high achievers.

4. Indicators of change.
   (a) Past and current attempts to improve the situation
       — client activity.
       — worker activity.
   (b) Interest in effecting change (motivation).
5. Alternatives or options available in this situation.
6. Summary statement.
7. Recommendations, if appropriate.
8. Date of report and signature.

Endnotes

1. *Cross on Evidence*, 4th ed. (London: Butterworths, 1974) at 9.
2. *Ibid.*, at 16.
3. H.J. Glasbeek, *Evidence: Cases and Materials* (Toronto: Butterworths, 1977) at 28.
4. Child and Family Services Act, S.O. 1984, c. 55, as amended.
5. Evidence Act, R.S.O. 1980, c. 145, ss. 33-35; Canada Evidence Act, R.S.C. 1985, c. C-5, ss. 29-31.
6. Cross, note 1 above, at 381.
7. *R. v. Fisher*, [1961] O.W.N. 94, 34 C.R. 320. Affirmed [1961] S.C.R. 535, 35 C.R. 107, 130 C.C.C. 1; *R. v. German*, [1947] O.R. 395, 3 C.R. 516, 89 C.C.C. 90, [1947] 4 D.L.R. 68 (C.A.). See also S.A. Cohen, "The Role of the Forensic Expert in a Criminal Trial" (1978), 1 C.R. (3d) 289.
8. J. Sopinka and S. Lederman, *The Law of Evidence in Civil Cases* (Toronto: Butterworths, 1974) at 291.
9. Glasbeek, note 3 above, at 325, discussing *Carter v. Boehm* (1876).
10. *Brownlee v. Hand Firework Co.*, 65 O.L.R. 646, [1931] 1 D.L.R. 127 (C.A.).
11. Glasbeek, note 3 above, at 352-8.
12. *Davie v. Edinburgh Magistrates*, [1953] S.C. 34.
13. For example, the Child and Family Services Act, note 4 above; Provincial Offences Act, R.S.O. 1980, c. 400.
14. *R. v. Silverlock*, [1894] 2 Q.B. 766.
15. *R. v. Bunniss*, 44 C.R. 262, 50 W.W.R. 422, [1965] 3 C.C.C. 236 (B.C. Co. Ct.).
16. Daley, Timothy T., "Guidelines for the Expert Witness", *The Social Worker*, Vol. 65, Summer, June 30, 1996, p. 1, 3- 5.
17. Canada Evidence Act, note 5 above, s. 4; Evidence Act, note 5 above, s. 11. See *R. v. Lonsdale*, 24 C.R.N.S. 225, [1974] 2 W.W.R. 157, 15 C.C.C. (3d) 201 (Alta. C.A.).

18. *Dembie v. Dembie* (1963), 21 R.F.L. 46 (Ont.).
19. *Mortlock v. Mortlock* (1980), 17 R.F.L. (2d) 253 (N.S. Fam. Ct.).
20. Health Disciplines Act, R.S.O. 1980, c. 196.
21. Child and Family Services Act, note 4 above, Part VIII, deals with confidentiality and access to records.
22. *Tarasoff v. Regents of the University of California.*
23. *R. v. R.S.* (1985), 45 C.R. (3d) 161, 19 C.C.C. (3d) 115, 8 O.A.C. 241 (C.A.). Leave to appeal to S.C.C. refused (1985), 61 N.R. 266 (note), 11 O.A.C. 317 (note) (S.C.C.).
24. *Cross*, note 1 above, at 226-7.
25. Dr. E. Vizard, "Interviewing Young Sexually Abused Children — Assessment Techniques" (1987), 17 Family Law 38.
26. K. Marron, "Ritual Abuse" (Toronto: Seal Books, 1988).
27. R. Albert, *Law and Social Work Practice* (New York: Springer Co., 1986) at 180.
28. Image is important even if social workers feel affronted by emphasis on externals such as dress or hair style. Judges and juries, influenced by the solemnity of the courtroom, tend to hold standards that reflect accepted social norms. Any appearance or behaviour that deviates from these norms contains a risk for the client.
    See also J. Hogarth, "Sentencing as a Human Process: An International Review Symposium" (1972), 10 Osgoode Hall L.J. 233.
29. J.L. Herman, *Father-Daughter Incest* (Cambridge: Harvard University Press, 1981) at 11, cited in M. Wells "The Child Witness: Issues and Strategies" Law Soc. of U. Can. seminar "Representing Children", 28 March 1987.
30. M. Wells. Unpublished paper, based on work at Justice for Children.
31. Criminal Code, s. 486(2.1).
32. Jacqueline Castel, "The Use of Screens and Closed Circuit Television in the Prosecution of Child Sexual Abuse", *Canadian Journal of Family Law*, Vol. 10, No. 2.
33. *Wakaluk v. Wakaluk* (1976), 25 R.F.L. 292 at 299 (Sask. C.A.).

Bibliography

Bloomfield, Miriam. "Application for Records Held by Third Parties in Sexual Assault Prosecutions" (Nov. 1995) 3 Crown's Newsletter, 1-49.

Ewashchuk, Eugene G. "Hearsay Evidence" (1978), 16 Osgoode Hall L.J. 407.

Fuerst, Michelle. "When Societal Interests Outweigh a Right to Confrontation: Charter Protection for Child Witnesses", in *The*

Charter's Impact on the Criminal Justice System, ed. Jamie Cameron (Toronto: Carswell, 1996) at 166-179.

Gertner, E. "The Unsworn Evidence of Children and Mutual Corroboration." (1978), 16 Osgoode Hall L.J. 495.

Gothard, Sol. "Power in the Court: The Social Worker as an Expert Witness." *Social Work*, Vol. 34, No. 1, January 1989, at 65.

Leonoff, Arthur and Robert J. Montague, *Guide to Custody and Access Assessments* (Toronto: Carswell, 1996).

Marron, Kevin. "Ritual Abuse" (Toronto: Seal Books, 1988).

McDonald, Hon. Mr. Justice D.C. "Opinion Evidence." (1978), 16 Osgoode Hall L.J. 321.

Rosenberg, E., J. Kleinman and J.I. Brantley. "Custody Evaluations: Helping the Family Reorganize." Soc. Csewrk., 63(4): 203-8, 1982.

Vizard, Eileen. "Interviewing Young, Sexually Abused Children — Assessment Techniques." (1987) 17 Family Law 28.

PART II

THE LEGAL LIFE CYCLE OF THE FAMILY: ISSUES IN FAMILY LAW

8

Defining the Family: Social Transitions and Legal Construction

> In an attempt to fill the gap created by the decline of the city and the urban forms of social intercourse it had once provided, the omnipotent, omnipresent family took upon itself the task of trying to satisfy all the emotional and social needs on its members. Today, it is clear that the family has failed in its attempts to accomplish this feat, either because the increased emphasis on privacy has stifled the need for social intercourse or because the family has been so completely alienated by public powers.[1]

The International Covenant on Civil and Political Rights, to which Canada became a signatory in 1976, states at Article 23:

1. The family is a natural and fundamental group unit of society and entitled to protection by society and the State.
2. The rights of men and women of marriageable age to marry and to found a family shall be recognized.
3. No marriage shall be entered into without the free and full consent of the intending spouses.
4. States which are parties to the present Covenant shall take appropriate steps to ensure equality of rights and responsibilities of spouses as to marriage and its dissolution. In the case of dissolution, provision shall be made for the necessary protection of any children.

In the decades since this Covenant was drafted, the family, then considered a natural group, has become difficult to define, both its composition and its function. In reality, family constellations are rarely biologically determined in a fixed way nor can family function be easily defined. While there appears to be a universal need and desire for a source of nurture, the provision of nurture is not dependent on a specific living arrangement nor must the provider be of a specific gender.

Elements contained in a definition of family include procreation, sexual fidelity, socialization, residential arrangements and economic and emotional support and interdependence. Each of these elements can be realized across a broad spectrum of relationships that include childless unions, sexual arrangements such as celibacy or promiscuity, couples who may work in different locations and reside separately or together as work permits, children who may reside away from their parents in a school or foster home, mutual economic independence of the partners, and dysfunctional or abusive families where there is an absence of emotional support. It is apparent that conventional notion of the normative family unit of provider father, nurturing mother, and biological children is not supported by observable variations in legal, sociological, and emotional indicators. Modern reality must recognize single parenthood, reconstituted families with children from former marriages who are either living with the reconstituted family or with a former spouse. Single parent families may be the result of marriage breakdown, but they may also be single parents by choice of both biological parents. The normative assumption of heterosexual unions ignores or marginalizes same sex unions. A growing number of grandmother-headed families is a result of structural or systemic influences on families, such as chronic unemployment.[2]

Notwithstanding these profound changes, family law is quite literally law which relates to the basic social group, husband, wife, parent and child. Family law is different from other branches of law simply because the legal conflicts arise out of intimate relationships within family units. Those who practise family law must become involved with situations in which complex emotional components both confound and compound a purely legalistic approach. Because of the difficulty in defining the contemporary family and because of the rising incidence of marriage breakdown and problems of custody and support, the courts are confronted with increasing numbers of children in need of protection, women and children who have been abused physically and emotionally, children who have broken the law, and children in need of care which their families are unable to provide. Judges and child protection workers must often make emergency decisions about whether a child would be better served by providing intensive service to the family while the child remained within the family or by placement away from the family in a custodial or treatment facility, knowing that resources in support of their alternative are starkly inadequate. At the other end of the life cycle is an aging population who may frequently require legal and social intervention to protect their persons, their rights, and their property.

Surveying the family from a life cycle approach, the normal developmental milestones require legal processing. For example, legal procedures regulating marriage, birth registration, school entry and progress record, public health innoculation requirements and exceptions, renting, buying, or selling shelter accommodations, routine goods and services contract negotiations, making and changing of wills may require legal assistance but are all relatively universal and routine life transitional processes. It is interesting to note that the legal age at which adolescence ends and adulthood begins varies from jurisdiction to jurisdiction and from law to law and often leaves persons from ages 16 to 21 in a curious state of fragmented legal identity,

Unexpected life events that affect individuals and families selectively but not universally cause the utmost stress, whether they are chronic situations or the result of sudden crises. For example, both individuals and families are stressed when chronic disability or illness of a family member requires support from external resources often circumscribed by laws. Crises such as separation and divorce, death and sudden loss of employment frequently require legal and social assistance. Adoption has always been a legal and social issue. Recent and developing advances in reproductive technology have created a new arena for medical, legal, and social intervention as all of the parties including the courts and lawmakers struggle with an array of ethical issues. In addition, individuals and families faced with coping with civil wrongs or criminal breaches of law can be plungedinto crisis at any point along the life cycle and be forced into rapid learning about legal procedures.

It has been said that the family has been accorded benign parliamentary neglect and "the judiciary sanctioned the prevailing social assumptions as it saw them."[3] Attempts to enforce legal norms which affect intimate personal behaviour can be interpreted as attempts by specific minorities or professional experts to impose their values on society. Such attempts are frequently met with controversy and resistance as a means to safeguard diversity of beliefs, values, and custom.[4] This is especially true of many urban Canadian communities where persons with diverse ethnic backgrounds may experience the weight of traditional mainstream Canadian institutions as oppressive and intolerant.

Law must in any event provide minimum safeguards for the family. If one takes a broad view of responses to family stress situations, it is possible to identify two processes which interact. One is found in laws, which use the coercive powers of the legal system and the courts. The other process relies upon legal support for voluntary associations which attempt to find solutions outside of the court system, such as counselling, or dispute settlement through mediation.[5] Clearly no single approach provides definitive solutions to family need, dysfunction, or breakdown. The basic function of family law is to provide protection and support when families break down or become dysfunctional. Family law in every province contains laws which are supportive, protective of vulnerable members, and relatively flexible. However, all systems are seriously stressed and too many lives remain at risk.

To intervene effectively when crisis occurs at any point in the life cycle of the family, those practising social work and social law will recognize the rapid ripple effect of crisis and learn to move quickly to deal with the most pressing aspects of the crisis while helping the family to identify and anticipate other concerns where coping strategies will be needed. Social law requires sharing of knowledge, accessing resources, and mutual professional cooperation to help clients construct a supportive legal and social helping network. Such a network involves formal systems such as courts and appropriate legal and social services and informal systems within the community such as extended family. Young families living in relative isolation from extended family support would benefit if community based support sensitive to relevant ethnic and cultural values were available to provide outreach to such families and to offer whatever help is needed such as child care, accessing of resources, and ongoing support. Community family resource centres which should receive public funding but retain local decision-making power could be seen as family cycle resource centres. As aging parents place new strains on families, appropriate information, support, and resources could respond to the needs of the middle and later stages of the family life cycle.

In addition, it seems apparent that current laws drafted to provide protection to families in crisis and to protect children are failing to provide the protection to many families experiencing overwhelming stress. Many are unable to provide basic needs such as safety, nutrition, and shelter, nor can they provide sufficient emotional nurture or intellectual stimulation when basic survival needs are a daily challenge. The number of people living in poverty as defined by the National Council of Welfare has increased to 4.8 million in 1993. Their report cites a continued increase of children living in poverty, more than 1.4 million Canadian children, with children under seven years faring the worst.[6] Not only those families living on the edge of poverty, but also some middle income families are finding it difficult to provide adequately for their families. Though there is a cherished popular belief in the notion of the autonomous nurturing family unfettered by official social policy and control, it is a vision without foundation in reality. Many observers note that it takes a village to bring up a child.

The current political emphasis on the primacy of market forces in shaping social policy has sharpened the debate about public responsibility for the family. Given the widening gap between rich and poor, the erosion of traditional, gender defined family roles, and conflicting values and beliefs of a multi-ethnic population, a national and provincial policy is needed. Perhaps a way to balance public interest and privacy rights of families is to envision a partnering contract between families and government throughout the family life cycle. For example, a guaranteed income benefit, tied to cost of living index and sufficient to maintain families above the poverty level as well as the maintenance of community family support centres. Those who practise family law recognize the interrelationship between human behaviour and the choices we make in structuring institutions and systems that create a negative or positive social environment.

Endnotes

1. Aries, P., "The Family and the City" *Daedalus*, Vol. 106, No. 2, Spring 1977, 227.
2. Eichler, Margrit, *Families in Canada Today: Recent Changes and Their Policy Consequences* (Toronto: Gage, 1988); and also Abella, Judge R.S. (as she was then), "Family Law in Ontario: Changing Assumptions" (1981), 13 Ottawa L. Rev. 1.
3. Eekelaar, J., *Family Law and Social Policy*, 2nd ed. (London: Weidenfeld and Nicholson, 1984) 74 (1978).
4. *Ibid.,* at 45 (1978).
5. *Ibid.*, at 44 (1978).
6. *Globe and Mail*, April 6, 1995

Bibliography

Baker, Maureen, *Canadian Family Policies: Cross-National Comparisons* (Toronto: University of Toronto Press, 1995).

Boyd, Susan B., "Can Law Challenge the Public/Private Divide?: Women, Work, and Family" (1996), 15 Windsor Yearbook, Access to Justice 161-185.

Eichler, Margrit, *Family Shifts: Families, Policies, and Gender Equality* (Don Mills, Ontario: Oxford University Press, 1996).

Findlay, Barbara, "All in the Family Values" (1947), 14 Canadian Journal of Family Law 129-196.

Knowles, Caroline, *Family Boundaries: The Invention of Normality* (Peterborough, Ontario: Broadview Press, 1997).

Takach, George F., "All Hail the Family" (1996), 21 *Law Now*, No. 3, 8-9.

Teghtsoonian, Katherine, "Work and/or Motherhood: The Ideological Construction of Woman's Options in Canadian Child Care Debates" (1995), 8 Canadian Journal of Women and Law 411-439.

Wooley, Alice, "Excluded by Definition: Same-Sex Couples and the Right to Marry" (1995), 45 *University of Toronto Law Journal* 471-524.

9

Family Courts: Resolving Family Disputes

In Canada, family law matters may fall within federal or provincial jurisdiction, or concurrent federal-provincial jurisdiction depending upon the nature of the matter before the court. The Constitution Act[1] establishes divorce as exclusively a federal matter, which is therefore always heard in a Superior Court before a federally appointed judge. Family property matters are entirely within provincial power but are also always heard before federally appointed judges in Superior Courts. On the other hand, all matters dealing with children are also exclusively provincial but may be heard by a federally appointed judge in Superior Court or by a provincially appointed judge in a provincial family court. The only federal jurisdiction over children occurs as corollary relief in a divorce action in the form of support, custody and access orders.

Judith P. Ryan has written that:

> A 1938 reference to the Supreme Court of Canada[2] established that large areas of family law could be administered by inferior courts presided over by provincially appointed judicial officers. Accordingly, in many provinces, such courts exercise jurisdiction over adoption, child protection, guardianship, affiliation, custody and maintenance.[3]

The Supreme Court of Canada reaffirmed that jurisdiction in guardianship, custody, access, and maintenance of children can be exercised by an "inferior" (meaning provincially-appointed) provincial judge. The decision held that these powers may be vested in provincial court judges by the provinces and their decisions in these matters are therefore valid.[4]

Though the court system has already been discussed in a previous chapter, this chapter will identify those courts which deal with family law matters. The reader should be aware that each province has a slightly different designation of its family courts.

FAMILY LAW DIVISION OF THE SUPERIOR COURT

Some provinces have established family law divisions so that matters pertaining to the family could be conducted at "one step". In Ontario the family law division has jurisdiction over divorce and corollary relief. In addition, under the Family Law Act and Children's Law Reform Act,[5] the Family Law Division of the Ontario Court (General Division) has power to hear all matters concerning family property, the matrimonial home, custody and access involving children, and support of dependants. It has exclusive jurisdiction over annulment of marriages, and the power to determine questions of paternity.

In order to streamline the court process in family law matters, some provinces have additional layers of judicial officers in the form of Masters and Commissioners.

Interim Matters

While the parties and their lawyers are unwinding a family and its assets, interim proceedings may be brought to determine such necessary and urgent matters as interim custody and access, support of children and residence in the matrimonial home until trial or final resolution of the family breakdown.

Pre-Trials and Case Conferences

Before a family dispute can proceed to trial in a Superior Court, the parties may be required to attend at a pre-trial or case conference whose function is to attempt to settle an action on the basis of a summary of the evidence which would be led at trial. The vast majority of cases, over 80 per cent, settle at the pre-trial stage, either in whole or in part. There are relatively few trials in family law matters.

SURROGATE COURT

This court has now been integrated into the Superior Court of the province, in Ontario this is the General Division. Judges of this court formerly had exclusive jurisdiction over guardianship of children under the former Infants Act, replaced by the Minors Act, now both superseded by the Children's Law Reform Act.[6] They also had power over applications for custody comparable to the Supreme Court. This court also has jurisdiction over wills, trusts, and estates. It may order support for dependants from the assets of an estate, under some circumstances.

PROVINCIAL FAMILY COURTS

Passage of the Family Law Reform Act, 1978, the Family Law Act 1986 and supporting legislation such as the Family Support Plan Act and the Child and Family Services Act[7] in Ontario and similar legislation in other provinces had the effect of broadening the jurisdiction of the provincial courts. They are now empowered to enforce support of dependants by garnishing wages and pensions and to issue judgment summons with the power to imprison for default. This court may also make orders of supervision and wardship of children in need of protection and may make adoption orders.

Provincial family court judges may also exercise limited jurisdiction over criminal charges that involve family members. Under provisions of the Provincial Courts Act,[8] and the Young Offenders Act,[9] they have jurisdiction over young offenders under the age of 16 in Ontario and under 18 in some provinces.

Mediation and Conciliation Services

Some provincial family courts have mediation and conciliation services attached to the court to assist parties to make decisions about custody and access to their children. These services are provided by skilled social workers and frequently divert the parties from custody battles which are devastating to both parents and children. There may be no cost to the parties for this service, and it has had the effect of reducing substantially the number of trials. At this point, these services are far from universally accessible across the provinces.

UNIFIED FAMILY COURT

The Unified Family Court Act[10] created a model court in the Ontario district of Hamilton-Wentworth. The judges of this court are accorded the powers of a judge of the provincial family court, of a surrogate court judge, and of a judge of the superior court. They are also *ex officio* justices of the peace. This court has *parens patriae* power to award custody of children.[11] The governing Act confers upon the court power to hear matters which it would otherwise have no power to hear, providing that such matters are within the authority of the judge. This has been an important experiment in creating a court empowered to deal with all family dispute matters. At the present time, Ontario has established additional such courts, but they are not province-wide. Unified family courts have also been set up in New Brunswick, Saskatchewan, Manitoba, and Newfoundland, among other provinces.

FAMILY COURT REFORM

The Zuber Commission Report[12] strongly recommended that all family law matters be heard in one court, which he conceived to be a unified family court for the Province of Ontario and which would form part of the provincial court system. The underlying rationale is to make justice in all family law matters more accessible to the citizens throughout the province, economically, geographically and intellectually.

Such radical reform would require a constitutional amendment to permit the province to appoint judges with full powers to deal with family law matters. In effect, the power of a unified family court should be conferred upon the provincial court in family matters. Understandably, this recommendation has met with resistance. Such diverse groups as the Family Law Section of the Canadian Bar Association (Ontario), Superior Court judges and a group concerned with poverty have objected to all family law matters being transferred to the provincial court. The consensus appears to be that transfer to an "inferior" court would diminish the status and importance of family law matters in the justice system. However, extensive family court reform is expected to occur because of the court backlogs that persist throughout Canada.

Endnotes

1. Schedule B of the Canada Act, 1982 (U.K.), 1982, c. 11.
2. *Reference re Adoption Act, Children's Protection Act, Deserted Wives' and Children's Maintenance Act*, [1938] S.C.R. 398, 71 C.C.C. 110, [1938] 3 D.L.R. 497.
3. J.P. Ryan, "The Overlapping Custody Jurisdiction: Co-Existence or Chaos" (1980), 3 Can. J. Fam. L. 95 at 132.
4. *A.G. Ont. v. A.G. Can*, [1982] 1 S.C.R. 62, [1982] 3 W.W.R. 1, 26 R.F.L. (2d) 113, 36 B.C.L.R. 1 (*sub nom. Reference re s. 6 of Family Relations Act*), 131 D.L.R. (3d) 257, 40 N.R. 206 (*sub nom. Re Family Relations Act of B.C.*); *Polglase v. Polglase*, [1980] 2 W.W.R. 393, 16 B.C.L.R. 378, 12 R.F.L. (2d) 296, 12 C.P.C. 217, 106 D.L.R. (3d) 601 (S.C.).

5. R.S.O. 1990, c. F.3 and R.S.O. 1990, c. C. 12.
6. R.S.O. 1970, c. 222 replaced by R.S.O. 1980, c. 292, superseded by R.S.O. 1980, c. 68.
7. Family Law Reform Act, note 5 above; Family Law Act, S.O. 1986, c. 4; Support and Custody Orders Enforcement Act, S.O. 1985, c. 6; Child and Family Services Act, S.O. 1984, c. 55.
8. R.S.O. 1980, c. 398.
9. R.S.C. 1985, c. Y-1.
10. S.O. 1976, c. 85 [now R.S.O. 1980, c. 515].
11. *Parens Patriae* is the traditional function of Superior Court judges to safeguard the welfare of children of the state. Literally it means father of the country. It refers to the sovereign power of guardianship over persons under disability, such as minors, insane, and incompetent persons. The jurisdiction evolved from the English Courts of Chancery. Judith Ryan has pointed out that one fact that is overlooked by Canadian courts is that traditionally in the English Courts of Chancery, the *parens patriae* power was exercised only when the *estate* of the child concerned was at issue. Only wealthy children received such consideration. She believes that the protection of the child's moral, intellectual, and physical well-being derives not from *parens patriae* but from the English *Poor Laws*. Under these statutes, parish authorities were required to provide shelter for the children of the destitute and to put them and their parents to work in special workhouses. This distinction has never been reconciled. See Ryan, note 2 above, at 114-6.
12. The Hon. T.G. Zuber, "Report of the Ontario Courts Inquiry" recommendations 29-31 (Toronto: Queen's Printer for Ontario, 1987).

Bibliography

Hotel, Carla, and Joan Brockman, "The Conciliatory Adversarial Continuum in Family Law Practice" (1994), 12 *Canadian Journal of Family Law* 11-36.

"Marriage, Separation, Divorce, and Your Rights: For Wives, Husbands, Children, and Common-Law Spouses in Ontario", David Botnick, 7th ed. (Self Counsel Legal Series) (North Vancouver, B.C.: International Self Counsel Press, Ltd., 1994).

Steinberg, David M. *Family Law in the Family Courts*. 2nd ed. (Toronto: Carswell Co., 1981).

Zuber, The Hon. T.G. "Report of the Ontario Courts Inquiry" (Toronto: Queen's Printer for Ontario, 1987).

10

Marriage, Cohabitation, Divorce and Corollary Relief

MARRIAGE DEFINED

> I will be the master of what is my own. She is my goods, my chattels, she is my house, my household stuff, my field, my barn, my horse, my ox, my ass, my anything.[1]

The most commonly referred to judicial definition of marriage is ". . . the voluntary union for life of one man and one woman to the exclusion of all others."[2] This definition is legally simplistic and leaves many questions unanswered. Consider the language used in the 1915 Swedish marriage ceremony, in which couples are told, "live together in mutual love, confidence and respect, and consider your responsibilities for future generations."[3] The reader will recall that the federal Parliament has power to make laws respecting marriage and divorce but the provinces have power over the solemnization of marriage.[4]

What constitutes a valid marriage is equivocal but there are certain criteria that are not disputed. If one of the parties has a prior valid marriage existing at the time of the marriage, then he or she lacks the legal capacity to marry. There is no legal capacity to marry under a minimum age which is, under the common law, 14 years for boys and 12 years for girls. Parental consent, however, is required for either party over 16 and under the age of 18 years.[5] Marriage between persons too closely related by blood or marriage is prohibited in most cultures, as it is in Ontario,[6] although in Canada, marriage to a deceased spouse's brother, sister, niece or nephew is permitted.[7] One must possess mental and physical capacity to understand marriage and to engage in normal sexual intercourse.[8] Finally, both parties must freely consent to marry.[9]

It is clear that the laws defining marriage are based on conventional views concerning the primacy of the nuclear family and they ignore the realities of current societal relationships. For example, the Marriage Act (Ontario) assumes a marriage between a man and woman of sufficient age and with the physical and mental capacity to marry, ignoring such alternative long term relationships as homosexual "marriages", communal "marriages" and consensual relationships without formal marriage. Our laws flow from the notions that marriage is a lifetime commitment, that procreation is an essential and natural feature of marriage, and that divisions of labour demand sex-related roles. Modern marriages do take other forms; for example, couples do elect not to marry or to remain childless, tasks are divided in unconventional ways, and marriages can essentially be economic or emotional partnerships. For the most part, the courts have been conservative in their interpretation of the law.

Several cases underscore the reluctance of the courts to extend the definition of family beyond its traditional boundaries. In the first instance, a person living in a lesbian relationship claimed medical coverage of her partner under the family provisions of the Ontario Health Insurance Plan. The court found against the claimant, stating that a couple living in a lesbian relationship could not be considered as having a spousal relationship as defined by law.[10]

In the second situation, the parties cohabited in a lesbian relationship for ten years during which time one of the women bore two children by artificial insemination with the consent of the other. The plaintiff claimed support for the children and an interest in matrimonial and other joint property. The British Columbia Supreme Court found that the Family Relations Act[11] does not address the legal responsibilities which homosexuals may have to each other or to children born to them. Neither did the fact of two persons living together satisfy the legal definition of step-parent. An argument suggesting that this provincial law violated the equality guarantee in the Charter of Rights and Freedoms,[12] which bars discrimination on the basis of sex, was dismissed on the basis of section 1 of the Charter, which refers to "such reasonable limits prescribed by law as can be demonstrably justified in a free and democratic society".

In the latter case, however, the claim over property succeeded. The judge noted that "the plaintiff's contribution to the global picture was significant and not only in the home by doing the housework (including painting, decorating, cooking and all the rest), but also in the defendant's office".[13] By using the remedy of constructive trust, which recognizes the shared effort in creating and maintaining property, the court prevented the title-holding party from being unjustly enriched at the expense of the other.

Persons who are classed as retarded are generally deterred from marrying either by direct or indirect means. Capacity to marry falls within the federal jurisdiction while solemnization is under provincial legislation. In Ontario, the law states that no person shall issue a licence to or perform a marriage for any person whom he or she believes lacks the capacity to marry.[14] The thrust of the province's marriage statute is to discourage such marriages despite recent studies in England and in the United States that have produced evidence that such marriages are feasible.[15] A statement by Betty Cochrane puts the issue eloquently:

> Every human being should be presumed to have these rights unless someone can show an almost certain probability of disastrous consequences if he exercises them. If this becomes the test, it should apply to retarded and non-retarded alike. An even more fundamental legal principle, which also demands a revision of the legal approach toward the mentally disabled, is that of individualization. There appears to be little legal justification for laws now on the books which deny persons with mental disabilities an entire set of rights on one omnibus finding of "incompetency" or mental retardation. What may be said of some does not apply to all. Retarded people, like all people, vary enormously in talent, aptitude, personality, achievement and temperament. . . . The law at present has no scientific or other basis on which to presume that any mentally retarded individual cannot do any or all things well. . . . Each person's capacities must be judged individually before he can be denied rights of citizenship or humanity.[16]

COHABITATION

Cohabitation is defined as living together as husband and wife. There is mutual assumption of those marital rights, duties and obligations which are usually manifested by married people, including but not necessarily dependent on sexual relations.[17] No rights or obligations arise from the simple fact of living together in a spousal relationship. However, mutual support obligations may be incurred if the cohabitation continues for more than three years, or a child is born to the couple. In that case, both have an equal obligation to support the child.[18]

In the Ontario Family Law Act, "cohabit" means to live together in a conjugal relationship whether within or outside marriage. The living arrangement must look like a marriage in order to qualify as "cohabitation". The courts have usually looked to the parties' relationship for evidence of their sexual, financial and social arrangements to determine if they lived together in a "marriage-like" relationship.[19]

Unlike married couples, unmarried couples do not automatically acquire property rights as a consequence of cohabitation. However, one should not assume that cohabitation will not result in rights and obligations respecting property. The Supreme Court of Canada found that a relationship that functions similarly to a traditional family and whose members face problems similar to a traditional family should be governed by similar law upon breakdown. This assumes that the law should promote and protect informal families to the same extent that it promotes and protects families, or at least that the law will not actively discourage informal families in extending private benefits to all family members.

A 1990 survey found that 28% of Canadians had lived or were living in common-law relationships compared with 16% in 1984. Those living common-law made up 22% of all unmarried, never married, divorced, separated, or widowed Canadians in the 18 to 64 age group. Provincial variations ranged from 33% (high) in Quebec to 15% (low) in the Atlantic provinces.[20]

It may now be that we have reached the point where a common-law relationship of some permanence will entitle a person to division of wealth or property by constructive trust/unjust enrichment approach that is available to married couples by legislation. However, since the legal provisions at common law always turn on the specific facts, rather than legislative formula, it may still be much more difficult to advance a property claim for an unmarried spouse.[21]

DIVORCE

Divorce is the legal separation of man and wife, effected by a judgment or decree of a court. Divorce pertains only to those spouses who have first been formally married, which is a prerequisite to obtaining a divorce.

The present Divorce Act[22] was enacted by the federal Parliament and came into force in July, 1986. The main relief provided by the Act is the granting of a judgment dissolving the marriage. Corollary, or accompanying relief provides for orders for inter-spousal support, custody of children and child support, including interim orders for relief. "Interim" is a word frequently used in law to denote temporary orders made to bridge the time until a permanent order has been issued. Since marriage and divorce are federal matters, applications for divorce are heard in the trial division of the Supreme Court of the province.[23]

DIVORCE JUDGMENTS

Under the Divorce Act, divorces are granted as judgments, or final orders, setting out the terms of the termination of the marriage. A divorce judgment may deal with only the severance of the marriage, or may also incorporate the terms of corollary or accompanying relief. It is possible to obtain a divorce without concluding the corollary proceedings for custody, access, and support if both parties consent. If they do not, the divorce may not be granted unless all matters are dealt with.[24]

A divorce is *not* effective until 31 days after judgment has been rendered unless the parties, by written consent, agree to abridge the waiting period and also undertake in writing not to appeal. In that event, the court *may* grant the divorce effective the day judgment is rendered, or when the court decides it is appropriate.

On taking effect, a divorce judgment has legal effect and is enforceable throughout Canada.

Residency Requirement

In order to have a petition heard, one of the parties, either the petitioner or respondent must have resided permanently in the province for at least one year immediately preceding the petition. Under the Divorce Act, a wife is not obliged to bring a petition for divorce in the province where her husband is resident but may bring it in the province where she lives. She is a person in her own right and can have an independent domicile.[25] At common law, the domicile of the wife was considered to be that of her husband.

Central Divorce Registry

Before a petition can be considered, it is necessary to establish that no other petitions have been filed. A Central Divorce Registry has been established which records all petitions on a computer and a routine process has been set up to check for duplicated petitions.[26] Where there is a prior petition concerning the same parties, that petition takes precedence over all others, unless it has been discontinued.

GROUNDS FOR DIVORCE

The two grounds for divorce in Canada are irreparable marriage breakdown and the commission of acts which are defined as matrimonial offences.[27]

Marriage Breakdown

In reality, marriage breakdown has more than a legal dimension. Six stations of marriage breakdown have been cited: emotional divorce, legal divorce, economic divorce, co-parental divorce, community divorce, and psychic divorce.[28]

Breakdown of a marriage is established when the divorcing couple have lived separate and apart for at least one year on the date the divorce is granted. They must also be living separate and apart when the divorce petition is commenced. The effect of this new provision is that a divorce on marriage breakdown grounds can be *commenced* at any time after separation, but the divorce judgment cannot be granted until one year after the date of separation. The secondary effect of this change is that an application for corollary relief, such as custody or support, can be brought immediately as part of the divorce, instead of bringing a separate action during the waiting period.

During separation, the spouses can attempt one or more reconciliations for a period of not exceeding 90 days without interrupting the one year requirement. The continuing policy in favour of reconciliation is preserved. However, for the purpose of calculating the separation, only one of the spouses must have the intention to live separate and apart. Agreement to separate is not required.

Fault Grounds

Fault grounds persist. There are are only two, namely adultery and serious mental or physical cruelty which would make continued cohabitation intolerable. Where a matrimonial offence is the ground for divorce, the divorce petition can be brought at any time; no waiting period is required.[29]

The standard of proof required by the court is the ordinary civil standard in which the allegations made by the applicant must meet the test of the balance of probabilities rather than the higher standard required in criminal cases where proof must be established beyond a reasonable doubt.[30]

Proof of Cruelty

A leading English case cited in establishing a definition of cruelty was one in which the question of law was whether non-injurious conduct was cruelty if it made living together impossible.[31] The House of Lords held that it was not and cited a definition established in a case heard in

1790, which said that in order to be cruelty, the acts complained of must have caused danger to life, limb, or health, bodily or mental, must go beyond the wear and tear of normal married life, and be "grave and weighty".[32] The Divorce Act permits a husband or wife to claim that the respondent has treated the petitioner with physical or mental cruelty of such a kind as to "render intolerable the continued cohabitation of the spouses." In Ontario, the Court of Appeal rejected the requirement of the "grave and weighty" definition and held that a spouse may be guilty of cruelty if in the marriage relationship his conduct causes wanton, malicious or unnecessary infliction of pain or suffering upon the body, the feelings or emotions of the other so as to render intolerable the continued cohabitation of the spouses.[33]

Spousal Compellability in Divorce Actions

The Ontario Evidence Act provides that in a proceeding involving an allegation of adultery, husbands and wives are competent to give evidence, but are not compellable. This means that a spouse can give such evidence but is not bound to answer any question tending to show that he or she is guilty of adultery unless that person has already given evidence in the same proceedings, and denied the adultery.[34]

Duty of the Court

Under the Divorce Act, the court has the obligation to delay a divorce judgment or deny it altogether in certain circumstances. If the court is not satisfied that reasonable arrangements have been made for support of the children of the marriage, the court must stay the granting of the divorce until satisfied that such arrangements have been made. Further, the court must deny a divorce where it has reason to believe that the petitioner who seeks the divorce has connived in creating the evidence of adultery or cruelty. Similarly, if the fault conduct has previously been condoned or approved of by the petitioner, she cannot later rely on that conduct to obtain a divorce.

The "no condonation" requirement may have the effect of barring a divorce to a woman who has been physically or mentally abused during a marriage, but appeared to condone the abusive conduct by remaining in the marriage. However, the marriage breakdown ground for a divorce can always be used after separation in such cases.

The court must also, in every case, satisfy itself that there is no possibility for reconciliation before granting a divorce and may actually choose to adjourn divorce proceedings to allow time for reconciliation through some form of counselling.[35]

Provision for Reconciliation

The Divorce Act specifies that every lawyer acting on behalf of a petitioner or a respondent on a petition for a divorce, except in those circumstances where it would be clearly inappropriate, must inform his client of those provisions which refer to the matter of reconciliation, must inform clients of appropriate resources providing marriage counselling and guidance, and must present to the court a certificate attesting to the fact that these conditions have been met.[36]

The main provisions of the Act which encourage reconciliation include: (1) allowance for a 90-day trial period of cohabitation without interrupting the required period of separation and without appearing to condone the respondent's conduct which has been presented as grounds for the petition to divorce; (2) empowering the court to adjourn the hearing to provide the opportunity for reconciliation; and (3) power to appoint a qualified person to assist the parties in reconciliation.[37] This person cannot be compelled in any legal proceeding to disclose admissions or communications made to him in his capacity as court-appointed expert in reconciliation, and discussions between husband and wife which relate to their possible reconciliation are protected from disclosure.

The intent of the law to promote reconciliation is clear and the means to execute that intent are specified, but attempts at reconciliation during a divorce action are often futile or observed in form only because the problems with the marriage seem unsolvable. The legislation appears to reflect a recognition by Parliament that family matters need something more than legal, adversarial remedies, but prevention is a concept of the social sciences. It is questionable whether contact between divorce client and lawyer is the optimal time for reconciliation. It is probably a case of too little, too late. However, it is a point at which cooperation between social work and law might give reconciliation a better chance. A social worker employed by a family law practice could not serve as a marriage counsellor since the firm acts for only one of the parties in dispute. However, the worker might help couples consider options and consequences, particularly when children are involved, with one option being to seek marital counselling from another source.

COROLLARY RELIEF

The Divorce Act also makes provision for custody and access of children, and support of both spouses and children, which may be claimed as relief that accompanies the divorce judgment which ends the marriage.

Child Custody and Access

The custody of and access to children of a marriage are addressed as accompanying relief in the Divorce Act.[38] "Child of the marriage" is defined as a child of the spouses or former spouses who is under the age of majority and has not withdrawn from parental charge, or if over the age of majority is unable to withdraw from parental charge because of illness or disability or other reason, such as education, or is unable to be self-supporting.[39] The spouses must be married to one another, or have been married, since the Divorce Act only applies to spouses who have been married.

Custody may be granted to either spouses, or to them jointly, either on an interim or permanent basis, or until the happening of an event.[40] Access is usually determined at the same time as custody in the first instance, but may be varied without variation of the custody order. Access generally includes the right of the non-custodial parent to information about the health, education and welfare of the children. In any event, the court is directed to consider the children's best interests and to ignore the past conduct of the parents unless such conduct is relevant to parenting of the children. The court must also promote maximum contact between the child and each spouse and the willingness of the custodial spouse to permit this contact.[41]

Custody and access orders are never considered to be permanent until the child reaches adulthood. They may always be varied on a material change in circumstances. Anyone seeking a variation should be aware, however, of frivolous variation applications. The courts are extremely loath to vary custody orders unless a major or profound change in parenting by the custodial parent has occurred. A child may be strongly bonded to a less than satisfactory parent, so that a change in custody may not be in the child's best interests. Access orders, on the other hand, are varied with some frequency, often on consent, as the child matures, to accommodate the child's changing needs, interests and schedule, and changing parental schedules.

Although the wording of custody and access provisions of the Divorce Act and provincial child custody and access legislation differ somewhat, the courts look to the children's best interests and the same standard in reaching decisions, so as to avoid inconsistency to the extent possible.

Spousal Support

The Divorce Act sets out the circumstances under which interim or permanent support is payable to a (married) spouse or former spouse. Some of the considerations which the court must consider are the length of the marriage and cohabitation, the roles adopted by the parties during marriage, a recognition of the economic advantages or disadvantages arising from the marriage and its breakdown, and any economic hardship resulting from the marriage breakdown.[42] The expectation of self-sufficiency of each spouse within a reasonable period of time has now been interpreted by the Supreme Court of Canada to be tempered by the other considerations. It may now be reasonable for a long-term traditional spouse to expect permanent spousal support on marriage breakdown, if her income earning capacity is permanently reduced.[43]

While the spousal support considerations in the Divorce Act vary to some extent from the Family Law Act, the courts tend to look to similar criteria and considerations in determining spousal support, the quantum and its duration.

Child Support and Guidelines

Amendments to the Divorce Act have ushered in a new era concerning child support, which at present applies *only* to child support orders made under the Divorce Act.[44] After many years of concern that child support orders did not provide adequately for children of the divorce, the federal government took action in the form of the Child Support Guidelines, which came into effect on May 1, 1997.

Prior to enactment of the Guidelines, child support payments were taxable under the Income Tax Act as income in the hands of the recipient (usually the wife) and a deduction from income for the husband. The usual result was that the custodial parent received less than the face amount of the support order, which was very often inadequate in the first instance. Under the Guidelines, support amounts geared to the income of the payor spouse are set out in Schedules for each province. The word "Guidelines" is a misnomer for all practical purposes, since the amounts to be paid under the Guidelines are mandatory, except in very limited circumstances. The only exception at present is *if* the payor can demonstrate a lower standard of living than the recipient, based on a mandatory formula.

The further significant feature of the support which is paid under the Guidelines is that it is no longer taxable as income to the recipient, and is not a deduction to the payor. All orders for child support made under the Divorce Act after May 1, 1997 are caught by this provision. However, child support orders made before that date are still taxable and deductible under the prior rules.

In trying to increase child support payments across the nation, parliament provided that support orders for less than the applicable Child Support Guideline amount could be varied by applying to the court for the Guideline amount.[45] Although there have been relatively few cases to date, the courts appear to be reluctant to depart from the Guidelines at this time.[46]

Additional enforcement provisions are the final feature of these far-reaching amendments. The federal government has introduced a range of measures to promote enforcement in full of child support orders.[47] It will be interesting to see whether sufficient resources are allocated to enforcement in support of the legislative enactments.

ROLE OF THE CHILDREN'S LAWYER

Under the Divorce Act, it is not mandatory to notify the Children's Lawyer in every divorce involving children, which was the prior practice. However, the presiding judge may appoint the children's lawyer as legal representative of the children in a divorce proceeding regarding custody and access. The child's representative thereby becomes a party to the proceeding. As a consequence, an investigator from the office of the Children's Lawyer may interview the parents and other significant persons and must then produce a report setting out the findings of the investigation, which may include recommendations about the children's custody and access. This report must be served on the parents and filed with the court. If either parent wishes to dispute the report, it must be made within 15 days. Interestingly, this report may contain hearsay which does not affect the admissibility of the report as evidence. This factor is a demonstration of the more relaxed standard of evidence in matters dealing with children.

Endnotes

1. W. Shakespeare, *The Taming of the Shrew* (1596), Act 3, Scene 2, as spoken by Petrucchio.
2. *Hyde v. Hyde and Woodmansee* (1866), L.R. 1 P&D 130, 14 W.R. 517, in Fodden, Simon, ed. *Canadian Family Law: Cases and Materials*. Toronto: Butterworths, 1977 at 2-1.
3. Quoted in Glendon, Mary Ann, "The New Marriage and New Property", in J. Eekelaar and S. Katz, eds. "Marriage and Cohabitation in Contemporary Societies" (Toronto: Butterworths, 1978), p. 59.

4. E.g., Marriage Act, R.S.O. 1980, c. 256, s. 4.
5. *Ibid.*, s. 5(2).
6. *Ibid.*, s. 19.
7. Marriage Act, R.S.C. 1970, c. M-5, s. 2.
8. Marriage Act, note 4 above, s. 7. See *D. v. D.*, [1973] 3 O.R. 82, 13 R.F.L. 1 (*sub nom. Dashevsky v. Dashevsky*), 36 D.L.R. (3d) 17 (H.C.); and *Miller v. Miller*, [1947] O.R. 213, [1947] 3 D.L.R. 354 (C.A.).
9. Marriage Act, *ibid.*, s. 6 — This appears to turn on the issue of mental capacity to understand the commitment and consequences, whether or not the marriage occurred under duress or was entered into for fraudulent purposes.
10. *Andrews v. Ont. Hospital Insurance Commission* (1988), 64 O.R. (2d) 258 (H.C.).
11. R.S.B.C. 1979, c. 121.
12. Part I of the Constitution Act, 1982, being schedule B of the Canada Act 1982 (U.K.), 1982, c. 11.
13. *Anderson v. Luoma* (1986), 50 R.F.L. (2d) 127 at 151 (B.C.S.C.).
14. Marriage Act, note 4 above, s. 7.
15. See W. Wolfensberger, *The Principle of Normalization in Human Services* (Toronto: National Institute on Mental Retardation, 1972).
16. B. Cochrane, "Conference Report: Conception, Coercion, and Control: Symposium on Reproductive Rights of the Mentally Retarded" (1974), 25 Hospital & Community Psychiatry at 289, quoted in B. Mecredy-Williams, "Marriage Law and the Mentally Retarded" (1979), 2 Can. J. Fam. L. 63 at 79-80.
17. *Boyd v. Boyd*, 228 Cal. App. 374, 39 Cal. RPTR, 400, 404.
18. Family Law Act, R.S.O. 1990, c. F-34, ss. 29 and 31.
19. MacDonald & Wilton, 1996 Annotated F.L.A.P. p.s. 1 at 5.
20. Globe & Mail, May 23, 1991.
21. McLeod, James G. and Alfred A. Mamo, "Annual Review of Family Law", 1995, Carswell, summarizing the present state of the law.
22. R.S.C. 1985, c. 3 (2nd Supp.).
23. *Divorce, Law and the Family in Canada* (Ottawa: Stats. Can., 1983) provides an excellent survey of the Canadian experience regarding divorce, past and present.
24. *Schulenberg v. Schulenberg* (1987), 59 O.R. (2d) 798, 17 C.P.C. (2d) 252 (Mast.).
25. For a good review, see H.W. Silverman, "Conflict of Laws: Some Matrimonial Problems" (1979), 2 Fam. L. Rev. 103.
26. Divorce Regulations, S.O.R./68-200 [now C.R.C. 1978, c. 557], ss. 3-7.

27. Divorce Act, note 22 above, s. 10.
28. Bohannen, Paul, noted in Family Law, Vol. 1, University of Toronto.
29. Divorce Act, note 22 above, s. 10.
30. *Smith v. Smith,* [1952] 2 S.C.R. 312, [1952] 3 D.L.R. 449.
31. *Russell v. Russell,* [1897] A.C. 395 (H.L.).
32. *Evans v. Evans* (1790), 1 Hag. Con. 35, 161 E.R. 466.
33. *Knoll v. Knoll* (1970), 2 O.R. (2d) 169, 1 R.F.L. 141, 10 D.L.R. (3d) 199 (C.A.).
34. Ontario Evidence Act, R.S.O. 1980, c. 145, s. 10.
35. Divorce Act, note 15 above, s. 10.
36. Divorce Act, note 15 above, s. 9.
37. *Ibid.*, ss. 8(3)(b)(ii), 10(1),(2).
38. Divorce Act, as amended by S.C. 1997, c. 1 and by R.S. (2nd Supp.), c. 3 at ss. 15-26.1
39. Divorce Act, as amended, s. 2.
40. *Ibid.*, s. 16.
41. *Ibid.*, ss. 16 and 17.
42. *Ibid.*
43. *Moge v. Moge*, 43 R.F.L. (3d) 345, [1992] 3 S.C.R. 813.
44. Please refer to the amendments at note 38.
45. Divorce Act, as amended, s. 17.
46. For example, *Buck v. Russell* (unreported) October 7, 1997, Ontario (Minden J.), where a hardship claim by the payor was dismissed.
47. Amendments to the Family Orders and Agreements Enforcement Assistance Act, R.S. (2nd Supp.) c. 4; 1992, c. 1; 1993, c. 8.

Bibliography

Baxter, Ian F.G. "Family Law Reform: a historical perspective of the Ontario experience" (1987), 6 Can. J. Fam. Law 247-269.

Bedont, Barbara C. "Gender Differences in Negotiations and the Doctrine of Unconscionability in Domestic Contracts" (1994), 12 Canadian Family Law Quarterly, 21-44.

Birklein, Brenda M. "Living Together/Splitting Apart: Common Law and Legal Marriages and the Law" (1994), 18 Law Now, No. 9, 9-12.

Blindor, M. "Marital Dissolution and Child Custody: A Primer for Family Therapists and Divorce Attorneys." *Family Therapy,* 9(1). 1-20, 1982.

Chipeur, G.D., Bailey, T.M. "Honey, I Proselytized the Kids: Religion as a Factor in Child Custody and Access Disputes" (1993), 4 *National Journal of Constitutional Law* 101-121.

Grassby, Miriam. "Spousal Support: Assumptions and Myths versus Case Law" (1995), 12 Canadian Family Law Quarterly 187-239.

Langer, Rosanna. "Postmarital Support Discourse, Discretion, and Male Dominance" (1994), 12 Canadian Journal of Family Law 67-90.

Payne, Julien D. *Payne on Divorce,* 3rd ed. (Toronto: Carswell, 1993).

Rusk, Peter. "Same-Sex Spousal Benefits and the Evolving Conception of Family" (1993), 52 University of Toronto Faculty Law Review 170-205.

Steward, Dana C., McFadyen, Linda E. "Women and Economic Consequences of Divorce in Manitoba: An Empirical Study" (1992), 21 Manitoba Law Journal 80-99.

11

Reform of Family Law

In the past three decades most provincial legislatures across Canada devised statutory schemes that have brought family law into line with contemporary modes of family interaction.[1] Before this period there was a half-century of benign parliamentary neglect which permitted courts to sanction notions of matrimonial misconduct and to render decisions based on prevailing assumptions as they saw them.[2] Notions of morality have evolved in favour of consideration for principles of equity in property and support matters and in regard to the best interests and needs of children. Federal law, embodied in the Divorce Act, still retains notions of morality and fault as grounds for divorce but not concerning division of property. Conduct is not now reflected in provincial family law reform. Prevailing provincial concepts of male-female relationships and parent-child responsibilities are built on principles of equality and demonstrated need as is the present federal legislation.

The case of *Murdoch v. Murdoch*,[3] which went to the Supreme Court of Canada, seemed to shock the provinces into moving toward reform and so is a watershed case that led to a new era in family law. The facts of this case are these:

> The plaintiff wife sought a beneficial interest in certain properties and assets vested in the name of her defendant husband. These properties were ranch properties acquired over a period of 18 years, and upon which the plaintiff carried out her duties as ranch wife. It was found as a fact by a majority of the court that "what the appellant had done, while living with the respondent, was the work done by any ranch wife". Although the plaintiff had from time to time advanced money to the defendant for the purpose of acquiring lands

> and chattels, these were recorded as loans and paid back. The plaintiff founded her claim on the basis of a trust.

It was held by the court that the plaintiff's claim must fail. A dissenting opinion was filed by Mr. Justice Laskin, the late Chief Justice of the Supreme Court of Canada, who wrote that the plaintiff should be entitled to a proprietary interest in the properties. Such share was to be determined upon a proper inquiry and report. The plaintiff, in fact, had acquired substantial household furnishings for the matrimonial home, advanced money towards the acquisition of properties and assets, and contributed labour far in excess of ordinary housekeeping duties. This was a case where the spouses over a period of some 15 years improved their lot in life through progressively larger acquisitions of ranch property to which the plaintiff contributed the necessary labour in seeing that the ranches were productive. There was no reason to treat this contribution as any less significant than a direct financial contribution, which to a lesser degree she also made. The relations of husband and wife in such circumstances should not be allowed to rest on the mere obligation of support and shelter which arose from the fact of marriage where the husband was able to provide for an impecunious wife nor be allowed to rest on her statutory dower rights under the law of Alberta. They represented a minimum and reflected the law's protection for a dependent wife. However, this should not be regarded as exhausting a wife's claim upon her husband where she had, as in the instant case, been anything but dependent. The appropriate mechanism to give relief to a wife who could not prove a common intention that she had an interest in the property, or to a wife whose contribution to the acquisition of property was physical labour rather than purchase money was the constructive trust[4] which did not depend on evidence of intention. The basis of the constructive trust was the unjust enrichment which would result if the person having the property were permitted to retain it.

In another case, following the dissent in Murdoch, Mr. Justice Dickson said:

> Many factors, legal and non-legal, have emerged to modify the position of earlier days. Among these factors are a more enlightened attitude toward the status of women, altered life-styles, dynamic socio-economic changes. Increasingly, the work of a woman in the management of the home and rearing of the children, as wife and mother, is recognized as an economic contribution to the family unit.[5]

The pressure for reform gained momentum and in Ontario the Family Law Reform Act was proclaimed in 1978 as were similar statutes in other provinces. The preamble stated:

> Whereas . . . it is necessary to recognize the equal position of spouses as individuals within marriage and to recognize marriage as a form of partnership;
> And Whereas in support of such recognition it is necessary to provide in law for the orderly and equitable settlement of the affairs of the spouses upon the breakdown of the partnership; and to provide for other mutual obligations in family relationships, including the equitable sharing by parents of responsibility for their children.[6]

This Act also provides for division (or equalization) of all property acquired by the parties during marriage and cohabitation, regardless of the registered ownership. Upon separation, divorce or death, a married spouse is legally entitled to claim equalization of all such property. The Family Law Act, 1986, contained several significant amendments to the common law. It established the independent legal personality of all married parties and gave each equal legal status (s. 64(1), (2), (3)).

In effect, this Act swept away many of the old common law inequities concerning the status of women and children by affirming that each spouse has the right to support from the other when need is demonstrated, that there exists an expectation that each will become self-supporting to the extent of his or her ability, and that there will be a fair sharing of assets. The old common law rules were disadvantageous to women by presuming that the spouse who holds title, usually the husband, had a primary right to property of a marriage unless the other spouse could produce evidence of legal title or direct financial contribution. Men were disadvantaged with respect to custody of the children of a marriage because of a presumption that children of "tender years" should remain with their mother. It was also presumed that a father had continuing support obligations toward his wife and children. In addition, children born outside of marriage had no right to inherit property and fathers of such children had no right to custody.

The Family Law Reform Act in Ontario, and similar legislation in other provinces, meant that married women have equal entitlement to a division of property at the point of marriage breakdown. It also created new responsibilities for support for both spouses and for their children. The operative phrase is the determination of need and capacity. Men have acquired an equal right to custody of and access to their children and a right to claim support from their spouse on the basis of need. For children, the distinction between children born inside or outside of marriage was abolished and all children are equally entitled to care, support and inheritance of property.

These egalitarian concepts have now been further confirmed by the Family Law Act in Ontario[7] together with similar legislation in other provinces, moving from partial division of property on marriage breakdown to provide a full equalization of the value of property acquired during the course of the marriage upon marriage breakdown, divorce or death. With few exceptions, the value of all property must be divided equally.

FAMILY LAW ACT, Ontario

This Act is divided into five parts, which deal with property division, special rules respecting the matrimonial home, child and spousal support obligations, domestic contracts and dependents' claims for damages in the event of accident, injury or death. The whole is preceded by a definition section.

The Act defines a child as one born within or outside marriage and includes a person to whom the parent has demonstrated a settled intention to treat as a child of his or her family. This includes both adopted and biological children and step-children, but does not include a child placed in a foster home by a person having lawful custody.[8] To cohabit is to live together in a conjugal relationship, whether within or outside marriage.[9] Spouse is defined in the Act in two ways depending upon the context. In property matters, spouse refers only to a man or a woman who is or has been married to the other. In regard to support obligations, this definition is extended to include an unmarried man and woman who have lived together as husband and wife continuously for at least three years, or in a relationship of some permanence where a child is born to them and they have lived together as husband and wife during the preceding year.[10]

Property for purposes of the Act has a very broad definition and includes virtually everything — the home, pensions, money in bank accounts, property over which a person may exercise some control now or in the future, regardless of ownership and whether or not a third party has an ownership interest. The value of property is determined at the date of separation, divorce or death, whichever first occurs. Gifts or inheritances from third parties during marriage are excluded, but very little else. The effect of the property provisions is to require spouses to value all of their property at marriage breakdown, deduct the value of debts and liabilities and arrive at the net family property of each of them. The spouse with the smaller total is entitled to one-half the difference between their net family properties. In order to enforce property entitlement, a person may have to apply to a superior court to have his or her property rights determined by the court.[11]

Formal recognition is given to a concept of marriage as a partnership and it obliterates the traditional assumptions of sex-linked roles and tasks. Child care, household management and financial provision are the joint responsibilities of the spouses. Inherent to the marital relationship is joint contribution, whether financial or otherwise in assuming these responsibilities, entitling each spouse to share equally in the value of property.

It is on the dissolution of a marriage (or a common law relationship) that the law is strained. Since both partners did not begin the relationship as equals in their capacity to earn, and since the physical care of children is still the principal responsibility of women, separation and divorce agreements still leave many women and children disadvantaged.

Social workers may wish to use the statutory concept of shared responsibilities as a model of community standards in working with couples experiencing difficulties in their family relationships. Indeed, children become part of the family unit as their capacity to make a contribution to its everyday function develops and they are included in family counselling sessions. The Act has extracted the essential components of a marital partnership, that is, child care, household management, and financial maintenance. It has not indicated which partner shall perform these tasks, or, of course, in what spirit they shall be performed. A discussion centred on how they shall be divided and the feelings surrounding the division may uncover discrepancies in each family member's concept of appropriate roles and functions which can open new channels of communication and new models for family roles.

COMMON LAW RELATIONSHIPS

The Family Law Act, when dealing with property rights, defines spouse narrowly as spouse by marriage. In other words, couples who are not or have never been married have no claim under the legislation to a share of property owned in the name of the other. For example:

> Carol and Bob lived together for nine years but were never married. Both worked but Carol, having been brought up to believe that the man was the head of the house, always let Bob look after their finances. Everything was in his name. In the fullness of time they separated. Carol wanted to claim her share and discovered she had no claim under the Family Law Act to any part of the furniture, bank account or car.

If a remedy were to be sought, one may be available at common law through a claim under the doctrine of constructive trust.[12] This may be a long and costly procedure; the moral is apparent. Clients should be advised to make sure that joint assets are always in the name of both partners to a common law relationship or that they enter into a cohabitation agreement that includes division of property upon separation.

An important case testing the scope of family law legislation is the following:

> A man and woman lived together as man and wife for approximately 20 years. The woman supported the couple during the first five years while the man saved so as to be able to acquire a farm. The woman aided the man in obtaining and maintaining his bee-keeping business and helped with the farm labours. The man subsequently purchased additional land on which a home was built. The farm was then sold and the proceeds deposited into the man's bank account. The woman maintained that she was entitled to one-half interest in the property and business. The trial judge dismissed her claim. She appealed and the appeal was allowed on the principle of the constructive trust. The man appealed to the Supreme Court of Canada but the appeal was dismissed and the principle upheld.[13]

Common law relationships do imply support obligations. Spouse is more broadly defined to include either a man or woman not being married to each other who have cohabited continuously for a period of three years or in a relationship of some permanence where there is a child born of whom they are the natural parents.[14]

HOMOSEXUAL RELATIONSHIPS

Since spouse is defined throughout the Family Law Act as man and woman who cohabit, it is clearly the intent of this Act to include only heterosexual relationships. Legislation does not now extend to include homosexual partners as spouses for family law purposes.

At the present time, adultery, cohabitation outside of marriage, or homosexual relationships do not disentitle a person to custody. The Court is interested in the effect of conduct and environment on the child and whether the alleged conduct is within the parameters of what is considered normative and reasonable within the society.

DEATH OF A SPOUSE

The Family Law Act expressly continues support obligations after the death of the payor spouse. If the payor dies leaving a will, the surviving spouse must elect to take as provided as a beneficiary of the will *or* to receive equalization of their net family properties. If the will does not make provision for pre-existing support obligations, a court may impose that they become a charge against the deceased person's estate. The intent is clear: support obligations cannot be avoided, even on death. Imagine the following circumstance:

> A man dies, having a support obligation to his two teenaged children and his first wife which was not insured at his death. In his will, he left everything, which comprised his home and a small pension to his second wife. Are the first wife and children entitled to anything?
>
> On application by the first wife, a court awarded her and the children the continuing support to which they were entitled as a first charge against the estate. The second wife became obliged to share her inheritance with those to whom her husband had a support obligation.

Death of a spouse is also a triggering event for division and equalization of the property of the parties.

POSSESSION OF THE MATRIMONIAL HOME

Spouses are equally entitled to possession of the matrimonial home which includes rental accommodation. Common law spouses are not eligible since they are excluded by the definition of "spouse". In the event of emergency need, the court is empowered to make orders for temporary possession of the home. This decision is usually based on protecting the best interests of the children or to prevent the eviction of a helpless wife and children, a scene from melodramas of an earlier era which could occur in real life prior to family law legislation.

PROVISIONS FOR SUPPORT

In our traditional social structure we expect that the wife will be the one who must make application for support. Prior to the enactment of the Family Law Reform Act and the present Family Law Act, a wife who was separated from her husband because of personal differences or having grown apart had no claim to support. She had to prove she was a deserted wife to justify a claim under the former Deserted Wives' and Children's Maintenance Act.[15] Incompatibility was not seen as an acceptable reason for separation because a wife's duty was to make her marriage function. She was expected to return to her husband or to become dependent on public welfare. Therefore, the only recourse available was to attempt to establish fault on the part of her spouse since legal liability for support was predicated upon fault. A wife had to prove that she had been deserted by her husband or that cruelty had been inflicted or that adultery had been committed. It also had to be established that these faults could not be condoned and that no reconciliation was possible. Moreover, she had to prove that she was the innocent party or that he was more guilty than she before she could succeed in her application for support.

Social workers and lawyers alike were disturbed and frustrated by laws which did not serve the values of contemporary society. The dominant Canadian culture views marriage as a partnership in which both husband and wife share responsibilities, in particular a responsibility to make the marriage work. Finding fault is destructive to all persons involved and, given the complexities and ambiguities of intimate relationships, very difficult to determine. Cruelty and desertion are the manifest symptoms of a troubled relationship. The Family Law Act recognizes the dynamic aspect of relationships by eliminating the necessity to establish that one spouse is at fault. The law has withdrawn from sitting in moral judgment in order to mete out punishment to the offending partner in marital relationships. The dissolution of a marriage produces sufficient vindictiveness, anger, sense of failure and guilt which do not need to be compounded by outmoded laws. The law accepts the dissolution of the partnership and provides for equity in so far as possible in the division of mutual responsibilities and obligations. The guiding principle now is support which is based on the need of either spouse and dependent children. Support obligations of unmarried spouses, as has been pointed out, are the same as if they had been married.

Family law legislation has established in law the notion that function follows form and that dependency is defined by the particular division of labour in any given union. For example, a woman who has employment outside the home and is the principal wage earner must contribute to the support of the spouse and dependent children. The critical factor is to determine the relative needs of each spouse and of the children.

COHABITATION

Brief separations during cohabitation are not considered to be interruptions in the continuity of cohabitation because the parties have not arrived at a settled state of mind in regard to their union. In common law relationships, as with any support application, it is essential to a claim for support that it be made within two years of the date that cohabitation is ended and separate living begins.

A man who cohabits with a woman in circumstances where he does not become a spouse does not have a legal obligation to provide support. If an application is made, the court will base the decision on the specific facts of each situation. For example, in Ontario, if cohabitation was for less than three years and no child was born, no support obligation would arise. It may never have amounted to cohabitation, although there was intimacy from time to time. If a child is born, it must be established that it was the natural child of the couple in question, in order for the man to incur support obligation as a spouse.[16]

In a 1994 case in Manitoba, the Court of Appeal held that where the applicant had applied for support more than a year after separation, the Manitoba court now lacked jurisdiction to hear the application because the definition of "spouse" under the Act could not be understood to include former cohabitees where their former period of cohabitation had ended more than a year before the date of the application. This decision emphasizes the importance of precision in drafting legislation because in this legislation the drafters had tied a limitation period to bringing a spousal support application to the definition of "spouse". If it had appeared elsewhere in the legislation, the court could have considered the application.[17]

CRITERIA FOR DETERMINING NEED FOR SUPPORT

In determining the degree of need, the court will consider a number of variables. These include consideration of the needs and capacities of both the parties to support the other, with consideration given to age and health, the length of cohabitation, accustomed standard of living, ability of the dependent spouse to become self-supporting, the desirability of one spouse to remain in the home to care for the children, and to provide for their support, having regard to their care and educational needs including continuing care for an ill or disabled child over the age of eighteen. Consideration is given to the period of time contributed by the non-working spouse in household and child care responsibilities.[18]

Before the advent of family law reform, conduct of the spouse took on primary importance and in Ontario, in cases where there were no grounds for divorce, women had to make an application for alimony. Entitlement to support is now determined solely on the basis of capacity and need without consideration of the conduct of either spouse.[19] In effect, support has assumed the status of a right rather than privilege to be earned by good conduct.

APPLICATION FOR ORDER TO SUPPORT WHERE FAMILY IS RECEIVING PUBLIC SUPPORT

An order for the support of a dependent spouse or child may be made to the appropriate court by government or by a municipal corporation if payments for the support of dependants are already being provided by these bodies.[20] Welfare authorities generally seem unwilling to initiate such proceedings to recoup funds for support. Instead, the wife is told she must initiate legal proceedings against her spouse if she wishes to receive benefits. Many recipients find this harassing and degrading. Some welfare workers feel it is coercive to have to insist that their clients take this initiative. Section 33(3) of the Family Law Act may be used in spite of the fact that the Family Benefits Act[21] states as a condition of eligibility that a woman seeking mother's allowance may be required to bring an action for support.[22]

POWERS OF THE COURT IN MAKING SUPPORT ORDERS

The court has wide discretion to order:

1. periodic payments, for a definite or indefinite period or until a specified event occurs, such as remarriage, or a child becoming 18 years of age;
2. a lump sum payment;
3. a property transfer or exclusive possession of the matrimonial home, either absolutely or for a specified period;
4. payment of expenses to cover prenatal care and birth of a child;
5. that the payor's obligations become a debt upon his estate, should he die; otherwise the order ends with death;
6. that a spouse or child be designated an irrevocable beneficiary of a life insurance policy;
7. that reimbursement be made to a public welfare agency if the recipient applies for or is receiving public assistance;
8. that payments be made into court. This arrangement has several advantages. The authority of the court may impress the payor with the seriousness of the order. Compliance can be monitored through the court process. Finally, the payor is relieved of potential resentment of having to make out a cheque to an estranged or former spouse;[23]
9. indexation of support payments in accordance with the cost of living increase published by Statistics Canada.[24]

However, it should be noted that there are limitations on the jurisdiction of the provincial family court to order lump sum payments, property transfers or charges upon property. Generally, this type of relief must be sought in the Superior Court.

OBLIGATION OF PARENTS TO SUPPORT CHILDREN

All parents have an obligation to the extent of their capability to provide support for children who are unmarried and under the age of 18 years in accordance with need.[25] This obligation to provide support does not extend to a child 16 years or more who has withdrawn from parental control. In an interesting case,[26] the appeal judge held that this provision means that a child must leave parental control voluntarily. In this case, the son could not remain with the mother because it would jeopardize her mental well-being; therefore, he did not leave her home voluntarily and so could not be denied support. In another instance, the court upheld the son's application for support from the parents because the evidence did not support the parent's claim that he had withdrawn voluntarily or that an intolerable situation existed. Consequently, they were obliged to pay support.[27]

OBLIGATION OF CHILDREN TO SUPPORT PARENTS

A child is now obligated to provide for a parent who has cared or provided support for him. However, it does not impose an obligation upon children to pay debts incurred by their parents. The support provisions set up a mutual support obligation. However, section 32 is not applicable where there has been no direct interdependency between the parties.[28]

VARIATION OF ORDERS

In the normal course of human affairs, circumstances never remain static. Where an order has been made, for example, for custody, support, access or exclusive possession, any person named in that order can bring an application to vary. There must be evidence of material change in circumstances, or new evidence in support. An application to vary cannot be brought within six months except with leave of the court in order to prevent frivolous applications. If the recipient of payments receives public assistance, the relevant provincial or municipal officer may also initiate an application to vary.[29]

PRIORITY GIVEN THE DIVORCE ACT

The reader will recall that federal legislation takes precedence over provincial legislation. Therefore, if there is an existing application for support or custody under provincial legislation and a divorce petition is filed, the provincial application is stayed until the divorce is settled by the court. For example, where a couple separate, the father applies for custody under provincial legislation and the mother files for divorce, the custody application is suspended until the divorce matters are concluded. Currently, all matters may be joined in a petition for divorce.

IMPACT OF FEDERAL CHILD SUPPORT GUIDELINES

At present, the Child Support Guidelines enacted by changes to the Divorce Act[30] do not affect provincial support applications. However, the provinces are expected to enact complementary support legislation so as to avoid inconsistency between the federal and provincial statutes. In the meantime, courts are taking cognizance of the federal Guideline amounts in setting provincial child support amounts.

DOMESTIC CONTRACTS

The Family Law Act (Ontario) provides that the parties may enter into various domestic contracts, establishing rules that determine validity and enforceability of the term of the contract, and in some cases gives the court jurisdiction to override the terms of the contract to promote a social value seen to be compelling.[31]

Family law legislation regulates domestic contracts in the form of marriage contracts, cohabitation agreements and separation agreements.[32] The distinction between them is based on the status of the parties at the time the contract is made. A marriage contract, for example, is valid only so long as the parties remain married unless the contract states otherwise. Parties to an agreement, which must be in writing and signed by the parties, are free to make any arrangements they consider suitable to regulate their own relationships, lives and property, including the right to direct the education and moral training of their children. Separation agreements may also include the right to decide custody and access to children. The court is authorized to disregard any agreement concerning support, education, moral training, or custody and access to children where it considers the contractual provisions are not in the child's best interests. The Family Law Act now requires full financial disclosure between spouses before a domestic contract is signed, otherwise the contract is at risk of being set aside for material non-disclosure of financial assets.[33]

In an elegant display of magnanimity, the former Family Law Reform Act swept away a final vestige of the double standard. *Dum casta* clauses in domestic contracts, literally "while chaste", are now void.[34] This has eliminated the need to maintain a facade of chastity in order to receive support. However, this does not refer to a change in status through remarriage or cohabitation, which may still affect the right to support or other benefits under the agreement.

In Ontario, property rights falling within the scope of the contract are seen as valid and enforceable. There is nothing in Parts 1 or 2 of the Family Law Act that allows the court to override valid and enforceable provisions of a domestic contract. However, in Ontario, support agreements may be overridden if they are seen as not in a child's best interests. The Family Relations Act, R.S.B.C. 1979, allows the B.C. court to override property provisions if the contractual division is deemed to be "unfair".[35]

DEPENDANT'S CLAIM FOR DAMAGES

The provision for dependant's claim for damages becomes available upon the injury or death of a person who has an obligation to support another, whether spouse, children, grandparents, grandchildren or siblings. Damages which may be claimed include all expenses incurred as a result of the injury or death, together with a compensatory amount for loss through the person's injury or death. Where a primary recipient advances a claim, subsidiary claims for loss of care, guidance and companionship may also be brought in the same court action. Interestingly, an unborn child is entitled to advance a claim and recover damages respecting injury incurred before birth.

FAMILY PROPERTY

Property law in Canada is a provincial matter under the Constitution Act.[36] Nevertheless, property claims can be joined with other claims in a Petition for Divorce. Property matters are always brought in the Superior Court of the province where the property is situated.

All provinces have community of property regimes which require equal division of property upon marriage breakdown, although the definitions of property may vary from province to province. In Ontario, the definition of property is extremely broad and all-encompassing, including real property, money, shares, R.R.S.P.s, pensions, rights, warrants, life insurance, retirement benefits, and more — virtually everything acquired by the parties during marriage and cohabitation. There are exceptions to property which must be divided with a spouse, including property owned by a spouse before marriage (except a matrimonial home) and property received by gift or inheritance from third parties during marriage and cohabitation.

The matrimonial home is treated differently. Regardless of registered ownership, a spouse is entitled to share in the value of a matrimonial home upon marriage breakdown, even if it was owned by the other spouse before marriage. The definition of "matrimonial home" is as broad as the definition of property, and includes every residential property in which a spouse has an interest and was ordinarily occupied by the spouses or children at the time of separation as their family residence. There can be more than one, and the courts have found that a boat with sleeping accommodation, ski chalet, cottage, Florida condominium, trailer, camper, apartment and residence above a restaurant and the part of the restaurant where the family ate their meals were all matrimonial homes.

It should be noted that statutory property rights only apply to *married* spouses on a marriage breakdown. Unmarried spouses have no property rights under statute. However, the law of trusts at common law may give some of the same rights to a common law spouse in similar circumstances. The unmarried spouse must show actual contribution to the acquisition of the property. In a famous case which was heard by the Supreme Court of Canada, a long-term unmarried spouse who had cared for and worked with her common law husband and contributed to his welfare for many years, while raising her own children, was given title to the husband's house, even though he had always been the registered owner.[37] The case attempted to redress and recognize the woman's contribution to the family by equitable distribution of the family resources.

Family property law is an exceedingly complex area of law which requires expert legal advice in order to protect the rights of the spouses and children upon separation or divorce. Without such advice, separated spouses may unwittingly give up important and valuable property rights until it is too late to claim their entitlement.

We have not attempted to define family property law in any depth because of its very complexity. Social workers are urged to direct their clients to obtain legal advice about their property rights in the event of a significant change in their status, such as at cohabitation, marriage, separation, divorce or death.

Endnotes

1. See the Tables of Concordance.
2. Judge R.S. Abella, "Family Law in Ontario: Changing Assumption" (1981), 13 Ottawa L. Rev. 1.
3. [1975] 1 S.C.R. 423, [1974] 1 W.W.R. 361, 13 R.F.L. 185, 41 D.L.R (3d) 367.
4. Constructive trust — A trust is created when money or property is held by one person for the benefit of another. When there is no express intention to create a trust, but in fairness or equity a trust should exist, the court may construe (construct) a trust. See *Becker v. Pettkus* (1978), 20 O.R. (2d) 105, 5 R.F.L. (2d) 344, 87 D.L.R. (3d) 101. Affirmed [1980] 2 S.C.R. 834, 19 R.F.L. (2d) 165, 8 E.T.R. 143, 117 D.L.R. (3d) 257, 34 N.R. 384.

5. *Rathwell v. Rathwell,* [1978] 2 S.C.R. 436 at 443, [1978] 2 W.W.R. 101, 1 R.F.L. (2d) 1, 1 E.T.R. 307, 83 D.L.R. (3d) 289.
6. R.S.O. 1980, c. 152, preamble.
7. S.O. 1986, c. 4.
8. Note 6 above, s. 1(a).
9. *Ibid.*, s. 1(b).
10. *Ibid.*, ss. 1(f) and 14.
11. *Ibid.*, s. 3(b). In discussing this Act, we have selected those provisions of particular interest to social workers and their clients. It is strongly recommended that the Act be read in its entirety. It can be found in any library or obtained from the Ontario Government Publications, Bay Street, Toronto.
12. See the definition of constructive trust, note 4 above.
13. *Becker v. Pettkus*, note 4 above.
14. Family Law Act, note 6, s. 14. For a comprehensive examination of common law unions, see W.H. Holland, *Unmarried Couples: Legal Aspects of Cohabitation* (Toronto: Carswell Co., 1982).
15. R.S.O. 1970, c. 128, repealed [1978, c. 2, s. 76] effective March 31, 1978 except in cases where proceedings had already commenced under this Act.
16. *Stoikiewicz v. Filas*, [1978] 3 A.C.W.S. 227 (Ont. U.F.C.).
17. *Patterson v. Torrence* (1994), 2 R.F.L. (4th) 74 (Man. C.A.).
18. Family Law Act, note 7 above, s. 33(5).
19. *Ibid.*, s. 33(10).
20. Family Law Act, note 7 above, s. 33(3).
21. R.S.O. 1980, c. 151.
22. See N.M. Fera, "“Children” Suing “Children” for the Support of Children: The Welfare Push" (1979), 2 Fam. L. Rev. 90.
23. R. Komar, "Enforcement of Judgments and Orders in the Ontario Provincial Courts (Family Division)." A paper presented to the Young Lawyers Division of the Canadian Bar Association — Ontario, November 30, 1983.
24. Family Law Act, note 7, above, s. 34.
25. Family Law Reform Act, note 6 above, s. 16.
26. *Re Haskell and Letourneau* (1979), 25 O.R. (2d) 139, 100 D.L.R. (3d) 329, 1 F.L.R.A.C. 306 (Co.Ct.).
27. *Ades v. Ades* (1979), 9 R.F.L. (2d) 318 (Ont. Prov. Ct.).
28. S. 32 of the Family Law Act, (Ontario) as discussed in Macdonald, J. and Ann Wilton, *Ontario Family Law Act* (Toronto: Carswell, 1996).
29. Family Law Act, note 7 above, s. 21.
30. Divorce Act, as amended by S.C. 1997, c. 1 and R.S. (2nd Supp.), c. 3.

31. Family Law Act, Part IV.
32. *Ibid.*, ss. 50-59.
33. *Ibid.*, s. 55(1).
34. *Ibid.*, s. 55(2).
35. McLeod, James G. and Alfred A. Mamo, "Annual Review of Family Law" (Toronto: Carswell, 1995) at 278-283.
36. Constitution Act, s. 92.
37. *Peter v. Beblow* (1993), 44 R.F.L. (2d) 329 (S.C.C.).

Bibliography

Abella, Judge Rosalie Silberman. *Family Law: Dimensions of Justice* (Toronto: Butterworths, 1983).

Bala, Nicholas. "Spousal Support Law Transformed: Fairer Treatment for Women", (July, 1994) 11 Canadian Family Law Quarterly 13-56.

Baxter, Ian F. G. "Family Law Reform: a historical perspective of the Ontario experience" (1987), 6 Can. J. Fam. Law 247-269.

Menear, Michael A. "Effectiveness of Domestic Contracts" (July, 1995) 13 Canadian Family Law Quarterly 1-24.

Mossman, Mary Jane. "Running Hard to Stand Still: The Paradox of Family Law Reform", (Spring, 1994) 17 Dalhousie Law Journal, 5-34.

Pulkingham, Jane, and Gordon Ternowetsky. "Rethinking Child and Family Policies: Struggles and Options", ed. (Halifax: Fernwood Publications, 1996).

Watson, Jack. "Construction and Reconstruction of Family Life". (Feb. 1996), *Law Now* No. 4, 34-35.

12

Custody, Access and Support in Separation and Divorce

Custody jurisdiction in Canada is a function of both federal and provincial legislation, and custody cases may be tried in at least two different courts within a province. In the majority of cases, jurisdictional or constitutional questions do not arise, but some confusion may arise in regard to the best court in which to initiate a custody action. However, if custody is sought as corollary relief in a divorce petition, it will always initiate in the superior court of the province.

Under the Divorce Act,[1] former spouses, as well as current spouses can apply for a custody order. Under the 1985 Act, a corollary relief proceeding has an independent status and can be heard separately from a claim for divorce and may be brought at some time later than the time of divorce. The 1985 Act enables a proceeding that is brought "by either or both spouses" for a custody order.[2]

Where no divorce is claimed, or the parents have never been married, then provincial legislation will govern custody and access issues. In Ontario the governing Statute is the Children's Law Reform Act.[3] Similar legislation has been enacted in every other province, and both superior and provincial courts have authority to decide these issues.

DEFINITION

There is no complete definition of custody *per se* as it is differentiated from guardianship. Custody may entail the daily physical care of the child, while guardianship is broader and may encompass decisions about the child's education, the management of his estate, and the child's religious upbringing, and may also involve representing the child in court. Guardianship evolved from Roman law and was limited to minors born into wealth where property was concerned. Guardians provided support for the child using the child's own funds. Under common law, support and maintenance of children was a purely moral obligation for parents until it was legislated through the English Poor Laws in 1834.[4] A common definition of custody in a contemporary context declares that it refers to the sum total of the rights, duties, and powers with respect to the person of the child. Among other things this includes physical care and control of the child, involving feeding and clothing, the choice of residence, control of his or her social life, choice of a name, determination of his education and so on.[5] Lord Denning has said of custody, that it "is a dwindling right which the courts will hesitate to enforce against the wishes of the child, and the more so the older he is. It starts with the right of control and ends with little more than advice."[6]

Canadian courts have moved away from the notion that children are prizes to be awarded to the most deserving parent. Until the early 1920s, fathers were the preferred custodians and would lose only if there was evidence of gross harm to the child. Around 1925 both parents had equal entitlement to custody but psychological studies on child development began to exert influence on decisions in favour of mothers where a child of "tender years" was involved. It was felt that girls, in particular, should remain with their mothers if at all possible.[7]

The "tender years" doctrine is merely a factor to be considered in custody cases. It is not a rule of law.[8] Neither the tender years doctrine nor the argument that the needs of female children are best met by their mother retain validity today.[9]

FACTORS IN DETERMINING CUSTODY

The most important test in current usage is the "best interests of the child". The question to be determined is whether a parent is competent to perform parenting functions regardless of the conduct that may have led to the breakup of the marriage. The courts have made varied interpretations of the meaning of fitness to parent. Both the Divorce Act and the Ontario Children's Law Reform Act state clearly that the past conduct of a person is not relevant in making a determination of custody of or access to a child unless that conduct has relevance to the capacity of the person to act as a parent.[10] This gives the courts wide discretion in making a determination of fitness to parent.

Conduct of the Parties

A wealth of decisions demonstrate how the courts view conduct of the parties in determining thorny custody disputes.

In *Fullerton v. Fullerton*,[11] the parents had separated after seven years of marriage with two children, aged four and two. The mother had custody of the children on condition that she not cohabit with any male. When the mother had a casual affair with a man in the home, the father brought a successful divorce petition against her on the ground of adultery and was awarded custody of the children. Although the mother had always had primary care of the children and was a good mother, the trial judge emphasized her conduct in having an affair in depriving her of custody. The New Brunswick Court of Appeal allowed the mother's appeal and awarded her custody on the ground that the welfare of the children would be better served by their being with their mother where they were of tender years and the father was not as capable of looking after them. The Court of Appeal held that the trial judge placed too much emphasis on the conduct of the mother.

Two recent cases are instructive. Where the husband was involved in a stable relationship at the time of his custody claim, his past adultery was found to be irrelevant.[12] Where the husband had shown great animosity to the wife and had involved the children in the dispute, his application for custody was refused. The children had lived with their mother most of the time as a result of a joint custody arrangement and their best interests were seen to be better served with their mother as the custodial parent.[13]

An important and frequently cited case which went to the Supreme Court of Canada is one in which custody was originally awarded to the mother.[14] The father appealed and won because in the opinion of the judge Mrs. Talsky "could have solved the trivial marital problems but chose to break up the home instead". Therefore, Mrs. Talsky did not deserve custody and was punished for her moral intransigence by losing her child. Mrs. Talsky appealed and the Supreme Court of Canada reversed the decision because in the words of the judge, a wife who is "well-nigh impossible" as a wife may nevertheless be a satisfactory mother. It will be noted that the interests of the child at no time entered into these deliberations.

There is evidence that sexual orientation may be separated from the ability and capacity to parent. The nature of the evidence presented at the trial is crucial to the outcome. The testimony of the psychologist in one case[15] contained the statement that her research supported her opinion that "the manner in which one fulfills one's sexual needs does not relate to the abilities of being a good parent . . .". The court in awarding the child to the mother stated that "one must guard against magnifying the issue of homosexuality as it applies to the capacity for performing the duties of a parent."[16]

In a study on custody decisions three interesting trends were presented. It was found that fathers will receive custody more often when they are petitioners than when they are respondents and that female petitioners receive custody more often than female respondents. It was also noted that petitioners using fault grounds will receive custody more often than those using breakdown grounds. Finally, it was found that when a petition is contested, the respondent spouse will gain custody more often than when there is no answer or response.[17] It seems that punitive judicial attitudes towards the offending spouse may not yet be laid to rest.

Best Interests Test

We have long since abandoned the belief that children belong to their fathers and we have almost set aside the more recent belief that young children are always better cared for by their mothers. Our age is guided by the principle of the "best interests of the child". The emotional, physical, financial, social, and psychological needs of the child are to be considered in determining the best interests.

Though the needs of children for ongoing support, protection, and education are traditional concerns of the courts, the idea of the importance of the emotional needs of children has only recently been recognized. The burgeoning literature of the mental health profession has established the importance of a nurturing climate for children. In a home disrupted by separation, divorce, and the loss of one parent through a change in status, the court has a difficult task giving consideration to emotional factors in custody decisions. Lawyers and judges are looking to experts in mental health, such as social workers, psychologists and psychiatrists to provide information and guidance in the form of assessments. Unless these assessments are filled with psychojargon, the opinions and recommendations are given serious consideration in determining the best interests of the child. The "best interest" doctrine has been used as an almost automatic response against an abusing parent where the court has reason to believe that abuse has occurred. In dealing with allegations of child abuse in custody disputes, the court should err on the side of caution. The evidence of a professional, even if based upon hearsay, should not be easily rejected where the children's safety is at stake.[18]

Representation of Children

The courts have assumed power to appoint counsel to represent the child's interests when it is felt to be required in custody and access litigation and also to order assessments when required.

In Ontario, the office of the Children's Lawyer has been given the responsibility of representing the child in custody and access litigation, however, there has been some disagreement over the proper role of the lawyer in these cases. The question has been whether the role of counsel should include stating the child's views and preferences in court without providing any corroborating evidence. Justice Granger addressed this issue when he held that the then Official Guardian had no more rights or role than any other lawyer to the proceedings. The Children's Lawyer must follow the child's instructions where possible, whether or not he agrees. On appeal, it was held that unless the parties consented, the child's counsel cannot merely state the child's preferences or counsel's observation without presenting corroborating evidence or calling witnesses.

There is also the recognition that long and bitterly disputed courtroom battles for custody of children are a drain on financial and emotional resources and are most harmful to children. Agreements negotiated through conciliation are to be encouraged as are alternatives such as joint custody arrangements.

JUDICIAL DISCRETION

The following cases may serve to illustrate the difficulties inherent in arriving at decisions in custody hearings and the wide discretion of judges.

The parties in *Yeoman v. Yeoman*[19] were divorced and at that time custody of the child of the marriage was granted to the mother. In his application, the father sought an order granting him custody of that child. A social worker prepared a report favourable to the father being granted custody, but the Superintendent of Child Welfare disagreed and filed an amended version of the social worker's report with the court. The Superintendent of Child Welfare felt that the child should remain with its mother for reasons of continuity. The social worker, on the other hand, felt that the home environment provided by the mother was unstable, citing the fact that she had moved twelve times in two years and was on welfare. The judge granted the father's application and observed that the recommendations made by the Superintendent of Child Welfare should be weighed heavily and not disregarded without cause. In this case, however, the court preferred the conclusion of the investigating social worker who gave evidence at the hearing. The social worker was the person directed by the Ministry of Human Resources to conduct a home study ordered by the court. His report was submitted to the court but his "Social Worker's Evaluation and Conclusion" was omitted. The court felt that the mother's attitude was debilitating in all respects, particularly her assertion that she wished to remain on welfare.

Another case contains some very strong comments from a Canadian judge in support of the claim of parental right to custody. In this case the mother had been neglectful and had threatened to kill herself and the children. McDonald L.J.S.C. said:

> I am satisfied that under this arrangement it would be the grandmother who would have the care and upbringing of these children for the time being at least and should the father remarry then the care and upbringing of the children to a large extent would be in the hands of a stepmother. As regards the paternal grandmother, while she would care for and look after the children, the fact remains that children of this age need their mother; it is nature's way.[20]

Though custody and access are generally arranged together, the parent who has custody has been awarded much more than simply the care and control of the child. Mr. Justice Thorson, writing for the majority of the Ontario Court of Appeal said:

> In my view, to award one parent the exclusive custody of a child is to clothe that parent, for whatever period he or she is awarded the custody, with full parental . . . responsibility for the care, upbringing and education of the child, generally to the exclusion of the right of the other parent to interfere in the decisions that are made in exercising that control or in carrying out that responsibility.[21]

JOINT CUSTODY AND CO-PARENTING ARRANGEMENTS

There has been considerable attention paid to joint custody in which both parents remain actively involved in the care of their children. It must be noted that the Divorce Act, s. 16(4), allows the court to make an order awarding custody of children of the marriage to any one or *more* persons. However, parliament stopped short of enacting a presumption of joint custody which would assume that such an arrangement would ensure unless one of the parties satisfied an onus that he or she should be awarded sole custody. This preserves the primacy of the "best interests" doctrine. The wording of s. 16(4) in the Divorce Act, 1985, is similar to s. 28(a) of the Ontario Children's Law Reform Act which states that "by order, the court may grant the custody of or access to the child to one or more persons."

Experts in child welfare cannot agree about the advisability of joint custody and its effect on the child. Solnit, Goldstein and Freud[22] feel that one consistent caretaker is to be preferred, while other experts feel that healthy development of a child is predicated on close contact with both parents.[23] In order for joint custody to be successful, it is essential that both parents be able to work together in a co-operative manner in matters concerning the child and to put aside their differences and hostility toward each other at least where the children are involved. Clearly, joint custody cannot be ordered by a court before a willingness to co-operate has been achieved and this is not a precondition that can occur frequently or be easily demonstrated. Joint custody does not always require a split residence for the child; one parent may provide a permanent address so that one parent has care and control, subject to generous visits to the other parent. Both parents, however, retain the right to participate in the upbringing of the child through consultation over major decisions affecting the child. Another model of shared parenting is one where each parent has alternate designated periods of care and control which may be a few days at a time, or every other week or month, or in accord with school terms or vacations. Both parents, again, retain the right to participate in the upbringing of the child through consultation over major decisions affecting the child, including education, health factors, and religious training. Shared custody goes further and includes not only joint decision- making but also a sharing of physical custody.[24]

Joint custody is not an appropriate order when there is hostility between the parties or where communication between the parents is governed primarily by hostility. However, it has been found that where the parents, in spite of personal differences, can demonstrate an ability to cooperate to meet the children's needs, joint custody may be awarded.[25]

In Ontario, an important case where joint custody was thought not to be feasible is that of *Baker v. Baker*.[26] The marriage deteriorated quickly after the birth of the child. The respondent wife drank excessively. Sexual relations between the parties ceased. The wife left the matrimonial home with the child in 1975. The husband petitioned for divorce and the wife counter-petitioned. Both claimed custody of the child. The trial judge granted the wife's counter-petition for divorce and awarded joint custody and child support. The husband appealed. The appeal judge ordered a new trial on the basis that there was no evidence to support the conclusion that the parents were able and willing to cooperate with respect to the child.

An annotation on this case written by B. Hovius states:

> The *Baker* case raises two fundamental issues concerning joint custody, the first definitional and the second substantive. Anglo-Canadian jurisprudence has distinguished between "joint custody", "divided custody" and "split custody". In the High Court decision of *Baker v. Baker* Boland J. described "joint custody" as follows: "Joint custody is shared parental responsibility. A joint custody award gives legal custody to both parents, with care and control to one and liberal access to the other." This definition appears to have

been accepted by the Ontario Court of Appeal. It encompasses custody arrangements which do not provide for the frequent lengthy periods of actual companionship with each parent that is envisaged by advocates of joint custody.[27]

The Ontario High Court has used the term "divided custody" to describe a situation where care and control, but not necessarily legal custody, is alternated between the parents. "Split custody" or a "split order" describes the situation where one parent has custody while the other has care and control.[28] Joint involvement in the raising of children after separation and divorce may indeed be a viable solution where two mature, fit and co-operating parents favour it.[29] However, as Leonoff and O'Neil point out, only effective legal and psychological counselling are likely to produce such parents.[30] Whether separated parents will choose such counselling in order to help them agree to a non-traditional form of custody remains problematic. The same authors observe that capacity for joint parenting can be demonstrated during the separation period prior to the hearing.

Additional cases demonstrate the fact that decisions for joint custody are dependent on many factors. In *Silver v. Silver*,[31] application was made by a mother and father to the Nova Scotia Supreme Court, Trial Division, for advice with respect to the custody of a five-year-old boy. The Trial Division rejected joint custody in the circumstances. Cowan C.J.T.D. said:

> In my opinion, however, the circumstances resulting from separation and divorce are so different from those found in the home of happily married parents that the analogy attempted to be drawn is not appropriate [i.e. the normal situation of two parents]. Where parents are joined by mutual love and affection and have a mutual concern for the welfare of the child, if differences arise, as sometimes happens, as to the way in which the child should be brought up and disciplined, such matters should be resolved by discussion and primary regard should be had for the welfare of the child. If the parents are separated or divorced, they are often not prepared to discuss, and settle amicably, points of disagreement with regard to the upbringing of the child. In many cases, there is bitterness between the parents and little disposition to have regard only for the welfare of the child. If, in fact, there is no bitterness and the parents can settle amicably any questions arising as to the upbringing of the child, there is no need for an order for joint custody. If, on the other hand, they are not disposed to settle such matters by agreement, it is, in my opinion, necessary that one parent have the right to make such decisions.[32]

In *McNeil v. McNeil* where the parties held disparate views on religion, education, and recreational activities of their children, it was held that a joint custody order was inappropriate.[33]

The case of *Fontaine v. Fontaine*[34] reinforces a belief that mature people can share parenting successfully. On an application for custody, the trial judge ordered that legal custody would continue to be jointly exercised by both parents with each having physical custody for part of every week. The mother's appeal was dismissed. The appeal court felt that in custody disputes, an order awarding legal custody to both parents was usually to be avoided. However, in this case the trial judge arrived at a practical solution for the care of the child that would provide regulation and order for the mutual benefit of husband, wife, and child. The parents of the child in issue were mature and sensible people and seemed able to cooperate with each other in matters of custody and child care. The order of joint custody was appropriate and the arrangements as to physical custody were realistic given the activities and availability of the parents. There was no ground to interfere with the award. But, in *Rezansoff v. Rezansoff*, in a highly idiosyncratic decision the court noted that the husband had displayed a propensity for violence but was not "a bad person" and an order for joint custody was made with primary care and control awarded to the wife.[35]

Although social workers will agree that parents cannot divorce their children, a cautionary note should be sounded about proposing joint custody in every case. In some cases, women and children may be severely disadvantaged by a joint custody arrangement. For example, a husband who has been an indifferent father may become a joint custodian of the children, with a concomitant reduction in his support obligation. In another circumstance, joint custody may permit a controlling father to continue to exercise control over the upbringing of the children without the corresponding obligation to participate in the responsibilities of their day to day care. The wife may find she is bearing the major burden of child care without adequate financial support.

ACCESS

Access refers to the physical arrangement for the non-residential parent to see, be with, enjoy and have information about the child, including the right to make inquiries and to be given information as to the health, education and welfare of the child, unless a court orders otherwise.[36] The sole criterion is the best interests of the child and access is not for the primary benefit of the parent.

The courts may grant an order for access under the authority of a provincial statute or by way of corollary relief pursuant to the Divorce Act. Under the Divorce Act, the superior court also has the discretionary power to vary or rescind any order it has made in respect to access under the divorce judgment. Provincial legislation contains similar provisions to vary an access order.

When custody is granted to one parent, the order usually provides for "reasonable access" to the other parent. If the parents cannot agree on how to work out the specific details, the court will specify the times. The order might call for access on particular weekends such as alternating weekends and specify the division of holiday time. The parent who has access must not change the child's basic mode of life or conduct during the period of access. That parent may only exercise that control which is necessary to safeguard the child while they are together. For example, the access parent cannot unilaterally determine or alter the arrangements made for the child's schooling, medical treatment, or religious training. Religious differences between spouses are not of necessity bars to access orders.[37] The court may make access orders for a definite or indefinite period, or until the occurrence of a specified event, and may impose terms and conditions at its discretion. For example, the court may require the custodial person to give the person with access notice (or a specified period of notice) of any change of residence.[38] It is uncertain whether the access parent is authorized to obtain information by subjecting the children to medical, educational, or other tests.[39]

An estranged Saskatchewan couple who were disputing the right of the custodial parent, Ms. Gordon, to take their daughter to Australia, formed the basis of a landmark decision of the Supreme Court of Canada in May, 1996.[40] The mother and daughter resided in Australia since early 1995 as a result of lower court rulings which granted her a variance in the access agreement. The Supreme Court of Canada, in a 7-2 decision said that "the child's best interests are not merely paramount, they are the only consideration", and that "the rights and interests of the parents, except as they impact on the best interests of the child, are irrelevant". In this case, the child was permitted to remain with her mother because the father had the means to maintain his access visits.

This decision, which reaffirms the principle of the best interests of the child as the overriding test in any custody and access dispute, means that a custodial parent wishing to move for any reason, job relocation, education, or new relationship, could run the risk of losing custody if such a move were seen by the court as a serious disruption in the life of the child.

The two dissenting justices argued for more weighting of the rights of the custodial parent based on the principle that the original decision to award custody is a major one from which subsequent decisions will flow. The key to the majority decision lies in the finding that a geographical move constitutes a "material change in circumstances" which according to existing law can automatically result in a court evaluation of custody and access in the light of the new circumstances.

This decision seems to mean that courts will have greater decision-making power over the freedom of custodial parents to make life decisions with which the access parent does not agree and may result in costly litigation. The courts have been directed to consider *only* the best interests of the child and not the merits of the custodial parent's plan.

Goertz v. Gordon effectively overruled a decision in the Ontario Court of Appeal which held that where the custodial parent, usually the mother, has good reason to move to a new location, such a move will be considered consistent with the best interests of the child. Madam Justice Abella wrote in her decision, "We must . . . forcefully acknowledge that the custodial parent's best interests are inexplicably tied to those of the child". The non-custodial father lost his petition at the appeal court to keep his wife and daughter from moving to the U.S. where the mother planned to remarry. The ruling, said the court, applies not only to decisions about family moves, but to other decisions from "the trivia; to the dramatic" and includes "whether to change neighbourhoods, or provinces, or partners, or jobs, or friends, or schools, or religions".

The access parent frequently feels quite peripheral to the developmental decisions and tasks of parenting, a spectator in the life of his own child. Consequently, such a parent may resent making support payments and may consciously or unconsciously sabotage the authority of the custodial parent. Cases where one parent is given custody and the other parent the power of care and control are rare but have occurred. In such an order, one parent would have all the rights of custody but the other parent would have physical care and control.

Access schedules are hard on the spontaneity of relationships but worth the time to work out through guidance to both parents. As a result of their research, Wallerstein and Kelly feel strongly that children's self-esteem is connected to a continuity of relationship with the non-custodial parent.[41] Many jurisdictions have provided space where visits between the non-custodial parent and the child take place under supervised conditions. For example, a parent who is alleged to have a harmful effect on his child, may apply to the court for access under supervised conditions ordered by the court. In a case known to the authors, the custodial mother was convinced that the father would harm the children in some way and had succeeded in communicating her fears to the children. Under an arrangement of supervised access visits to which she reluctantly agreed, the children did begin to form a relationship with the father that was based on the father's genuine feelings for his children. This arrangement was subsequently confirmed by a court order.

Sometimes parental access rights have been recognized even when the children do not wish contact with a specific parent. In *Re Stroud and Stroud*, Lieff J. stated:

> In this case, the court must balance the right of a parent to access, the benefits to the child which would flow from such a relationship against what is in the best interests of the child in terms of his welfare and stability.[42]

In two other cases, the court reached differing conclusions in regard to children's wishes not to see their father. In one instance the judge determined that it was in the children's best interest to develop a relationship with the father and in the other case, the judge said that teenaged children should exercise their discretion as to whether they saw a father with whom they had difficulty in communication.[43]

In some cases, however, the wishes of the children have been respected. Generally the courts regard continued access as presumptively beneficial to the child and the responsibility falls on the custodial parent to demonstrate that to deny access is justifiable. Some judges have considered it the right of the child to see the non-custodial parent rather than the other way around. Other decisions in regard to access are of particular interest. The court rejected the wife's application that the husband, a homosexual, who had AIDS, be granted supervised access only. There was no evidence indicating that the children were likely to contract the virus and it was in their best interest to have regular contact with their father.[44] In another case, a parent who was thought to present a physical danger to the child was permitted access by the judge. The mother had killed three of her children but she had been released from the hospital by order of the Lieutenant Governor and there was, therefore, no further basis for denying her access. The judge felt she should have access rights to her child but visits should be carefully supervised.[45] In order to make accommodating arrangements for access where substantial distances and costs are involved, the court may order either parent to compensate these costs. A custodial parent who contravenes an order of the court by wilfully refusing access may be found in contempt or imprisoned. Such denial of access is not an offence under the Criminal Code but is civil contempt and therefore the court can take action to compel the custodial parent to permit access. Unfortunately, these proceedings may be complex and are often unsuccessful. Payne and Kallish have observed that "where the parents continue to play 'war games' using a child as ammunition in the emotional conflict arising from their unresolved personal hostilities, the court defines access with precision."[46]

An adulterous relationship is not usually, in itself, sufficient ground to deny access because the children's welfare will not of necessity be affected adversely by the adulterous relationship. In one instance, the custodial mother wanted the access order made conditional on the absence of the father's girlfriend. The request in this instance was denied by the court.[47]

Access disputes present a stellar opportunity for appropriately involved social workers to exercise neutrality in order to assist children caught in an access dispute. Rather than identifying with one or another parent, if the focus of assistance is the child, the worker can play a significant role in reducing the tension and hostility between the custodial parent and the access parent. The worker's identification with one parent or the other can inadvertently result in fuelling the fires of revenge, rather than dampening them for the child's benefit. Whatever can be done to decrease a child's fear and guilt by defusing the conflict between child and parents will minimize his emotional damage.

SUPPORT

> After 15 years of marriage Sam A. has deserted the matrimonial home to live with another woman. His wife, Ann, has filed for divorce. Her immediate needs are for support for herself and their two children and for funds to cover mortgage payments on their home.

Access and support are necessarily interdependent one upon the other. The custodial parent cannot in law deny access for the reason that the non-custodial parent is in arrears in support payments. The non-custodial parent cannot legally use support as a lever in relation to access. Once ordered, support must continue and the custodial parent who denies the other parent access places his or her custodial rights in jeopardy. Though there are American precedents for withholding support funds if access is denied by the custodial parent, in Canada this is not defined by statute as an adequate defence. McDonald and Komar point out that some American cases have held that where a child refused to see a non-custodial parent, then support payments are automatically suspended during the period that the child's refusal is current. Canadian courts, however, appear to be reluctant to force an unwilling child to see a non-custodial parent and hold that such refusal should not jeopardize support.[48] However, an interesting decision, the father's access to the children was made conditional upon his payment of child support, a condition that may be seen as using the children as a bargaining chip to ensure payment. It may also be seen as an appropriate condition because support is without doubt in the child's best interest.[49]

Child Support

The court recognizes that there is a positive obligation on both parents to support their children. For support purposes, a "child" is defined as a person under the age of 16 or over that age of 16 who is unmarried and continues to be dependent because of education, illness or disability, and this definition may extend to children whom the parent or custodian has treated as a child of the family. Children who have voluntarily withdrawn from parental control are no longer considered children for support purposes.[50] It should be noted that in Sweden and France, the state will pay child support to a child and will then undertake the pursuit of the debtor, thereby reducing the danger of putting children at risk of falling into poverty.[51]

The need for an increase in child support payments has resulted in action from the government and the courts to establish support guidelines because of the high costs of litigation. Non-payment of child support frequently forces women and children to seek welfare. Increases in the amount of child support may also result in the non-custodial parent seeking more control over how the money is spent and unwillingness to tolerate limitations or interference with access to the child. In one case, the Court held that it is unjust to allow a wife to ignore and thwart an access order. In addition to permitting the husband to hold the wife accountable for other funds, the husband was entitled to make direct third party payments.[52]

The federal government through the office of the Attorney General for Canada, has introduced child support legislation which came into effect on May 1, 1997. Please refer to Chapter 10, Corollary Relief in Divorce, for a full discussion of the new Guidelines. The Child Support Guidelines under the legislation set out basic child support amounts payable in each province for one or more children, which is dependent on the gross income of the payor parent. In addition to basic support, the court is directed to consider additional child cost factors such as child care costs, education, health and extraordinary expenses which are in addition to the basic child costs. The courts have adopted them in setting child support, both under federal and provincial law, although at present they are only mandatory under federal legislation for support orders under the Divorce Act.

Since coming into force, child support payments are no longer included in the recipient's (usually the mother's) income. Nor are they deductible from the payor's (usually the father's) income. A custodial mother had petitioned all the way to the Supreme Court of Canada, claiming that her child support payments should not be included in her income which reduced the amount she actually received for the support of her child. She lost.[53] The Government of Canada remedied this inequity to custodial parents by the Child Support Guidelines. Although this is federal legislation, the provinces have supported the guidelines and will likely adopt them through provincial legislation.

Spousal Support

The Supreme Court of Canada wrought a radical change in the law of spousal support in December, 1992.[54] Spousal support is not conditional upon the good conduct of a spouse during cohabitation or marriage, but is determined by the need and economic capacity of the spouses, tempered by the length of the cohabitation and the functions performed by the spouses in the course of their cohabitation. Courts have recognized the economic advantages and disadvantages of the marriage and the hardship created by the marriage breakdown. Perhaps the most significant factor was the expectation that each spouse will become economically self-sufficient within a reasonable period of time.[55]

The courts interpreted "reasonable period of time" narrowly in some instances. This has created hardship for women in particular, who, after long periods of absence from the workplace, are expected to secure adequate paid employment in relatively short periods of time. Such women frequently require retraining and education before they have any chance of finding employment. If the breakdown occurred after 20 or more years of marriage, they face the prejudices the workplace accords middle-aged women. It must be added that in some cases, men have needed to be supported because of some inability to earn a living and their wives are even less inclined to want to pay spousal support.

In order to justify variation of an existing order or separation agreement which deals with spousal support, the Supreme Court of Canada earlier determined that there must be a causal connection between the changed circumstances which precipitated the application for support and the marriage itself.[56] In other words, the changed circumstances must be rooted in a pattern of economic dependency created by the marriage. Otherwise, the applicant spouse, usually the wife, was not entitled to support or to an increase in established support.

The law governing spousal support where there is no pre-existing separation agreement or order was less clear. The applicant's need for support must be established together with the payer's ability to pay. There is considerable variation in judicial interpretation about the need to establish a causal connection between the marriage and the present need as a precondition to an award of spousal support.[57] It is therefore unwise for social workers to assume that spousal support will be available to a client, even when need and capacity to pay are demonstrated.

Support from Other Family Members

The Ontario Court of Appeal has ruled that a woman can sue her estranged inlaws for support for herself and her three children. The decision permitting this to occur is a unique one. In this case, the wife argued that her inlaws had demonstrated a "settled intention" to look upon the grandchildren as children of their family and had assumed financial and physical responsibilities for their care as well as for herself. This arrangement occurred within a patriarchal culture wherein the grandparents retained control of the household.[58]

Another Ontario case decided that adult children may have an obligation to support parents if the parents had cared for and provided for the children, even if the parenting was not ideal.[59] There is no such obligation, however, if there has been no dependency of the child on the parent.[60]

INTERIM ORDERS

Interim relief may be granted pending hearing of a petition for divorce or other claim.[61] Interim orders may include support of either husband, wife, or children, or custody of children.

As with a final order, the court has wide discretion respecting the relief which it can order. Generally, the court will not inquire closely into the merits of an application for interim support unless it appears to be grossly inappropriate.[62] The court has power to make orders which it considers to be "fit and just", displacing the earlier principle that an interim support allowance should only permit a wife to live "modestly and in retirement" until the trial of an action.[63] However, interim support orders may still be inadequate because only the necessary interim expenses may be allowed.[64]

VARIATION OF JUDGMENTS AND ORDERS

Provision is made in the Divorce Act and provincial legislation to vary the terms and conditions of an order, including custody and support orders.[65] Applications to vary the judgment or order are brought in the court which made the original order. An inferior court has *no power to vary* an order under the Divorce Act. The order may only be varied if there is a substantial change in circumstances.[66] Examples of such changes include significant increase or decrease in the supporting spouse's income, or remarriage of the supporting spouse, putting additional strain on his income, or a major change in the circumstances of the custodial parent.

Judicial interpretation reflects the court's attempt to clarify the permissible reasons for a request to vary the terms of support. The principal test is whether the changed circumstances are causally related to the marriage and thus affected by the marriage breakdown. Custody variations are always determined by the test of the child's best interests.

Variation of Spousal Support

In a major decision which addressed variation of spousal support after a marriage was terminated by a final judgment of divorce, the Supreme Court of Canada ruled in the "family law trilogy" that variation would only be granted where there is a material change in circumstance which is a direct consequence of a dependency created by the marriage.[67] If the applicant spouse (usually the wife) could not demonstrate such a dependency, her application would be unsuccessful. For example, if parties were divorced and all spousal support obligations ended, and the spouse suffers major financial reverses resulting from a business venture commenced after marriage, an application to vary spousal support would not likely be successful. However, if the spouse who was receiving spousal support lost employment and could not obtain a new job because the ability to be employed was diminished during the marriage, that spouse *may* be successful in varying the judgment if the court finds that it is a dependency created by the marriage. More recently, however, the courts have largely abandoned the "causal connection" test in favour of an analysis of the economic need of the dependent spouse and the economic disadvantage created by the breakdown of the marriage.[68]

Variation of Child Support

Child support can always be varied by the court in accordance with the child's need and the capacity of the parent to pay support. Please note that child support may also be reduced on the basis of a material change in circumstances of the payor parent, whose means to pay is reduced. The coming into force of the Child Support Guidelines entitles the custodial parent to an automatic variation to the Guideline support amount if she is receiving less than the Guideline amount.[69]

Orders and judgments for custody and support, including those under the Divorce Act are now enforceable through an automatic process established under the Support and Custody Order Enforcement Act in Ontario[70] and reciprocating legislation across Canada and elsewhere. This Act is discussed in detail elsewhere in this book.

Endnotes

1. R.S.C. 1985, c. 3 (2nd Supp.) as amended.
2. Macdonald, James and Ann Wilton, *The Annotated Divorce Act*, ss. 16(1), (2)1 (Toronto: Carswell, 1993).
3. *Children's Law Reform Act*, R.S.O. 1990, c. 12.
4. See J. Ryan, "The Overlapping Custody Jurisdiction: Co-Existence or Chaos" (1980), 3 Can. J. Fam. L. 95.
5. See W. G. W. White, "A Comparison of Some Parental and Guardian Rights" (1980), 3 Can. J. Fam. L. 219.
6. *Hewer v. Bryant*, [1970] 1 Q.B. 357 at 369, [1969] 3 All E.R. 578 at 582 (C.A.).
7. *Talsky v. Talsky*, [1976] 2 S.C.R. 292, 21 R.F.L. 27, 62 D.L.R. (3d) 267, 7 N.R. 246.
8. *Lancaster v. Lancaster* (1992), 38 R.F.L. (3d) 373, 109 N.S.R. (2d) 88, 297 A.P.R. 88 (C.A.).
9. *Williams v. Williams* (1989), 24 R.F.L. (3d) 86 (B.C. C.A.).
10. Children's Law Reform Act, R.S.O. 1990, c. 12, s. 24(3).
11. (1980), 31 N.B.R. (2d) 661, 75 A.P.R. 661 (C.A.).
12. *McNeil v. McNeil* (1989), 20 R.F.L. (3d) 52 (B.C. S.C.).
13. *Nelson v. Nelson* (1990), 86 Sask. R. 10 (Q.B).
14. *Talsky*, note 8 above.
15. *K. v. K.*, [1976] 2 W.W.R. 462, 23 R.F.L. 58 (Alta. Prov. Ct.).
16. *Ibid.*, at 64.
17. B. Prentice, "Divorce, Children and Custody: A Quantitative Study of Three Legal Factors" (1979), 2 Can. J. Fam. L. 351.
18. *Migliore v. Migliore* (1989), 23 R.F.L. (3d) 131 (B.C. S.C.). Cited in MacDonald, J. and A. Wilton, *Annotated Divorce Act* (Toronto: Carswell, 1994).
19. (1979), 13 B.C.L.R. 10 (S.C.).
20. *Bratland v. Bratland* (1976), 29 R.F.L. 34 at 42 (B.C. S.C.).
21. *Kruger v. Kruger* (1979), 25 O.R. (2d) 673 at 677, 11 R.F.L. (2d) 52, 2 Fam. L. Rev. 197, 104 D.L.R. (3d) 481 (C.A.).
22. J. Goldstein, A. Freud, and A. J. Solnit, *Beyond the Best Interests of the Child* (New York: The Free Press, a division of Macmillan, Inc., 1973). Also see: Sheff, David, *If it's Tuesday, it Must be Dad's House*, New York Times Magazine, March 26, 1995.
23. J. Grief, "Access: Legal Right or Privilege at the Custodial Parent's

Discretion" (1980), 3 Can. J. Fam. L. 43. See also J. B. Kelly and J. S. Wallerstein, "The Effects of Parental Divorce Experiences of the Child in Early Latency" 46 Amer. Jr. of Orthopsychiatry (1976): 20; J. S. Wallerstein and J. Kelly, "The Effects of Parental Divorce: Experiences of the Pre-School Child" Jr. of the Amer. Academy of Child Psychiatry, Autumn 1976, 600-616; and J. S. Wallerstein and J. Kelly, "The Effects of Parental Divorce: The Adolescent Experience," in the Child and His Family, 3, 1974.

24. See *Simmchen v. Potter* (1991), 33 R.F.L. (3d) 430 (N.B. Q.B.), affirmed (1992), 120 N.B.R. (2d) 447, 302 A.P.R. 447 (C.A.).
25. *Colwell v. Colwell* (1992), 38 R.F.L. (3d) 345 (Alta. Q.B.).
26. (1979), 23 O.R. (2d) 391, 8 R.F.L. (2d) 236, reversing 3 R.F.L. (2d) 193, 95 D.L.R. (3d) 529, 1 Fam. L. Rev. 226 (C.A.).
27. *Ibid.*, at 8 R.F.L. 237-238.
28. J. Payne and P. Boyle, "Divided Opinions on Joint Custody" (1979), 2 Can. J. Fam. L. 163.
29. J. Payne, "Co-Parenting Revisited" (1979), 2 Can. J. Fam. L. 243.
30. M. O'Neill, and A. Leonoff, "Joint Custody: An Option Worth Examining" November and December 1977. *Perception* 28 at 29.
31. (1979), 35 N.S.R. (2d) 88, 62 A.P.R. 88, 104 D.L.R. (3d) 689 (T.D.).
32. *Ibid.*, at 102-103.
33. *McNeil v. McNeil* (1989), 20 R.F.L. (3d) 52 (B.C. S.C.).
34. (1980), 18 R.F.L. (2d) 235 (Man. C.A.).
35. *Rezansoff v. Rezansoff* (1991), 32 R.F.L. (3d) 443 (Man. Q.B.).
36. Divorce Act, R.S.C. 1985, c. 3 (2nd Supp.) as amended, s. 16(5); Children's Law Reform Act, note 10 above, s. 20(5); Education Act, R.S.O. 1990, c. E.2, s. 124.
37. *Friesen v. Friesen* (1988), 156 Man. R. (2d) 303 (Q.B.); *Hockey v. Hockey* (1989), 21 R.F.L. (3d) 105, 69 O.R. (2d) 338, 60 D.L.R. (4th) 765 (Div. Ct.).
38. S. 16(7), *Droit de la Famille — 663*, [1989] R.J.Q. 1550, [1989] R.D.F. 544 (C.A.).
39. *Ibid.*, s. 16(5).
40. *Gordon v. Goertz* (1996), 19 R.F.L. (4th) 177 (S.C.C.).
41. Wallerstein and Kelly, note 23 above.
42. *Stroud v. Stroud* (1974), 4 O.R. (2d) 567 at 574, 18 R.F.L. 237, 48 D.L.R. (3d) 527 (H.C.) quoted in J. D. Payne, and K. L. Kallish, "A Behavioral Science and Legal Analysis of Access to the Child in the Post-Separation/Divorce Family" (1981), 13 Ottawa L. Rev. 215. This is an excellent and comprehensive review.
43. *Stowbridge v. Stowbridge* (1992), 4 R.F.L. (3d) 154, 10 O.R. (3d) 540, 95 D.L.R. (4th) 540 (Gen. Div.); and *Katz v. Katz* (1989), 21 R.F.L. (3d) 167 (Ont. U.F.C.).

44. In *Droit de la famille — 663*, [1989] R.J.Q. 1550, [1989] R.D.F. 544 (C.A.).
45. *O. v. O.* (1976), 28 R.F.L. 389 (Ont. H.C.).
46. Payne and Kallish, note 42 above, at 257.
47. *Brown v. Brown* (1973), 10 R.F.L. 379 (Sask. Q.B.).
48. M. McDonald, and R. D. N. Komar, "Access Rights to Children and Maintenance Obligations: a *Quid Pro Quo?*" (1979), 2 Can. J. Fam. L. 299.
49. *Rodger v. Rodger*, [1988] N.W.T.R. 163 (S.C.).
50. Family Law Act, R.S.O. 1990, c. F.3.
51. Zweibel, Ellen B.: "Child Support Policy and Child Support Guidelines; Broadening the Agenda". 6 *Canadian Journal Women and the Law*, p. 386.
52. *Welstead v. Bainbridge*, [1994] W.D.F.L. 576 (Ont. Prov. Div.).
53. *Thibaudeau v. R.* (1995), 12 R.F.L. (4th) 1 (S.C.C.).
54. *Moge v. Moge* (1992), 42 R.F.L. (3d) 345 (S.C.C.).
55. *Ibid.*
56. *Pelech v. Pelech*, [1987] 1 S.C.R. 801, 14 B.C.L.R. (2d) 145, 17 C.P.C. (2d) 1, 7 R.F.L. (3d) 225, [1987] 1 W.W.R. 481, 38 D.L.R. (4th) 641, 76 N.R. 81; *Richardson v. Richardson*, [1987] 1 S.C.R. 857, 17 C.P.C. (2d) 104, 7 R.F.L. (3d) 304, 38 D.L.R. (4th) 699, 77 N.R. 1, 22 O.A.C. 1; *Caron v. Caron*, [1987] 1 S.C.R. 892, 14 B.C.L.R. (2d) 186, 7 R.F.L. (3d) 274, [1987] 4 W.W.R. 522, 38 D.L.R. (4th) 735, 75 N.R. 36.
57. See, for example: *Newson v. Newson* (1986), 3 B.C.L.R. (2d) 1, 2 R.F.L. (3d) 137, 27 D.L.R. (4th) 738 (B.C. C.A.); *Madill v. Madill* (1988), 15 R.F.L. (3d) 181 (Ont. Fam. Ct.).
58. *Cheng v. Cheng*, May 23, 1996 (unreported), *Globe and Mail* — April 26, 1996.
59. *Godwin v. Bolsco* (1993), 45 R.F.L. (3d) 310 (Ont. Prov. Div.) and s. 32, Family Law Act, R.S.O. 1990, c. F.3.
60. *Berendt v. Berendt* (1987), 11 R.F.L. (3d) 69 (Ont. U.F.C.).
61. Divorce Act, note 37 above, ss. 15 and 16.
62. *Nishikawa v. Nishikawa* (1971), 6 R.F.L. 191 (Ont. C.A.).
63. *Gibbs v. Gibbs*, 56 O.L.R. 614, [1925] 2 D.L.R. 880.
64. *Sugar v. Sugar* (1976), 12 O.R. (2d) 327, 23 R.F.L. 248 (C.A.).
65. *Globe and Mail* (June 30, 1989) A-3, s. 17.
66. See, for example, *McDougall v. McDougall* (1973), 11 R.F.L. 266, affirmed 13 R.F.L. 62 (C.A.); *Johnstone v. Johnstone*, [1967] 1 O.R. 211, 60 D.L.R. (2d) 26 (C.A.); *Eves v. Eves* (1974), 6 O.R. (2d) 203, 17 R.F.L. 57, 52 D.L.R. (3d) 331; and *Osborne v. Osborne* (1974), 14 R.F.L. 149 (Ont.).

67. Note 56 above.
68. See note 54 above.
69. S.O. 1985, c. 6 as am.
70. Note 1, ss. 16-19.

Bibliography

Bala, Nicholas. "Spousal Support Law Transformed: Fairer Treatment for Women." (July 1994) Can. Fam. L.Q. 13-56.

Bala, Nicholas and Jane Anweiler. "Allegations of sexual abuse in a parental custody dispute: smokescreen or fire?" (1987/88) 2 Can. Fam. L.Q. 343-415.

Bala, Nicholas and Susan Miklas. *Rethinking Decisions about Children: Is "the Best Interests of the Child" Approach Really in the Best Interests of Children?* Toronto Policy Research Centre on Children, Youth and Families, 1993.

Bayda, E.D. "Procedure in Child Custody Adjudications: A Study in the Importance of Adjective Law." (1980) 3 Can. J. Fam. L. 57.

Bedont, Barbara C. "Gender Differences in Negotiations and the Doctrine of Unconscionability in Domestic Contracts". (Dec. 1994) 12 Can. Fam. L.Q. 21-44.

Bene, Eva. "The Nature of Attachment Children Have Towards Their Parents in Contested Custody and Access Cases." (1980) 38 Advocate 281.

Birklein, Brenda M. "Living Together/Splitting Apart: Common Law and Legal Marriages and the Law", (June 1994) 18 Law Now, No. 9, 9-12.

Brownstone, Harvey. "The Homosexual Parent in Custody Disputes." (1980) 5 Queen's L.J. 199.

Cano, Marlene. "Reflections on Recent Trends in the Analysis of Custody and Parental Authority in Canada." (Jan. 1994) 10 Can. Fam. L.Q. 269-289.

Chang, P.N., and A.S. Deinard. "Single Father Caretakers: Demographic Characteristics and Adjustment Processes." (1982) 52:2 Amer. Jr. of Ortho. 236-43.

Derdeyn, Andre P. and Elizabeth Scott. "Joint Custody: A Critical Analysis and Appraisal." (1984) 54:2 Amer. Jr. of Ortho. 199-209.

deSousa, Maria Linhares. "Family Law Reform in Ontario: Towards Economic Partnership." (Dec. 1994) 12 Can. Fam. L.Q. 1-20.

Doskoch, Bill. "Intrigue, Tears and Burnout: Family Law in the 90's". (August 1993) 2 National No. 6, 25-29.

Ehrcke, Ann. "Limiting Judicial Discretion in Custody Proceedings on Divorce." (1987) 6 Can. J. Fam. L. 211-246.

Engel, Susan. "Compensatory Support in Moge v. Moge and the Individual Model of Responsibility: Are We Headed in the Right Direction?" (1993) 57 Sask. L. Rev. 397-413.

Ernst, T. and R. Altis. "Joint Custody and Co-parenting: Not by Law but by Love." (1981) 60:10 Child Welfare, 669-77.

Evaluating Child Support Policy: A Brief to the Federal/Provincial/Territorial Family Law Committee by the Canadian Advisory Council on the Status of Women. Ottawa, 1992.

Ewaschuk, E.G. "Abduction of Children by Parents." (1979) 21 Cr.L.Q. 176.

Fineberg, A.D. "Joint Custody of Infants: Breakthrough or Fad?" (1979) 2 Can. J .Fam. L. 417.

Goodfellow, Walter R.E. "Spousal Support after Moge (S.C.C.), Child Support after Thibaudeau (S.C.C.) and Levesque (Alta. C.A.): Do These Decisions Really Change Support Law?" (July 1996) 14 Can. Fam. L.Q. 1-47.

Grief, J.B. "Access: Legal Right or Privilege at the Custodial Parent's Discretion?" (1980) 3 Can. J. Fam. L. 43.

Holmes, Sheila M. "Imposed joint legal custody: children's interests or parental rights?" (1987) 45 Univ. of T. Fac. of Law R. 301-323.

Hovius, Berend. "Mobility of the Custodial Parent: Guidance from the Supreme Court". (July 1996) 19 R.F.L. (4th) 292-319.

Klassen, Claire M. "Can a Husband Apply for Spousal Support?" (Dec. 1994) 19 L. Now No. 3, 27-29.

Kline, Marlee. "Complicating the Ideology of Motherhood: Child Welfare Law and First Nation Women" (Summer 1993) 18 Queen's L.J. 306-342.

Kurtz, Linda and Jeffrey Derevensky. "Child Custody and Public Policy: A Contemporary Debate Revisited." (July 1994) 11 Can. Fam. L.Q. 57-70.

Langer, Rosanna. "Postmarital Support Discourse, Discretion, and Male Dominance". (1994) 12 Can. J. Fam. L. 67-90.

Legal Status of Children Born Outside of Marriage in Nova Scotia: Final Report by the Law Commission of Nova Scotia, Halifax, L.R. Commission, 1995.

Leonoff, Arthur and Maureen O'Neill. "Custody Decisions: Psychological Aspects." (1979) 2 Fam. L. Rev. 192.

Leonoff, Arthur and Maureen O'Neill. "Custody Decisions: Some Psychological Factors." (1979) 8 R.F.L. (2d) 179.

Mackinnon, V.J. and J.R. Groves. "Some Proposals to reform custody litigation, (Ont.)" (1988) 3 Can. Fam. L.Q. 287-314.

Mayers, Nadine. "Effective Processes in Custody/Access Assessments." (Oct. 1994) 11 Can. Fam. L.Q. 147-157.

McDonald, Margaret and Roman N. Komar. "Access Rights to Children and Maintenance Obligations: *A Quid Pro Quo?*" (1979) 2 Can. J. Fam. L. 299.

Mnookin, R.H. and D.K. Weisberg. *Child, Family, and the State*. (2d) 1989.

Morgan, Laura W. "Child Support and the Anomalies of the High- Income and Low-Income Parent: The Need to Reconsider What Constitutes "Support" in the American and Canadian Child Support Guideline Models" (1996) 13 Can. J. Fam. L. 161-214.

Mossman, Mary Jane. "Running Hard to Stand Still: The Paradox of Family Law Reform", (Spring 1994) 17 Dal. L.J. 5-34.

Mowatt, E. Ann. "Maintenance for Common Law Spouses." (Summer 1994) 10 Solicitors' J. No. 3, 4.

Nicholas, Michael C. "The Case Against Joint Custody, *Baker v. Baker.*" (1980) 5 Queen's L.J. 326.

Payne, Julien D. *The Divorce Decisions Workbook: A Canadian Planning & Action Guide*. Whitby, Ontario, McGraw-Hill Ryerson, 1994.

Penfold, Susan P. "Questionable Beliefs about Child Sexual Abuse Allegations During Custody Disputes", (1997) 19 Can. J. Fam. L. 11-30.

Pulkingham, Jane. "Private Troubles, Private Solutions, Poverty Among Divorced Women and the Politics of Support Enforcement and Child Custody Determination." (Fall 1994) 9 Can. J.L. and Society 73- 97.

Rathberg, B. "Joint Custody: Parental Problems and Satisfaction." (1983) 22:1 Family Process 43-52.

Rosnes, Melanie. "The Invisibility of Male Violence in Canadian Child Custody and Access Decision-Making", (1997) 19 Can. J. Fam. L. 31-60.

Rosenberg, E., J. Kleinman and J. Brantley. "Custody Evaluations: Helping the Family Reorganize." (1982) 63:4 Soc. Csewrk. 203-8.

Schmidt, Gregory B. "Legal Strangers: How do Grandparents Get Access?" (Dec. 1993) 18 L. Now No. 4, 11-13.

Stewart, Dana G. and Linda E. McFadyen. "Women and the Economic Consequences of Divorce in Manitoba: An Empirical Study." (1992) 21 Man. L.J. 80-99.

Zarb, Lise Helene. "Allegations of Childhood Sexual Abuse in Custody and Access Disputes: What Care is in the Best Interests of the Child?" (1994) 12 Can. J. Fam. L. 91-114.

Zemans, Frederick H. "The Issue of Cultural Diversity in Custody Disputes." (1983) 32 R.F.L. (2d) 50.

13

Enforcement of Family Court Orders

Orders for custody, access and support under the Divorce Act are enforceable across Canada since they issue from federal legislation.[1] By the simple expedient of registering an order obtained under the Divorce Act in the province where a party to the divorce is resident, the order is enforceable in that province. Orders made under provincial statutes and in particular under the Children's Law Reform Act[2] may be enforceable across Canada through the operation of reciprocal legislation. However, the actual process of enforcement can be time-consuming, frustrating, costly and ineffective.

CUSTODY ENFORCEMENT

Removal of a Child to Another Province

In an increasingly mobile society, the parent who has lost a court battle and is unwilling to accept the result may take the child to try his or her luck in another jurisdiction, in effect, to make an "end run" around the court's order. Most provinces have enacted legislation which authorizes the court to enforce the custody order of another province.[3] These provisions require the application for enforcement to be brought where the child is living and requires the services of a lawyer practising in that province. The court may vary the order of another province where it is satisfied that serious harm may befall the child, or that there is no real and substantial connection with that province or state and there is a real and substantial connection with the province where the application to vary custody is brought.

The Family Responsibility Act,[4] which is primarily directed to support, has no provisions for enforcement of custody orders. The Act provides that the Director may be requested to enforce an existing support order only. Since the primary focus is the enforcement of support, there is no provision for enforcement of custody orders through this Act at the present time.

Provincial custody legislation provides for the reciprocal enforcement of custody or access orders. A person who is deprived of rights can seek the court's help to locate the other parent or seek police assistance to locate and return the children. In addition, the extra-provincial enforcement rules have restricted a parent's ability to remove a child from one jurisdiction and obtain custody in another. A custodial parent cannot unilaterally change the child's residence without the consent of the other parent or the court.[5]

While the legislation varies from province to province, in general, it provides that the local court should recognize a foreign order if that order was made in a place where the child habitually resided, and was based on the best interest doctrine.

Removal of a Child to Another Country

If the child has been removed to a foreign country, recourse may be had to The Hague Convention on the Civil Aspects of International Child Abduction, if that country is a signatory. The present signatories represent 37 countries including Canada.[6] Enforcement provisions of the Criminal Code[7] may also be helpful. With these provisions, the client's chances to regain the child are improved but by no means can success be assured.[8] In any event, retrieval is a complex and costly process when the non-custodial parent is determined to have the child. Expert legal advice is always needed.

Changes to the Children's Law Reform Act in Ontario and some other provinces give both the provincial and superior courts the power to take preventive measures against the possibility of kidnapping the child or for contempt of a custody order. For example, it is now possible for the court, upon the application of the aggrieved party, to direct peace officers to apprehend the child.[9] Because most of the evidence regarding the child's best interest is available in the country of habitual residence, it is held that custody and access matters are best determined in that jurisdiction, which is the basis of the request to return the child.

FAILURE TO COMPLY WITH AN ORDER

Consequences of default in support under the Divorce Act can include attachment of wages, a fine, or imprisonment for continued default or other refusal to comply with the court's orders. Penalties have also been imposed for denial of access on the part of the custodial parent. The former Ontario High Court has committed a mother to jail for 24 hours for this reason.[10]

In a custody and access matter, a father absconded with the children during a period of interim access and was apprehended by the police after being charged under the Criminal Code with unlawfully detaining a child. He was sentenced to 90 days in prison as a deterrent.[11] It must be emphasized that the court's jurisdiction to enforce support and custody orders only exists when an application is made by one of the parties to the original order or a party lays charges under the Criminal Code.

In reference to support, should the child be removed to another province by the custodial parent, a leading case in Ontario pointed out, by way of *obiter dicta*, that even if there was an implied condition that the child would remain in the province, the support orders could not be suspended and support payments must be continued.[12]

ACCESS ENFORCEMENT

There was no specific statute in Canada which provided expressly for enforcement of access orders until The Children's Law Reform Amendment Act was passed by the Ontario legislature in 1989. In many ways the enforcement of access is the most troublesome aspect of an order and is frequently used as leverage by one spouse against the other in a continuing post-separation battle. The only loser in many instances is the child.[13]

While the court may cancel or restrict access as a result of the access parent's action, it is usually not realistic to change custody because of the importance of the child's attachment to the custodial parent and the familiar environment. If the parents' relationship deteriorates to the point where they cannot work cooperatively, a court may cancel access arrangements.[14] However, the court always reserves the right to vary custody to enforce access in an extreme case.

SUPPORT ENFORCEMENT

In Ontario, the Family Responsibility Act and the previous Family Support Plan Act has facilitated the process of guaranteeing compliance with support orders. The Ontario Acts provide for enforcement of support and custody orders as well as marriage contracts, cohabitation agreements, and separation agreements filed with the courts after March, 1992. Prior filed cases may be transferred if there are arrears and an income source. The plan provides for automatic support collection through employee payroll deductions.[15] In general, the experience with such legislation has been positive. Newspaper reports have indicated that there has been a reversal from an 85% non-compliance rate to an 85% rate of compliance with support orders in provinces where legislation has been in place for a number of years.

The Ontario legislation has established an Office and a Director of Enforcement who monitors orders for support and is empowered to take steps to enforce payments when they fall into arrears. Orders made prior to 1985 must be filed with the Director while orders made after that date are filed automatically unless withdrawn from the Director by the parties under very limited circumstances. If persons are receiving family benefits or general welfare assistance and orders for support of that person are in default, the Director of Community and Social Services may file with the Office of Enforcement on that person's behalf. Payments will continue to the spouse while the defaulter is sought.

The Director may initiate a search for a missing spouse and may request information or provide information to another jurisdiction. A support order has priority over other judgment debts regardless of when the enforcement action is commenced. The Director may also file a garnishment of a defaulter's wages, bank accounts, pensions or other assets. The court may make an order restraining the defaulter from wasting or disposing of assets and may issue a warrant for the arrest of a debtor whom it believes is attempting to leave the province for the purpose of evading a support order.

The court, unless satisfied that a defaulter has valid reasons for nonpayment, may order the debtor to be imprisoned for not more than 90 days either continuously or intermittently. Imprisonment does not constitute a discharge of the arrears. Some defaulting spouses have felt that the bureaucracy of the enforcement process has created injustice and that freezing of assets and imprisonment work against the ability to produce the support ordered by the court.

Merely creating new legislation does not guarantee automatic justice. Legislation without adequate administrative resources to follow through promptly may produce more frustration when new expectations for redress cannot be met. For example, in Ontario there can be up to six months delay in commencing enforcement orders. Defaulting spouses, particularly the self-employed, have created schemes to evade payment of support, which are often successful.

Endnotes

1. Divorce Act, R.S.C. 1985, c. 3 (2nd Supp.) as amended.
2. Children's Law Reform Act, R.S.O. 1990, c. C.12.
3. See Tables of Concordance.
4. Family Responsibility Act, S.O. 1997.
5. *Carter v. Brooks* (1990), 30 R.F.L. (3d) 53 (Ont. C.A.).
6. The present signatories include Australia, Argentina, Austria, Bahamas, Belize, Burkino Faso, Bosnia, Canada, Chile, Croatia, Denmark, Equador, France, German Federated Republic, Greece, Honduras, Iceland, Israel, Luxembourg, Macedonia, Mauritass, Mexico, Monaco, Netherlands, New Zealand, Norway, Panama, Poland, Portugal, Rumania, Slovenia, Sweden, Spain, Switzerland, United Kingdom and United States.
7. Criminal Code, R.S.C. 1985, c. C-46.
8. Such a case, *Charmasson v. Charmasson* (1982), 27 R.F.L. (2d) 241 was argued in the French courts. Mrs. Charmasson, the custodial parent of a six-year-old boy under an Ontario custody order, petitioned for return of her child by her French husband who had failed to return the child after a visit. The French court ordered the child returned to the mother, whereupon the father abducted the child. The intervention of the French authorities was required to return the child to his mother in Canada.
9. Note 2 above, ss. 18 and 37.
10. *Re Petryezka and Petryezka*, [1973] 2 O.R. 866, 10 R.F.L. 321, 35 D.L.R. (3d) 526 (C.A.).
11. *R. v. Hart* (1978), 7 R.F.L. (2d) 85 (Ont. Co. Ct.).
12. *Wright v. Wright* (1973), 1 O.R. (2d) 337, 12 R.F.L. 200, 40 D.L.R. (3d) 321 (C.A.).
13. S.O. 1989, c. 22 [not proclaimed in force]. See chapter 9, Enforcement of Access.
14. See *M. (B.P.) v. M. (B.L.D.E.)* (1992), 42 R.F.L. (3d) 349 (Ont. C.A.), leave to appeal to S.C.C. refused (1993), 48 R.F.L. (3d) 232 (note) (S.C.C.); *Abdo v. Abdo* (1993), 50 R.F.L. (3d) 171 (N.S.C.A.); *Pollon v. Pollon*, [1993] W.D.F.L. 1632 (B.C.S.C.).
15. See note 4, above.

Bibliography

Johnstone, Bruce. "Parental Child Abduction under the Criminal Code." (1987) 6 Can. J. of Fam. L. 271-286.

Niman, Harold. "Custody, Access and Parental Mobility Rights (Ont.)." (1988/89) 11 Advoc. Q. 117-125.

Wilton, Anne and Miyauchi. "Enforcement of Family Law Orders and Agreements". Carswell, Toronto (1989) is an excellent loose-leaf service which summarizes provincial and federal enforcement regimes.

14

Violence in the Family

Social workers and lawyers are no different from any other segment of our society which views the family as basic to a stable social structure and defines the family in conventional terms where father, mother, and children form a nurturing circle against the outside world. Society at large feels threatened when cracks appear in the family structure, and it responds with outrage and confusion. Front line systems such as the police, legal, and mental health systems are either unresponsive or lack adequate resources and remedies.

When an assault occurs between non-family members, legal consequences flow naturally to restrain and punish the attacker and protect the victim. Assault is viewed differently when it occurs within the intimacy of the family. Intra-familial violence is seen as more private than public and family members may be encouraged or counselled to reconcile their differences. In general, there is wariness toward using authority to invade family privacy and in particular male-female spousal relationships. Women and children have all too often been fearful about seeking help from external sources. Even when women assert their independence by leaving a threatening spouse, they still face inadequate financial support and often unavailable emergency shelter.

Domestic violence, unlike other criminal cases of assault, is more difficult for law enforcement, precisely because it is domestic; that is, the victim is or has been intimately involved with the perpetrator. Legal intervention, from initial investigation to sentencing, is affected by this distinction.[1] The Criminal Code is now clear about assault, but it is the descriptive modifier "domestic" which can cloud the issue. The Criminal Code now defines assault more precisely, thus facilitating legal prosecution of abuses, by clearly delineating manifestations of abuse. Section 266 of the Criminal Code states that it is an offence to threaten or to actually apply force intentionally to another person. The Code provides for the following circumstances:

- **Assault Causing Bodily Harm**

  Assault that causes injury to the complainant that interferes with the health or comfort of the complainant and that is more than very minor in nature and causes more than minor distress. The maximum sentence is 10 years.

- **Aggravated Assault**

  Assault that wounds, maims, disfigures, or endangers the life of a person. The maximum sentence is 14 years.

- **Assault With a Weapon**

  Assault during which the accused carries, uses, or threatens to use a weapon or an imitation weapon. The maximum sentence is 10 years.

- **Uttering Threats**

  Occurs when there is a verbal threat to cause harm or death to someone. The maximum sentence is 5 years.

- **Criminal Harassment**

  An anti-stalking law was passed in the fall of 1993 which makes it a crime to follow or intimidate or harass a person, either in person or over a phone, against their wishes. This includes watching the other person's home or workplace and engaging in threatening conduct. The maximum sentence is 5 years.

- **Sexual Assault**

  This ranges in severity from an assault of a sexual nature to include rape. The maximum sentence is 10 years.

- **Sexual Assault With a Weapon**

  This is a sexual assault during which the accused carries, uses, or threatens to use a weapon or an imitation weapon. The maximum sentence is 14 years.

- **Attempted Murder**

  This is an intentional attempt to kill another person. The maximum is life imprisonment.

Offences against the person and the consequences of a criminal conviction are also discussed in Chapter 22.

Social work has also had difficulty in responding effectively to domestic violence, principally because assault in the family is met first by police intervention within boundaries set by the law. Coordination between police and judicial systems and social services is not routinely built into the system. Responses of either or both systems are neither consistent nor timely. There is little doubt that domestic abuse is a gendered problem. In the first quarter of 1993, in Alberta alone, police laid 95% of the criminal charges against men, about 3% against women, and in about 2%, both parties were charged.[2]

To call this chapter family or spousal violence is to obscure the specific gender of the victim. The statistics are indisputable and overwhelming. Almost one in ten Canadian women is involved in a battering relationship, although some women's shelter workers estimate the figure at one in six or even five. Close to 600,000 Canadian women sought help for beatings in 1985.[3] The difference in domestic assault is that the perpetrator can manipulate the victim in order to protect himself. It is the nature of the relationship and its complexity that separates this type of assault from all other assaultive incidents.

Reporters looked at 133 cases of domestic violence in Toronto. They found that, out of 100 completed investigations of the 133, there were 40 acquittals and 60 convictions, 90% resulting from guilty pleas. Of the 40 cases resulting in acquittals, 37 of the cases had victims who either recanted or did not attend court. It is possible that these victims were stayed by fear engendered by power and control behaviour of the abuser. The report revealed that within a day or two of the assault, 85% of the accused persons were released on bail, usually under a number of conditions which required the accused to stay away from the victim. Close to half of these accused broke their bail conditions by either harassing, stalking, or going back to live with the victims. In the 37 cases where the victim recanted or failed to attend court, the Crown did not once use any injury photographs, 911 calls, statements to the police, or other witnesses including police officers at the scene to prove the case. In addition, it was noted that most victims were never contacted by the Victim Witness Assistance Program or by Crown Attorneys in regard to their cases.[4]

Batterers use violence as only one weapon in their control and power repertoire. Other strategies include coercion and threats, intimidation, using emotional abuse, isolation, minimizing, denying, and blaming, using children, using male privilege, and using economic abuse. These characteristics of abusive relationships have been defined by the Duluth Domestic Abuse Intervention Program, a coordinated community response to domestic assault cases developed in Duluth, Minnesota. Each of these is defined by placing them as spokes along a wheel whose centre is power and control. Each spoke can be expressed through physical or sexual abuse in the following ways:

- **Using Coercion and Threats**

  Examples include: threats to leave; to commit suicide; to report the victim to welfare; to deny that the abuse occurred or to pressure the victim to drop charges.

- **Using Intimidation**

  Examples include: promoting fear through use of looks, actions, or gestures; displaying weapons; or destroying the victim's property.

- **Using Emotional Abuse**

  Examples include: making the victim feel diminished; attempting to humiliate; suggesting craziness or being deserving of abuse.

- **Using Economic Abuse**

  Examples include: preventing the victim from getting or keeping a job; withholding household money; witholding information on family income or assets.

- **Using Isolation**

  Examples include: control over what the victim may do, or may see or talk with, or may go, or may read.

- **Using Children**

  Examples include: threats to take the children away; using the children to relay messages; usurping power to make decisions about the children.

- **Using Male Privilege**

  Examples include: defining male and female roles as master/servant; usurping decision making, imposing financial penalties.

Morris notes that victim blaming pervades the entire court process. The woman's family may say they told her not to marry that man, the investigating officer may note that she had been drinking, or that she might have provoked the attack.[5] These attitudes are pervasive, even though in Ontario the Policing Standards Manual contains a chapter that outlines the police response to wife assault wherein police are instructed to lay charges in all instances of wife assault where there are reasonable grounds. Police are provided guidance in what factors constitute reasonable grounds.

A London, Ontario study has found that women are more likely to follow through as witnesses when police lay charges. As well, the courts tend to be tougher on offenders when police lay charges. The study suggested that experienced police are more likely to lay charges than are junior officers.[6] If charges are to be laid by the police, it is especially important that coordinating support services be in place, because many women may face serious censure and further abuse from families and community because of cultural attitudes about appropriate female behaviour and the fear that public exposure will shame an entire family. Social support services that are culturally acceptable to specific communities should work closely with police, the justice system and the extended family so that women in this situation are not subject to further abuse if they follow through with court proceedings or refuse to testify.

In some situations, women have been placed in double jeopardy by the systems designed to protect them. An abused wife who sought compensation from the Criminal Compensation Board was given a reduced award because she had not left her husband and because she had thrown his clothes into a suitcase, presumably provoking him.[7] In another case, a woman who refused to testify against her husband after she had laid a complaint against him for abuse was arrested and imprisoned for five days. She was eventually awarded compensation for humiliation and distress because of the particularly insensitive aspect of her treatment, but only one of the three courts involved noted awareness of her experience as an abused wife fearful of the consequences of her taking direct action against her husband.[8]

REMEDIES AVAILABLE WHEN VIOLENCE ERUPTS

Exclusive Possession

A lawyer or the victim herself can apply for a restraining order that prevents the husband from contacting her for a specified time, usually three months. In an urgent situation, a restraining order can be granted without prior notice to an abuser. If she wishes to start a legal action, she can obtain a non-molestation order. If she wishes to remain in the matrimonial home with her children, a lawyer can file a claim under The Family Law Act, Ontario seeking exclusive possession of the home, household goods, and a vehicle. Such an order can both force the husband out of the home and keep him away when she moves back in.

Exclusive possession of the matrimonial home can be ordered if it is in the best interests of the children to do so.[9] Application for exclusive possession of the family home must be brought in a superior court. It cannot be brought in the provincial family court since it is a property matter.[10] Courts are generally sympathetic on an interim basis where violence has been inflicted on a wife and children.

Personal Protection Orders

If the husband has been charged, application may be made to a justice of the peace for a peace bond under the Criminal Code. The wife needs only to swear that she fears her husband will cause injury to her or her child, or will damage property. The justice of the peace needs only to find reasonable grounds for these fears.[11]

A charge may be laid under the Criminal Code by any person, including a common law spouse. A peace bond may be issued by the court if the applicant can prove "fear of injury". Alternatively, the justice or the summary convictions court before which the parties appear may order that the defendant "enter into a recognizance . . . to keep the peace and be of good behaviour for any period that does not exceed 12 months, and comply with such other reasonable conditions prescribed in the recognizance as the court considers desirable for securing the good conduct of the defendant".[12] The defendant may be imprisoned for breach of the recognizance, since this is a criminal order.[13] In practice, the enforceability of a peace bond or recognizance varies and the victim of assault cannot always rely on their protection.

Restraining Orders

A victim may apply for an order restraining a spouse from molesting, annoying, or harassing the applicant, and this order may be obtained in conjunction with exclusive possession of the matrimonial home if it is brought in a superior court.[14] Breach of this order may result in civil contempt proceedings. The effectiveness of a restraining order may be of limited effectiveness to provide protection. A spouse intent upon harassment or revenge may frequently succeed, since the police cannot provide full-time supervision to any person.

Restraining Orders — Common Law Spouses

Relief to an unmarried spouse is available only in the form of non-molestation orders. In Ontario, the common law spouse may be forced to flee a shared home to find shelter elsewhere. The Act arbitrarily excludes from protection those victims of violence who fail to meet the three-year minimum for cohabitation or have cohabited for less than one year and produced a child of that union. Further, the cohabitation as spouses must have occurred during the preceding 12 months. If a couple is childless and has cohabited for two years, no relief is possible under the Family Law Act. A peace bond would be the appropriate remedy.

If the woman is not married, she can apply for a restraining order by filing a claim, but cannot seek exclusive possession of the home unless she is a named tenant on the lease or a registered owner.

POWERS OF ARREST

The Family Law Act does not provide for the powers to arrest; however, it does grant quasi-criminal powers to the provincial court in the event of wilful contempt or resistance to its orders and specifies that the court may punish by fine or imprisonment. There is no threat of immediate arrest since the applicant would have to initiate a complaint to obtain relief. Since no rules in Ontario indicate that the local police need to be informed that an injunction exists, the police cannot provide a sense of security. However, the Supreme Court of Canada has held that any lawful order is enforceable and a person failing to act may be held in contempt and punished.[15]

Ontario announced that it has established two domestic-violence courts which would operate as a team involving prosecutors, police, and counsellors. Each court will prosecute a different level of spousal abuse. One is to focus on all types of domestic assault cases, especially cases of stalking and failing to comply with previous court orders. The other court is to hear cases where no injury has occurred, where the abuser has no previous arrests, and where both parties wish their relationship to continue. Remedies to be employed in this court include counselling, a group for male batterers which will be available to those who plead guilty in place of the imposition by a court of a fine or incarceration. Police will be required to collect evidence such as videotaping victim statements, photographing injuries as well as the crime scene, and submitting tapes of the original 911 call as evidence. This will minimize the victim's reluctance to testify and the frequency of the victim withdrawing charges. The police will have evidence to press charges. Similar special court approaches are already operating in Winnipeg. A year after Manitoba opened its special court in 1990, the number of domestic assault cases reaching the provincial courts had increased by a third.[16]

A preferred approach to serving the needs of victims of family violence is an interdisciplinary team of police, law and social work to develop expertise regarding needed resources and available legal remedies. Some municipalities have established domestic violence units and employ social workers to accompany police where domestic disputes or violence are reported. Others have developed special training programmes for selected police personnel to better enable them to cope with volatile family situations. The participation of lawyers as instructors or resource persons would enhance both the appropriateness and confidence of the police/social worker team.

WHAT TO DO AFTER THE POLICE HAVE LEFT

> Mrs. C. is seated in your office crying. Her face is bruised, one eye blackened, and she has lost a tooth. Last night, neighbours again called the police who arrived and warned her husband that if they were called one more time, he would be charged. Mrs. C. refused to go to the hospital because she was afraid to leave the children, twin boys, aged 11, and a 10-month-old infant. This morning she arrived carrying the baby and said she did not know what to do next but she does not want to return home.

Clearly, she needs emergency shelter for herself and her children. Though she has several legal remedies available to her, one has to be certain that a particular course of action is appropriate to all of the specific circumstances. A referral to a community legal centre, legal aid (if available), or a lawyer should ensure that all factors will be considered. These may include exclusive possession of the matrimonial home, a degree of protection from further harm, and access to quality counselling for this family. It may be appropriate for the social worker to remain involved in order to provide support, community referral and counselling beyond the scope of the legal proceeding.

There is serious question whether a legal response, and especially a criminal sanction, is the most appropriate response to domestic violence. The primary goal, to stop the violence, is only temporarily achieved. The victim continues to suffer the consequences of this legal response in the form of economic deprivation, loss of the spousal relationship where it is not beyond repair, and loss of assistance for parenting the children.

The fallout from family violence is of a different order from violence and assault occurring outside the family and while society may feel relieved that the perpetrator has been brought to justice, the remaining family members too have been sentenced and will be punished. The base of financial support has been altered if not eliminated, mortgage or rental payments on the matrimonial home may be affected, the home lost and the family forced to move to less desirable accommodation. Complex emotions of children who have seen a parent punished and removed from the home can create problems of child management at home, the school and in the community. For these and other reasons, some spouses elect to return to an abusive spouse and thus perpetuate the cycle. Nevertheless, both lawyers and social workers have an obligation to discuss the various alternatives which are available, the likely consequences of each, and to support the client in her decision.

Examining all the sources of violence, however, is only the beginning of the process of response. It is not enough to be aware and informed, but also, it is important to question personal world views that we assume to be universal and correct, and to examine and challenge institutional practices and policies starting from the most basic levels.[17]

In summary, law and social support services must devise a coordinated system to meet the needs of each community whether rural or urban, ethnic specific or cosmopolitan. Each part of the system must attach to a coordinating body with appropriate communication protocols in place. Clearly, legal remedies are important, but in domestic situations they do not provide sufficient protection. Social workers and a range of social services from readily available and safe shelters for women and children, sensitive medical services, and immediate response counselling for the woman, her children and, if necessary extended families must work closely with the legal and justice systems. Counselling may be needed for an extended period in order for an abused woman to build up self-respect and instill and support feelings of empowerment that will enable her to make decisions for her future that will not result in re-entry into the abusive system. For the abusers, therapy based on anger management is not an approach that is universally appropriate or effective, though it is helpful to some abusers. Participation in group therapy which addresses individual differences as well as common patterns of behaviour has proven to be helpful for some abusing men. Domestic violence can only be reduced by a concerted effort on the part of the government and local communities to provide a comprehensive network of response that includes a coordinated range of legal and social intervention.

Finally, in analyzing violence as a pervasive social phenomenon, it is necessary to look beyond individual violence wherein someone is physically and emotionally assaulted by another person. Violence may also be found at less visible or obvious levels; for example where it is institutionalized in settings such as schools, prisons, mental institutions, the military, welfare bureaucracies, and government bodies. Violence at this level is less discernible than individual violence because the perpetrators are camouflaged by bureaucratic procedures or by policies that do not reflect the daily reality of those they direct and control. Violence can also be embedded at a deeper structural level where social and cultural bias blindly support inequity. Society, in general, tolerates substantial levels of unemployment, substandard housing, food banks, children at risk where arrangements for care are lacking or dangerous. Overt family violence often takes root in institutional and structural violence. Lawyers and social workers, among others involved at the direct level of intervention deal with symptoms and social consequences, but rarely examine the less obvious sources of violence.[18]

CHILD ABUSE

Child abuse does not fit comfortably within the purview of any single profession, whether medical, legal or social work. No one profession can explain, treat, or contain child abuse. It seems to be a learned behaviour comprised of poor parenting experiences and unrealistic expectations of the abuser toward herself and toward the child. These factors may be compounded by persistent poverty and parental isolation. The act of abuse is probably precipitated by some crisis which may not be readily identified.[19]

Our society is not prepared to countenance abuse of its children although parental correction in the form of physical punishment as well as corporal punishment meted out by teachers, continues to be condoned in the Criminal Code.[20] A strong statement about our wish to protect children would be delivered by the elimination of the section of the Criminal Code which continues to authorize lawful correction of children by physical punishment. Child welfare legislation is the primary legal vehicle for intervention when abuse is alleged. A succeeding chapter will outline the procedures to be followed by child protection and health workers. The reality remains that child abuse is a troubling and dangerous problem whose resolution seems to elude the policy planners.

Though society deplores child abuse and is prepared to prosecute the abuser and to take steps to protect the child who has been abused, there has been reluctance to take preventive steps based on the strong association between abuse and poverty and isolation. This issue will be discussed under Child Welfare and Protection.

Child sexual abuse has taken hold in the public mind, not only as a social reality, but also as a trauma whose negative effects can be felt years later when the victimized child becomes an adult. An extensive literature has sprung up proclaiming the prevalence of repressed memories of childhood sexual abuse that becomes manifest usually through a therapeutic experience where abuse may be suggested as an explanation for current troubles. As memories are recalled, the perpetrator may remember events in which the victims were too frightened or too intimidated to speak about abusive behaviour at the time it was occurring. In Canada, we have examples in the court cases involving adults now empowered to name the perpetrators of sexual and physical abuse that happened when they were children in residential schools. Repressed memory syndrome, however, is not without its voluble critics who question the validity of memories of sexual abuse that are recalled suddenly many years later as part of a therapeutic process which may be unreliable as evidence in a court proceeding.

There can be no generalized guides to how society is to deal with sexual abuse. Children must be protected from such assault and perpetrators do face criminal proceedings. It is a difficult task for lawyers and social workers involved in these situations to consider each situation as unique and to search for ways to respond appropriately. If prosecution and incarceration are our only responses, we have a negative fallout. Shame, anger, guilt, loss of income, and loss of parent must be professional concerns along with protection of the child and punishment of the perpetrator.[21]

ELDER ABUSE

The abuse of elderly persons can occur within or without institutions, but a study released by the British Columbia and Federal health departments has concluded that the abused elderly are usually mistreated by loved ones. The study looked at 542 cases of "elder abuse" across Canada. The most common perpetrator cited in the study was a son, followed by a husband, and to a lesser degree a daughter. Other perpetrators included grandchildren, neighbours, and employed caretakers. Nearly a third of seniors surveyed reported being physically abused, but the most common abuse reported was psychological, such as being subjected to demeaning comments or being tolerated as a burden.[22] Another study reported that in 1989, four percent of Canadian seniors living in private dwellings were abused by a partner, relative or other close contact after the age of 65.[23]

Elder abuse often takes the form of neglect by family or caregivers who are themselves physically and economically over-extended. Add to this fact their concern that good care of the elder family member will deplete assets. The result is neglect and sometimes physical abuse in the form of malnutrition, poor hygiene and lack of physical and mental attention. Such neglect may be a result of the caregiver's reluctance to draw upon the elder's financial resources or where the elder person has no resources. A further result may be conversion of the elder's assets to their own use, while depriving the elder of the right to their own property.

Both social workers and lawyers may learn of the abuse of an elderly person by accident, in the course of a routine visit or interview. The most appropriate response in such circumstances is to discuss the observations with the family (if there is a family) or caregiver. If abuse or neglect continues, the Office of the Public Guardian and Trustee, or the official charged with supervision of the affairs of the elderly in the province, should be notified.

Endnotes

1. Morris, Robert N., "Prosecuting Domestic Assault Cases: A Time for New Approaches", *Crown's Newsletter* (April, 1996), p. 38.
2. Boll, Rosemarie and Sybil Bohonas, "When Home is Where the Hurt Is", 20 *Law Now*, No. 4, (Feb., 1996).
3. McGillvray, Ann, "Intimate Violence and Manly Men", C.J.L.S., (Spring, 1994), p. 233.
4. Daly, Rita, Jane Armstrong and Caroline Mallon, "Seven Days: A Chronicle of Domestic violence in Metro", *Toronto Star*, March 9-16, 1996; discussed in Morris, Robert N., "Prosecuting Domestic Assault Cases: A Time for New Approaches"; 1 *Crown's Newsletter*, April, 1996.
5. Morris, op.cit. p. 137.
6. *Globe and Mail*, July 5, 1991
7. [1991] 5 W.W.R. 315 (Sask. Q.B.).
8. *Pigeau v. Crowell* (1991), 101 N.S.R. (2d) 231 (T.D.) "assessment decision", (1990), 96 N.S.R. (2d) 412 (C.A.) "appeal decision", (1989), 91 N.S.R. (2d) 318 (T.D.) "trial decision", reported in Hughes,

Patricia, "How Many Times a Victim?", 1993, C. J. Woman and Law, pp. 502-512.

9. Family Law Act, R.S.O. 1990, c. F.3, s. 24(b).
10. See *A.G. Ont. v. A.G. Can.*, [1982] 1 S.C.R. 62, [1982] 3 W.W.R. 1, 26 R.F.L. (2d) 113, 36 B.C.L.R. 1 (*sub nom. Ref. re s. 6 of Family Relations Act*), 131 D.L.R. (3d) 257, 40 N.R. 206 (*sub nom. Re Family Relations Act of B.C.*).
11. Boll, Rosemarie and Sybil Bohonas, "When Home is Where the Hurt Is", *Law Now*, Feb./March 1996, pp. 6-7.
12. Criminal Code, R.S.C. 1985, c. C-46, s. 810(3)(a).
13. *Ibid.*, s. 811.
14. *Ibid.*, s. 14.
15. *R. v. Clement*, [1981] 2 S.C.R. 468, [1981] 6 W.W.R. 735, 23 R.F.L. (2d) 225, 23 C.R. (3d) 193, 10 Man. R. (2d) 92, 61 C.C.C. (2d) 449, 127 D.L.R. (3d) 419, 38 N.R. 302.
16. *Globe and Mail*, November 5, 1996.
17. Vayda, Elaine and Marion Bogo, "A Teaching Model to Unite Classroom and Field: the ITP Loop", *Journal of Social Work Education*, Vol. 27, No. 3, Fall, 1991, pp. 271-78.
18. Van Soest, Dorothy and Shirley Bryant. "Violence Reconceptualized for Social Work: The Urban Dilemma". *Social Work*, Vol. 40, No. 4, July, 1995. pp. 549-56.
19. See D. J. Lange, "Child Abuse and Ontario's New Reporting Register" (1980) 3 Fam. L. Rev. 3.
20. Criminal Code, R.S.C. 1985, c. C-46, s. 43.
21. See Terr, Lenore. *Unchained Memories: True Stores of Traumatic Memories, Lost and Found*, Basic Books; Loftus, Elizabeth and Katherine Ketcham, *The Myth of Repressed Memory: False Memories and Allegations of Sexual Abuse*, St. Martin's; Bass, Ellen and Laura Davis, *The Courage to Heal: A Guide for Women Survivors of Child Sexual Abuse (3rd Edition)*, Harper Perennial; Ofshe, Richard and Ethan Watters, *Making Monsters: False Memories, Psychotherapy, and Sexual Hysteria*, Scribner's; Pendergrast, Mark, *Victims of Memory: Incest Accusations and Shattered Lives*, Upper Access; MacLean, Harry N. *Once Upon a time: A True Story of Memory, Murder, and the Law*, Harper Collins, 1993.
22. *Globe and Mail*, May 10, 1997.
23. "CASW Report: Elder Abuse in Ethno-Cultural Communities", *Newsmagazine*: Journal of the Ontario Association of Social Workers, 23, No. 2, Summer 1996, 19.

Bibliography

Bala, Nicholas. "Spousal Abuse and Children of Divorce: A Differentiated Approach" (1996), 13 Can. J. Fam. L., 215-285.

Bala, Nicholas. "Criminal Code Amendments to Increase Protection to Children and Women: Bills C-126 and C-128", Institute for the Prevention of Child Abuse (Case Law Series) Toronto, 1993.

Boll, Rosemarie and Sybil Bohenas. "When Home is Where the Hurt Is", 20 Law Now, No. 4, (Feb. 1996) 6-9.

Browne, Angela and Sharis Bassuk. "Intimate Violence in the Lives of Homeless and Poor Housed Women: Prevalence and Patterns in an Ethnically Diverse Sample", *American Journal of Orthopsychiatry*, Vol. 67, No. 2, April, 1997, 261-278.

Ciraco, Joseph. "Domestic Violence: A History Unfolded", (Aug. 1996) 2 Crown's Newsletter, 24-42.

Coughlan, G. *et. al*. "Mandatory Reporting of Suspected Elder Abuse and Neglect", (Spring, 1996) 19 Dalhousie Law Journal, 45-70.

Ginn, Diana. "Wife Assault, the Justice System and Professional Responsibility", (Aug. 1995) 33 Alberta Law Review, 908-919.

Golden, Gail K. and Phyllis B. Frank. "When 50-50 Isn't Fair: The Case Against Couple Counselling in Domestic Abuse", Social Work, Vol. 39, No. 6, Nov. 1994, 636-637.

Goodwin, Gail S. and Betty L. Bottoms. "Child Victims, Child Witnesses: Understanding and Improving Testimony", New York: Guilford Press, 1993.

Lenton, Rhonda L. "Power vs. Feminist Theories of Wife Abuse" (July, 1995) 37 Canadian Journal of Criminology, 305-330.

Martin, Dianne L. and Janet Mosher. "Unkept Promises: Experiences of Immigrant Women with the Neo-Criminalization of Wife Abuse", (1995) 8 Canadian Journal of Women and the Law, 3-44.

Mills, Linda. "Empowering Battered Women Transnationally: The Case for Post-Modern Interventions", Social Work, May, 1996, Vol. 41, No. 3, 261-268.

Morris, Robert N. "Prosecuting Domestic Assault Cases: A Time for New Approaches", (April, 1996) 1 Crown's Newsletter, 35-57.

Mosher, Janet. "Wife Abuse: Assessing the Interventions of Law and Social Work", 1996, ed. Toronto Faculty of Law, University of Toronto, Student use only.

Mulroy, Elizabeth A. "Building a Neighborhood Network: Interorganizational Collaboration to Prevent Child Abuse and Neglect", Social Work, May, 1997, Vol. 42, No. 3, 255-264.

Penfold, Susan. "Questionable Beliefs about Child Sexual Abuse

Allegations during Custody Disputes", (1997) 14 Canadian Journal of Family Law, 11-30.

Seuffert, Nan. "Hanging Out at the Gap: A Dialogue Reading of Experience of Survivors of Domestic Violence with Legal Representation" (1995) 8 Canadian Journal of Women and the Law, 290-336.

15

Mental Health and Substitute Decisions

The last quarter of this century has seen growing recognition of the need to achieve a delicate balance between individual rights to autonomy and the public duty to treat and protect those who may be at risk. The conflict weighs the right of the individual to be protected from state imposed restriction on freedom and the public interest in safety. Mental health professionals too, have an interest in providing care to those who may benefit from that care. A complicating factor is the extent to which one believes in the efficacy of psychiatric treatment and decision making. It is certainly true that many problems, diagnosed as mental disorders, have overriding social components which do not respond to psychiatric or medical intervention. In order to bridge the gap between the competing interests in mental health issues of capacity, consent to treatment, substitute decisions, and involuntary commital to hospital, the concept of therapeutic jurisprudence provides a useful link.[1]

Therapeutic jurisprudence attempts to construct mental health law so that it advances therapeutic outcomes where they are supported by current empiric research. Both mental health lawyers and caregivers need to keep an open mind which is informed by empirical literature about therapeutic claims.[2] For example, the movement toward deinstitutionalization of mental patients based on strong psychiatric belief coupled with limited public resources, has met with evidence of stressful outcomes for all parties. In reality those involved face inadequate community care resources, inadequate housing and employment opportunities, isolation and stigmatization. Therapeutic jurisprudence should be collaborative, not adversarial, and must include solid research and policy review and evaluation in formulating decisions. Wexler has cautioned "that the law's use of mental health information to improve therapeutic functioning cannot impinge upon justice concerns."[3] It should not be equated with a return to the therapeutic state that prevailed at mid-century.[4]

Ontario has enacted the Health Care Consent Act, 1996, which along with the Substitute Decisions Act,[5] has brought significant changes to the healthcare system. The Health Care Consent Act[6] consolidates rules regarding consent to treatment that apply consistently in all settings including hospitals, both psychiatric and acute care, homes for the aged, nursing homes, and long term care homes, as well as setting regulations regarding consent to personal care services. In general, this legislation has as its purpose the enhancement of individual automony through establishing precise procedures in assessing incapacity, appointing substitute decision makers, and guaranteeing the right to review of a finding of incapacity. Where an individual while capable and over the age of 16 has expressed a wish in regard to the assignment of power of attorney, those expressed wishes take precedence unless the review should find otherwise.

Consent and Capacity Review

The Consent and Capacity Review Board functions under the Health Care Consent Act. The members sit in panels of one, three, or five to hear applications for review, usually within seven days of receipt of an application for review. Any person may apply to the Board for a review of a health practitioner's finding that he or she is incapable, provided that no guardian or attorney has been appointed. The decisions of the Board in regard to capacity may be appealed to the Ontario Court (General Division). The Board may, when requested, give directions to a substitute decision-maker.

Treatment

Persons are considered capable of making decisions about their treatment if they can understand information relevant to making a decision and are able to foresee reasonable consequences of a decision or refusal to make a decision. The elements required for consent to treatment include the following: the consent must be informed, must be given voluntarily, and must not be obtained through misrepresentation or fraud. Informed consent requires that a person be told the nature of the treatment, its expected benefits, material risks and side effects, alternate courses of action and the likely consequences of not having the treatment.

Substitute Decision-Maker

Where a person is found incapable of making a decision, a substitute decision-maker must be identified. It is important to remember that such a decision-maker should be identified while an individual is capable and over 16 years of age wherever this is possible. A substitute decision-maker is that person's guardian who has authority to give or refuse permission for treatment. The Consent and Capacity Review Board may also appoint a person's representative as a substitute decision-maker if no other person has been given this authority.

There is a ranking of persons who may be named as substitute decision-makers. These are a person's spouse or partner, a parent or child of the person, a Children's Aid Society who has assumed parental authority, a sibling or other relative.[7] Where none of these persons meet the requirements either because they are under 16 years or are legally prohibited, or are not available or willing to assume such responsibility, then the Public Guardian and Trustee shall be the decision-maker. All substitute decision-makers are entitled to all information needed to make a decision, must always consider the best interests of the incapable person and make the least restrictive decision given the circumstances.

Emergency Treatment

Emergency treatments may be undertaken without the consent of a substitute decision-maker where delay will place the incapable person at serious risk unless there is sufficient reason to believe that a person does not want that treatment and was capable and over 16 years when that wish was expressed.

Admission to a Psychiatric Facility

If the incapable person is 16 years or over and objects to being admitted to a psychiatric facility, consent to the admission may only be given by a guardian of that person or the attorney with power to decide about personal care. This person has the authority to use necessary and reasonable force to enable the admission. The incapable person may apply to the Board for a review of the decision to consent to that person's admission to a hospital, psychiatric or other health facility, but the admission may take effect and the treatment may be administered until the application for review has been disposed of.[8] In the case of a person between the ages of 12 and 16 who objects to admission to a psychiatric facility as an informal patient, no permission for review will be granted.[9]

Admission to Care Facilities

If a person is found by an evaluator to be incapable to make a decision in regard to admission to a care facility, a substitute decision-maker may make the decision based on the following criteria; where a wish has been expressed by the person while capable in regard to such admission, that wish be respected, where there is no knowledge of such a wish, the decision-maker must consider the values and beliefs held by the person while capable and must consider whether the quality of life will be enhanced by the admission and negative consequences reduced, and whether any option exists that would be less restrictive than admission.

All persons affected by a decision may make application for review to the Board if they disagree with the decision-maker. If a review is pending, the admission will not take place until the review has been resolved unless the administrator of the care facility believes that a crisis situation necessitates immediate admission. A substitute decision-maker may apply to the Board for directions if the incapable person expressed a wish about admission while capable and was at least 16 years.

Personal Assistance Services

In regard to personal assistance services, procedures similar to those defining treatment and admission to treatment and care facilities are covered in the legislation. In general, no consent can be given on behalf of an incapable person to the use of confinement, monitoring devices or types of restraint unless such use is considered essential to prevent serious bodily harm to the recipient, to others, or would provide for the recipient greater freedom or enhancement of life quality. No guardian may use or give consent to use electric shock or aversive treatment unless consent is given in accordance with these provisions of the Health Care Act.[10]

Secure Treatment of Children

Where a child who has been admitted to a secure treatment program described in the Child and Family Services Act is a party to a Board hearing, the children's lawyer must provide legal representation for the child where no legal representative has been provided for the child.

Assessment

A person has the right to refuse to be assessed and must be informed of the right to refuse assessment by the assessor. If the court is satisfied that there are reasonable grounds to believe that a person is incapable, the court may order that an assessment must take place.

Estate Considerations/Property Management

The Substitute Decisions Act, 1992, deals with persons incapable of managing their property.[11] It grants authority to give power of attorney to a person of their choice or to name the Public Guardian and Trustee. A continuing power of attorney is valid if the person is capable of giving it even if incapable of actually managing the property. This statutory power of attorney comes into effect when the attorney is notified that an assessor has found the giver of the power to be incapable of managing property. Note that the Public Guardian and Trustee is the statutory guardian only where no other qualified person such as a spouse or partner, a child over 16 years, relative, personal attorney or Trust company has been designated by the person needing assistance in estate or property management. No person who provides health care or residential, social, training, or support services to an incapable person for compensation may be appointed guardian because of a potential conflict of interest.

HOSPITALIZATION FOR MENTAL DISORDERS

Mental health legislation which deals with involuntary civil commitment to a mental hospital is a complex and troubling area which has a number of dimensions. The best that mental health legislation can do is to provide safeguards in the nature of procedural review for the individual patient while not unduly fettering psychiatric assessment and intervention where such intervention may benefit the patient.

THE PATIENT ADVOCATE

Ontario has established a network of patient advocates situated in every provincial hospital. These advocates are not necessarily lawyers. There may be a number of advocates in a hospital, depending on its size. They are available to any patient or staff member speaking on behalf of a patient concerning any aspect of treatment and placement of the patient within the facility. Their express function is to ascertain that the patient receives appropriate treatment and if he feels an injustice has occurred, either by commission or omission of the facility, he is assured of due process and a review of his situation. The significance of patient advocates is that they are not hospital employees and are independent of the hospital system.

COMMITAL FOR INVOLUNTARY ASSESSMENT

The Mental Health Act of Ontario[12] provides for an application for a psychiatric assessment where a physician believes a person may cause bodily harm to himself or another person, or shows a lack of competence to care for himself.[13] This application must be issued by a justice of the peace and may authorize that the person be detained for an assessment for a period not to exceed seven days. The physician who completes a certificate for involuntary admission after the period of assessment cannot be the same physician who completed the application for assessment.[14]

It is always open to any person to admit themselves to a mental health facility as a voluntary patient either for assessment or treatment.

TIME CONSTRAINTS

Once assessed, an involuntary patient may be detained, restrained, observed, and examined in a psychiatric facility for not more than two weeks, plus one additional month under a first certificate of renewal, two additional months under a second certificate of renewal, and three additional months under a third certificate of renewal.[15] An involuntary patient whose authorized period of detention has expired automatically becomes an informal patient who cannot be detained in hospital against his will.[16]

Where a judge has reason to believe that a person before him who is charged or convicted of a criminal offence suffers a mental disorder, he may order a psychiatric assessment.[17] Any person who is remanded in custody under the Criminal Code for observation and is detained may be admitted to a psychiatric facility as an involuntary patient.[18]

COMMUNICATIONS TO AND FROM IN-PATIENTS

Correspondence to or from a patient cannot be interfered with except under circumstances provided by the legislation. The apparent intent is to protect the rights of the patient, but in effect, the interpretation of the special circumstances gives hospital staff broad discretionary powers. Communications can be withheld, for example, if the content would prejudice the best interests of the patient, be offensive to the addressee, interfere with treatment or cause the patient unnecessary distress.[19] On the other hand, correspondence to or from a lawyer or member of an advisory or review board is excluded from discretionary interference, and must not be detained, delayed or interfered with in any way.[20]

TREATMENT

Psychiatric treatment cannot be given to an involuntary patient without the patient's consent. However, if a patient consents, the treatment provided is at the discretion of the psychiatrist. In view of the setting and the mental condition of the patient, the voluntariness of the consent may be questionable. Where the patient is a minor or not mentally competent, consent must be obtained from the nearest relative, unless it is ordered by a regional review board after notifying the patient or nearest relative that such an order is being sought. Psychosurgery may *not* be performed on an involuntary patient.

In spite of the provisions of the Act, some persons feel that a person, once labelled as a mental patient, is not sufficiently protected from loss of civil liberties. Voluntary associations and self-help information and advocacy groups, some composed of former mental patients, have developed in many localities. Community legal aid centres can usually provide information about these groups.

ESTATE CONSIDERATIONS

The Mental Health Act (Ontario) addresses the estates of persons deemed not competent to manage their own affairs. Families are frequently concerned about property matters where their relative is not competent. Social workers should advise families to seek legal advice regarding trusteeship of the assets of a certified mental patient.

REVIEW BOARDS

The Mental Health Act (Ontario) provides for a review board to review the status of certified, involuntary patients.[21] An involuntary patient or someone acting on his behalf may apply for a review of his involuntary status.[22] The patient is permitted to attend the hearing or may have a person appear as his representative. Witnesses may be called and cross-examined with the permission of the chairman.[23] The decision of the review board determines whether or not there is a change in status. The chairman of the board must prepare a written report of the decision and must provide a copy to the applicant and to the hospital director.[24]

Every patient detained in criminal proceedings and found not guilty because of mental illness must be reviewed at least once each year or earlier if requested. The Review Board has power to make orders regarding the disposition and privileges of the accused ranging from absolute discharge, discharge with conditions, or committal to a mental hospital with conditions.[25]

In *R. v. LePage*, the court found that section 672.54 of the Criminal Code was struck down as a violation of the rights of the accused under subsection 15(1) of the Charter. The court reasoned that the test of "significant threat" is vague and difficult to define with no clearly stated standards to determine the risk to public safety. The court suspended its declaration in order to allow Parliament to remedy the "deficiencies" of section 672.54 of the Code which empower the Board to determine that a person is a significant threat to the public and should not be given an absolute discharge. This decision was reversed on appeal. The court held that the section did not violate the Charter.[26]

JUDICIAL REVIEW

Review boards may be subject to review by the courts in certain circumstances. The following case demonstrates a judicial response to both a psychosocial and medical problem, which places mental patients in the twilight zone between inadequate community resources and admission to a mental hospital.[27]

This was an application to a review board for an order discharging the patient from a mental health facility. The petitioner stated that he was not receiving active medical treatment for his mental disorder and did not require treatment and that the burden of proof for detention rested with the director of the facility. The petitioner's counsel said his client was a difficult person who presented a housing problem but that he was merely being "warehoused" in the mental hospital and should be discharged.

The court reviewed the medical and social work findings, in particular the affidavit of the social worker which showed that over the past year prior to his committal to the hospital, the patient had moved his lodgings a minimum of 40 times. She stated that "in my opinion, Jeffrey Robinson is impossible to house in the community and is at risk from assaults, malnutrition, disease, and exposure and others are at risk from his unpredictable verbal and physical outbursts."[28] The judge found that though the social worker was not qualified to render a medical judgment, her report corroborated or supported the doctor's evidence. The judge accepted her statement that, "because of his behaviour it is impossible to find accommodation for Jeffrey Robinson in the private rental sector of the community."[29] The judge stated that the key question was "whether the petitioner requires medical treatment and care in a provincial mental health facility."[30]

In order to satisfy the court, the Director must show that the patient is a mentally ill person, that is, a person who is suffering from a disorder of the mind that seriously impairs his ability to function properly in society and that requires medical treatment or makes care, supervision, and control of the person necessary for his protection or welfare or the protection of others.[31] The term "medical treatment" is not restricted to medication and therapy but includes psychiatric nursing care where a patient has been involuntarily admitted to a mental facility and psychiatric or other evidence shows that, by reason of his paranoid tendencies, he neglects his person and health and is unable because of his personality to care for himself or to retain housing outside of a mental health facility and that he requires psychiatric nursing for his welfare. The burden of showing that he should be detained in a mental health facility was satisfied. As a result, Mr. Robinson remained in the hospital. If suitable housing in a supervised group home had been available in the community, the court may have found this setting to be the least restrictive setting that would serve the needs of the public and the patient.

GROUP HOMES

A problem for mental health workers in many jurisdictions across Canada is that of finding adequate housing for patients able to be discharged from mental hospitals. Group homes exist in some municipalities but community suspicion and fear have prevented homes from being established in many neighbourhoods. Group homes capable of housing small groups, 6 to 12 persons, plus resident staff have proven to be an essential part of the trend toward deinstitutionalization in the last two decades. People needing this type of shelter include children, adolescents, and adults coming from child protection and treatment settings, mental hospitals, and correctional facilities.

These homes can provide the measured independence and sense of group sharing necessary to a plan for re-entry into mainstream society for people emerging from such institutional settings. The resistance to group homes, however, is formidable.

Positive enabling legislation can be a powerful tool in overcoming resistance so that group homes can become realities against which irrational fears can be tested. In Toronto, such assistance has been provided through an amendment to the City of Toronto Zoning Bylaws[32] which states that a residential care facility is a residence for accommodation of 6 to 10 persons, exclusive of staff, who by reasons of their emotional, mental, social or physical condition, or legal status, require a group living arrangement for their well-being and (a) such facility is supervised and the members of the group are referred by a hospital, court, or government agency, or (b) such facility is funded wholly or in part by any government other than funding provided solely for capital purposes, or (c) such facility is regulated or supervised under any general or special Act.

In addition, a residence must be at least 800 feet from any similar facility. This last stipulation is intended to prevent group homes from being established in close proximity so that the concept of neighbourhood integration will not be defeated.

Social workers can join with others in advocating a similar law in their communities which permit property to be purchased for use as group homes. These homes, however, cannot do their job without the backup of essential services and support programmes providing social, vocational, and educational opportunities for the residents.

CHILDREN IN MENTAL HEALTH FACILITIES

In the United States, the attitude towards the rights of children was brought sharply into focus by the landmark decision in *Re Gault*.[33] The United States Supreme Court in that case found that children must be entitled to the same due process guarantees as adults. In Ontario, the Child and Family Services Act[34] expressly provides safeguards to the child in a mental health treatment facility. If the child is admitted as a voluntary patient by his parents or on the recommendation of a physician, the child may apply at any time to have his hospitalization reviewed. Such a review must occur automatically six months after admission, in any event. The function of the formal review is to determine whether continued hospitalization is necessary. The review board must render a written decision directing either discharge or continued status as an informal patient in the facility.[35]

In order to admit a child under 16 as an involuntary patient to a secure treatment programme, application must be made by the child's parent, caretaker or society and must be confirmed by the court.[36] In effect, involuntary committal is a very serious matter permissible only where a child has a mental disorder and is a serious risk to himself or others and the court so finds. The court must also be satisfied that such a treatment programme will be effective to prevent harm to the child or others. In the case of a child of 16 and over, the child or a physician must consent to the application.

Children who are committed to secure mental health treatment facilities are guaranteed extensive procedural and personal rights under the Child and Family Services Act of Ontario which include rights to privacy, freedom from corporal punishment, privacy of mail, right to participate in the plan of treatment, and right to adequate meals, clothing, education and physical care.

The Children's Law Reform Act (Ontario) has established the principle of the best interests of the child as the test for all decisions involving children. It has yet to be determined whether this test will be applicable or sufficient to protect children who are placed in treatment facilities voluntarily or to provide them with treatment when their parents do not consent.

AGE OF CONSENT TO MENTAL HEALTH TREATMENT

The very question of the age of consent is a confused one in Canada. In Ontario and British Columbia, 16 years is considered to be the age at which consent can be vested in the person in regard to medical or surgical procedures. In Quebec, the age of consent is 14 years. The Conference of Commissioners on Uniformity of Legislation in Canada recommended that 16 be the age of consent.[37]

In order for consent to be valid, four crucial tests should be met.[38] The person must have the capacity to give consent; the consent must be voluntarily given; it must be informed consent; and it must be directed toward a specific act or set of acts. Landau points out that certain exceptions exist; for example, in the case of an emergency where life is endangered and where the minor is an emancipated minor, living outside the parents' home, is self-supporting, married, or in the armed forces.[39] The prevalent view in Canada seems to be that age is not a conclusive test of the capacity to give consent. It is generally believed that 15 year olds have ability to give consent, that between 11 and 14 there is varying ability with the tendency to defer to an adult, and that below the age of 11 capacity to give consent is limited. Landau recommends that all minors over 16 should have automatic right of consent, between the ages 14-16 a rebuttable presumption of capacity should be applied, and under age 14 the rebuttable presumption should be that the child is not fully competent to give consent, but must be consulted and provided with an independent representative. Under the Child and Family Services Act, a child over 16 need not consent to any treatment.[40]

Among the recommendations acted on by the Government of Ontario in response to the omnibus legislation contained in the Child and Family Services Act, was the suggestion that the province establish an Office of Child Advocacy and a network of lay advocates. In effect this has resulted in the establishment of an advocacy office for children's services and a special chilren's ombudsman.[41]

CONTRACEPTION IN REGARD TO MINORS

The dilemma facing health professionals when a minor seeks contraceptive counselling is not resolved by Canadian case law. It would seem that the central issue is concerned with the consensual capacity of the child, in other words, whether there is informed consent. This suggests that the minor must be able to understand the nature and consequences of the request. Recent authoritative writing suggests that there is no rule in tort law linking the capacity to provide consent to the age of majority. Although some authorities say that the situation is akin to contract law which excludes minors, the general rule in Canada holds that informed consent is all that is required and that a health professional will not be liable in tort law for providing information about contraceptives if informed consent exists.[42] There is no public policy against advertising, selling, or counselling contraception. It is now possible for a child of 16 years or more to consent to be treated for venereal disease without the approval of a parent or guardian.[43]

MENTALLY IMPAIRED ELDERLY

Where elderly persons are mentally impaired, three serious problems may arise which have legal implications. The person may have lost the capacity to manage assets properly, and may either use money in irrational ways or insist that there is no money for basic needs when adequate funds do exist. Secondly, the person may no longer be able to manage at home or may become unmanageable to the family caregivers and may need permanent placement in a nursing home. In addition, the person needing help at this stage may not be able to obtain it as quickly as desired, which can create much stress for family members who may disagree over who should be vested with legal responsibility for decisions and asset management.

These legal issues often carry much emotional baggage as adult children are faced with parental aging and incapacity and their own guilt and fears. Life transitions are usually destabilizing times where old and familiar coping patterns are no longer effective and new ones must be painfully developed. This natural process is often exacerbated when an older person undergoes a marked personality change, possibly due to Alzheimer's disease so that a spousal caregiver is suddenly the target of rage and physical violence. Legal advice is often helpful to family members in assisting them to make decisions through gaining an understanding of the law as it pertains to the elderly, legal procedures, and their own rights and responsibilities.

When adult children face the prospect of providing long-term care and the possibility of nursing home or institutional placement, they should ensure (to the extent possible) that the parent's affairs are in order *before* the parent becomes impaired and unable to arrange his own affairs. At the very least, parents should be urged to make sure they have a valid will, a continuing power of attorney for the management of their finances and property if they become mentally impaired, and a power of attorney for personal care so that someone close to them is authorized to make health care decisions if the parent cannot make them for himself. Although anyone can make their own wills and powers of attorney, legal advice is recommended. Social workers should always advise their clients that in the absence of valid powers of attorney for property and personal care, the Public Guardian and Trustee is authorized to assume control of the impaired person's assets and care.

Endnotes

1. Wexler, D.B. and Winick, B.J. (eds.), 1991, *Essays in Therapeutic Jurisprudence*, Durham, N.C.: Carolina Academic Press.
2. Sales, Bruce D. and Shuman, Daniel W. "Mental Health Law and Mental Health Care: Introduction", *American Journal of Orthopsychiatry*, 64(2), April, 1994, p. 177.
3. Wexler, D.B. and Winick, B.J. (eds.), 1991, *Essays in Therapeutic Jurisprudence*, Durham, N.C.: Carolina Academic Press, 17.
4. Kittrie, N. (1971) *The Right to be Different: Deviance and Enforced Therapy*, Baltimore, Md.: Johns Hopkins University Press, cited, in Perlin, Michael L., "Law and the Delivery of Mental Health Services in the Community", *American Journal of Orthopsychiatry*, 64(2), April, 1994.
5. 1992, S.O. 1996, c. 2, Schedule A as amended.
6. 1996, S O. 1996, c. 2, Schedule A, s. 32.
7. Substitute Decisions Act, S.O. 1992, c. S-30, s. 1.
8. S. 34(3).
9. Health Care Consent Act, 1996, S.O. 1996, c. 2, Schedule A, s. 32.
10. 1992, s. 66 at 12.
11. Part 1, s. 4, c. 6.
12. R.S.O. 1990, c. M.7. See also Table of Concordance.
13. *Ibid.*, s. 9(1).
14. *Ibid.*, s. 14(2).
15. *Ibid.*, s. 14(4).
16. *Ibid.*, s. 14(6).
17. *Ibid.*, s. 15(1).
18. *Ibid.*, s. 19.
19. *Ibid.*, s. 20(1) and (2).
20. *Ibid.*, s. 20(3).

21. *Ibid.*, s. 30(2).
22. *Ibid.*, s. 31.
23. *Ibid.*, s. 32(2) and (3).
24. *Ibid.*, s. 33(1).
25. Criminal Code, s. 672.54.
26. (1995), 40 C.R. (4th) 43 (Ont. Gen. Div.), reversed on appeal [1997] O.J. No. 4016.
27. *Robinson v. Hislop* (1980), 24 B.C.L.R. 80, 114 D.L.R. (3d) 620 (S.C.).
28. *Ibid.*, at 93.
29. *Ibid.*, at 95.
30. *Ibid.*, at 94.
31. Mental Health Act, R.S.B.C. 1979, c. 256, s. 1.
32. Amendments to 20623 — Amendments 333-335-78, sec. 112B and C.
33. (1967), 387 U.S. 1, 87 Sup. Ct. 1428.
34. R.S.O. 1990, c. C.11. This Act sets out procedures for the admission of mentally disturbed children to secure treatment facilities and regulates the use of secure isolation, intrusive measures and psychotropic drugs regarding children receiving care.
35. Mental Health Act, note 12 above, s. 8(*a*).
36. Child and Family Services Act, note 34 above, s. 110.
37. B. Landau, "Barriers to Consent to Treatment: The Rights of Minors in the Provision of Mental Health Services" (1979), 2 Can. J. Fam. L. 245.
38. *Ibid.*, at 256.
39. *Ibid.*, at 257.
40. *Ibid.*, at 264-5.
41. "Response to the Children's Act: A Consultation Paper." Justice for Children, June 1983 at 30. See note 34 above, ss. 105 and 106.
42. M. G. McLeod, "Birth Control: The Minor and the Physician." (1980), 5 Queen's L.J. 269.
43. W. G. W. White, "A Comparison of Some Parental and Guardian Rights." (1980), 3 Can. J. Fam. L. 219.

Bibliography

Advocacy in Psychiatric Hospitals: Evaluation of the Psychiatric Patient Advocate Office. Centre for Research and Education in Human Services (Toronto: Ontario Ministry of Health, 1987).

Bourque, Paul C. "Mental Disorders Amendments in the Criminal Code". Health Law Canada, Vol. 14, No. 4, 1994, 108-114.

Brissenden, R. Bernadette. "On Adolescence and Informed Consent". (1994) 14 Health Law Canada at 68-73.

Caulfied, Timothy. "Suing Hospitals, Health Authorities and the Government for Health Care Allocation Decisions". Health Law Review, Vol. 3, No. 1 (Spring, 1994), 7-11.

Cavill, Mary. "Aging and the Law: What Does this Mean to You?" (Nov. 1993) 18 L. Now 3, 6-9.

Chernin, Susan, Joan Jenkinson, Taivi Loba. 1995 revisions: Judith Wahl, "Every Resident: Bill of Rights for People Who Live in Ontario Long-Term Care Facilities." 2nd ed. rev. (Toronto: Advocacy Centre for the Elderly; Community Legal Education, Ontario, 1995).

Glass, Kathleen Cranley. "Informed Decision-Making and Vulnerable Persons: Meeting the Needs of the Competent Elderly Patient or Research Subject". *Queen's Law Journal*, Vol. 18, No. 1, Spring, 1993.

Hislop, M.W. "Guardianship and Mental Health Legislation: Interface Issues and Options". (1988/89) *Health Law in Can.* at 39-41.

Hoffman, Brian F. "Competency to Consent to Psychiatric Treatment". (1987/88) *Health Law in Can.* at 100-101.

Kaufman, Miriam. "The Impact of the Ontario Consent to Treatment Act (B.11 109) on Adolescent Health Care". Health Law Canada, Vol. 15, No. 2 (1994) 31-32.

Silberfield, Michel, and Arthur Fish. *When the Mind Fails: A Guide to Dealing With Incompetency* (Toronto: University of Toronto Press, 1994).

Solomon, Phyllis and Jeffrey Draine. "Issues in Serving the Forensic Client", *Social Work*, Vol. 40, No. 1, January, 1995, 25-33.

Ticoll, Ellen. "The Comfort of My Old Age: Must Children Support Their Parents?" (Dec. 1993) 18 L. Now No. 4, 22-24.

16

Financial Safety Nets and Social Assistance Review

GENERAL WELFARE ASSISTANCE ACT

In Ontario, the financial safety net includes the Canada Pension or the Quebec Pension,[1] Old Age Security, Ontario Guaranteed Annual Income, General Welfare Assistance,[2] and Family Benefits.[3]

A person in need of assistance by welfare is defined as someone who is unable to obtain employment, or receives insufficient income from employment, is head of a family where the spouse is absent, lacks a parent for support and maintenance, has a disability, or has reached old age. An unemployable person is defined as a person whom a physician has certified is unable to engage in remunerative employment because of physical or mental disability.

Those entitled to receive family benefits include persons 65 years and over who are not eligible for a pension under the Old Age Security Act (Canada), a woman who is 60 and is a widow or unmarried, a woman whose husband is a patient in a mental hospital or chronic care facility or a nursing home, or in a Home for the Aged, or in prison, or a woman whose husband has deserted her for three months or more and whose whereabouts are unknown, a woman who has divorced and not remarried, or is separated for a continuous period of five years or more, a person who is 18 years or more and is blind or otherwise disabled, a sole mother with a dependent child, or a dependent father with a child, or a foster parent with a foster child.

Social welfare agencies exercise considerable discretion in making decisions about the allocation of resources, both monetary and service. There is need, therefore, to monitor discretionary interpretation of general guidelines, rules, and regulations. Discretion has been defined as the power to make a decision that cannot be determined to be right or wrong in any objective way.[4] It creates rights and privileges upon which there are said to be four restrictions on its use. They are: that the discretionary power be exercised in good faith; that it be uninfluenced by irrelevant considerations or motives; that it be exercised reasonably; and that it be exercised within the statutory bounds of the discretion.[5]

The day to day decisions that administrators must make is an area of interest for both social workers and lawyers. Davis points out that more justice is administered outside courts and that injustice occurs "when officers who are not judges exercise unreviewed discretionary powers".[6] Discretion, however, can and should be controlled. Arthurs has argued that rather than more judicial review of administrative decisions, there should be clear statements of legislative purpose, more open participation, more careful training of administrative decision-makers, clearer systems of internal appeal and external and politically accountable authorities.[7]

Davis believes that discretion can be controlled by limitation, structuring and checking. Limiting puts boundaries on discretion by tightening up statutes, regulations and rules. Structuring relates to how power is exercised. It should be open in all aspects, proceedings should be fair though informal and arbitrariness avoided. The third method, checking, places a fetter on discretion through the option of appeal. The client must be informed of the existence of an appeal process and the steps which must be taken to initiate and follow through with an appeal.

In a discussion of decision-making by welfare tribunals, Mossman suggests that the Social Assistance Review Board has a difficult job because:

> The substance of correct decisions in the welfare context depends on the interaction of law and discretion. Welfare statutes frequently set out only general guidelines for determining eligibility, leaving a myriad of details to administrators through regulations or departmental policy manuals.[8]

She adds that terms such as "deserted wife" or "not living with a man on a *bona fide* domestic basis" need defining so guidelines are established which then must be subject to review. That review body then has three choices open to it, namely, to ensure that both the law and guidelines have been observed, or to use its discretion in the weighing of these two facts, or to attend only to the legislation by asking if the legislative purpose has been met or affected by the decision. In the latter instance, departmental guidelines can be considered but they are not the sole determining factor.[9] For example, one might feel that the legislation clearly established a right to welfare, but the departmental guidelines may have restricted the intent. Regulations, if strictly applied, can have the effect of subverting the intention of the legislation, which is to provide emergency and short-term income maintenance to persons with no means of support. A situation formerly familiar to every social worker is the guideline which prevents payment of welfare assistance to an applicant with no fixed address. This is no longer true in Ontario. No person can be refused assistance solely because he or she does not have a permanent address.[10]

Social Assistance Review

Anyone having waited for justice to be dispensed through the courts will understand why alternative forms of adjudication have proliferated in recent years through the establishment of administrative tribunals, appeal boards and a variety of regulatory bodies. It can be argued that administrative law is public law. Unlike private law which generally involves a dispute between two individuals over rights, in public law the conflict more often is between the right of the individual and the public interest.

As a general rule, the courts will only review administrative decisions if it can be shown that there were gross violations of natural justice based on the notion of the duty of a tribunal to act fairly. Under some circumstances, restrictive clauses can exclude judicial review, which generally means there can be no recourse to the courts to substitute the court's opinion for that of the body that made the ruling. Such restrictive clauses state that the Statutory Powers Procedure Act does not apply to proceedings of a welfare administrator under this section of the Act. However, if it can be demonstrated that there was a serious procedural error or that the tribunal exceeded its authority or was obviously biased in its decision-making, a review by the courts may be available. Expert legal advice is required in these situations.

Social workers need to be informed concerning the procedures of specific legislation which most frequently affect clients' benefits or rights. Social workers are often in a position to advise clients about rights and procedures, about preparation for a hearing or review and in some cases may represent the client at the hearing. Though we will look at the procedures contained in Ontario legislation, readers are again advised to consult their corresponding provincial legislation for the applicable appeal procedure.

Social workers should be aware of the competing issues in any review arising from a client's entitlement to financial assistance. On one hand, having demonstrated her need, the client should be entitled to receive, and to continue to receive, assistance. On the other hand, society at large and the government of the day must be satisfied that the need is genuine and the public purse is not being defrauded. Often the procedures by which evidence is obtained about an applicant and how the hearing is conducted clearly violate the client's civil rights and may also lead to an unjust result. For example, a visit to a recipient's home to verify eligibility criteria may occur with or without notice but is restricted to what can be seen in plain view.[11] Snooping is not permitted, nor should overly zealous attempts to uncover evidence of fraud be condoned. It is in these kinds of circumstances that an informed social worker can be an appropriate advocate of a person applying for or at risk of being denied social assistance.

As a result of the community legal workers' concern in Ontario and advocates involved with clients whose appeals had been denied, a Social Assistance Review Board Standing Group was formed which has now become the Social Assistance Action Committee. This group was successful in their push for basic changes in the composition of the Board, their terms of services and procedures to be followed. There was concern that the members of the Board were not representational of the general public and were perceived as elitist, that they were part-time appointees paid a per diem for their work, and that they did not always write their own decisions so that decisions could be written by persons not actually present at the hearing. Currently, the members of the Board are full-time appointees paid a salary. They are interviewed by the Chairperson of the Board before being appointed to ascertain, in so far as possible, values and attitudes which could bias their decisions against welfare recipients. They are required to write their own decisions.

The Social Assistance Review Board (Ontario) has jurisdiction to review decisions of administrators under the Family Benefits programme (which includes Mothers' Allowance), General Welfare Assistance, Vocational Rehabilitation Services, the Ontario Guaranteed Annual Income programme, and Co-payment for Chronic Care Services under the Health Insurance Act. The purpose of the board is "to provide, on appeal by an applicant or recipient, an objective review of an administrator's decision to deny, suspend, cancel or reduce assistance, or where there is dissatisfaction with the amount of assistance granted".[12]

The hearing may be requested by filling out the appropriate forms within 30 days of receiving the Director's decision. The hearings are held in the applicant's local community and at times in the applicant's home. They are closed to the press and general public and are conducted in an informal manner, although it is possible to request an appeal on the record and to submit a written appeal. The applicant may be represented by counsel or an agent, may bring an interpreter if a language other than English or French is spoken, and may call witnesses, present submissions and cross-examine witnesses.

After hearing the applicant and reviewing the decision being appealed, the board may affirm the decision, rescind the decision and order the Director to make another decision, or refer the matter back for reconsideration.

The board is expected to give its decision in writing and to give the reasons for its decision. The applicant who feels the board's decision is in error may ask for a reconsideration within 30 days of the date on which the decision is received. This is done by completing the proper form. There may be a further appeal to the Divisional Court (Ontario) on a question that is not a question of fact alone. Notice of such an appeal must be made within 15 days of receiving the board's decision. This requires legal advice. In special circumstances, applicants may get temporary financial assistance while waiting for a hearing, but only if the board is convinced that hardship would result without assistance.[13] There is strong opinion that benefits should remain in force until the hearing is held.[14]

In Ontario, regulations which became effective in 1995, stated that all live-in partners of the opposite sex were considered a spouse with support obligations. A Charter challenge was launched by four recipients of family benefits who had been disqualified because of this regulation. The regulations prior to 1995 had stated that determination of whether a person of the opposite sex residing continuously with a recipient for three or more years is considered a spouse would not be determined by sexual factors. If the recipient supplied evidence that the economic, social, and familial aspects of the relationship did not amount to cohabitation, the person would not be considered a spouse. The court, in replying to the challenge to the new definition stating that all partners of the opposite sex *were* spouses with support obligations, upheld the legality of this definition. There was a dissenting opinion, in which Mr. Justice Rosenberg stated that the amended "spouse in the house" rules should be declared unconstitutional because they violated the Charter guarantee of freedom from discrimination of sole support parents and their children.[15]

The dilemma for many social workers is the situation of the single woman receiving assistance who is suspected of having a man living with her in her home. Does the protection of the public purse demand that a woman on welfare be deprived of companionship and sexual relationships and must a man involved on this basis be assumed to be shirking his responsibility to support the woman and her children? There are several other interesting cases dealing with this issue. In the case that follows, the issue is neatly avoided by the circumstances of the appeal.

The applicant, an unmarried woman with dependent children, had her family benefits terminated for allegedly cohabiting with a male person contrary to the Family Benefits Act (Nova Scotia). The decision to terminate was affirmed by the Appeal Board. The Director's appeal report failed to disclose either the name of the man or the period of cohabitation in question, with the result that the applicant first received this information at the appeal hearing itself. She applied for *certiorari* to quash the decision of the Appeal Board on the ground that she had been denied natural justice. Failure to inform the applicant of the man's name and the period of cohabitation amounted to a denial of natural justice because the applicant was not given sufficient information on which to base her case. The Nova Scotia Supreme Court, Trial Division, allowed the application and ruled that a new board should hear the appeal.[16] Another case in Nova Scotia involved a fraud prosecution of a sole support parent for living with an undisclosed spouse. A successful argument held that the oppressive stereotyping of women was a violation of the equality clause, s. 15 of the Charter. The decision was not appealed.[17]

Two other cases deal with this question of a woman living with another person. In one, a woman was receiving Family Benefits and living with a man as his housekeeper. The court held that the woman was not disentitled to receive welfare assistance because she had not ceased to live as a single person.[18] The second case involved an appeal to the court from the Board of Review which had found that the woman was living as the wife of the man with whom she was residing and therefore was not entitled to Family Benefits as a permanently unemployed person. The court found that she was not a spouse on the grounds that the woman was living in his home as a boarder who paid no rent and that the man with whom she lived had assumed no financial responsibility for her and was therefore not to be considered a spouse. The case turned on a narrow interpretation of spouse by looking only at economic arrangements.[19]

Another case that should be noted dealt with an appeal from a Review Board decision that the appellant was not entitled to general welfare benefits as a person in need due to his inability to obtain regular employment. In determining whether a person in need is eligible for benefits under the General Welfare Assistance Act,[20] consideration must be given to whether continuing unemployment is due to circumstances beyond the control of the applicant. The question before the court was whether a welfare administrator could look at the past record of an applicant, in this case, an applicant who had been dismissed from his previous employment for absenteeism. The court found that the important determination was whether the applicant was "a person in need" within the meaning of section 7(1) and as such entitled to assistance in accordance with the regulations if he was otherwise eligible for such assistance.[21] The essential effect of the decision is to focus determination of need for support on a person's current situation regardless of past performance so long as all other criteria for eligibility set forth in the statute are met.

It is necessary for anyone wishing to assist a client with a legal proceeding to be familiar with the procedure details embedded in all regulations. They are bureaucratic and arbitrary and frustrating, but they are very real and failure to follow the prescribed timing and the prescribed form can result in delay or even loss of the review without any consideration of its intrinsic merit. Social workers who would be advocates must have a broad view of the issues and a familiarity with the legal details.

The steps that a worker can take on behalf of a client to ensure that her rights are fully protected include the following:

1. obtain and read the relevant legislation (in Ontario, the Family Benefits Act and Regulations);
2. assist the person requesting a review of an unfavourable decision to fill out the appropriate form. If it is a first review it must be Form 1; if a subsequent review, it is Form 2;
3. be sure the request for a review is filed in the time required. This often creates difficulties because the form is not available. In that case be sure a letter is written within the appeal period, requesting both a form and an extension of the appeal time;
4. be certain that the client receives written notice of the review hearing at least four days before the hearing;
5. the notice of the hearing must be accompanied by the evidence or names of witnesses on which the Director intends to rely. If not, the worker should immediately advise the Board and request an adjournment, since the client is always entitled to know the case to be met;
6. the client is entitled to be "assisted" by legal counsel or an agent, who cannot capriciously or arbitrarily be asked to withdraw by the chairperson;
7. help the client to marshal her evidence and witnesses (if any) to rebut the allegations made by the Director;
8. at the hearing itself, the client or her lawyer or agent may wish to question the Director's witnesses. Prepare the questions in advance and be sure they are related to the Director's evidence;
9. review the materials with a lawyer before the hearing if at all possible; legal consultation may be available at local community legal clinics;
10. if the decision is unfavourable, be aware of the client's entitlement to a further review if the facts of the case warrant.

While the foregoing is certainly not a complete guide, a worker who is well prepared and has access to legal advice and consultation can be of considerable practical assistance at a review hearing.

In Ontario, the Social Assistance Reform Act has been introduced, which proposes to create two separate statutes: the Ontario Works Act and the Ontario Disability Support Program. This first Act will introduce workfare, to be administered by the municipalities, which will require the mandatory participation in work programs of sole support parents with children in school, with assistance provided for child care expenses. If the legislation is passed, the two Acts will replace the General Welfare Assistance Act, the Family Benefits Act, and the Vocational Rehabilitation Act.[22] These Acts will alter the political intent and eligibility criteria for social assistance in Ontario. The practical effect will be to increase the burden on those who require social assistance.

Holes in Our Safety Nets

A last word in this section on financial safety nets concerns some thoughts on society's attitude towards welfare assistance. We are becoming more polarized toward rich and poor with more people dropping toward the lower end of the scale. A book, based on in depth interviews with 214 welfare mothers living in Camden, New Jersey, reports that all but one had an unreported income and still could barely get by each month. The researchers' conclusion is that "the poor simply can't survive on welfare alone". They found that eight in ten women had severe housing problems, one in six had recently been homeless, one-third ran out of food at least once in the previous year.

Conditions were not improved for those who held an entry-level job, in fact, they found that conditions were sometimes worse for the women who held entry-level jobs. These women needed more clothing, child care and transportation. Those who did make it to an improved situation had "relative" privilege, that is, they had family or a close friend to babysit or help with care bills.[23]

Whether sociologists interviewing sole support mothers on welfare in Canada would make similar findings is not known but is quite probable. It may be that the dismantling of the welfare system across Canada and the United States is a short term effort to decrease the deficit and reward taxpayers, but at a human cost of degrading and relentless poverty for too many women and children. It may be that the way to break the cycle of welfare dependency cannot be found by decreasing benefits and relentlessly searching out fraud or demanding entry level work for welfare. We may need to maintain a real safety net that does not jeopardize the development of children whose daily needs for nuture cannot wait.

Endnotes

1. R.R.O. 1990, Reg. 537, s. 2.
2. R.S.O. 1990, c. G.6.
3. R.S.O. 1990, c. F.2.
4. J.H. Grey, "Discretion in Administrative Law" (1979), 17 Osgoode Hall L.J. 107.
5. *Ibid.*, at 114.
6. K.C. Davis, *Discretionary Justice in Europe and America* (Chicago: University of Illinois Press, 1976) at 3.
7. H.W. Arthurs, "Rethinking Administrative Law: A Slightly Dicey Business" (1979), 17 Osgoode Hall L.J. 1.
8. M.J. Mossman, "Decision-Making by Welfare Tribunals: The Australian Experience" (1979), 29 U.T.L.J. 218 at 228.
9. *Ibid.*, at 230.
10. General Welfare Assistance Act, R.S.O. 1990, s. 1(8).
11. General Welfare Assistance Act, R.S.O. 1990, s. 7 (10), (12)
12. Twelfth Annual Report — Social Assistance Review Board, 1980-81 at 1.
13. Family Benefits Act, R.S.O. 1990, c. F.2.
14. Parkdale Community Legal Services, in Metropolitan Toronto, listed the following recommendations, among others, in Social Assistance Review Board (SARB) Study Group, "The Social Assistance Review Board in Ontario: A Critical Analysis and Proposed Changes." Autumn, 1981.
    1. Benefits should remain in force until the hearing is held and decision rendered.
    2. Board members should be trained for their jobs.
    3. Applicants should be fully informed of their right to be represented at a hearing.
    4. Applicants should have powers to subpoena witnesses and evidence.
    5. Decisions should be clearly stated and reasons given.
    6. The hearings should be recorded.
15. *Globe and Mail*, October 30, 1996.
16. *R. v. Rehberg* (1993), 127 N.S.R. (2d) 331 (N.S. T.D.).
17. *Smith v. Fam. Benefits App. Bd.* (1980), 42 N.S.R. (2d) 200, 77 A.P.R. 200 (T.D.). See also *Re Ellis and Min. of Community & Social Services* (1980), 28 O.R. (2d) 385, 110 D.L.R. (3d) 414 (C.A.).
18. *Warwick v. Min. of Community & Social Services* (1978), 21 O.R. (2d) 528, 5 R.F.L. (2d) 325, 91 D.L.R. (2d) 131 (C.A.).
19. *Re Proc and Min. of Community & Social Services* (1974), 6 O.R. (2d)

624, 19 R.F.L. 82, 53 D.L.R. (2d) 512. Affirmed without written reasons 6 O.R. (2d) 624n, 53 D.L.R. (3d) 512n (C.A.).

20. R.S.O. 1980, c. 188.
21. *Re Brown and Social Assistance Review Bd.* (1978), 18 O.R. (2d) 405, 83 D.L.R. (3d) 95 (Div. Ct.).
22. *Community Action*, July 14, 1997.
23. DeParle, Jason. "Learning Poverty Firsthand", *New York Times Magazine*, April 27, 1997. The book, *Making Ends Meet*, Katheryn Edin and Laura Lein, will be published by Russell Sage Foundation, May, 1997.

Bibliography

Carruthers, Errlee. "Prosecuting Women for Welfare Fraud in Ontario: Implications for Equality" (Fall, 1995) 11 *Journal of Law and Social Policy*, 241-262.

Doyle, Robert and Livy Visano. "Equality and Multiculturalism: Access to Community Services." (1988) 3 *Journal of Law and Social Policy*, 21-35.

Ellsworth, Randall, et. al. "Poverty Law in Ontario: the Year in Review", (Fall, 1993) 9 *Journal of Law and Social Policy*, 1-61.

Jackman, Martha. "Poor Rights: Using the Charter to Support Social Welfare Claims", (Fall, 1993) 19 *Queen's Law Journal*, 65-94.

Turner, Joanne C. and J. Francis. *Canadian Social Welfare*, ed. 3rd ed. (Scarborough, Ontario: Alleyn and Bacon, Canada, 1995).

PART III

CHILDREN AND THE LAW

17

Rethinking Child Welfare Issues

The basic premise of this third edition is that the life cycle of the family is the arena in which law and social work meet most naturally. The cycle can be entered at any point, but childhood and adolescence have been accorded special interest, particularly in this century. The intense focus on childhood derives from the development of psychology as a social science coupled with the notion that children have rights as individuals. Psychology asserted that early childhood experiences influence the behaviour of the adult, and that adverse experience, physical or emotional deprivation or abuse can limit or impede the child's present and future functioning in every sphere. Since such serious consequences, both personal and public, can flow from noxious early rearing, the idea developed that the state had a vested interest in protecting children from parents or caregivers whose behaviour might be dangerous to a child's well-being. This is a significant development but it is still limited and narrow in scope. The legislation expressing the state's concern for protecting children is reactive in that it is designed to intervene when a breakdown in the standard or quality of care can be demonstrated. What is lacking is a proactive policy that would address the basic needs of child rearing, freedom from poverty, adequate nutrition, accessible day care where one or both parents work, safe shelter, and supportive community services. Children need nurturing parents, and our child welfare legislation falls short of providing the supports needed by many parents. Until society demands social policy that provides basic resources, we are still deficient in our commitment to child protection and welfare.

Prior to this century, children, if they were given special consideration at all, were viewed as chattels to be used as parents saw fit until they reached the legal age of majority. Children are now seen as having rights independent of their parents and parents are charged, by law, with specific responsibilities toward their children.

In Ontario, most child welfare matters are encompassed by two pieces of legislation, the Child and Family Services Act[1] and the Children's Law Reform Act.[2] The first Act has caused enormous controversy within both the legal and human service professions. The controversy centres upon the intent and consequences of child welfare policy and the extent to which the state or its agents are authorized to intervene in family life. In dispute are the respective roles of lawyers as protectors of children's rights, and social service professionals as protectors of the physical and social well-being of the children at risk. Also at issue are the rights of parents to make decisions involving their children, such as voluntary placement in a treatment facility and the right of a child to informed consent, and the conditions of third-party review of treatment and placement decisions.

British Columbia has recently enacted the Child, Family and Community Service Act. This legislation incorporates two new mechanisms for planning; mediation and the family conference. The family conference includes the immediate family group, extended kin, and carefully selected members of the family's social support network. This model was originally developed in New Zealand and was incorporated into legislation in B.C. Newfoundland has also evaluated a two year pilot of the model.

When children are found to be in need of protection, they can be referred by a society social worker to a conference coordinator who organizes a conference. The conference is generally divided into three stages. In the first stage, non-family members present relevant information, and can elicit expert knowledge, to assist the family in making plans. In the second and most lengthy stage, the family is left to deliberate in private. Usually only family members meet at this time, thus ensuring that the plan of care that emerges is "owned" by the family. In so far as possible, all information produced in the conference is confidential, though any new information that indicates a need for protection of the child must be reported to the Ministry. In the final stage, the coordinator is presented with the proposed plan which is then discussed and a concensus of approval from the family and social worker is reached. The social worker can only veto a plan which is clearly not in the best interest of the child; that is, the child would remain at risk. Studies of the process from other jurisdictions have found that agreement is reached in over 90% of such conferences. The court process remains available when it fails.[3]

This model mediates family autonomy with the legal systems of the child welfare agency and the court. The effectiveness of the conference model is determined by how well all parties are willing to work collaboratively. In addition relevant services and resources must be available to assist the family. Finally, the family conference has been found to be effective in curtailing family violence.

We seem to be struggling to find a balance between the guarantees of fairness in proceedings involving children and parents and the right of children to adequate care, protection and, in some cases, treatment, which are generally considered to be necessary to healthy growth and development. It should be self-evident that both legal rights and physical and emotional protection are necessary, but no one yet knows which aspect should be given greater importance. For example, where a child is neglected, abandoned, or abused it seems obvious that someone should intervene to protect the child from harm. But, from a legal perspective, what do "neglect" and "abandonment" and "abuse" mean? When is intervention justified and who shall decide — parent, child, mental health professional, or the court?

In Chapter 12, we discussed what can happen to children involved in custody and access disputes resulting from the dissolution of the marriage. In Chapter 18, we consider those aspects of law concerned primarily with the welfare of children when they appear to require protection from their parents, caregivers, or sometimes from themselves.

CHILDREN'S LAW REFORM

Incredible as it may seem, a statute which grants equal legal status to all children and demands that their best interests be given primary importance in all matters affecting them was only enacted in the past twenty years. The Children's Law Reform Act (Ontario)[4] was enacted in two parts, 1978 and 1982, coming into full force and effect in the fall of 1982. Primarily, it abolishes for all purposes any legal distinction between children born inside and those born outside marriage.[5] A child is presumed in law to be the child of both parents, and the child has status as their child, independent of their marital status.[6] Both parents are equally entitled to custody, care and control of the child, and both are equally responsible for the child's support and education.[7]

A second aspect, which is an important development, stipulates that this Act applies in all circumstances where the welfare or entitlement of children is at issue. For example, notice provisions under the Child and Family Services Act are now governed by the expanded definition of "parent" in the C.L.R.A., and the children born outside of marriage are equally entitled to inherit from a natural parent.[8] Consequently, all legal matters which might affect children must be considered in light of the provisions of the Children's Law Reform Act.

Since the rights and protection of children are central to this Act, an expanded definition of "best interests" is included, which contains emotional and non-tangible considerations such as love and affection, emotional ties with other family members, familiarity of surroundings and the child's own preferences. All matters affecting children must be determined by the courts in accordance with this definition.

BEST INTERESTS OF THE CHILD

The overriding concern of judges in courts across Canada is directed toward finding what would serve the best interests of the child. This principle, which now guides all decisions involving children, has replaced the conflicting traditional assumptions that fathers had unquestioned right of control over their children or that all children of tender years always belonged with their mothers. The best interests standard, however, is difficult to define. Katherine Catton has observed that unfettered discretion leads to individual judgments and that the best interests of the child is no test at all.[9]

Compare the definition of "best interest of the child" as stated in the Child and Family Services Act with the Children's Law Reform Act. The Child and Family Services Act requires consideration of all factors in the light of individual circumstances, including:

> 37.(3) Where a person is directed in this Part to make an order or determination in the best interests of a child, the person shall take into consideration those of the following circumstances of the case that he or she considers relevant:
>
> 1. The child's physical, mental and emotional needs, and the appropriate care or treatment to meet those needs.
> 2. The child's physical, mental and emotional level of development.
> 3. The child's cultural background.
> 4. The religious faith, if any, in which the child is being raised.
> 5. The importance for the child's development of a positive relationship with a parent and a secure place as a member of a family.
> 6. The child's relationships by blood or through an adoption order.
> 7. The importance of continuity in the child's care and the possible effect on the child of disruption of that continuity.
> 8. The merits of a plan for the child's care proposed by a society, including a proposal that the child be placed for adoption or adopted, compared with the merits of the child remaining with or returning to a parent.
> 9. The child's views and wishes, if they can be reasonably ascertained.
> 10. The effects on the child of delay in the disposition of the case.

11. The risk that the child may suffer harm through being removed from, kept away from, returned to or allowed to remain in the care of a parent.
12. The degree of risk, if any, that justified the finding that the child is in need of protection.
13. Any other relevant circumstance.

(4) Where a person is directed in this Part to make an order or determination in the best interests of a child and the child is an Indian or native person, the person shall take into consideration the importance, in recognition of the uniqueness of Indian and native culture, heritage and traditions, of preserving the child's cultural identity.[10]

However, it should be noted that the "best interests" definition in the Child and Family Services Act becomes applicable only after a child has been found by the court to be in need of protection, or whose placement or supervision by the C.A.S. is being reviewed by the court under the Act.

In contrast, the Children's Law Reform Act says that the court shall consider all the circumstances of the child including:

1. love, affection, and emotional ties between the child and all persons claiming custody or access to the child, other members of the family who live with the child or persons involved with the care of the child;
2. the views and preferences of the child where they can be ascertained;
3. how long the child has lived in a stable home environment;
4. the capacity of persons wanting custody to provide guidance, education, the necessaries of life and any special needs of the child;
5. any proposed plans for the care and upbringing of the child;
6. the permanence and stability as a family unit of any proposed custodial home;
7. the relationship by blood or adoption between the child and parties to the application.[11]

The "best interests" test in the Children's Law Reform Act has much broader application and applies in all circumstances under provincial jurisdiction where the legal interests of children may be affected. Words such as love, affection, and emotional ties, uncommon to legislative drafting, charge the court with the responsibility to consider the emotional as well as the physical needs of the child.[12]

The "best interests" test is the standard guide for child welfare decisions in every province. The overriding importance of the "best interests" doctrine is demonstrated by the following case.[13]

The Supreme Court of Canada considered the nature and permissible extent of state intervention in the case before them. It involved a child of Jehovah's Witness parents who was apprehended by the Children's Aid Society in order to receive a blood transfusion which was deemed necessary by a pediatrician. Since the parents' religion forbade blood transfusions, they objected on two grounds: freedom of religion guaranteed by s. 2(a) of the Charter and their right to raise their children as they saw fit, a protected liberty interest under s. 7 of the Charter.[14] A majority of the Supreme Court found that the Child and Family Services Act in giving the Society the right to intervene in these circumstances, was a reasonable limit on parental authority. While the right to raise one's children is a liberty interest by s. 7 of the Charter, the state has the right to intervene to protect the child when parental conduct falls below a standard seen as acceptable by the community.

Another case illustrates that best interests are specific to the individual child, so that dispositions within the same case may vary greatly in relation to the characteristics of the child and the parents. The Society applied for Crown Wardship with no access for the natural mother to two children. The mother was 15 when the youngest child was born and both children were apprehended. The court made an order for Crown Wardship for one child because he had a limited attention span and aggressive behaviour and the court said that he could not be adequately protected in his natural home as could the other child who was returned under a supervision order.[15]

In another case, the Catholic Children's Aid Society removed three native Indian children from their parent's home and placed them with foster families. At a subsequent status review hearing, the Society sought Crown wardship. The Trial Judge believed that the children would be best served by sending them to the reserve because of their native status. The Society appealed requesting Crown wardship. The appeal was dismissed because, although the Trial Judge had erred in ruling that the Child and Family Services Act makes a Crown wardship order more difficult to obtain for native children, there was no doubt that the judge had considered the best interests of the children in his finding that they be placed on the reserve. The Act states that native status must be considered but is not the sole determinant.[16]

The best interests principle is a broad concept which reflects the paramount importance of the child. The determination of what constitutes the best interests of a specific child is still a difficult task. Other disciplines have looked at the concept from a fresh perspective. In their book, *Beyond the Best Interests of the Child*, Goldstein, Solnit, and Freud suggest that the court should consider the least detrimental of the possible resolutions available to it. They say:

> Whether the problem arises in separation, divorce, adoption, neglecting parent, foster care, or even juvenile delinquency proceedings, the overall guide-

> line for decision which we propose is to select "that placement which is the least detrimental among available alternatives for the child." To use "detrimental" rather than "best interest" should enable legislatures, courts, and child care agencies to acknowledge and respond to the inherent detriments in any procedure for child placement as well as in each child placement decision itself. It should serve to remind decision makers that their task is to salvage as much as possible out of an unsatisfactory situation. It should reduce the likelihood of their becoming enmeshed in the hope and magic associated with "best", which often mistakenly leads them into believing that they have greater power for doing "good" than "bad" .[17]

In their subsequent book, these authors express concern for the current trend toward a legalistic approach in the matter of child welfare and protection. They believe the delays which often accompany legal proceedings work against the child's best interests which must be provided by a consistent and continuing caregiver.[18] They propose a concept of the "psychological parent", who is the one who provides the day-to-day care, affection, and stimulation for a child. They argue that this person is more important to the child's sense of well-being than is an absent or inadequate biological parent and that the bonding of the child to caregiver occurs with the psychological parent. They add that "an absent biological parent will remain, or tend to become, a stranger." A psychological parent is one who "on a continuing basis, through interaction, companionship, interplay, and mutuality, fulfills the child's psychological needs for a parent, as well as the child's physical needs."[19] This view has created controversy among those concerned with child welfare. It would seem to imply that emotional stability is only possible with one consistent caregiver and that this stability might be threatened by contact with a non-custodial parent. This concept runs counter to the current notion that children benefit from continued contact with natural parents either through joint custody or visits with parents while living with foster parents or adoptive parents in the case of older children.[20] It also denies the changing developmental needs of children where desired contacts with estranged parents at a later stage of development are difficult to establish after prolonged separation.

Another concern with the thesis of Goldstein, Solnit and Freud is that it assumes the primacy of the value of the autonomy of the family with the role of the state being the court of last resort in the cases of severe abuse or neglect. They see no legitimate role for the State as the initiator of prevention programmes that might support the family in its task.

A landmark case which dealt with the issue of the importance of the psychological parent is that of *Re Moores and Feldstein.*[21] This case involved an appeal from a decision awarding a four-year-old girl to her natural parents. The child had been living with the appellants, Mr. and

Mrs. Feldstein since she was 10 days old. The trial judge awarded the child to the mother and said, "natural parents have a right to custody which they can lose only by abandoning the child or so misconducting themselves that in the opinion of the court it would be improper that the child should be allowed to remain with them." At appeal, Dubin J. reviewed the facts of the case and held that the child's best interests would be served if she remained with the Feldsteins who had cared for her since infancy, when the natural mother, Mrs. Moores, had placed the child with the Feldsteins.

In a comment on this case, Weiler and Berman set out some guidelines for determining the best interests of the child.[22] These include physical well-being and psychological needs, which encompass affection of a reciprocal nature, stimulation, continuity of relationships, lifestyle, and stability of the home. Other factors may be important, for example, in the case of *Re Moores*, the mother put her interests over that of the child.

> Despite the valiant attempt of the Ontario Court of Appeal to make it seem otherwise, the decision in *Re Moores and Feldstein* is a departure from precedent. It is a landmark decision in Ontario not only because it extends the principle that the welfare of the child is the paramount consideration to be considered in custody disputes between parent and non-parent, but because it considers the welfare of the child apart from the wishes of the natural parent. The decision of the Court of Appeal is also remarkable because it has given effect to views respecting custody which have not hitherto been considered "legal" views. It is hoped that the decision will form the basis for a new, more realistic view of the best interests of the child by considering the effects of a resolution of a custody dispute on the child himself apart from the merits of the competing parents.[23]

The following case also upheld the principle of the best interests of the child based on the evidence presented at the hearing.[24] From a social work perspective, however, the service provided to the mother was inadequate and the power of the state vested in both social work and legal institutions, created an apparent unequal contest between parent and state. The child in question was made a Children's Aid Society ward. The Society brought a status review application to have the child made a Crown ward. On a status review hearing of the Society wardship order, the Act provides that the court must only consider the best interests of the child. The child was an adoptable child and if made a Crown ward, the Society's plan was to place him for adoption. The mother's home life was unstable, she lacked parenting skills and did not have a good relationship with the child.

The mother was 16 when the child was born and 18 years old at the time of the trial. She had had a chaotic childhood and no adequate instruction in parenting. The judge found her to be "a very likeable young lady, although somewhat naive, passive and immature". When the Society took the child on a voluntary agreement basis, the mother agreed to a psychiatric assessment and a programme of parental modelling which ran into difficulties almost from the beginning. The reasons for this included the fact that the child was placed in a foster home in a municipality some distance from the mother's home, the foster parent was not skilled in managing the modelling job and the child was thrown into confusion as he began to bond to the foster mother. The mother had problems getting to the foster home, such as lack of money for bus fare, fear of buses because she had been raped on a bus when she was younger, and confusions about the times of the visits, none of which she communicated to the Society. The modelling programme was eventually moved to the mother's home with the child brought to her and the sessions supervised by a visiting homemaker. These sessions were unsuccessful, the child was confused and upset and the mother was judged to be unaware of potential dangers to his safety. On balance, though the Society's plan was poorly conceived and not effective in spite of the mother's genuine attempts to co-operate fully, the judge had to make a decision based solely on the child's best interests and his need for consistent care. The child was made a Crown ward. It is interesting to add that the mother was about to give birth to the child of a man with whom she was living and who had established a good relationship with the mother's first child.

An appeal heard in Manitoba[25] has established a test beyond the "best interests" test. This was an appeal against a decision to give permanent custody of two children to the local authority based on the children's best interests. The appeal court held that when a child is taken into a Society's temporary custody, either under a consent order or after finding that the child is in need of protection, the court should decide the issue of a subsequent Society request for permanent wardship on something more than the interests of the children alone. This something more would be the need to satisfy the court that the child is or continues to be in need of protection. This reaffirms the principle that the onus is on the Society to make such a case against the parent.

CHILD AND FAMILY SERVICES ACT

The Child and Family Services Act[26] sets out in its Declaration of Principles that it endorses maintaining the integrity of the family unit through emphasis on minimal intervention. It sets up a series of steps which the Society must observe before removing a child from the care of parents. Even with a finding that a child is in need of protection, the court must be satisfied that its intervention is also required to protect the child, that is, the court must be satisfied that the parents are unwilling or unable to make and maintain required changes. A parent is entitled to a hearing within five days from the time a child is apprehended. Before a child can be removed from his or her caregivers, the court must be assured that less intrusive measures have been refused, have not worked, or will not likely be effective.[27]

In Part II, Voluntary Access to Services, the Child and Family Services Act makes provision for a service provider to offer counselling to a child 12 years of age or older with the child's consent, but adds that if the child is less than 16 years of age, the service provider must discuss with the child the desirability of involving the child's parent.[28] The only exclusion to the requirement of voluntary consent from a child 16 years or over in the case of residential service is where the court orders the service to be provided.[29]

These provisions can become important in a child protection hearing. If a parent is willing to seek these services voluntarily and follow through, the court should be reluctant to make a finding that a child is in need of protection which a Children's Aid Society may be seeking.[30]

Temporary care agreements state that a Society can make no temporary care agreement in respect of a child 16 years of age or older or 12 years of age or older unless the child is a party to the agreement. The exception is where the child has been found not to have the capacity to participate in an agreement based on an assessment made not more than one year before the agreement. Again, the Society must demonstrate that a less restrictive plan has been tried and proved not feasible in the circumstances. A Society may make written agreements with children of 16 and 17 who are not living with parents and have a special need.[31] These agreements are terminated when the child turns 18.[32] Part III of the Child Welfare Act is described at length in the following chapter.

Endnotes

1. R.S.O. 1990, c. C.11.
2. R.S.O. 1990, c. C.12.
3. Scheiber, Aler, "Collaborative Decision Making in Child Protection Cases", *The Social Worker*, Vol. 63(4) Winter, 1995, p. 153-56.
4. R.S.O. 1990, c. C.12.
5. *Ibid.*, s. 1(4).
6. *Ibid.*, s. 1(1).
7. *Ibid.*, s. 20.
8. *Ibid.*, s. 4.

9. K. Catton, "Children in the Courts: A Selected Empirical Review" (1978) 1 Can. J. Fam. L. 329.
10. Child and Family Services Act, note 1 above, s. 37(3).
11. Children's Law Reform Act, note 2 above, s. 24(2).
12. Child and Family Services Act, note 1 above, adopts the criteria for "best interests" of both the old Child Welfare Act and the Children's Law Reform Act, and adds these additional significant criteria to the determination of "best interests": cultural and religious background, Indian or native heritage, and the relative merits of plans proposed by a society, the effects on the child of delay in disposition, the relative risk to a child of removal from, prolonged absence from, or return to the parents, and the degree of risk, if any, that justified the finding that the child is in need of protection.
13. *Catholic Children's Aid Society (Metro. Toronto) v. M. (R.)*, 62 O.R. (2d) 535, [1988] 4 C.N.L.R. 55 (Dist. Ct.). Affirming 57 O.R. (2d) 551, [1987] 3 C.N.L.R. 39 (Fam. Ct.).
14. *B.(R.) v. Children's Aid Society of Metropolitan Toronto* (1994), 9 R.F.L. (4th) 157, [1995] 1 S.C.R. 315, 21 O.R. (3d) 479 (note), 122 D.L.R. (4th) 1, 26 C.R.R. (2d) 202, 176 N.R. 161, 7 O.A.C. 1.
15. *Children's Aid Society of Kingston (City) v. V.(T.)*, [1994] W.D.F.L. 673 (Ont. Prov. Div.). Affirmed [1995] W.D.F.L. 1330 (Ont. Gen. Div.).
16. Child and Family Services Act, s. 37(4). See also *Children's Aid Society of Sudbury and Manitoba (Districts) v. T. (W.)*, [1993] W.D.F.L. 148, for another consideration of this issue.
17. J. Goldstein, A. Freud and A. Solnit, *Beyond the Best Interests of the Child* (New York: Free Press, 1973) at 62-63.
18. J. Goldstein, A. Freud and A. Solnit, *Before the Best Interests of the Child* (New York: Free Press, 1979).
19. *Ibid.*, at 17.
20. See H.J. Folberg and Marva Graham, "Joint Custody of Children Following Divorce," in H.H. Irving, ed. *Family Law: An Interdisciplinary Perspective* (Toronto: Carswell Co., 1981), p. 71.
21. *Re Moores and Feldstein*, [1973] 3 O.R. 921, 12 R.F.L. 273, 38 D.L.R. (3d) 641 (C.A.).
22. K.M. Weiler (as she then was) and G. Berman. "Re Moores and Feldstein — A Case Comment and Discussion of Custody Principles." (1974), 12 R.F.L. 294.
23. *Ibid.*, at 304-5.
24. *Catholic Children's Aid Society v. J.* (1981), 24 R.F.L. (2d) 195 (Ont. U.F.C.).

25. *Re D.L.C. and C.W.C.; Western Man. Children's Aid Society v. D.A.C.* (1983), 34 R.F.L. (2d) 225 (Man. C.A.).
26. R.S.O. 1990, c. C.11.
27. Mang and King, p. 4.
28. C.F.S.A., s. 28.
29. C.F.S.A., s. 27(1).
30. Mang and King, pp. 34-35.
31. C.F.S.A., s. 31.
32. C.F.S.A., s. 32.

Bibliography

Bala, Nicholas. "Mental Health Professionals in Child-Related Proceedings: Understanding the Ambivalence of the Judiciary" (Mar. 1996) 13 Can. Fam. L. Quar. 261-312.

Bernd, Walter, Janine A. Isenegger, and Nicholas Bala. " "Best interests" in Child Protection Proceedings: Implications and Alternatives", (1995) 12 Can. J. Fam. L. 367-439.

Deleury, Edith and Andre Cloutier. "The Child, the Family and the State: Seeking to Identify the Best Interests of the Child" in *Matrimonial Themes in Family Law*. M. Hughes and D. Pask, eds. Toronto: Carswell, 1988.

In the Interest of Native Child Welfare Services: Recommendations from the Working Committee on Native Child Welfare. Edmonton: Alberta Social Services, 1987.

18

Child Protection

The Child and Family Services Act, Part III,[1] together with the Children's Law Reform Act,[2] set minimum standards for care of children in Ontario. Each province has enacted similar legislation designed to protect the welfare of children living within that province. We will examine the Ontario legislation, but readers should refer to the legislation in their respective provinces.[3] The Child and Family Services Act enables the province to vest its authority in its agent, the Children's Aid Society, when there is an allegation that care provided to a child has fallen below the standards prescribed by law. A Children's Aid Society is empowered to intervene in the family care of the child and, where it is deemed necessary, remove the child from his parents to a place of safety. Society's interference with the natural family is only justified when the level of care of the child falls below minimum community standards set out in the legislation. Social workers employed by Children's Aid Societies are empowered by law to act as agents of the Minister and are given the authority to take whatever action is deemed necessary to protect a child living in circumstances defined by the Act as constituting harm or risk of harm.

The Child and Family Services Act, Ontario, was the culmination of a long process on the part of the provincial government to solicit a broad range of discussion and opinion regarding the precise definition of a child in need of protection. The current Act contains words which underscore a deliberate intent to sharpen and limit the wide powers of child welfare workers. Justification for intervention is defined by the use of modifiers such as "serious" or "severe" and places upon child welfare workers the burden of defining the boundary between "serious" and "severe" and a potential to develop to the point of becoming "serious" and "severe" unless some intervention occurs. The Act considers a child to be in need of protection when it can be demonstrated that there is actual harm to the child; risk of harm to the child; parental incapacity to remedy the harm or risk to the child.[4] The balance between the protection of the privacy of the family and the interest of the state in prevention shift slightly in either direction from decade to decade so that the law can only represent philosophical compromise between the early interventionists on behalf of the child and those who would have the family deal with its own, whether or not the child is placed at risk.

Child protection agencies, notably in Ontario and British Columbia, but in reality in all provinces, are beset by reports in the media that children in their care are subject to continuing abuse and neglect, resulting in some instances in death. Inquests, investigations, and recommendations for prevention of such tragic outcomes occupy public attention for brief periods and then drop from the glare of media attention. Inadequate resources resulting from decreased provincial funding, and too few workers responsible for too many children and families, as well as inadequate training and supervision of front line workers are frequently cited as reasons for the failure to protect children. In addition, legislation that favours protecting families as the least intrusive, least onerous intervention is often cited as the reason some children are returned by the courts to families where risk is high.

All of these factors may be valid explanations for why children continue to slip through systems set up to protect them. However, we do not have a federal or provincial policy that creates a comprehensive plan for child welfare and support. Such a policy would establish cooperative links between health, education, community and social services, and corrections ministries. These links are essential to the provision of community based outreach services to work with families on a preventive as well as a crisis basis. Abusive and neglectful situations generally have a long history of inactivity or inadequate response and generally reveal on investigation that nothing was done to reach out to prevent the abuse or neglect through a network of human and material resources. As a further consideration, the enormous cost of lengthy child welfare trials and appellate litigation might better be devoted to front-line child supervision and family support on behalf of the child, but these services often fall victim to reduced agency budgets.

WHICH COURT

Child welfare proceedings usually take place in a provincial family court or Unified Family Court. The Children's Law Reform Act of Ontario extends tbe court option to the Superior Court.

DEFINITION OF A CHILD IN NEED OF PROTECTION

The Ontario Act defines a child as a person under 16 years of age. If a child, however, is already under a protective court order, the Act permits protection of the child until that child reaches 18 years of age. A child in need of protection is defined as one or more of the following:

1. a child has actually suffered harm or neglect at the hands of the legal caregiver or is at substantial risk of such harm;
2. the child has been sexually molested or exploited by the legal caregiver or in circumstances where the caregiver knew or should have known that sexual interference with the child would or could occur;
3. the legal caregiver fails or refuses to provide medical treatment considered necessary to maintain the child's well-being or prevent suffering;
4. the child has suffered emotional harm demonstrated by *severe* anxiety, depression, withdrawal or self-destructive or aggressive behavior and the legal caregiver fails or refuses to provide treatment to remedy the harm or the child is at substantial risk of such harm;
5. the child suffers from an emotional or developmental condition for which the legal caregiver fails or refuses to provide treatment or remedy which may prevent the serious impairment;
6. the child has been abandoned or his parents have died or are not available to care for him, or the child is in a residential placement and his legal caregivers are unwilling or unable to resume his care;
7. the child is under twelve and has killed or seriously injured someone or caused serious damage to property and his legal caregivers are unwilling or unable to provide necessary treatment to prevent a recurrence; or where the legal caregiver has encouraged such behaviour in the child; or
8. the child's legal caregivers are unable to care for him and the child is brought before the court with the caregiver's consent and with the consent of a child over twelve.[5]

HOW PROTECTION PROCEEDINGS ARE INITIATED

A child who is believed to be in need of protection may be apprehended with or without a warrant and detained in a place of safety such as a receiving home or shelter for children or a foster home.[6] The Children's Aid Society may also obtain an Order to Produce from the court which compels the parent or custodian to bring the child before the court at a specified time,[7] or may obtain a warrant authorizing entry of a home to apprehend a child.[8] The Act also authorizes the placement of a homemaker in the child's home rather than removing the child.[9]

BY WHOM AND WHEN A CHILD MAY BE APPREHENDED

Persons who have the right to apprehend a child are a police officer, a Director of Child Welfare, a local director of a Children' s Aid Society, or a person authorized by a director or local director.[10] These persons have the right to enter the premises by force, if need be, and to apprehend with or without a warrant. Within five days of apprehension, the Children's Aid Society must either bring the matter before the court for a ruling on the alleged need for protection, or return the child to the person having charge prior to the apprehension, or enter into a voluntary care agreement with the child's parents. If none of these options has occurred within five days, the child's custodian can seek return of the child. If this occurs, the Society can reapprehend within seconds after the child's release and can begin proceedings again. During adjournments, the court has no authority to remove a child from his legal caregivers if the court is satisfied that the child will be adequately protected and is not at risk of harm in his own home. The onus is on those who apprehend to persuade the court.

In general, the courts have held that only when a child is confronted by real and immediate danger should apprehension be undertaken. Section 40(9) of the Act deals with the right of a worker who has reasonable and probable grounds to believe that a child is in need of protection to apprehend the child without a warrant and take the child to a place of safety, which includes a hospital. Where a child is too young to consent to a physical examination, the worker may act on the child's behalf. In one case, a father's action for assault and battery against a worker who apprehended a child did not succeed.[11] A worker is immune from civil prosecution where a child is removed to a place of safety before a warrant can be obtained if that worker was acting in good faith.

An important ruling articulated the competing arguments which underline the irreconcilable demands of legal justice and child welfare workers' concerns.[12] The Children's Aid Society brought wardship proceedings in regard to three infant children. The parents agreed with the wardship for the two boys, but disputed the wardship proceedings for their daughter. Two of the children, Peter and Amy, were under an existing order of supervision, and the third child was also in care. Inconclusive and contradictory evidence was raised at the trial about the conduct of the parents, and in particular the mother, toward the children. The Children's Aid Society social worker and a nurse produced sufficient evidence to support their allegations that Amy was abused by her mother, but two physicians who had attended the child and her mother testified that they did not feel Amy had been abused by her mother. The Society was granted wardship over the two boys, but supervision only over the daughter. The judge commented:

> While I have not been able to find any clear evidence of abuse, I suspect that the C.A.S. is attempting to take preventative steps. It seems to me that in such a situation the potential for real and immediate abuse must be clear before the state should be permitted to intervene by removing the child from her parents. If it were otherwise, it would allow a C.A.S. to be the final arbitrator in a so-called child abuse case and would leave the parents and the child with no real recourse to a really independent and impartial court. In adopting this principle, I realize that there is always the danger that some real and even irreparable harm may be inflicted upon the child if the parents are really potential child abusers, but the C.A.S. has not been able to prove that fact because of the unavailability of witnesses who can testify to the alleged abuse and therefore has not been able to meet the standards of proof required by the court. I think that this risk must still give way to the greater risk of the irreparable harm that can be inflicted upon a child and the danger to society of the serious undermining of the parents and the family if a C.A.S. is permitted to act in an arbitrary way, even though its intentions are motivated by the highest ideals and concerns.[13]

Two cases are significant in determining the standard of proof of allegations that a child is in need of protection. In the first case, "substantial risk" has been defined as being an actual risk rather than a speculative risk of harm to the child.[14] The other case defines admissible evidence in protection proceedings and includes hospital records and nurses' notes as well as social workers' notes and records.[15]

Of interest is a further case in which a trial judge dismissed a Society's protection application and this decision was upheld by the appeal court who also upheld a judgment awarding costs against the Society. The trial judge had not believed allegations of sexual abuse and had questioned the child extensively. Judicial questioning had formed the basis of the appeal. The appeal court noted that a protection proceeding is not the same as a two-party litigation. The community also has an interest in the proceedings and the judge must inquire into the facts to determine whether the child is in need of protection.[16]

VOLUNTARY CARE AGREEMENTS

The Act provides for voluntary care by agreement. They are: (1) a temporary care agreement for children under 16 if the Society has an appropriate placement available and is satisfied that no less restrictive course of action such as care in the child's own home is possible; (2) a special needs agreement in those instances where the parents are unable to provide the child with the necessary services required for special needs created by physical, mental, emotional, behavioural or other handicaps; and (3) a special needs agreement where the person is 16 or 17 years of age and requires special services.[17]

The consent of the involved child is required where the child is 12 years of age unless he or she cannot give consent because of a developmental handicap. The consent of the Director of Child Welfare is required for an extension of any temporary care agreements. No initial temporary care agreement may exceed six months, and extensions, if granted, must not usually exceed 12 months and in no circumstance shall it ever extend 24 months. A special needs agreement may not extend beyond the child's 18th birthday.[18]

Either the parent or the Society may terminate a temporary care or special needs agreement by giving at least 21 days written notice. A child who is at least 12 years of age and the subject of an agreement may make a written request for a review of the agreement by the Society or the Minister. If no new agreement is reached, then the existing agreement automatically terminates at the end of the 21-day period. If this occurs, then the Society must either return the child to the previous custodian or submit the matter to the court for a determination of the child's need for protection.

A social worker must make certain that the agreement for temporary care and custody contains a statement about the Society's responsibilities and the parents' responsibilities during the time of the agreement in order to ensure that both parties comply with the terms. In addition, it must state that responsibility for the child is transferred to the society by voluntary agreement of all parties on the basis that the legal caregiver is temporarily unable to provide care. The Society, for its part, must keep the parents informed of the child's progress, notify the parents of any emergency concerning the child, and help the parents and the child to plan for their reunion. The parents, for their part, must maintain contact with the child.

Special needs agreements can be extended for a period of time exceeding six or twelve months. In the case of a child 16 to 18 years who has a developmental handicap, the agreement can be entered into by the child on his or her own behalf.[19] A 16 or 17-year-old not yet before the courts is permitted under the Act to obtain service from the Society.

PARTIES TO A CHILD WELFARE PROCEEDING

Parties always include the applicant who is usually the Children's Aid Society, the parents, which always means the mother and may also include the father if he is the recognized or acknowledged male parent, the legal caregivers and the actual caregivers. This broad definition of parent also includes foster parents. The Director may also be added as a party on his application. A child of 12 or more now has full party status unless the court is satisfied that his attendance would cause emotional harm, whereas a child under 12 does not usually have party status.

Where the child is an Indian or native person, a representative chosen by the child's band or native community is also a proper party and has extended status during welfare proceedings. These rights include rights to seek access, apply for a status review, receive notice of proceedings including adoption and to appeal of any decision. The declaration of principle in the Act recognizes the distinct culture and heritage of native children, including the concept of extended family.[20]

The complexity of cultural identity in our acculturated society is demonstrated in this situation. Parents, who were Status Indians, but who had elected to leave their culture and live in the "white" community, were charged with chronic neglect and brought to court in a protection hearing. The band was notified and attended the hearing but offered no plan. The court found that the parents had voluntarily left their Indian heritage and so the child's best interests could not be served by returning him to a culture totally unknown to him.[21]

NOTICE OF HEARING

A proceeding may be initiated by filing an application, whereupon the clerk must set a date and must issue a notice of hearing. Persons entitled to notice of the hearing of a protection application include:

1. parents or legal caregivers having actual custody of the child;
2. foster parents who have been caring for the child for a continuous period of more than six months;
3. a child over 12, unless the Court directs that the child not be served because the hearing might negatively affect the child's emotional health; or
4. a child under 12, at the discretion of the Court.[22]

The Act defines a parent as:

1. a person under a legal duty to provide for a child which includes the natural parents, a guardian or person who has demonstrated a settled intention to parent the child, but excludes foster parents and the Children's Aid Society;
2. the mother of a child and either the natural father or other person who has been ordered by the court or agreed to support the child or has acknowledged parentage and supported the child.[23]

In addition, as a consequence of the Children's Law Reform Act, any person who has assumed a parenting role or is a biological parent is entitled to notice, which may include grandparents, foster parents and the natural father where the child was born outside of marriage.[24] A court may dispense with notice to any party if it is satisfied that delay might endanger a child's health and safety.[25]

CUSTODY OF THE CHILD PENDING A HEARING

Pending final disposition of the protection application, the onus is on the Society to "show cause" or present evidence why the child should remain in its temporary care and custody. Unless this motion is made or if it fails, the child will be returned to the person who had charge before his apprehension. In order to determine where the child will live, the court may consider evidence which is ordinarily inadmissible, that is, hearsay evidence as long as the other party has a fair opportunity to correct or contradict it. The court may also consider the legal caregivers' past conduct toward any child in his or her care in reaching a decision about continuing residence of the child.

THE HEARING

The provincial family court is a statutory court. It has no *parens patriae* power because this jurisdiction arises out of the equitable jurisdiction of the old Courts of Chancery and no provincially appointed judge can exercise this power. However, many family court judges seem to act on the basis of the equitable *parens patriae* doctrine. Child protection hearings are always held in private unless the court orders a public hearing. They must also always be held separately from hearings in criminal matters, including those under the Young Offenders Act.[26] Two representatives of the news media are entitled to be present at a hearing, but the court may exclude them if their presence would be injurious to the child's emotional health.

THE COURT PROCESS

A protection application is brought before the courts by:

1. an application,
2. an order to produce, which compels the parent or guardian to attend the court hearing,
3. apprehension of a child,

4. termination of an agreement for temporary care, or
5. a third party application.

In general, the Children's Aid Society elects to proceed by an order to produce rather than apprehending the child if the child is not in immediate danger. The Society may be seeking an order for supervision in order to keep the child with the family.

The Two Part Nature of the Hearing

The hearing in child protection matters has two distinct stages. The Children's Aid Society carries the burden of proof in both stages. In the first stage, the Society must establish that the child is in need of protection, which means it has to prove that the custodial parent has failed to maintain minimum community standards in one of the ways listed in the Act. The second stage is the disposition, which cannot be made unless there is a finding that the child is in need of protection at the first stage. The best interests test only applies at the second or disposition stage, after the court has first found that the child is in need of protection.

Show Cause

In general, after the first appearance before the court, the proceedings may be adjourned to give the Children's Aid Society time to assess the situation, which may include medical examination of the child without parental consent, and to give the parties time to retain counsel. This adjournment cannot exceed 30 days without the consent of all parties. An interim order for the temporary care and custody of the child must be made at this time and the onus is on the Society to show cause why the child cannot remain with the custodial parent.

This "show cause" hearing is not a full trial, and the introduction of hearsay evidence is permitted.[27] The family service worker will usually present evidence *viva voce*[28] which contains that person's concerns as well as those of other professionals such as public health nurses, teachers or daycare workers. This is an important hearing since the child can be kept out of his home and in a temporary place of safety by the Society until the trial is held, if the judge is convinced that such a temporary order is necessary. A social worker might suggest that the parents work out an alternative plan to satisfy the court of the child's safety — for example, placement with a relative or a friend. This alternative may spare the child the trauma of placement in a totally unknown environment. Alternatives to removal from the home must be canvassed by the Society before a child is removed by court order. The court may vary or terminate any interim order at a later date, but the onus is then on the party seeking the variation to convince the court to make the order to vary.[29]

Pre-Trial Conference

After the show cause hearing, a pre-trial conference may be convened. The effect has been to greatly reduce both the number of trials and the delay in disposing of a child welfare proceeding, to the child's benefit. These conferences are very informal. Counsel summarize their cases, indicate what evidence they intend to present and hear an opinion from the judge about the probable legal outcome, which may facilitate a settlement without going to trial.

Plan of Care

Before making an order, either for supervision, society wardship, or Crown wardship, or a status review of the child under an order, the court must have before it a plan for the child's care prepared in writing by either the Society or a person applying for change in the current order.[30]

The criteria stated in these sections is somewhat confusing. An order under s. 57(9) permits the court to make a finding of the need for protection. In the case cited below, the court concluded that an order was not required on the basis of the evidence presented for the child's future protection where s. 65, which deals with status reviews, states that decisions should be guided by the best interests of the child. In effect, there appear to be different criteria on status review.

The child in this situation was in a foster home and the placement was prolonged by protracted litigation. Over the course of this time, she bonded with the foster parents who wished to adopt her. In support of this plan, the Society brought an application for Crown Wardship without access to the natural mother, stating that to separate the child from the foster parents would cause emotional damage to the child. The judge ruled that the child's best interests were not a factor, that the Society had not made a case for the need for future protection and ordered that the child be returned to the natural mother.

The Society appealed and the appeal judge found that the best interests were relevant but would be served by returning the child to the natural mother. On an appeal by the Society to the Court of Appeal in which the Society cited new evidence on the extent of the bonding to the foster parents, the court found not only that the best interests argument was relevant, but that the Society should succeed. The mother appealed this decision to the Supreme Court of Canada who dismissed the appeal finding that protection in a status review must include protection of the best interests of a child which may not have been applicable at the initial stage of the case for protection. Thus, the passage of time in care created the bonding with the foster parents that supported the argument that emotional damage to the child might occur if the bonds to the foster parents were to be severed by returning the child to the mother.[31]

Dispositions

The following are possible dispositions at a hearing of a protection application where the court has found that a child is in need of protection.

Supervision order

A supervision order places the child with the parent or caretaker subject to the supervision of the Children's Aid Society. The minimum period of supervision is three months and the maximum is twelve months. A supervision order will expire upon the child's marriage or upon the child's 18th birthday, or unless the order is terminated earlier at a status review hearing. The court may impose terms and conditions in the order relating to the method of supervision. The courts have interpreted this provision very broadly and have used it to impose detailed conditions on the parent or person in charge of the child. In one recent case, the judge ordered the mother to continue in therapy with a specific psychiatrist as a condition of her continuing to retain custody of her child.[32]

Society wardship order

A Society wardship order commits a child to the care and custody of the Society which initiated the proceedings. No order may exceed 12 months, but if a previous order has existed no period of continuous temporary care may exceed 24 months. This order will expire upon the child's marriage or upon the child's 18th birthday or upon an earlier termination decided by the court. This order gives the Society the authority to place the child wherever it is felt the child's needs will be met, depending upon the adequacy and availability of community resources.

The Society must also ensure not only that the child receives a proper education in accordance with both Ontario law and his intellectual capacity, but also that provision is made for the child's occupational training and total development such as a good parent would provide.

Crown Wardship Order

A Crown wardship order commits the child to the care of the Society which brought him before the court. It can expire upon the child's marriage, the child's 18th birthday, the child's adoption, or a termination of the wardship determined by the court. Where a Crown wardship order expires as a result of the child reaching his 18th birthday and that child is enrolled as a full time student in an educational institution or is mentally or physically handicapped, the Society may provide continuing care and maintenance under some circumstances.[33]

In every case, the court is enjoined from removing a child from the care of his legal caregivers unless it is satisfied that less restrictive alternatives, including non-residential services and other alternatives have been tried and proven unsuccessful or were refused by the legal caregiver, or would not adequately protect the child. The court must also consider placement with a relative, neighbour, community or extended family. Native children must always be placed with a member of the child's extended family, band, native community or other native family unless a substantial contrary reason exists.[34]

Status Review Proceedings

The court must review all orders for supervision and for Society wardship prior to their expiration. Orders for Crown wardship may be reviewed providing the child has not been placed for adoption.[35] The Children's Aid Society can apply for a review at any time, but the parent of a child or a child himself who is 12 years or over can apply for a review only after the expiration of six months from the making of the order. The Director must now review the status of every child who is a Crown ward at least once in each calendar year.[36] The court in general must consider the best interests of the child on a status review, although there is some question about whether, on a status review, a court must make a fresh finding that the child is in need of protection.[37]

Once a finding of the need for protection has been established, the question of disposition must be dealt with by the court. The following cases demonstrate the reasoning used in making distinctive dispositions.

By statute, children can only be kept for two years under a Society wardship order before a disposition must be made. The original reason for taking them into care was the mother's physical neglect and unclean living conditions. The children were healthy, well-adjusted and bonded with the mother. The Society asked for Crown Wardship to clear the way to adoption. Evidence was produced that the mother had taken steps to improve herself and her housekeeping. The court was satisfied that the minimum standards in which protection of children could be demonstrated was sufficient and that there was no evidence that the children faced a substantial risk of harm if returned to the mother providing that supervision from the Society was provided for a 12 month period.[38]

In another case, a child was placed at birth with foster parents, but the case took nearly two years to come to trial, by which time, the child had bonded with the foster parents and they wanted to adopt. The court refused to consider the question of the child's best interests until the initial question of the need for protection from the parents had been decided.[39]

In a further case, a child, having suffered physical abuse from the mother, was apprehended and placed with foster parents. The father and paternal grandfather had access to the child and an attachment developed between them and the child, as well as an attachment to the foster mother. The court found that the child's best interest would be served if he were placed with his extended family, in this case, the paternal grandparents, in spite of the bond to the foster mother as primary caretaker.[40]

Evidence at a Child Welfare Hearing

> Since the immediate health and/or life of a child may hang in the balance, the ordinary rules of evidence as to admissibility should be modified to reflect the gravity of the situation, consistent with as fair a hearing as is possible. . . . [In considering] the balance of probabilities, . . . if the balance does not tip either way, then the resulting doubt should be determined in favour of the safety of the child.[41]

The prevailing practice in child protection matters in regard to evidence is to relax the rules of evidence so that every opportunity to consider any information that might assist the court in protecting the best interests of the child can be heard. Any party to the proceedings may request a judge or a justice of the peace to summon any person to appear before the court to give oral testimony or produce any relevant documents in his possession, including the presiding judge.[42] Such documents may include agency files, workers' notes, case and treatment summaries, school records, financial statements, and any other written materials which may shed light on the issue before the court. The court may also receive affidavit evidence on any matter providing the affidavit[43] is confined to facts, not opinion, which is within the personal knowledge or belief of the person swearing the affidavit. The following case is an interesting example of the court's thinking about the introduction of evidence in the form of Children's Aid Society files.[44]

The Catholic Children's Aid Society apprehended the child from the mother and placed the child as a temporary Society ward with his grandparents. The grandparents applied to adopt the child, the Society applied for Crown wardship and the parents attempted to regain custody. The parents' counsel asked for the production of Catholic Children's Aid Society records respecting supervision of the child by the grandparents.

In his decision, Fisher Prov. J. noted that the C.C.A.S. file was a "business record" and thus admissible under the Ontario Evidence Act and that the legislation considered that prior parenting (by the grandparents) was certainly relevant and admissible in certain circumstances. He also noted that there was no privilege between social workers and their clients, and that the evidence upon which a social worker as expert gives an opinion can be cross-examined as to the source — for example, the files.

Against the relevancy and admissibility it was argued that the relationship between the grandparents and the C.C.A.S. was confidential. If this material could be introduced it would result in families being reluctant to seek help if the interchange could be used against them. However, the best interests of the child would dictate that a social worker, at trial, would have to disclose information and that this should be understood by families and the Society at the outset.

Further, it was argued that the file would offend the hearsay rule. The counsel for the grandparents stated that in her experience, information in C.A.S. files was on occasion "outrageous and inaccurate". The judge found that if this was so, it was all the more important to open the files to the scrutiny of the courts and litigants. Further, the judge noted that disclosure by experts that is hearsay is admissible to show the basis upon which the opinion is formed but not as proof of the facts stated. The Child and Family Services Act now makes express provision for the introduction of Children's Aid Society files into evidence.[45]

Past Conduct Evidence

Under the Children's Law Reform Act, which now applies to the Child and Family Services Act, the past conduct of a person is not relevant to a determination of an application in respect to custody of or access to a child unless the conduct is relevant to the capacity of the person to act as a parent of a child.

It is interesting to note that low parental intelligence does not, in itself, determine the child's need for protection. The question is whether these parents are able to meet their parental responsibilities given their intellectual capacities. A negative answer requires that the judge consider whether the parents can be provided with the services and knowledge necessary to care adequately for their child within the home.

CONFIDENTIALITY AND ACCESS TO RECORDS

Consent to disclosure of records must be obtained from all persons over the age of 16 except under certain conditions and to persons specifically described in the Child and Family Services Act.[46] A person who is 12 years of age or older has a right of access to his or her own records, the records of his or her child who is under the age of 16 years, and the records of a child who is in his or her custody. The exception is counselling records which may be disclosed to a parent only with the child's written consent. A parent may also designate specific information they wish withheld from the child. Parental consent is not required for a child's access to his or her own record. Service providers may refuse to disclose all or part of the record of a child under 16 years of age if they hold the opinion that to do so would cause the child physical or emotional harm.[47]

Clinical Records

Clinical records such as psychiatric assessments, which are usually confidential between patient and clinician under the Mental Health Act, may be ordered to be produced before the court.[48] If the Society can demonstrate that there are reasonable grounds to believe they are relevant to fitness to parent where a request by a local director to inspect such records has been refused, the court may order production.

ASSESSMENTS

In Ontario, the family court may order a child and family to undergo a psychological or psychosocial assessment which becomes evidence in the proceeding.[49] The court may also decide who shall conduct the assessment. Paradoxically, as the demand for assessments from mental health professionals increases, the literature of both law and mental health reveals a parallel increase in scepticism about their value.

Assessments, particularly those done to inform legal proceedings, must wary of opinion that it is not supported by evidence. Since lawyers must present this evidence to the court, assessments must be able to stand against scrutiny of their objectivity, particularly in areas of human interaction where ambiguity defies objective reporting. Some guidelines can be offered, however, which can provide structure in formulating assessments. Assessments should contain a clear statement about why the assessment was undertaken which should be mutually agreed to by all parties. It should state where the assessment took place, who was present, what reports will be prepared, who will have access to those reports and a statement of conclusions based on observed fact and professional interpretation of these facts.

The social worker preparing an assessment who is aware of ambiguous feelings will strive to create a climate in which a parent can express negative feelings and doubts. Parental ambivalence is a factor that underlies parent-child interaction, even in untroubled families, and such ambivalence is amplified when there is a custody dispute or when fitness for parenting is brought into question. The same parents may appear alternately warm and caring, and insensitive and rejecting, reflecting the parents' desire to both win and lose. Yet ambivalence in an assessment often seems vague and contradictory and the results may be viewed with frustration and scorn by the lawyer who must present the report in court. Communication between lawyer and social worker may help to clarify the importance of weighing the parents' conflicting feelings in relation to their capacity to parent.

APPEALS

Any decision made under the Child and Family Services Act, except an assessment order, is subject to appeal to a single Judge of the Ontario Court (General Division).[50] An appeal may be launched by the child, the parent, the person in charge of the child, a Director of Child Welfare, a local director of a Society, a friend on behalf of the child or a representative of the child's Indian band. The appeal must be filed within 30 days of the decision. There is a positive obligation to expedite child welfare appeals. If the parents had custody of the child at the time the original hearing granted them custody, then the child would automatically remain in their custody pending the appeal.

The ground on which the appeal court can take action depends upon whether the appeal judge finds any error either in fact or in law in the decision of the trial judge. The appeal court's responsibility is not to re-try the protection application, but must be based on a specific error which would change the information upon which the decision was made.

The appeal judge has several options. If no error is found to exist, the appeal may be dismissed. If the appeal is allowed on the basis of a demonstrable error, the children may be returned to the person in whose care they were when they were apprehended. The court may also rule that a new trial take place where an appeal has been allowed and may, upon the review of additional evidence, substitute the appeal court's decision for that of the trial judge. It is possible to launch a further appeal to the Ontario Court of Appeal with the permission of that court, with the possibility of further appeal to the Supreme Court of Canada.

LEGAL REPRESENTATION FOR THE CHILD

A child may be represented by counsel at any stage of any proceeding under the Child and Family Services Act[51] which provides that the child must have legal representation if any of the following circumstances are present, unless the court is satisfied that the child' s interests are adequately protected without legal counsel. The circumstances are:

1. where there is a difference between the views of the child and those of either the parents or the Society and the Society is recommending either that the child be removed from his parents' home or that he remain in the Society's care as a Society or Crown ward;
2. where a child is in the care of the Society and a parent is not present at any stage of the proceedings;
3. where the child is in the care of the Society and is alleged to have suffered abuse;
4. where an order excluding the child from the hearing is made.

If any or all of these conditions are present and the court fails to consider legal representation for the child, there may be a basis for an appeal of any resulting order.

If the child is not represented, the judge must determine whether separate representation is needed to protect the child's interests. A Society will frequently make a referral to the Children's Lawyer Child Representation Programme or the court may so order. This programme will then either assign a staff lawyer or refer the matter to a lawyer in private practice who is a member of the Child Representation Programme panel.

Accessibility of counsel to the child, and the capacity of the child to give instructions are essential to the provision of representation to a child. The approach assumed by the lawyer is also of crucial importance. The approaches that are possible are *adversarial*, in which the lawyer takes instruction from the child as from an adult client, a *guardianship* role, in which the lawyer examines the available information and then advocates a position which he sees as in the child's best interests in spite of the child's instructions, and that of *amicus curiae*, in which the lawyer maintains a neutrality and acts as an intermediary between the child and the court, providing the court with facts, reports, and important information. A decisive factor is, of course, the age of the child and the child's capacity to understand the proceedings and their consequences, and to give instructions. In general, children 10 years and over are considered capable to give instructions and to see consequences, while younger children may be more or less capable of such understanding. The lawyer of a young child might therefore serve as an advocate of the child's legal rights and social needs.

In determining the child's capacity for competent choice, one authority has stated that such capacity is present when the child

> [I]s able to appreciate the nature and purpose of the proceeding, the alternatives available to the court, the risks to him if he is permitted to remain at home, and . . . appears to possess sufficient maturity to weigh these factors with a reasonable degree of dispassion and objectivity.[52]

Another commentator has recommended that:

> A child's right of privileged communication with counsel should be established through legislation and this privilege should reside with the child and not the lawyer, and the role of the Superintendent of Child Welfare should be broadened to encompass the best interests of the child, and that where conflict exists between the expressed wishes of the child and the judgment of the lawyer, the wishes of the child should prevail.[53]

Judge Steinberg had this to say:

> [T]he development of a valid concept of child law advocacy requires meaningful interaction between the legal and social work professions . . . [I]t is a joint function of both the legal and social work professions to define and to strike a proper balance of the legal and social rights of children both within the family and before the courts in order to make our concept of child advocacy work.[54]

A clear articulation of the complex task of providing legal representation of a child is contained in the court's remarks in the following case.[55] The Children's Aid Society applied for an order of Crown wardship of a 7-year-old girl. The girl expressed ambivalence about where she wanted to live and offered no clear instruction to her lawyer. An issue arose as to the role of the child's lawyer in the proceedings. The child's counsel had indicated she would be representing the child by presenting not only the child's wishes but her own perception of the child's best interests as well. Abella Prov. J., as she then was, in articulating guidelines for the role of the child's counsel, had this to say:

> In a trial it is for a Judge to determine ultimately what is in a given child's best interests. The bases for this determination include, among other evidence, the child's wishes.
>
> There must undoubtedly be a degree of flexibility in a child's lawyer's role as articulator of his or her client's wishes. The child may be unable to

> instruct counsel. Or the child may be, as in this case, ambivalent about her wishes. Or the child may be too young. Although there should be no minimum age below which a child's wishes should be ignored — so long as the child is old enough to express them, they should be considered. . . In the absence of clear instructions, protecting the client's interests can clearly involve presenting the lawyer's perception of what would best protect the child's interests. In this latter role of promulgating the infant client's best interests, the lawyer would attempt to guarantee that all the evidence the Court needs to make a disposition which accommodates the child's best interests is before the Court, is complete, and is accurate. There could in this kind of role be no inconsistency between what is perceived by the lawyer to be the child's best interests and the child's instructions. Where there is such conflict, the wishes of the child should prevail in guiding the lawyer.
>
> In the case of a child who is capable of coherent expression the lawyer's role in representing the child's wishes does not preclude the lawyer from exploring with the child the merits or realities of the case, evaluating the practicalities of the child's position and even offering, where appropriate, suggestions about possible reasonable resolution to the case. Offering advice is part of the lawyer's obligation to protect the client's interests. Obviously, however, given the vulnerability of most children to authority in general and given the shattered sensibilities in family disputes in particular, great sensitivity should be exercised during these exploratory sessions. The lawyer should be constantly conscious of his or her posture being an honest but not an overwhelming one.[56]

In April, 1980, the Professional Conduct Committee of the Law Society of Upper Canada appointed a sub-committee on the legal representation of children. In its report, the subcommittee recommended that counsel in child welfare proceedings should reflect the child's wishes, concerns, and opinions in the same manner as would a lawyer representing an adult. If the child is unable to express wishes, the lawyer should protect the child's interests.[57]

The following cases are instructive about the role of legal counsel as interpreted by the courts.

A Society had applied for supervised access. At the hearing, counsel for the child advised that the child wished to return to her parents but did not want supervised visits. Counsel then added her opinion that the child was emotionally incompetent to instruct counsel and so counsel would call witnesses in the child's best interests. The respondent parents' counsel objected. The court held that counsel was an advocate and so her personal opinions about the child's best interests should be disregarded. If the child could give instructions, they should be presented; if the child was unable to give instructions, counsel might apply for removal from the case but could not act as *amicus curiae*.[58] However, the court in another case found that child's counsel must not only relay the child's instructions but must also call evidence as to the child's wishes; for example, a social worker or other person who has knowledge of the child's wishes.[59]

Role of the Children's Lawyer

In Ontario, a Children's Lawyer is made responsible for an independent investigation concerning the circumstances of certain children whose custody is in question. The standard practice is for the office of the Children's Lawyer to be served with notice of the proceedings. Questionnaires are sent to the parties, from which a determination can be made about whether further investigation is required. The actual legal representation comes from a series of geographically based panels. Local lawyers on these panels have taken special training workshops conducted by the Ministry of the Attorney General. It is possible, at times, for the child to have legal representation under this programme, in advance of the court hearing, so that needless delays and adjournments can be avoided. Such delays and adjournments can have a devastating effect on children whose sense of time does not yet encompass an accurate concept of future. Social workers are employed as staff in the office of the Children's Lawyer in order to investigate and report to the court concerning custody and access, support and education of the child.

The role of the Children's Lawyer is perceived as that of advocate for the child and he therefore does not generally express a view other than the child's instructions, or what he considers to be in the best interests of the child if the child cannot give instructions. He may call witnesses, and may cross-examine witnesses of opposing parties.

Presence of the Child at the Hearing

The court is empowered to determine whether a child should be present or excluded from any part of the hearing. If the child is 12 years old or more, the child is entitled to attend and generally attends the hearing unless the court feels attendance would be injurious to the child's emotional health.

PRESENCE OF MEDIA AT THE HEARING

In general, all persons are excluded from the hearing unless they are parties or unless the parties wish them to be present. However, two or more representatives of the media may be present unless excluded by the presiding judge. However, the names of the children cannot be disclosed or published; neither can information which would tend to identify the parties be disclosed.

STATUS OF THE CHILD

In child protection and custody matters the status of the child is less than clear, mainly because it is at the discretion of the court, unless the child is over 12. Even then he may be excluded if his presence would cause the child emotional harm. In Manitoba and Quebec, a child in a protection hearing has a statutory right to participate through legal counsel. In Newfoundland, there is a provision permitting a judge to "consult the wishes of the child" in respect to the order to be made and in Alberta a child can make an application for his own custody. Ontario gives a child 12 years or older party status.

In Ontario, the Child and Family Services Act provides for a judge, at his discretion, to hear any person on behalf of the child which might include the child himself. Those empowered under the rules to represent a child in court include a lawyer, an articling student, a supervised law student with the permission of the court, and any other person with the permission of the court.

The Children's Law Reform Act, Ontario, authorizes the court to interview the child when considering an original application for custody or access to a child, or application for variance of an order previously given or to supersede an order of an extra-provincial tribunal. The court may interview the child to determine his views and preferences, and the interview must be recorded. The child is entitled to be advised by and to have his counsel present.

RIGHTS OF CHILDREN

The concept of children's rights is relatively new to our thinking about children. Those involved with the traditional social agencies such as the Children's Aid Societies may feel that they alone can represent the child's best interests. They may fear that legal representation will create delays and will fail to appreciate the child's situation as understood by the worker through long involvement with the child.

It has been observed that the social service system developed as a quasi-legal system, in part because of deficiencies in the court system, such as overloaded dockets and delays which were costly and damaging to the parties involved. In addition, it has also been demonstrated that social agencies do not always represent the child's best interests because of bureaucratic concerns, unavailability of beds, restrictive administrative policies, and adherence to prevailing theories of child care which may subsequently be abandoned but may have consequences for the children who are considered in the light of these theories.[60] Neither are parents always reliable to represent the child's best interests because of the primacy of their own needs and their fear of self-incrimination.

The discretion of the social service system, which went unexamined for so long, has now been brought under scrutiny by the introduction of legal representation for children. The current belief of many child advocates is that there is a need for procedural safeguards protected by the lawyer. There must also be persons who can produce an appropriate investigation of the child's physical, social, and emotional needs and the fit of these needs with the resources of the competing parties, and who will be able to provide expert opinion evidence to the court. Obviously both legal and social work skills are required.

Rights of Children in Care

A specific section defining the rights of children in care and the creation of an Office of Child and Family Service Advocacy are now embedded in the Child and Family Services Act.[61] This is a significant development and the specific rights that are listed in the Act should be carefully noted by child welfare workers. Rights are meaningless unless enforced and monitored. If they are ignored or overridden, children in particular have little power to sound an alarm, even if aware that their rights have not been observed. Children in vulnerable situations need an advocate to ensure that these rights are protected and that the needs of a large care system do not obscure or ignore these rights.

The children referred to in the section on rights are those receiving residential services, such as care from foster parents, temporary detention placement, or in secure or open custody under the Young Offenders Act. Their rights include:

1. the right not to be placed in locked premises except under specified circumstances;
2. the right to be free of corporal punishment in any circumstances;
3. the right to privacy in visits with family unless the child is a Crown Ward where visits can occur only with a specific access order;
4. the right to privacy in visits with a lawyer or other advocate or representative and to complete privacy of written communication;
5. the right to send and receive mail that is not read or censored by another person unless opened in the presence of the child for the reason of protecting the child from emotional or physical harm or for the inspection for contraband articles;

6. the right to reasonable privacy and possession of personal goods;
7. the right to receive religious instruction and to participate in religious activities with parental consent where authorized;
8. the right to participate in a plan of care which must be prepared within 30 days of admission;
9. the right to meals that are well-balanced and of good quality;
10. the right to clothing that is appropriate to age and activity and is of good quality;
11. the right to medical and dental care in a community setting whenever possible;
12. the right to an education that corresponds with ability in a community setting whenever possible;
13. the right to participate in recreational and athletic activities that correspond to ability and interest, preferably in a community setting;
14. the right to be consulted and heard whenever significant decisions are made respecting education, religion, medical treatment, and discharge, placement, and transfer plans; and
15. the right to be informed of these provisions in the Act in language suitable to the child's level of understanding.

The Act provides specific complaint and review procedures that are available to children and families of children in care in order to ensure that the child's rights while in care are protected where the Society takes an opposing view. An independent advocate for the child is essential to protect his rights.

CHILD ABUSE

The guiding principle in a child protection matter where abuse is alleged is whether it is improbable that an accident, injury or condition could have been caused in any way other than through the action or negligence of the parents or caregivers. Where no reasonable explanation can be produced, the child is deemed in need of protection from the abusing person.

The Ontario Act has extensively defined children in need of protection, which includes those who have been abused physically, sexually and emotionally. Emotional harm is demonstrated where there is *severe* anxiety, depression, withdrawal, or self-destructive or aggressive behaviour. A worker may intervene if there is substantial risk that the child will suffer abuse and that the person in charge of the child cannot or will not provide or consent to services or treatment to prevent the harm.[62] The standard of proof and the quantum of evidence required to substantiate an allegation of abuse is not entirely clear. Guidelines which the court may follow in making a determination of child abuse have been stated in *Re S*:[63]

> The applicable standard of proof should be the ordinary civil test of the balance of probabilities. In making its determination the court should have available to it all possible evidence relevant to the issue of "abuse". Since the immediate health and/or life of a child may hang in the balance, the ordinary rules of evidence as to admissibility should be modified to reflect the gravity of the situation consistent with as fair a hearing as is possible. The court must be both vigilant and careful and the approach to the assessment must be one of common sense and not hysteria. Where physical "abuse" is alleged there must be tangible evidence of the damage suffered by the child. Intention to "abuse" does not have to be proven. Negligence or the lack of an application of a reasonable standard of care, if proven, will support a finding. However, if what appears is as the result of an accident which could not be avoided with the application of a reasonable standard of care, then "abuse" has not been proven. If the court is satisfied that on the balance of probabilities there has been "abuse" then it should be quick to act to protect the child. If the balance does not tip either way, then the resulting doubt should be determined in favour of the safety of the child.[64]

Two further cases are instructive about the role of the judge on hearings involving abuse. In the first, a child was apprehended at birth because the mother had been found criminally responsible for physical abuse of an older child. The father sought custody, but, on review, the court found both parents to have demonstrated poor parenting skills, with little evidence that change would occur. The child could not be protected from the mother if the father had custody. The court concluded that Crown wardship was in the child's best interests and was the least restrictive alternative.[65]

The other involved a father who applied corporal punishment with a belt to his six-year-old son who had been diagnosed as having Attention Deficit Hyperactivity. The court deemed the punishment inappropriate and found the child to have been abused and in need of protection. The court, however, adjourned the case for a probationary period to give the father a chance to seek assistance in learning how to employ alternate methods of discipline and control.[66]

REPORTING SUSPICION OF CHILD ABUSE

The Ontario legislation requires everyone who has reasonable and probable grounds to believe that a child has been abused to report it to a Society. Professionals who become aware of abuse in the course of their professional duties must immediately report their suspicion. Professionals include physicians, nurses, dentists, pharmacists, psychologists, teachers, principals, social workers, family counsellors, clergy, day nursery operators, youth workers (but not volunteers who would still be included in the "everyone" clause), peace officers, coroners, lawyers, service providers and their employees.

A Children's Aid Society worker who obtains information that a child in care or under Children's Aid Society supervision may be experiencing abuse must report the information to the Director. The *only* exception to the positive duty to report child abuse is provided by the solicitor-client privilege.

Failure to report such suspicion is punishable by a fine of up to $2,000.[67] and might also result in a charge of liability under the Criminal Code[68] if the child should subsequently suffer a predictable injury. In making a report of abuse, a check list, "Indications of Abuse" may be obtained from a Children's Aid Society.[69]

In a well publicized case, a family physician was charged under the former Child Welfare Act with failure to report sexual abuse of a child.[70] The child's mother had informed the doctor that the stepfather had fondled the child over a period of time. The doctor did not question the child or report the incident to the Children's Aid Society, but had referred the family for counselling. However, the stepfather had withdrawn after a few sessions. The Society was subsequently alerted, the stepfather was arrested and the doctor was charged for failing to report the abuse of a child to the Society. The court found that the law is unclear in its definition of child abuse and therefore was unable to make a finding that the doctor had failed to comply with the Act. In addition, the sketchy second-hand description reported by the mother was not sufficient to establish beyond a reasonable doubt that the doctor should have reported the abuse at that point. The court concluded that where such reasonable doubt exists, the matter must be resolved in favour of the doctor.

The significance of this case lies in the dangers of a broad definition of sexual abuse that intrudes into the intricate and varied expressions of love to be found within families. Children do need legal protection against excess and assault within the family, but can the law deal with behaviour that moves into the grey areas of community moral standards? The second aspect is whether or not a professional using his or her best judgment on information available, will be held liable for failure to report abuse according to an equivocal legal standard.

Members of the public too can be charged with an offence for failure to report immediately to a Society any information concerning abandonment, desertion, need for protection, or abuse of a child.[71] No legal action can be taken against an informant unless it can be shown that the information was given maliciously or in the absence of reasonable grounds to suspect that the information was true. One study looked at the effect of provincial and territorial legislation and the authors concluded that provincial legislation should be more explicit in order to provide optimum protection for children.[72]

Ontario Abuse Register

In Ontario, a central register was created by statute[73] with a minimum storage time of 25 years. The register contains the names of those who have been reported to the Society as suspected abusers. A person whose name is entered in the register must be given written notice of this fact and may request a hearing in order to expunge his or her name from the register.[74] Access to the register is limited to persons on the staff of the government Ministry concerned, the Children's Aid Societies, extra-provincial child protection agencies, or a person providing treatment or service to a registered person.

A registered person may request removal from the register, whereupon a hearing may be held to determine whether or not the person's name should be removed. Such a hearing is subject to the requirements of procedural fairness and a decision may be appealed by the applicant.[75]

There is much controversy about the value of the register because it is limited to what is reported and it tends to give the appearance that official action has been taken. In reality, the register is not considered to be helpful by workers concerned with case-by-case child protection. From a legal point of view, it is generally considered that the state should intervene to protect children only in the most severe cases so as not to interfere with the civil rights of parents.

A multidisciplinary approach has been advocated by many authorities including Bernard Dickens, who writes:

> Such professionals as physicians, nurses, social workers, day-care attendants and, regarding the older child, school teachers, may be considered in the forefront of identification of child abuse. It is therefore realistic for legal schemes addressed to control of child abuse to gear their provisions to the skills and functions of such specialists, whether they operate in the private sector of social organization as independent practitioners or through private agencies, or in the public sector, for example, as public hospital employees or officers of governmental agencies concerned with, for instance, school health services or social welfare. Similarly, legal implementation of social policy may be designed to serve child protection through recourse of professional expertise. The French policy of making financial child-support grants to families, for instance, is implemented not by rendering payments automatically through postal or banking facilities but by channelling grants

through child health clinics, to which children must be regularly presented for inspection as a precondition of child support payments.[76]

The critical issue for society is the balance between the right of the child to protection and the family's right to privacy and autonomy. This issue is further compounded in Canada where a pluralistic society makes difficult the task of determining acceptable community standards of child rearing practices. Since cultures vary in their attitudes toward physical discipline as a necessary part of child-rearing, confusion will persist unless the law states clearly that in this country physical force used against children is not condoned.

Offences related to sexual abuse have been created; sexual interference, invitation to sexual touching, and sexual exploitation.[77] In addition, changes have been made to the Criminal Code and to the Canada Evidence Act. Under certain conditions, there is the possibility of conviction based on a child's testimony without the legal necessity of corroboration of that testimony. A videotape of a child's disclosure of sexual abuse is admissible provided that the child also testifies. It is possible now for a child to give testimony outside of the court via closed circuit television or from behind a screen. There is also the possibility of the admission of unsworn testimony of young children where they can demonstrate "an ability to communicate and promise to tell the truth".

Under the new law, the spouse of a person charged with the new child abuse offences can be compelled to give evidence. Children under 14 years, either victims of sexual abuse or witnesses to abuse, may testify if the court is satisfied that they either understand an oath or affirmation or promise to tell the truth and have the ability to communicate.

Endnotes

1. R.S.O. 1990, c. C.11.
2. R.S.O. 1990, c. C.12.
3. See the Table of Concordance.
4. Mang, Ian and Jacqueline King. *Annotated Child and Family Services Act* (Toronto: Carswell, 1997), p. 46.
5. Child and Family Services Act, note 1 above, s. 37(2).
6. *Ibid.*, s. 41(2), (6).
7. *Ibid.*, s. 41(3).
8. *Ibid.*, s. 41(5).
9. *Ibid.*, s. 74(2).
10. *Ibid.*, s. 41(5).

11. *M.(J.) v. Toronto Bd. of Education* (1987), 59 O.R. (2d) 649, 38 D.L.R. (4th) 627 (H.C.).
12. *Re Chrysler* (1978), 5 R.F.L. (2d) 50 (Ont. Fam. Ct.).
13. *Ibid.*, at 58-59.
14. *Catholic Children's Aid Society of Metropolitan Toronto v. D.(A.)* (1994), 1 R.F.L. (4th) 268, 111 D.L.R. (4th) 151 (Ont. Gen. Div.).
15. *Ares v. Venner*, [1970] S.C.R. 608, 12 C.R.H.S. 349, 73 W.W.R. 347, 14 D.L.R. (3d) 4.
16. *Children's Aid Society of Hamilton-Wentworth v. M.(P.)* (1988), 17 R.F.L. (3d) 46 (H.C.).
17. Child and Family Services Act, note 1 above, s. 29.
18. *Ibid.*, s. 32.
19. *Ibid.*, s. 31.
20. *Ibid.*, s. 1(*f*).
21. *Family & Children's Services of Waterloo (Region) v. Y.(B.)*, [1995] W.D.F.L. 1011 (Ont. Prov. Div.)
22. *Ibid.*, s. 39.
23. *Ibid.*, s. 37.
24. *Ibid.*, s. 37.
25. *Ibid.*, s. 39(7).
26. *Ibid.*, s. 41(3).
27. *Ibid.*, s. 46.
28. "With living voice" (*i.e.,* orally).
29. Child and Family Services Act, note 1 above, s. 47(6).
30. Sections 56, 57(9) and 65(3).
31. *Catholic Children's Aid Society of Metropolitan Toronto v. M.(C.)* (1993), 47 R.F.L. (3d) 109, 13 O.R. (3rd) 227, 101 D.L.R. (4th) 766 (C.A.), affirmed 2 R.F.L. (4th) 313, [1994] 2 S.C.R. 165, 18 O.R. (3d) 160 (note), 165 N.R. 161, 71 O.A.C. 81, 113 D.L.R. (4th) 321.
32 *Re F.M.* (1979), 11 R.F.L. (2d) 120 (Ont. Fam. Ct.). See also Child and Family Services Act, note 1 above, s. 53(1).
33. Child and Family Services Act, note 1 above, ss. 53(3) and 67.
34. *Ibid.*, s. 53(3), (4), (5).
35. *Ibid.*, s. 60(9).
36. *Ibid.*, s. 62.
37. See *C.A.S. of Winnipeg v. Olson* (1980), 19 R.F.L. (2d) 384, 5 Man. R. (2d) 75 (C.A.); *C.A.S. of Ottawa-Carleton v. D.J.L.* (1980), 15 R.F.L. (2d) 102 (Ont. Fam. Ct.); *Re D.L.C. and C.W.C.; Western Man. C.A.S. v. D.A.C.*, 34 R.F.L. (2d) 225, [1983] 5 W.W.R. 1, (*sub nom. C.A.S. of Western Man. v. Corrigan*) 22 Man. R. (2d) 18, 148 D.L.R. (3d) 114 (C.A.).

38. *Children's Aid Society of Haldimand-Norfolk v. L.(C.B.)*, [1995] W.D.F.L. 1015 (Ont. Prov. Div.).
39. *Children's Aid Society of Peel (Region) v. K.(D.)*, [1991] W.D.F.L. 264 (Ont. Prov. Div.).
40. *Children's Aid Society of Kingston (City) & Frontenac (County) v. C.(T.)*, [1994] W.D.F.L. 1325 (Ont. Prov. Div.).
41. *Re S.* (1979), 10 R.F.L. (2d) 341 at 350 (Ont. Prov. Ct.).
42. Children's Law Reform Act, R.S.O. 1980, c. 68 [am. 1982, c. 20], s. 45.
43. Affidavit evidence is a statement sworn on oath.
44. *Re M.R.* (1979), 14 R.F.L. (2d) 289 (Ont. Fam. Ct.).
45. Child and Family Services Act, R.S.O. 1990, c. C.11, s. 46.
46. *Ibid.*, ss. 181-182.
47. *Ibid.*, ss. 184-185.
48. *Ibid.*, s. 50.
49. R.S.O. 1990, c. C.12, s. 28.
50. Note 45 above, s. 65.
51. Note 45 above, s. 50.
52. J. Leon, "Recent Developments in Legal Representation of Children: A Growing Concern with the Concept of Capacity" (1978) 1 Can. J. Fam. L. 375 at 411, quoting J. Dick, "The Role of Counsel in Neglect and Dependency Proceedings" in *Juvenile Court in Transition — A Workshop*, 49th Annual Legal Aid and Defender Conference, 5 November 1971, Denver, Colo. This article continues to be relevant.
53. Maczko, "Some Problems with Acting for Children" (1979) 2 Can. J. Fam. L. 267.
54. M. J. J. McHale, "The Proper Role of the Lawyer as Legal Representative of the Child" (1980) 18 Alta. L. Rev. 216 at 236, quoting D. Steinburg, "Children's Rights" in British Columbia, *Fifth Report of Royal Commission on Family and Children's Law, Part III: Children's Rights*. Vancouver, 1975, at 238-9.
55. *Re W.* (1979), 27 O.R. (2d) 314, 13 R.F.L. (2d) 381 (Fam. Ct.).
56. (1979), 27 O.R. (2d) 314 at 317-318.
57. Report of Subcommittee on the Legal Representation of Children in Law Society of Upper Canada Professional Conduct Committee, May 1981.
58. *Children's Aid Society of Metropolitan Toronto v. S.D. and J.D.*, [1993] O.J. No. 148 (Ont. Prov. Div.).
59. *Strobridge v. Strobridge* (1992), 42 R.F.L. (3d) 54, 10 O.R. (3d) 540, 94 D.L.R. (4th) 503 (Gen. Div.).
60. J. Tator and K. Wilde, "Child Abuse and the Courts: An Analysis of

Selected Factors in the Judicial Processing of 'Child Abuse' Cases" (1980) 3 Can. J. Fam. L. 165.
61. Child and Family Services Act, note 45 above, Part V, ss. 95-106.
62. *Ibid.*, s. 37.
63. (1979), 10 R.F.L. (2d) 341 (Ont. Fam. Ct.).
64. *Ibid.*, at 350.
65. *Children's Aid Society of Kingston (City) and Frontenac (County) v. H. (R.)* (1994), 5 R.F.L. (4th) 457 (Ont. Prov. Ct.).
66. *Children's Aid Society of the Regional Municipality of Waterloo v. D. (S.)*, [1995] W.D.L.F. 1221 (Ont. Prov. Ct.).
67. Note 45 above, s. 85.
68. Criminal Code, R.S.C. 1985, c. C-46, ss. 218 and 219.
69. Children's Aid Societies maintain current information on child abuse which is available to the public.
70. *R. v. Cook* (1983), 37 R.F.L. (2d) 93 (Ont. Fam. Ct.).
71. Note 45 above, s. 85.
72. See note 68 above.
73. Note 45 above, s. 71.
74. *Ibid.*, s. 71(8).
75. *Ibid.*, s. 71(7), (8).
76. B.M. Dickens, "Legal Responses to Child Abuse in Canada" (1978) 1 Can. J. Fam. L. 87 at 97-98.
77. R.S.C. 1985, c. 19 (3rd Supp.), ss. 151, 152 and 153.

Bibliography

Bala, Nicholas. "Developments in Family Law: The 1993-94 Term [of the Supreme Court of Canada]: The Best Interests of the Child", (1995) 6 Supreme Court Law Review 753-774.

Bernstein, Marvin M. and Lynn M. Kirwin, *Child Protection: Practice and Procedure* (Toronto: Carswell, 1996).

Christopher, Catherine, "Laudable Goals: Process and Problems in Child Welfare" (Dec., 1993) 18 *Law Now*, No. 4, pp. 14-18.

Freedman, Elaine. "Parents' Rights and Best Interests of Children Under the Child and Family Services Act" (Oct. 1994) 11 *Canadian Family Law Quarterly* 215-251.

Freeman, Michael, "Whither Children: Protection, Participation, Autonomy?", (1994) 22 *Manitoba Law Journal* 307-327.

Kline, Marlee, "Child Welfare Law, 'Best Interests of the Child' Ideology and First Nations", (Summer, 1992), 30 *Osgoode Hall Law Journal* 375-425.

O'Neill, John, *The Missing Child in Liberal Theory: Towards a Covenant*

Theory of Family, Community, Welfare and the Civic State. (Toronto: University of Toronto Press, 1994).

Scheiber, Alex, "Collaborative Decision-Making in Child Protection Cases", *The Social Worker*, Vol. 63(4), Winter, 1995, pp. 153-56.

Schmidt, Dennis and M. Jerry Metfale, "The Child, Family, and Community Service Act: Rule 2: Mandatory Case Conferences" (Sept., 1996) 54 Advocate (Van.) 733-737.

Sherrot, Geoff, "Foster Care for Abused Children: An Unacceptable Solution", (1993) 57 *Saskatchewan Law Review* 479-491.

Ward, Robin (Translator) "The Legal Representation of Children", (Consultation Paper) prepared by the Quebec Bar Committee (1996) 13 *Canadian Journal of Framily Law* 49-141.

Wharf, Brian, *Rethinking Child Welfare in Canada* (Toronto: McClelland & Stewart, 1993).

19

Adoption

INTRODUCTION

Adoptions existed under Roman law where the adopted person acquired all the benefits of a natural son, including inheritance of the family name, the family religion, and the family wealth. However, in England, Roman style adoption only became possible in 1926. Modern adoption in England and North America was motivated by a concern for the welfare of the child and problems of the illegitimate child and of the abandoned or neglected child.[1] Adoption has never become part of the common law and so the regulations and practices governing adoption are statutory and vary in some respect from province to province. We will cover relevant aspects of Ontario law concerning adoption and again suggest that readers in other provinces consult their specific legislation.[2]

Adoptions — Ontario

The best interests of the child remains the primary concern of the court in adoption matters, as it is in all matters concerning the welfare of children under the Child and Family Services Act.[3] However the circumstances governing adoptions have changed substantially in the past fifteen years. There are far fewer children to adopt because the natural mothers elect to keep their babies, or an unwanted pregnancy may be terminated by abortion long before the issue of adoption arises. No longer are there many unwanted infants awaiting adoption; adoption has become a last resort for the fortunate few who are able to locate an eligible child. The notable exceptions are older children whose families can no longer care for them and children with physical, mental or emotional handicaps.

Three types of adoption proceedings are:

1. Adoption of a child found to be in need of protection, where a Crown wardship order has been made;
2. A private adoption arranged through a licensee;
3. An adoption by a relative or other person known to the parents.

A child can come into the adoption system either by a finding of the need for protection and an order for Crown wardship without access; or on consent of the parties including the child where the child is over seven years of age, subject to any order dispensing with the consent of a parent of the child.[4]

Commencing an Adoption

All adoptions are initiated by filing an application, which is the formal document required by the court. An application may be filed personally by the adopters, by their agents, or lawyer. All applications are heard by the court *in camera*.[5] Part VII of the Child and Family Services Act deals with adoption. This part addresses the licensing of private adoption agencies, the role of the Children's Aid Society in the adoption of children and the procedure for adopting a child.

Residence of Adoptee

A child being considered for adoption (adoptee) must be a resident in Ontario.[6] The question of residence becomes important in the case where the adoptee is a foreign national. The court may be aware of the possibility that the adoption application is sought as a way to lend strength to a child's claim to remain in Canada as a permanent resident. Such "adoptions of convenience" have been viewed as an abuse in case law where no genuine parent-child relationship can be demonstrated.[7] The court, however, has recognized that the status of a child under immigration law does not necessarily affect the jurisdiction of the court, but may be a factor to be considered in determining an adoption order. In one instance the court found that the legislation requires a reasonable connection between the child and Ontario. The child must have lived in Ontario long enough for an investigation to be made of the prospective adoptive home so that the child's best interests could be served. Helping professionals whose clients are involved with questions regarding the status of prospective adoptees from other countries should be aware of the equivocal nature of the law in this matter and should advise their clients to seek legal assistance.

However there is now a special provision for intra-family adoptions which are an exception to the usual rules concerning residence and investigation provisions.

MARITAL STATUS OF THE APPLICANTS

Spouses, whether married or unmarried, are the preferred applicants in adoption proceedings but a single applicant may also apply and can succeed if there are special circumstances that justify an adoption order. In a special circumstance, the court permitted a Roman Catholic Priest to adopt two boys with whom he had established a parent-child relationship.[8] In another case the court said that a single woman of good character should not be denied the opportunity to adopt a male child.[9] However since adoptable children are scarce, the most stable adopting environment which closely meets the child's needs, is the most likely to be selected.

FOSTER PARENTS

A Crown ward's foster parents may make application to adopt the child where that child is residing with them at the time of the application, with the approval of the local Director of the Society and the Director of Child Welfare.

RELIGION OF THE APPLICANT

It is not an absolute requirement of the Act that a child be placed with people of the same religious faith. Even where the natural parent expresses wishes regarding the religious affiliation of the adoptive parents, the adoption agency or licensed person is not obligated to comply with these wishes but generally attempts to honour them where possible. However, religious affiliation or proposed religious upbringing of the child is one factor which the court will consider in granting an adoption order.

PROCEDURE FOR ADOPTION

Valid Adoption Consents

Consent to adoption must be obtained from every person who is a parent or has had lawful custody of the child. This of course would include the biological father but excludes foster parents.[10] Any person who has given consent may cancel the consent in writing within 21 days of the time it was given. An adoption consent will only be valid if it is a true and informed consent, not obtained through trickery, fraud, duress or through a mistake or misunderstanding of its true nature and consequences. In the case of a newborn infant, the consent cannot be taken until after the child is seven days old.

The consent of a child, parent or person with lawful custody of the child must be in writing. An employee of a Society or licensee must ensure that the consent reflects the true and informed wishes of the person giving the consent. A clear explanation should be given by the worker of the possible alternatives to adoption and the legal consequences of the adoption consent. It is not enough merely to tell the person that he or she is giving up all parental rights to the child. It is essential that the following points be covered:

1. the person giving the consent to the child's adoption has the right to cancel that consent in writing within 21 days of the time the consent was given;
2. after the 21-day period has expired, consent can be withdrawn only if the court is satisfied that it is in the best interests of the child, and only if the child has *not* already been placed for adoption and is residing with the prospective adoptors;
3. the person who consents has the right to consult an independent lawyer and must have had the opportunity to seek counselling;
4. the order for adoption, once made, will mean permanent surrender of all parental rights to the child, in other words, the child becomes the child of the adopting parents and ceases to be the child of the natural parents; and
5. the nature and operation of the voluntary disclosure registry and the right to participate.[11]

Consent of the Child

The written consent of a child seven years old or more is required. However, the child must have had the opportunity to obtain counselling and independent legal advice concerning the consent before consenting.

Dispensing with Consents

If the written consent of a particular person cannot be obtained, a court order dispensing with the consent may be sought.[12] An Ontario judge has held that:

> The power to dispense with consent has generally been viewed in the light of the two basic considerations of the child's best interests and the parent's

> rights. While the best interest rule has been on the ascendancy it is not the sole test and parental rights remain important.[13]

The judge also addressed the issue of affidavit evidence in lieu of a formal hearing and concluded:

> The fact that the Court can accept affidavit evidence would lend weight to the argument that a formal hearing with *viva voce* evidence is not required. Thus the child's psychologist, psychiatrist, and/or social worker would, in my view, be capable of attesting in written form to the fact that the child is capable of appreciating the nature of the application. One would think that such a professional would be just as capable and reliable as the presiding Judge's momentary appraisal of the child in his/her Chambers.[14]

After an adoption of a child with the consent of both parents had occurred in Ontario, the child's paternal grandparents sought custody under the Children's Law Reform Act. The application was dismissed on a jurisdictional finding because all matters concerning custody were controlled by the Child and Family Services Act, which provided jurisdiction only to the Ontario Court (Provincial Division) or the Unified Family Court. The Court of Appeal said that to permit the grandparents to assert a custodial claim under a provision of the Children's Law Reform Act would be inconsistent with s. 143(2) of the Child and Family Services Act, which states that once a child has been placed for adoption but no adoption order has yet been made, no person shall interfere with the parties to that placement. This decision should, however, be approached with caution, since the respective jurisdictions of the two statutes which deal with custody both rely on the best interests doctrine, and may be interpreted differently in another case.[15]

In a Manitoba case, the natural mother and her husband applied to adopt her child born out of wedlock, without obtaining the consent of the natural father and without serving him with notice of the application. The court found that the service of a notice was required although the consent of the natural father was not always required.[16]

The Native status of an Indian child was raised in a British Columbia case,[17] where a white couple attempted to adopt an Indian child with treaty status. The child had been apprehended on two occasions by the welfare authorities because he had been injured and neglected by his parents. The trial judge declined to dispense with the natural parents' consent and dismissed the application on the basis that "to the extent that the operation of the Adoption Act would affect the status of the child as an Indian, and so extinguish his rights as an Indian, it is inconsistent with the Indian Act". The British Columbia Court of Appeal reversed the decision, unanimously permitting the adoption. The Supreme Court of Canada dismissed the further appeal and allowed the adoption but held that the child could not be deprived of federally granted rights by provincial legislation such as the Adoption Act.

Another interesting case involving an application to adopt a Native infant also succeeded on appeal.[18] The mother, a native Indian, gave her 6-week-old child into the care of the Children's Aid Society who placed the child with non-Indian foster parents. The child was returned to the mother after two years. The mother, who was still emotionally upset, allowed the child to return to the care of the foster parents. The mother subsequently requested the return of the child and the foster parents, who wished to adopt the child, refused. During the next four years, the mother attempted to gain assistance from the authorities in obtaining custody, but had no direct contact with the child.

The foster parents applied for adoption and the mother applied for custody of the child. The trial judge found that the mother had abandoned the child and granted the adoption without the mother's consent. The Manitoba Court of Appeal overturned the adoption order, made the child a ward of the court and granted custody to the adoptive parents. The adoptive parents appealed and the mother cross-appealed. The Supreme Court of Canada allowed the appeal and reinstated the adoption order. There was evidence before the trial judge to justify her finding that the mother had abandoned the child during the four-year period when she had no contact with the child. The Court of Appeal put a different interpretation on the evidence than that of the trial judge. It was not the function of the appellate court to reinterpret the evidence. Furthermore, the court had the power to dispense with parental consent without finding that the natural parents abandoned the child. In the case of a *de facto* adoption, the adoptive parents had assumed the obligations of the natural parents and the consent of natural parents was not required.

The trial judge did not err in holding that the best interests of the child would be served by granting the adoption order. The trial judge addressed the issue of the child's Indian parentage in making her decision. Moreover, the child's heritage became less important as the bond with the adoptive parents developed. Finally, it was important for the court to make a final decision and put an end to the continued litigation and media exposure.

Homestudy and Report of the Director

The Director of Child Welfare must be notified of the proposed adoption. Upon notification, the Director is obliged to order that a homestudy be done and a report submitted before a child is placed in the adopting home. A homestudy is usually completed by a social worker and is an inquiry into both the suitability of the home and the capacity of the applicants to provide a nurturing environment for the child. The report recommends either approval or refusal of the adoption placement. If positive, the adoption can proceed. If it is negative, the applicants must be notified and informed of their right to a review of the decision of the Director and of their right to provide further evidence in support of the adoption.

FAMILY AND NATIVE ADOPTIONS

There is now a special provision for adoption of children by relatives, who include the child's grandparents, great uncles, or great aunts and uncles or aunts by blood, marriage or adoption.[19]

In the case of native children, their band and native community must be given advance notice of a proposed adoption.[20] Presumably, the band or native community is expected to advance an adoption plan for the child if one can be found.

The procedure for placement of children in family adoptions is far simpler than for extra-familial adoptions. Any family member may place a related child for adoption within or outside Ontario, with a relative, a parent or the parent's spouse. There is no longer a bar to bringing related children into Ontario for adoption without first notifying the Director or obtaining his prior approval, and such adoptions, once granted, do not have to be registered.

TERMINATION OF ACCESS ORDERS

When a child is placed for adoption by a Society or licensee, orders in regard to access to the child are terminated, *unless* that access order was made under child protection proceedings in Part III of the Child and Family Services Act and where the continuation of the access order is felt by the court to be in the child's best interests.[21]

STEPPARENT ADOPTIONS

Stepparent adoptions involve the petition of the stepparent to adopt the spouse's child of a former marriage.[22] Many problems arise when a mother who has custody of a child remarries, for example, changing the child's name on school records, denial of access to the natural father which may provoke withholding of maintenance payments, and the cessation of access between the child and the biological paternal grandparents and family. There are many reasons for the stepparent to petition to adopt his spouse's child. An adoption would guarantee that the child would have rights of succession and maintenance against his or her stepfather while giving the stepfather rights of custody over the child in addition to the psychological meaning of adoption to the child and stepfather.

Some authorities recommend guardianship by the stepparent as an alternative, because they are interested in the child maintaining his or her right to access to the natural parent.[23] The Ontario Law Reform Commission concurs with that view where one natural parent has died. The stepparent then acts jointly with the surviving natural parent, providing the court concurs that this is a viable alternative to adoption.[24]

The courts tend to rely for guidance in the matter of adoption on current psychiatric or psychological theory. Formerly, as a result of the least detrimental alternative theory of Goldstein, Freud, and Solnit,[25] the prevailing belief was that in order to create a stable home for the child, it was necessary to terminate contact with the non-custodial parent. More recent findings have considered the child's need to maintain relations with the non-custodial parent.[26] The following case illustrates the difference of opinion held by the mental health professionals and the presiding judge in regard to access between the child and the natural father.[27] The child's parents had married in 1969, and a daughter was born the following year. They divorced in 1974 with custody given to the mother and the right of reasonable access given to the father. The mother remarried in 1975 and petitioned with her new husband to adopt the child. The natural father refused consent. The judge felt the father's relationship with the child was affectionate and that his failure to see the child frequently was the result of the mother's animosity toward him. The child also had a good relationship with the paternal grandparents. The child's counsel and the Superintendent of Child Welfare, who based his opinion on the social worker's report, both recommended the adoption as "the least detrimental alternative possible". The judge, however, refused to dispense with the father's consent.

This perspective reaffirms an earlier case where the judge held that:

> [A] child has a right to the knowledge of the existence of its natural parents, to a normal association with those parents, and to the benefit of the love, understanding and guidance which may be developed in the intimate relationship between the child and its natural parents. No court should deny a child those rights without serious reasons.[28]

Many judges have also stated that they wished they could make access to the natural parent a condition of the adoption order.

Another aspect of the controversy has to do with the conflict between the paramountcy of the federal Divorce Act, and adoption which is a provincial matter. In one interesting case the judge made a distinction between access and adoption.[29] A father was granted custody of two children with reasonable access to the mother. Subsequently the mother moved to New Zealand and the father remarried and applied with his spouse to adopt the children. The mother could not be contacted. The judge dispensed with consent and ordered the adoption. When the mother returned, she sought an order from the court defining the terms of access. The court found in her favour using the principle of paramountcy. The court held that access is a right that does not depend upon a parental relationship and that adoption only alters the legal status between adopting and natural parents.

Generally, an outstanding order for access to the non-custodial parent is terminated at the point of adoption. If access is to continue subsequent to adoption, it must be specified in the order, but this is not the usual case.

Adoption orders

The court may order the adoption of a child by the person with whom the child is placed, or, in the case of a child over 16 or person over 18, upon the application of another person. The court may also order a family adoption by the child's relative, parent or step-parent.[30] In every case the order must be based on the best interests of the child. However, the court may not grant an adoption order where the consent of a person has been dispensed with until all appeal periods have elapsed.

An interesting case concerns four homosexual couples who each brought a joint application for adoption under s. 146(4)(b) of the Child and Family Services Act. This section states that an application can be made jointly by two individuals who are spouses of one another. One of the applicants in each of the applications was the natural parent through artificial insemination. The Act says that only the spouse of the natural mother can seek to adopt the child and guarantee that the natural mother would not lose the child to the applicant. In other words the definition of the word spouse is critical. When the Child and Family Services Act was revised in 1984, sexual orientation was not a bar to adoption because s. 136(1) states that "spouse" has the same meaning as in Parts I and II of the Human Rights Code where the definition of "spouse" includes persons living in a conjugal relationship outside marriage. The four couples claimed that s. 136 is still discriminatory and in violation of s. 15(1) of the Charter.

The appeal from the Ontario Court (Provincial Division) order succeeded and the appellate court granted adoption orders to the four couples, thus striking down the section of the Child and Family Services Act that prevented lesbians from legally adopting the children of partners. Question however whether this case would extend to the partner of the natural father?[31]

ADOPTIVE PARENTS RIGHT TO MATERNITY AND PARENTAL LEAVE

In 1996, the Ontario Court (General Division) ruled that sections of the Unemployment Insurance Act contravened the Charter by giving adoptive parents only 10 weeks of maternity leave compared with 15 weeks of maternity leave and 10 weeks of parental leave for birth parents. Mr. Justice Donald Cameron ruled that "adopted children are indirectly denied equal benefit of the law to the extent that their parents may be economically constrained to return to work after only 10 weeks". He added that the distinction between adoptive and biological parents was based on "an assumption that since the adoptive mother is highly unlikely to breast-feed, neither she nor her husband needs comparable bonding time with their child".[32]

LEGAL EFFECT OF AN ADOPTION ORDER

A legal order for adoption cannot obliterate emotional ties with a stroke of the pen, either for the biological parents or for an older child. However, the legal effect is abrupt, clear, and unequivocal. The child becomes the child of the adopting parents for all purposes as though he had been born into that family and ceases to be the child of his biological parents and family.

An important case involved a child who was a Crown ward in Ontario and sought access to her sister who had been adopted. The society refused her application on the grounds that the statute prohibits access to the former family once a child has been adopted. However, they were aware that they also had a responsibility to act in the best interests of the child under their jurisdiction, the Crown ward applicant, who turned to the court. The Provincial Court held that there was no bar to access and awarded costs against the society. Leave to appeal to the Supreme Court of Canada was refused but the question of the best interests of the child being served by contact with members of the former family after adoption has occurred has been opened and may need to be considered in new legislation. There is growing interest in "open" adoption and post-adoption access with former family members.[33]

THE VOLUNTARY DISCLOSURE REGISTRY

A voluntary disclosure registry has been established under provisions of Ontario legislation. It records the identity of birth parents who wish to re-establish contact with the child. The birth parent or a child who is at least 18 years old may apply to be registered in the disclosure registry. When the Director receives an application, he must determine if there is a complementary registration and must obtain consent to disclosure from the adoptive parents, the adopted child, and the person named as the birth parent. The Act states that it is the duty of every Society to provide guidance and counselling to persons who may be registered and are eligible for disclosure from the registry.[34] Some provinces have significantly different disclosure laws in which the rights of the adult adoptee are greater than those of the birth or adoptive parents.[35]

The Garber Commission recommended that the adoptee, upon reaching the age of 18 years, and the natural parent should be the only persons whose consent is required. The consent of the adopting parents should not be required since the adoptee is now an adult; neither should their withholding consent bar contact between child and natural parent.[36]

Disclosure of Non-Identifying Information

Non-identifying information is any information that would not reveal the identity of the person who is its subject. Anyone can make a request for such information but the Registrar must decide whether that person should be given it. Such requests may be made by the adopted person over 18, or under 18 with the written consent of the adoptive parents; an adoptive parent; a birth parent; a birth grandparent; a birth sibling (age 18 or older) or any other person with the written consent of the adoptive person where appropriate, or the written consent of the adoptive parent. The Registrar has a duty to ensure that counselling is made available to the person who receives the information.[37]

Adoption Disclosure Registrar

Once an adoption order is made, the Act sets out the terms governing disclosure of identifying information. An adopted person 18 years or over, a birth parent, a grandparent, a sibling, or any person deemed to be suitable by the Registrar can apply to be named in the Register. If both parties are named in the register and have had an opportunity to receive counselling, both may provide their consent in writing to the release of information. The Registrar also may disclose information, either non-identifying or identifying to any person if that information is relevant to the health, safety, or welfare of the parties involved.[38]

Searches

When an adopted child reaches the age of 18, that child may ask the Registrar to conduct a search for the person who consented to the adoption, the biological father, the grandparents, or birth siblings aged 18 or over. The purpose of the search is for the Registrar to ascertain whether the person wishes to be identified to the adopted person. Where the person who is the object of the search has died, lacks capacity or has not been located in six months, the Registrar may provide the information as if both parties had consented. If the Registrar, the Society, or licensee believes that disclosure might result in physical or emotional harm to any person, the information may be withheld with notice and reasons for refusal, and the person advised of the right to review.[39]

In 1996, British Columbia became the first province to open its adoption records. Adoptees are entitled to gain access to their original birth registration and learn the identity of their birth parents, as well as their own names at birth. Parents who gave up children are able to obtain copies of the adoption orders and learn the child's adopted names. Names of the adopted parents will be deleted to protect their privacy. This is a reversal of the procedure in Ontario and many other jurisdictions where a Registry has been established to determine whether both parties wish to be identified. British Columbia has simplified the process by giving adoptees and birth parents the right to veto the release of information about them, rather than promising them that their identities would be kept secret. The British Columbia law also creates a registry for birth fathers who may wish to be a party to an adoption proceeding, gives children over the age of seven a say in an adoption procedure, and a right to consent to a change in their legal name, and recognizes the right of same sex couples and common law spouses to apply to adopt children.[40]

Canada has ratified the Convention on Protection of Children and Cooperation in Respect of Intercountry Adoption. The Convention establishes safeguards aimed at preventing the abduction, or sale of, or trafficking in children. It also establishes consistent lower cost adoption procedures and seeks to eliminate improper financial gains. Approximately 20,000 intercountry adoptions occur each year, of which 2,000 involve Canadians. The legislation sets up a Central Authority to monitor the adoption process which will coordinate requests to adopt children from other countries. Five provinces have passed implementing legislation: British Columbia, Manitoba, New Brunswick, Prince Edward Island, and Saskatchewan.

CHANGE OF NAME

Most provincial legislation permits a child's name to be changed to that of the adopting parents. In Ontario, a given name or surname is changed to that of the adopting parents at their request and with the written consent of the child over 12 years. Both the surname and given names may be changed at the time of adopting.[41]

Endnotes

1. W. Oppel, "Step-Parent Adoptions in Nova Scotia and British Columbia" (1981), 6 Dalhousie L.J. 631.
2. See Tables of Concordance.
3. Child and Family Services Act, R.S.O. 1990, c.C.11.
4. *Ibid.*, s. 137.
5. *In camera* — literally in chambers or away from public scrutiny.
6. Note 3 above.
7. See *Re Rai* (1980), 27 O.R. (2d) 425, 106 D.L.R. (3d) 718 (C.A.); *Re Lee Yen Chum*, [1964] N.S.W.R. 854, 4 F.L.R. 296 (Sup. Ct.).
8. See *Re R.L. and B.L.*, Ont. Dist. Ct., October, 1980 (unreported).
9. *Re M.J.W.*, [1964] N.S.W.R. 1108 (Sup.Ct.). See, note 3 above, where s. 136(1) defines spouses by incorporating the broad definition in the Human Rights Code, and includes single, divorced, and widowed persons and couples living together in a conjugal relationship.
10. Child and Family Services Act, R.S.O. 1990, c.C.11, s. 137.
11. Child and Family Services Act, R.S.O. 1990, c.C.11, s. 137(4)(b) requires that the birth parents be given the opportunity to seek counselling and independent legal advice before consenting to their child's adoption.
12. Child and Family Services Act, R.S.O. 1990, c.C.11, s. 138.
13. *Re M.L.A.* (1979), 25 O.R. (2d) 779 at 795 (Fam. Ct.).
14. *Ibid.*, at 783.
15. *M. (R.) v. M. (S.)* (1991), 9 R.F.L. (4th) 372, 20 O.R. (3d) 621, 119 D.L.R. (4th) 757 (C.A.).
16. *Re B.M.F.*, ([1981] 4 W.W.R. 171, 8 Man. R. (2d) 331 (Co. Ct.).
17. *Natural Parents v. Supt. of Child Welfare*, [1976] 2 S.C.R. 751, [1976] 1 W.W.R. 699, 21 R.F.L. 267, 60 D.L.R. (3d) 148, 6 N.R. 491, affirming (*sub nom. Re Birth Registration No. 67-09-022272*) [1974] 2 W.W.R. 363, 14 R.F.L. 396, 44 D.L.R. (3d) 718 (*sub nom. Re Adoption Act*), which reversed [1974] 1 W.W.R. 19, 13 R.F.L. 244.
18. *Re W.; W. v. R.; R. v. W.*, 32 R.F.L. (2d) 153, (*sub nom. Woods v.*

Racine) 19 Man. R. (2d) 186, [1983] 2 C.N.L.R. 157. Reversed (*sub nom. A.N.R. v. L.J.W.*) 36 R.F.L. (2d) 1, [1984] 1 W.W.R. 1, 24 Man. R. (2d) 314, 48 N.R. 362 (S.C.C.).
19. Child and Family Services Act, R.S.O. 1990, c.C.11, s. 146(2).
20. *Ibid.*, s. 140(3).
21. *Ibid.*, s. 143(1)
22. *Ibid.*, s. 146(2)(c).
23. A. Bissett-Johnson. "Children in Subsequent Marriages — Questions of Access, Name and Adoption." (1980), 11 R.F.L. (2d) 289.
24. *Ibid.*, at 312.
25. J. Goldstein, A. Freud, and A.J. Solnit. *Beyond the Best Interests of the Child* (New York: The Free Press, a Division of Macmillan, Inc., 1973).
26. J. Grief. "Fathers, Children and Joint Custody". *Amer. Jr. of Ortho.*, 49(2): 311, 1979.
27. *Smallenberg v. Smallenberg* (1978), 5 R.F.L. (2d) 315 (B.C. S.C.).
28. *Re Kennette and Munro*, [1973] 3 O.R. 156 at 167, 11 R.F.L. 21 at 33 (*sub nom. Re Munro*), 36 D.L.R. (3d) 180 (Co.Ct.) and subsequent cases which have relied on it.
29. *Kerr v. McWhannel*, 16 R.F.L. 185, [1974] 6 W.W.R. 543, 46 D.L.R. (3d) 624 (B.C. C.A.).
30. Child and Family Services Act, R.S.O. 1990, c.C.11, s. 140.
31. *Re K.* (1995), 15 R.F.L. (4th) 129, 23 O.R. (3rd) 679, 125 D.L.R. (4th) 653 (Prov. Div.).
32. *Globe and Mail*, June 1, 1996.
33. *P.(M.A.R.) v. Catholic Children's Aid Society of Metropolitan Toronto* (1995), 9 R.F.L. (4th) 385 (Ont. Prov. Div.), affirmed (1995) 11 R.F.L. (4th) 95, 122 D.L.R. (4th) 719 (Ont. Gen. Div.). Affirmed (1995), 15 R.F.L. (4th) 330, 126 D.L.R. (4th) 673, 84 O.A.C. 308. Leave to appeal to S.C.C. refused (1995), 130 D.L.R. (4th) vii (note) (S.C.C.).
34. Child and Family Services Act, R.S.O. 1990, c. C.11, s. 167.
35. See the Table of Concordance.
36. Garber, R., "Disclosure of Adoption Information" (Toronto: Ministry of Community and Social Services, 1985).
37. Child and Family Services Act, R.S.O. 1990, c. C.11, s. 166.
38. *Ibid.*, s. 167.
39. *Ibid.*, s. 167.
40. Community Action, April 14, 1997 and see the Table of Concordance.
41. See the Table of Concordance.

Bibliography

"Adoption Rights for Same-Sex Couples: A Grammar Lesson?" (Sept. 1995) 10 *Money and Family Law*, 69-70.

Adoption Disclosure Services in Ontario, by the Ministry of Community and Social Services of Ontario (Toronto: The Ministry, 1996).

Adoption and the Indian Child (Ottawa: Indian and Northern Affairs Canada, 1993).

Black, Vaughn. "GATT (General Agreement in Tariffs and Trade) for Kids: New Rules for Intercountry Adoption of Children" (Oct., 1994) 11 Canadian Family Law Quarterly, 253-315.

Borgman, R. "The Consequences of Open and Closed Adoption for Older Children." *Child Welfare*, 61(4). 217-26, 1982.

Depp, C.H. "After Reunion: Perceptions of Adult Adoptees, Adoptive Parents and Birth Parents." *Child Welfare*, 61(2): 115-19, 1982.

Eade, Mark. "Intercountry Adoption: International, National and Cultural Concerns" (1993) 57 Saskatchewan Law Review 381-395.

Francis, Verlyn F. *In the Application of the "Best Interests of the Child" Test in Adoption, There Must Be a Place for the Consideration of Race* (Ottawa: National Association of Women and Law, 1994).

Garber, Ralph. "Disclosure of Adoption Information." Report of the Special Commissioner to the Minister of Community and Social Services, Ontario (Toronto: Ministry of Community and Social Services, 1985).

Hodgkinson, Terry L. "A Lifelong Dream: The Risks and Rewards of Private Adoption" (Dec., 1993) 18 Law Now, 19-21.

House, Jeannie. "The Changing Face of Adoption: The Challenge of Open and Custom Adoption" (March, 1996) 13 Canadian Family Law Quarterly, 333-363.

Klauer, Joan. "Open Adoption Records: A Question of Empowerment" (1993) 57 Saskatchewan Law Review 415-427.

Lightstone, Susan. "Adoption Law" (March, 1994) 3 National, No. 2, 30-35.

Phillips, Douglas W. et al. *Adoption Law in Canada: Practice and Procedure* (Toronto: Carswell, 1995).

Reynolds, Nancy T. *Adopting Your Child: Options, Answers and Actions*. 1st ed. (Self-Counsel Reference Series) (North Vancouver: Self-Counsel Press, 1993).

Ward, Margaret. "Culture Shock in the Adoption of Older Children." (1980), 78 Soc. Wkr. 8.

Williams, Catherine. "Step-Parent Adoptions and the Best Interests of the Child in Ontario" (1982), 32 U.T.L.J. 217.

20

Education

Social workers should have general knowledge of provisions contained in provincial Education Acts that affect the rights and responsibilities of children, parents, and school personnel. In practice, the system of ensuring fairness and informed consent is more apt to occur with the involvement of a social worker who will assume an advocacy role. School districts and individual schools vary greatly in the availability of resources and services and in the commitment to ensuring that all pupils and parents are apprised of their legal rights. For example, where psychological testing of a child occurs, the parent or guardian is entitled to attend the meeting to discuss the report and recommendations and to be advised about the ongoing process of review. Similarly, it is important to inform parents that they may attend special meetings set up by the board to discuss the proper placement of a child and that they may bring a friend or request that an interpreter be provided. The cultural diversity of Canada requires that new immigrants be given special consideration to help them to understand how and why decisions regarding their children are made, to understand the extent of their right to participate in those decisions, and to ensure that they see all reports and records concerning their children. School trustees can be helpful in advocating a special service or concern for a pupil in some situations where formal efforts have been exhausted.

In Ontario, the Education Act[1] is the relevant legislation which will be examined. Readers from other provinces are directed to consult their own provincial legislation.[2] The significant actors are pupils, parents or guardians, teachers, principals, supervisory officers, school boards, and various committees.

COMPULSORY ATTENDANCE

Children between the ages of 6 and 16 years are compelled to attend school.[3] The school attendance officer must inquire into every case where a child fails to attend school and must give written notice to the parent or guardian requiring the child to attend school.[4] This officer cannot enter a home without a warrant. A parent or guardian who neglects or refuses to get a child to school is guilty of an offence and on summary conviction is liable to a fine of not more than $100.[5] Formerly, a truanting child could be charged with delinquency under the Juvenile Delinquents Act. At present, the enforceability of school attendance is questionable. A child can be excused from school attendance if the Minister is satisfied that the child is receiving adequate home instruction.[6]

EARLY SCHOOL LEAVING

A pupil who is 14 years old may be excused from school attendance or may be required to attend only part-time on the recommendation of a committee which is composed of a supervisory officer, a provincial representative and a third appointee. Any school board employee involved directly with the pupil, including the teacher, principal, or social worker, as well as the child's parent or guardian, may attend meetings of this committee.

USE OF CORPORAL PUNISHMENT

The Criminal Code[7] permits substitute parents and school teachers to physically punish children, using force that is "reasonable under the circumstances" to enforce acceptable conduct. Many school boards have established policies restricting or prohibiting the use of corporal punishment.

SUSPENSION

A pupil may be suspended by a principal for a fixed period not to exceed 20 days[8] for persistent truancy, opposition to authority, habitual neglect of duty, wilful destruction of school property, use of profane or improper language, or conduct which is injurious to the moral tone of the school or to the physical or mental well-being of others. The principal must give written notice of the suspension to the pupil, his teachers, parent or guardian, the board, and the supervisory officer.[9]

The parent or guardian of the pupil or the adult pupil himself may, within seven days of the commencement of the suspension, appeal to the board against the suspension.[10] The board has the power to sustain or revoke the principal's decision.

EXPULSION

The board has the right to expel a pupil on the recommendation of both the principal and supervisory officer. Notification of expulsion must be in writing and must be made to the parent or guardian of the pupil or the adult pupil.

The board, at its discretion, may decide to re-admit a pupil after consideration of an appeal from the principal, parent or guardian, or supervisory officer.

PERSONS UNABLE TO PROFIT FROM INSTRUCTION

In the case of pupils who are alleged to be unable to profit from instruction, the board may appoint a three-person committee called a Special Education Programme Placement and Review Committee.[11] This committee is composed of a supervisory officer, a principal (but not of the school involved) and either a physician or a psychiatrist depending upon whether the problem is defined as emotional or physical. A review of the decision of this committee is permitted to be brought to another similar committee at a later time. These hearings can be especially important where there is concern that discrimination based on cultural or racial factors may be influencing decisions to stream students into special education programmes.

Recommendations of the committee may be for a withdrawal programme where the pupil is requested to spend less time in the classroom,[12] or assignment to a special education programme. There must be a review at least once every year of such a placement. A parent or guardian may request in writing a review at any time and such a review must occur within 30 days of receipt of the request.[13]

Once a placement is made, parents or an adult pupil must agree in writing to any major change in the placement.[14]

SPECIAL EDUCATION

The Ontario Education Act provides for compulsory special education programmes,[15] setting in place the concept of zero-reject. In effect, all children must be provided with appropriate education. This concept has already been established in law in Quebec, Nova Scotia, Manitoba,

Saskatchewan and Alberta, but the implementation falls far short of zero-reject.[16] The major objective is to ensure that all exceptional children in Ontario have available to them appropriate special education programmes and special education services without payment of fees by parents or guardians. The Act instructs a school board to establish special education programmes or to purchase them from another board. If children need a special placement not provided by a board, it will be paid for by the province. This placement must be in Ontario unless no placement suited to the needs of the pupil is available in the province. A placement outside the province may then be made.[17]

It should be noted that the decision of the three-member committee set up to determine the placement of the child and to conduct ongoing review is subject to appeal only under certain conditions. There is an appeal to a "Special Education Tribunal" against a decision that the pupil is hard to serve, or against the location of a placement.[18] However, if the decision is that a child is not hard to serve or that a board has an adequate programme for the child, there is no appeal possible. Recourse to the courts may be possible under the Judicial Review Procedure Act,[19] but only in cases of lack of jurisdiction or unfair procedure. The courts may not entertain an appeal on the ground that the committee has not appreciated the problem and has made an inappropriate decision. It has been noted by one commentator that there is still no duty to see that the special programmes are effective and no obligation in the Act to provide and train effective teachers.[20]

Under the Education Act, the Statutory Powers Procedure Act,[21] which guarantees procedural fairness applies only to the Special Education Tribunal and the Regional Tribunal. It does not apply to hearings at the first stages of the appeal process, which are the decisive and critical hearings before the school board and the Special Education Identification Placement, and Review Committees. At these hearings, the child and parent are not allowed to be represented by counsel, the hearing will not be open to the public, and witnesses may not be cross-examined.

A social worker can assist parents and children to understand the process of hearings and reviews so that they are well prepared for the initial round of hearings. Legal counsel should be consulted if irregularities occur and counsel should be retained if an appeal takes place at the Special Education Tribunal and Regional Tribunal levels.[22]

In an important case in Ontario, the issue of the right to education within the regular classroom for a child with a severe physical handicap was considered. The child, Emily, a 10 year old girl with cerebral palsy could not speak, had no other mode of communication, had some visual impairment, and spent most of her time in a wheelchair. During kindergarten and grade 1, she was in a regular class at her local school aided by a full time educational assistant assigned to her. At the end of grade 1, the Identification Placement and Review Committee (I.P.R.C.) ruled that she should be placed in a special class in another integrated school. Her parents appealed this decision, but it was upheld by the Special Education Tribunal established under the Education Act.[23]

The parents then applied for judicial review and the decision was again upheld by the Ontario Divisional Court. When internal appeals have been exhausted, parents can made a human rights complaint or go to court, but courts are traditionally loath to challenge educational expert opinion. The parents chose to appeal to the Ontario Court of Appeal. The court focussed on the question of discrimination and equality rather than on the education question. The Divisional Court held that the Canadian Charter of Rights and Freedoms created a presumption in favour of integration of handicapped persons into the mainstream of the community, and the integration of disabled students into a regular classroom.[24]

The Court of Appeal held that the Divisional Court had erred in holding that the Charter and the Ontario Human Rights Code did not apply to the situation. The court shifted the burden of proof from the parents to the school board to prove that the segregated placement they proposed is the appropriate pedagogy. The court found that s. 8 of the Education Act was discriminatory by giving the school board discretion to put a child identified as exceptional in a segregated environment without the parents' consent. They placed an onus on the school board to "provide a placement that is the least exclusionary from the mainstream and still reasonably capable of meeting the child's special needs".[25] The same court ordered that a new hearing be held by a different Special Education Tribunal in accordance with the new threshold test. Where parents do not consent to a segregated placement, the onus is on the board to prove that its recommendation is the only appropriate alternative. The decision makes a strong presumption in favour of integrated education for exceptional children.

The debate for inclusive education has been going on for over 20 years. In general, the legislation across Canada and the territories grants the preponderance of discretion to school administrators rather than to the disabled and parents.[26]

The Nova Scotia Education Regulations limit the right to education to students who are capable of benefitting from schooling. The Alberta and Newfoundland Acts include provisions which restrict the right for students with severe disabilities who are not considered to be educable. Decisions that only look at scarce resources and inadequately trained teachers fail to recognize the discriminatory aspect of these decisions. In the last decade, service delivery policies and practices have tended toward mainstreaming in some jurisdictions. New Brunswick, Quebec, and Saskatchewan and the two territories have passed legislative revisions in mainstreaming and integration dictated by a least restrictive orientation. In the United States, the Individuals with Disabilities Education Act was passed over 20 years ago. It gives very specific directives in contrast with a level of discretionary permissiveness in Canadian law. In reality, while procedural fairness must be demonstrated, substantive rules are difficult to legislate beyond general guidelines to consider the effects of discrimination in each situation. In many communities, parents and interested persons have formed action groups to advocate for inclusion into the mainstream of disabled children.[27]

HOME INSTRUCTION

When medical evidence is provided to the principal that a pupil cannot attend school, then on the recommendation of an Identification, Placement and Review Committee, the pupil may be referred for home instruction.[28] Generally two and one-half hours per week of home instruction is provided by the board with a review of this plan twice a year. A parent or guardian of the pupil must agree in writing to any major change in the plan for the child. Social workers are usually involved when home instruction is suggested for a child. There is also a trend towards home schooling, which is permitted under the Education Act (Ontario). These children must be supervised by the relevant School Inspector and are required to pass examinations related to their school grade.

RELIGIOUS EXERCISES

No pupil is required to take part in any religious exercises or be subject to any instruction in religious education where his parent or an adult pupil applies to the principal of the school for an exemption. It is worth noting that an exemption must be requested. The Supreme Court of Canada has ruled that Ontario's funding of Roman Catholic schools which is required by the Constitution, does not imply an obligation to fund other religious schools in the name of equality or religious freedom.[29]

ATTENDANCE IN ANY SCHOOL WITHIN THE SYSTEM

If the supervisory officer concurs, a pupil may attend another school in the system. If a pupil moves out of the district, that pupil may continue to attend the old school with the permission of the supervisory officer.[30] A person less than 18 years who is entitled to admission to school should not be refused admission because the parent or guardian is unlawfully in Canada. A person who has been enrolled in school for seven or more years may attend continuing education classes to earn a diploma required for advanced training or education without payment of tuition.[31]

PUPIL RECORDS

Pupil records are considered privileged communications. Parents or guardians or adult pupils have the right to review their records and submit corrections. If the principal refuses to include the corrections, the supervisory officer may order inclusion or a hearing is held before a person appointed by the Minister. That person's decision is binding and final.[32]

RIGHTS OF PARENT TO INFORMATION ABOUT CHILD'S EDUCATION

Many educators incorrectly assume that only a custodial parent, where the parents are separated or divorced, has a right to information concerning the child's education and progress in the school system. Consequently, a non-custodial parent who is interested may be denied access to the child's school records by teachers and principals. Teachers may find themselves drawn into the conflict between parents because the custodial parent insists that no information be released to the other parent. Teachers are frequently unaware that both parents have an equal right to access to school records and information about the child.[33]

In Ontario, the provincial government has introduced legislation that concentrates authority over education with the province by reducing the number of school boards and curtailing their tax-raising powers. Under the legislation which will take effect in 1998, Ontario boards will be reduced to 66 from 129. Community input will be restructured but curriculum program and service decisions will be subject to increased provincial control. This will include, for example, the number of school librarians, and library resources, guidance counsellors, psychologists, social workers, and teacher preparation time, as well as physical plant amenities. Paring down these resources may improverish schools in some communities.[34]

Studies have linked poverty and social class with school achievement and have reinforced a strong statistical association between socioeconomic status and educational achievement. Canada's poorest children are more than three times as likely as the richest children to be in remedial education classes; the richest pupils, aged 9 to 11, are almost twice as likely to be in gifted classes as the poorest, and the richest students are most likely to be rated near the top of their class by teachers in reading and in mathematics. In addition, the Canadian School Boards Association reports that children living in poverty drop out of school more often than children whose families live above the poverty level. These figures are consistent from 1987 to 1991.[35]

These outcomes should be unacceptable to a society that values equal opportunity as a democratic right and that needs an educated and thoughtful populace in a complex post-industrial economy. A needed approach might be to introduce legislation that declares that the state has an interest in education that begins at birth. A partnership could then be structured between ministries of health, education, community and social services, and corrections which would mandate cooperative systems to monitor the resource needs of families ranging from income and physical needs to psychological supports that would reduce isolation. Since multiculturalism is a reality of Canadian culture, sensitivity to multicultural values would be mandatory to prevent such an approach to children and families from becoming a form of social control by the dominant culture. The cost of this legislation would be short-term intensive. However, there would be long-term savings in the costs of supporting and advancing children and young adults whose family poverty condemns them to failure and the negative systems of marginalization.

Endnotes

1. R.S.O. 1990, c. E.2.
2. See Table of Concordance.
3. Note 1 above, s. 20(1).
4. *Ibid.*, s. 25(4).
5. *Ibid.*, s. 29(1).
6. *Ibid.*, s. 20(2)(*a*).
7. R.S.C. 1985, c. C-46, s. 43.
8. R.S.O. 1990, c. E.2, s. 23.
9. See note 1, s. 22(1).
10. *Ibid.*, s. 22(2).
11. Regulation under the Education Act, R.S.O. 1990, c. E.2.
12. *Ibid.*, r. 32.
13. *Ibid.*, r. 32(4).
14. *Ibid.*, r. 32(5).
15. Note 1 above, s. 32(5) and (6).
16. J. A. C. Smith, "The Right to an Appropriate Education: A Comparative Study" (1980), 12 Ottawa L. Rev. 367.
17. Note 1 above, s. 34.

18. *Ibid.*, s. 34(10).
19. R.S.O. 1990, c. E.2.
20. J. A. C. Smith. "The Education Amendment Act, 1980." (1981), 13 Ottawa L. Rev. 199 at 201.
21. R.S.O. 1990, c. C.32.
22. An excellent pamphlet has been prepared by the Ontario Association for Children with Learning Disabilities, entitled "Putting the Pieces Together: A Parent's Guide to Special Education in Ontario" written by K. MacGregor, S. Rosenbaum, and K. Skoutajan.
23. *Eaton v. Brant (County) Board of Education* (1995), 22 O.R. (3d) 1 (C.A.).
24. Greenstein, Bertha, "Exceptional Children's Right to Inclusion", Case Note, Educational Law Journal [7], p. 77.
25. Per Madame Justice Arbour (1995), 22 O.R. (3d) 1 (C.A.) at 21.
26. MacKay, Wayne A. and Vincent C. Kazmierski, "And on Eighth Day God Gave Us . . . Equality in Education: Eaton vs. Brant (County) Board of Education and Inclusive Education," 7.1 National Journal of Constitutional Law, August, 1996, 1-42.
27. *Ibid.*
28. Education Act, s. 21 and regulations.
29. *Adler v. Ontario* (1994), 19 O.R. (3d) 1 (C.A.), affirmed [1996] 3 S.C.R. 609.
30. Education Act, s. 41.
31. *Ibid.*, s. 49.
32. *Ibid.*, s. 266(2) and Children's Law Reform Act, R.S.O. 1980, c. 68, s. 20.
33. *Ibid.*, s. 266(10) and Children's Law Reform Act, R.S.O. 1980, c. 68, s. 20.
34. Bill 160, Ontario.
35. Statistics Canada, *Globe and Mail*, April 26, 1997.

Bibliography

Brown, Anthony F. and Marvin A. Zuker, *Education Law* (Toronto: Carswell, 1994).

Correia, Margaret, "Student Suspensions Case Note: *Skyrme v. Shuswap* — School District No. 89 (February 2, 1993) (Dec., 1993) 5 *Education and Law Journal* 262-64.

Dolmage, W. Rod, "One Less Brick in the Wall: The Myths of Youth Violence and Unsafe Schools" (Sept., 1996) 7 *Education and Law Journal* 185-207.

Ferguson, Margaret. "Parent Advocacy" (June, 1995) 19 *Law Now*, No. 6, pp. 25-26.

Greenstein, Bertha. "Exceptional Child's Right to Inclusion" (Nov., 1995) 7 *Educational Law Journal* 77-80.

Holloway, Joanna. "The Liability of the Local Education Authority to Pupils Who Receive a Defective Education" (May, 1996) 7 *Education and Law Journal* 95-106.

Holloway, Joanna. "The Rights of Individuals Who Receive a Defective Education" (July, 1995) 6 *Education and Law Journal* 279-99.

House, Jeannie. "Parent Power: Participation in Educational Decision-Making" (Sept., 1994) 6 *Education and Law Journal* 27-57.

MacKay, A. Wayne. "Principles in Search of Justice for the Young: What's Law Got to Do with It?" (March, 1995) 6 *Education and Law Journal* 181-202.

MacKay, A. Wayne and Vincent C. Kazmierski. "And on the Eighth Day, God Gave Us . . . Equality in Education: *Eaton v. Brant (County) Board of Education* and Inclusive Education" (August, 1996) 7 *National Journal of Constitutional Law* 1-42.

MacKay, A. Wayne and Pamela Rubin. "Study Paper on Psychological Testing in Education and Employment" (Toronto: Ontario Law Reform Commission, 1997).

MacKay, Wayne. "Human Rights and Education: Problems and Prospects" (Dec., 1996) 8 *Education and Law Journal* 69-88.

MacLellan, Duncan K. "The Legal Question of Extending Public Funds to Private Schools in Ontario" (Case Comm.) *Adler v. Ontario* (1994), 19 O.R. (3d) 1 (C.A.) in (Nov., 1995) 7 *Education and Law Journal* 77-80.

Response to Proposed Amendments to the Education Act (Bill 4) (Special Education, Suspensions) (Toronto; Justice for Children and Youth, 1993).

Richter, Christopher. "Separation and Equality: An Argument for Religious Schools within the Public System" (1996-97) 28 *Ottawa Law Review* 1-44.

Smith, William J. and William F. Foster. "Educational Opportunities for Students with Disabilities in Canada: A Platform of Rights to Build On" (Dec., 1993) 5 *Education and Law Journal* 193-223.

Smith, William J. and William F. Foster. "Educational Opportunity for Students with Disabilities in Canada: Beyond the Schoolhouse Door" (May, 1994) 4 *Education and Law Journal* 305-334.

Thorncroft, Kenneth W. "Do Teachers' Strikes Harm Students?" (May, 1996) 7 *Education and Law Journal* 127-47.

Watkison, Ailsa M. "Equality, Empathy and the Administration of Education" (May, 1994) 5 *Education and Law Journal* 273-304.

21

Children Who Break the Law

INTRODUCTION

"In my opinion, this child don't need to have his head shrunk at all. Juvenile delinquency is purely a social disease."
"So take him to a social worker . . ."
"The trouble is he's crazy.
The trouble is he drinks.
The trouble is he's lazy.
The trouble is he stinks."[1]

Is a child who breaks the law to be treated or punished? Or both? It seems that even Parliament cannot make up its mind.[2] The former Juvenile Delinquents Act, which survived for many years was a treatment-oriented statute.[3] The Young Offenders Act requires both punishment and treatment.[4] The pendulum swings back and forth, carrying the errant child with it as Parliament adjusts the balance. But equilibrium is elusive if not impossible; there will likely always be disproportionate emphasis on one or the other, treatment or punishment.

In the past few years the emphasis has been punishment in the form of stricter supervision, secure custody and more onerous dispositions. This emphasis has been accompanied by calls from the police and the public to amend the Young Offenders Act to provide for ever more stringent and onerous dispositions for youthful offenders. The prevailing view is that there has been a rapid and radical increase in the incidence of crimes by youthful offenders, which is not borne out by the statistics. For the period 1985 to 1990, there was no increase over the period 1980-1984 in the numbers of youths suspected of a crime and a small increase (about 10%) of youths actually charged. The number of convictions is not reported.[5]

ROLE OF LEGAL COUNSEL IN YOUNG OFFENDER PROCEEDINGS

The legal profession is equally confused about its proper role in youth court. Some lawyers propose that the only role for lawyers who defend children against criminal charges should be that of defence counsel — to provide the best possible defence, require strict proof of the allegations against the child and to make every effort to have the child found not guilty. Only after a finding of guilt should the lawyer engage in discussing treatment possibilities and only as appropriate to obtain the least onerous disposition for the client.[6] Other lawyers are of the opinion that an offending child is a troubled child and, once a charge has been laid, should receive counselling or treatment at all stages.[7] There is no easy answer. On one hand, do lawyers have any right to intervene in a child's life with referrals for treatment, because a criminal charge has been laid, but before there has been a finding that the child committed the offence? Is a child who has committed an offence necessarily a child in need of treatment? On the other hand, when the child is obviously troubled in his everyday life, can a lawyer ignore these problems and focus only on innocence or guilt? The same issues seem to have confronted Parliament when the Young Offenders Act was passed and continue to trouble the lawmakers. The late Judge Peter Nasmith proposed that both roles are appropriate, at different stages of the proceedings.[8] From the time that a charge is laid until a finding of responsibility for the criminal act, full procedural safeguards should be afforded to the child. The lawyer is in every sense defending the child. Only after a finding should counsel become involved in any assistance or treatment options. This is generally the prevailing view of defence counsel for youthful offenders.

At the disposition stage, a lawyer who is knowledgeable about community services can be of tremendous assistance to a client in obtaining the most beneficial disposition. Many lawyers, however, may not be familiar with the range of resources in a community. This is an area of natural collaboration between social workers and lawyers. There was for some time a project in Ottawa which permitted Legal Aid lawyers to engage a social worker to canvass services available to the client to facilitate disposition. The social worker thus became a member of the defence team.[9]

PROCEEDINGS AGAINST YOUNG OFFENDERS ARE CRIMINAL LAW

Both the former Juvenile Delinquents Act and the Young Offenders Act are procedural statutes which provide a legal means of dealing with criminal acts committed by children. The charge or information which is laid pursuant to the Young Offenders Act states that the child "Did commit (a named offence) . . . contrary to the Criminal Code of Canada and thereby contrary to the Young Offenders Act".

The procedural trial commences with reading of the charges and taking of a plea of "guilty" or "not guilty" and the rules of criminal procedure apply throughout the trial. If there is a finding of guilt, it is a criminal conviction.[10] The record which results is admissible in evidence if the child later commits a further offence as an adult, but the Young Offenders Act provides for the record to be destroyed at the police station upon good conduct for two years after satisfactory completion of the disposition or penalty.[11]

The significant feature of the Young Offenders Act is that it falls within the ambit of criminal law[12] unlike juvenile delinquency matters in the United States, which have been held to be civil law.[13] American law has been summed up in these terms ". . . the juvenile court is a civil court, not a criminal court, and an adjudication of delinquency is not conviction of a crime."[14]

The significant consequence to a Canadian child who is found to be guilty is that a criminal conviction results. If a child charged with an offence is also in serious conflict with his parents, or truanting from school, or is experiencing serious emotional problems, the immediate recourse would be to refer the child and his parents to an appropriate social agency, if they consent. If they do not, there is no authority to intervene unless the child is at risk of serious harm without intervention. Treatment planning should be pursued only when the court has found that the child actually committed the offence.[15]

THE YOUNG OFFENDERS ACT

Introduction

With the enactment of the Charter of Rights, a new statute concerning juvenile offenders was required. While the Juvenile Delinquents Act was clearly a treatment statute, the inescapable fact is that juvenile offences are criminal law. That being the case, children must be afforded at least the same procedural safeguards as adults, which the former Juvenile Delinquents Act did not do. Since the enactment of the Charter of

Rights, many of the sections of that Act were clearly contrary to its provisions. For example, the section granting authority to the court to retain control over a juvenile delinquent until the age of 21 was clearly contrary to the right not to be subjected to cruel and unusual punishment.[16] Inevitably, much of that Act became ineffective, and a new statute for children became mandatory.

Essentially, by the Young Offenders Act, a young person who commits an offence will be held responsible for his actions if he is convicted,[17] and will be subjected to one of the prescribed penalties in order to protect society.[18] But the concept of diminished responsibility of children is retained, as is the possibility of treatment.[19] New concepts of diversion outside the court system,[20] minimum necessary interference in the life of the child,[21] and parental responsibility for the child[22] are made explicit. Procedurally, the Charter of Rights is specifically made to apply to young persons as a minimum standard.[23]

There has been a clear shift from a "treatment of the child" emphasis to embrace the philosophy of "responding to the act", while vestiges of the treatment model are retained. The Act certainly affords full legal protection, which is an unquestionable benefit. The question remains, does it serve children who are in conflict with the law better than the former Juvenile Delinquents Act or does it formally "criminalize" the behaviour, making the legal response to young offenders indistinguishable from the response to adults? Does it have the effect of creating ever-younger "criminals"?

Specific Provisions

The court

The youth court, or the court designated by each province, has exclusive jurisdiction to hear and decide all federal offences committed by young persons over the age of 12 and under 18, unless the hearing is transferred to adult court. The youth court has authority to hear and determine criminal (federal) offences *only*. The provinces have enacted complementary legislation to deal with young persons who commit provincial offences. As a practical matter, young persons charged with provincial offences such as highway traffic violations or trespassing are generally tried by a youth court judge who assumes the status of a magistrate or provincial court judge.

Age

A "young person", which is the term for a youthful offender, is an adolescent over 12 and under 18 at the time the offence is committed. A "child" is a person under the age of 12.[24]

The consequences of the ages are significant for everyone involved with children and youth. Existing facilities have been expanded and reallocated to comply with the Act. Young persons between 16 and 18 who were under the jurisdiction of adult criminal courts and correctional facilities are now dealt with by the youth court in facilities designated for young persons. Children under the age of 12 have been taken out of the youthful offenders system entirely, to be dealt with through child welfare proceedings and facilities. These changes strain existing resources, demanding new facilities and staff allocation, and have created interministerial funding conflicts.

One consequence of the minimum age has been to create a groundswell of support to reduce the minimum, especially among police officers and law enforcement agencies. They maintain that children under 12 are being used by older offenders to carry out offences planned by their elders, since the children are effectively immune from criminal prosecution. However, children under the age of 12 who would otherwise be charged with a criminal offence *are* referred to child welfare authorities for appropriate attention and intervention.[25] The extent of such child criminality is questionable, and the legislators have so far resisted any attempts to lower the age of youthful offenders.

Notice to parents

Parents must be notified in writing, by the police officer in charge, of an arrest or criminal charge against their child as soon after the event as possible. If no parent is available, the notice must be given to an adult relative or other adult who can help the young person. If it is uncertain who should be notified, a youth court judge will give direction.[26] Failure to notify parents does not invalidate the proceedings, as was the case under the Juvenile Delinquents Act. Parents must not only be notified, but can also be compelled to appear before the court in a proceeding against their adolescent. If a parent fails to appear, that parent may be arrested and brought before the court, held in contempt and may become liable to be sentenced.[27]

Bail provisions

When a young person is detained in custody after being charged with an offence, he has the same right to bail as an adult under the Criminal Code.[28] However, he must be detained separately from adults unless the judge directs otherwise.[29] If a young offender is being held in custody after being charged, a bail application can be brought before a youth court judge.[30]

Diversion programmes as an alternative to trial

The Young Offenders Act explicitly provides for non-judicial means of dealing with the youthful offender, but only if certain criteria are met. Diversion programmes, usually in the form of mandatory, time-limited community service, are made available as an alternative to the judicial hearing and disposition process. If the young person fails to comply with the diversion disposition, he can be returned to court to have the offence dealt with in the usual way. There must be a diversionary programme for young persons in the province, such as a community service order or restitution programme. Diversion must be appropriate in the circumstances, both for the young person and for society, perhaps where the offence is not serious and little harm resulted. Obviously, a serious offence such as robbery or sexual assault would not be an appropriate case. The young person must understand and consent to participate, and before consenting, must have been informed of the right to legal representation. The young person must accept responsibility for the offence, which seems to require that he admit to committing the act and is prepared to accept the consequences. There must also be sufficient evidence to prosecute the offence.

A diversionary programme cannot be ordered if the young person denies the offence or wishes to have the charges dealt with by the court. In order to avoid double jeopardy, the statement accepting responsibility for the offence is not admissible in evidence against the youth in any court proceeding.[31]

The outcome of successful completion of a diversionary programme must be a dismissal of the charge. If there is only partial completion, the court may dismiss the charge or make another disposition.

Diversion was practised by juvenile court judges for many years, using the *sine die* (without date) adjournment at trial. The significance of the Young Offenders Act is that it provides for procedures that are separate from court proceedings and protects the young person from coercion by providing for legal counsel and by demanding sufficient evidence to support a prosecution *before* diversion is undertaken. Social workers, therefore, should not support a diversion proposal until they are certain there is evidence to support a prosecution, even if the proposal would be beneficial to the young person from their point of view. The law restates the principle that a person should not be required to admit guilt in order to avail himself of helping services.

Initially, Ontario and one other province did not adopt diversion programmes, which were therefore not available to youthful offenders in all provinces. The legal arguments for the failure to adopt alternative measures were interesting. The Attorney General and a number of Crown attorneys argued that the diversion option robbed the young person of full procedural due process, despite the safeguards provided by the Act. In effect, the young person might not be legally guilty, but wished to plead to avoid a trial and avail himself of diversion. The countervailing argument was that it was not due process which was being denied, but the right to apply to remove a first offender from the criminal process, thus reducing the risk of a criminal conviction. The appeal courts have not decided that each province must have diversion programmes in place, and that failure to provide such programmes does not violate the equality provisions of the Charter.[32] However, as a practical consideration, every province now has diversion programmes in place, although they are not identical in each province.

Procedural safeguards

The Act spells out two procedural safeguards for the youthful offender which are greater than those afforded to adults in any criminal statute. The right to counsel at any stage of the proceedings[33] is probably the most important. The presiding judge or justice has a positive duty to inform the young person of this right, and if the young person cannot retain a lawyer, he is entitled to a lawyer through Legal Aid or through other government funding. It is not unusual for the presiding judge to order legal representation for the young person before proceeding with trial of the charges. The youthful offender may also be represented by an agent if the court finds the person suitable. This right to his own lawyer also extends to situations where the judge feels the child's interest may be in conflict with those of his parents. The judge also has a positive duty to assure himself that an unrepresented youthful offender understands the charges against him, and if not satisfied, the judge must enter a plea of not guilty.[34]

Report to the court

Specific reports may be ordered to assist the court. Where there is an application to have the case tried in adult court, or where the young person's fitness to stand trial because of insanity is at issue, the court may order a medical, psychological or psychiatric report. These reports may also be ordered prior to disposition.[35]

After a finding of guilt, but before disposition, the court may order a pre-disposition report, which is similar to the pre-sentence report in adult court. These reports must be in writing and must include the results of (1) an interview with the young person and, where possible, his parents, (2) an interview with the victim, if there is one, where possible, and (3) other applicable information, including the age, character, behaviour and attitudes of the young person.[36] The young person's plans to change his behaviour, participate in activities or improve himself are also significant. This might include regular attendance at school, participation in recreational activity, or obtaining a part-time job, or, for a seriously dysfunctional young person, might comprise a comprehensive treatment plan. Previous findings of delinquency or diversion programmes and their outcome should also be noted. The young person, his parent in attendance at the proceedings, the defence counsel and prosecutor are entitled to a copy of the report on request. However, the report may be withheld if, in the opinion of the court, it might be prejudicial to the child and is unnecessary to the case.[37] A request to withhold reports should be made to the presiding judge rather than to the author of the report.

Dispositions available to the court

Upon a plea of guilty or finding of guilt, the court may order one or more consequences which include: (1) an absolute discharge; (2) a fine of not more than $1,000.00; (3) compensation for loss or a restitution order; (4) compensation by personal service to the victim or by community service; (5) prohibition of conduct connected with the offence; (6) a treatment order where a medical or psychiatric report has recommended it; (7) a probation order of up to two years; or (8) an order for custody in a facility for young persons not exceeding three years.[38] This maximum disposition has caused community concern and outrage in a few well-publicized cases. However, the Crown may always apply to have a very serious matter, such as murder, tried in adult court. This procedure is usually used to circumvent the three year maximum where the offence warrants such a proceeding.

The court must specify custody to be either "open custody",[39] such as a group home, community residential facility, child care institution or wilderness camp, or "secure custody",[40] which must be a setting which provides secure confinement. The latter is to be ordered only for serious offences, but has been used increasingly for less serious offences.

The important feature of custodial dispositions is that any change in the level of custody, from secure to open or the reverse, must occur with the approval *of the court*. A child may also have legal representation upon a review of the level of custody.

Length and form of sentence

The Act provides for dispositions for definite periods *only*, which cannot be longer than two or three years,[41] depending on the seriousness of the offence. In no case can the length of the disposition exceed the maximum sentence for an adult who commits the same offence.[42]

Young persons are eligible for temporary absences from custody for compassionate reasons and for such purposes as school attendance, employment and training programmes. They may also be ordered to serve custodial time intermittently,[43] for example, for a specified number of weekends. As with adults, a sentence continues in force until it expires, unless it is varied on appeal or terminated earlier by the court.

Unlike adults, young persons convicted of criminal offences are not eligible for earned remission or reduction of their sentences for good behaviour. In effect, a custodial sentence of one year means that the full year must be served unless the young person is released on the recommendation of the Review Board.

Review board

The Act creates a Review Board[44] which has less power than the Parole Board for adults. A progress report, similar to a pre-disposition report is required prior to a review, which is conducted by the board. The young person has the right to be present and to be represented by counsel. The board may recommend variation or termination of the disposition of a sentence to the court, which must confirm or vary a recommendation before a child can be released. The court also has the power to order continued detention in custody.

Appeals

A young offender has the same right of appeal under the Young Offenders Act as an adult in criminal matters, and appeals are heard in the same courts.[45] The severe limitation on appeals which existed under the Juvenile Delinquents Act is abolished.

Endnotes

1. "West Side Story." Copyright © 1957, 1959 by Leonard Bernstein and Stephen Sondheim. Used by permission of G. Schirmer, Inc., publishers.
2. See N. Boyd, "The Circularity of Punishment and Treatment: Some Notes on the Legal Response to Juvenile Delinquency" (1980), 3 Can. J. Fam. L. 419.
3. R.S.C. 1970, c. J-3, s. 3(2).
4. R.S.C. 1985, c. Y-1, s. 3(1).
5. "Youth Crime, Police Response and the Y.O.A.", Can. J. of Criminology, Jan. 1994, pp. 9-13, based on quarterly date, Canadian Centre for Justice Statistics.
6. See S. Av Ruskin, "The Role of Counsel in Acting for Juveniles or 'Kids are People Too' " Young Lawyers Division, Canadian Bar Association — Ontario, November 16, 1982, where Av Ruskin proposes that the single role of counsel is to defend the child in a fully adversarial criminal proceeding.
7. S. B. Feldman, "Role of Defence Counsel in Juvenile Court." Young Lawyers Division, Canadian Bar Association — Ontario, 16 November 1982. Feldman asserts that the Juvenile Delinquents Act asserts its own frame of reference outside the Criminal Code, with the objective of drawing social conclusions about the behaviour of children before the court. He suggests that the Act may be divisible into two stages: pre-adjudication, which is purely legal in scope, and post-adjudication, which contemplates a social resolution. He prefers an interpretation which is broader than the adversarial role whereby counsel for the child orchestrates the proceedings to obtain the most favourable social *and* legal result for the child.
8. The late Judge Peter Nasmith, Provincial Court (Family Division) as he then was, "Dispositional Alternatives for Young Offenders." Young Lawyers Division, Canadian Bar Association — Ontario, 16 November 1982.
9. (February 1982) 8:2 *Liaison* 11-16.
10. *Morris v. R.*, [1979] 1 S.C.R. 405, 6 C.R. (3d) 36, 43 C.C.C. (2d) 129, 91 D.L.R. (3d) 161, 23 N.R. 109.
11. Young Offenders Act, note 4 above, ss. 36 and 40-46.
12. See *A.G. B.C. v. Smith*, [1967] S.C.R. 702, 2 C.R.N.S. 277, 61 W.W.R. 236, [1969] 1 C.C.C. 244, 65 D.L.R. (2d) 82; and *Morris v. R.*, note 10 above.
13. See *Re Gault* (1967), 387 U.S. 1, 87 Sup. Ct. 1428; confirmed in *K.M.S. v. Georgia* (1973), 129 Ga. App. 683.

14. *K.M.S., ibid.*, at 684.
15. See further, E. Schur, *Radical Non-Intervention; Rethinking the Delinquency Problem* (Inglewood Cliffs, N.J.: Prentice-Hall, 1973).
16. Constitution Act, 1982 [en. by the Canada Act, 1982 (U.K.), c. 11, Sched. B.], Pt. I (Canadian Charter of Rights and Freedoms), s. 12.
17. Young Offenders Act, R.S.C. 1985, c. Y-1, s. 3(1)(*a*).
18. *Ibid.*, s. 3(1)(*b*) and (*f*).
19. *Ibid.*, s. 3(1)(*a*) and (*c*).
20. *Ibid.*, s. 3(1)(*d*).
21. *Ibid.*, s. 3(1)(*f*).
22. *Ibid.*, s. 3(1)(*h*).
23. *Ibid.*, s. 3(1)(*e*).
24. *Ibid.*, s. 2(1).
25. C.F.S.A., s. 42(1), (2), (3).
26. *Ibid.*, s. 9.
27. *Ibid.*, s. 10.
28. *Ibid.*, ss. 6, 8, 51 and 52. The bail provisions are difficult to find. The specific applicability of the Criminal Code, except where excluded, appears to import the bail provisions into the Y.O.A.
29. *Ibid.*, s. 7.
30. *Ibid.*, s. 8.
31. *Ibid.*, s. 4.
32. *R. v. S.(S.)* (1990), 57 C.C.C. (3d) 115 (S.C.C.).
33. Young Offenders Act, s. 14.
34. *Ibid.*, s. 12(3) and (4).
35. *Ibid.*, s. 13.
36. *Ibid.*, s. 14.
37. *Ibid.*, s. 14(5) and (7).
38. *Ibid.*, s. 20.
39. *Ibid.*, s. 24.1(1).
40. *Ibid.*, s. 24.1(6).
41. *Ibid.*, s. 20(3) and (4).
42. *Ibid.*, s. 20(7).
43. *Ibid.*, s. 20(1)(*k*).
44. *Ibid.*, s. 30.
45. *Ibid.*, s. 27.

Bibliography

Abramovitch, Rona and Juliane Duda. "Young Children's Legal Knowledge and Reasoning Ability" (April, 1997) 39 *Canadian Journal of Criminology* 145-170.

Bala, Nicholas. "The 1995 YOA Amendments: Compromise or Confusion?" (1994) 26 *Ottawa Law Review* 643-676.

Bolton, Janet. "The Young Offenders Act: Principles and Policy: The First Decade in Review" (Oct., 1993) 38 *McGill Law Journal* 939-1052.

Carrington, Peter and Sharon Moyer. "Interprovincial Variations in the Use of Custody for Young Offenders: A Funnel Analysis" (July, 1994) 36 *Canadian Journal of Criminology* 271-290.

Leschied, Alan W. "The Young Offenders Act: Law of Retribution or Restoration" (July, 1995) 6 *Education and Law Journal* 329-333.

McGuire, Maureen. "Getting Tougher?: [An Act to Amend the Young Offenders Act and the Criminal Code]" (April, 1997) 39 *Canadian Journal of Criminology* 185-214.

Platt, Priscilla. *Young Offenders Law in Canada*, 2nd ed. (Markham, Ontario: Butterworths, 1994).

Reitsma-Street, Marge. "Canadian Youth Court Charges and Dispositions for Females Before and After Implementation of the Young Offenders Act" (Oct., 1993) 35 *Canadian Journal of Criminology* 437-458.

Schissel, Bernard. *Social Dimensions of Canadian Youth Justice* (Don Mills, Ontario: Oxford University Press, Canada, 1993).

Silverman, Robert and James Creechan. *Canadian Young Offenders* (Scarborough, Ontario: Prentice-Hall, Canada, 1995).

Toward Safer Communities: Violent and Repeated Offending by Young People. Dept. of Justice, Canada, Ottawa, 1993.

Waters, Robert Craig. "Kids, the Law and You: Understanding and Using the Legal System to Protect Our Children: What Every Parent, Caretaker, Teacher and Social Worker Needs to Know (But is Seldom Told)" (Self-Counsel Legal Series) (North Vancouver, B.C.: International Press, 1994).

West, W. Gordon. *Young Offenders and the State: A Canadian Perspective on Delinquency* (Toronto: Harcourt Brace & Co., Canada, 1993).

Wilson, Jeffrey. *Children and the Law*, 3rd ed. (Markham, Ont.: Butterworths, 1979).

Winterdyk, John. *Issues and Perspectives on Young Offenders in Canada* (eds.) (Toronto: Harcourt Brace & Co., Canada, 1995).

PART IV

CRIMINAL LAW

22

Structure of a Crime

The structure of Canadian criminal law and some of the consequences of a criminal conviction need explanation because it is not unusual for social work clients to be charged with criminal offences. An understanding of the nature of a crime, the necessary elements, the defences available, and the consequences which may flow from a conviction may help workers to provide appropriate assistance. It should be stressed again that legal knowledge is not a substitute for legal advice and representation.

Every society identifies particular acts which it considers abhorrent or detrimental to the common good and prescribes either formal or informal penalties upon their commission. Early Innuit society severely punished the hunter who failed to share his kill by excluding him from the group, thereby exposing him and his family to almost certain starvation when his hunting was unsuccessful. Simply stated, a crime is behaviour which a society identifies as a crime.[1] The significant features of societal response to crime are the elements of social control over the proscribed behaviour, and the prescribed punishment for commission of the prohibited act. In Canada, as elsewhere in the western world, there has been a growing inclination to criminalize behaviour which we wish to control, most notably impaired driving, the use of non-prescription drugs, and family violence.

Canadian criminal law is created entirely by federal statutes, which were enacted under the federal criminal law power.[2] The most important of these are the Criminal Code,[3] the Narcotic Control Act,[4] which controls the use of true narcotics and marijuana, the Food and Drugs Act,[5] which controls the use of other restricted drugs and some foodstuffs, and the Young Offenders Act.[6] True crimes are acts which are considered to be harmful or dangerous to all citizens, including murder, arson, robbery, theft and illegal use of a controlled drug.

Provincially created offences, such as violations of the Highway Traffic Act, Trespass to Property Act and Landlord and Tenant Act,[7] among others, are acts which a province wishes to regulate and are often referred to as "quasi-crimes". The standard of proof for provincial offences is the criminal standard, beyond a reasonable doubt.[8]

NECESSARY ELEMENTS OF A CRIMINAL OFFENCE

> Peter, Paul and John, all aged 19, broke into an abandoned warehouse one night to get out of the cold, using a tire iron from John's car. They looked around, found some candles, which they lit, some boxes to sit on and some old maps and newspapers dating back to 1940. They were reading the papers and maps when they were interrupted by police sirens and whistles. In their panic to leave they kicked over a candle, igniting the papers and causing a fire. All three were caught and were charged with arson. All pleaded guilty to arson. Peter, who had no previous criminal record, received two years probation and a community service order. Paul and John, who had previous records, received 18 months in reformatory.

To constitute a criminal offence, the accused person must intend to commit a forbidden act (have the requisite "*mens rea*" or guilty mind), and must actually commit the act (have committed the "*actus reus*" or forbidden act). The two elements must co-exist and have a causal connection. In the case above, the three youths may not have intended to start a fire, yet they were convicted of arson. Were the two necessary elements of a crime present and did they co-exist?

Intention

The mental element alone is not enough, or the whole nation would be in prison. For example:

> Arthur was furious at the storekeeper for ejecting him from the store. He intended to return with a baseball bat and teach the man a lesson by cracking the bat over his head. But he did nothing. The intent to commit a crime was present, but not the act; therefore, Arthur did not commit an offence.

Neither is the act alone a crime.

> Martha is pedalling her bicycle down the street. Suddenly a child darts out of an alley, directly in front of her. She cannot stop in time and strikes the child. The child is seriously injured. Assuming Martha was cycling in an entirely lawful manner, no offence was committed.

Co-existence of the Elements

The intention to commit the act and the forbidden act itself must occur at the same time:

> Dorothy was so upset at Darlene for stealing her boyfriend that she planned to kill her. But she changed her mind. Three days later she lent Darlene her new make-up which caused such an acute allergic reaction that Darlene died. Since the two elements did not co-exist, no offence was committed.

A Causal Connection

Not only must the intention and the act co-exist, but the mental element must cause the forbidden act to occur:

> George intended to rob a bank. On his way to the robbery he spotted a canvas money bag which had just fallen from a Brinks truck. He scooped it up and returned home with the money. George did not commit robbery, since his intention to rob did not cause the theft of the money but he has committed theft if the money is not returned.

Where the intention is acted on and causes the offence, both necessary elements are present and co-exist:

> Andrea wanted a new sweater and planned to steal it. She went into Eatons for that purpose, tried on sweaters until she found one she liked, put it on under her own clothing and left the store. The offence is complete. Andrea has committed theft.

RECKLESSNESS, NEGLIGENCE AND OMISSIONS

In some circumstances, recklessness of the consequences of an act is sufficient to show a guilty mind and may constitute a criminal offence.[9] For example:

> A silver tea service is offered for sale by Barbara's cleaning man, at a fraction of its actual value. Barbara is suspicious but buys it anyway. The tea service is found to be stolen. Barbara is charged with possession of property obtained by crime. In these circumstances, Barbara's protestations that she did not know the tea service was stolen would be unlikely to be believed.

In a limited number of situations, negligence, or neglect of a legal duty, can also be a criminal offence. The most frequent example is criminal negligence in the operation of a motor vehicle, which results in injury or death to another person.[10] Where the law imposes a legal duty to act in a certain way and the person fails to do so, the omission may constitute a criminal offence. For example, parents are under a legal duty to provide the necessaries of life for their children[11] and to protect them from physical harm.[12] If they fail to do so, they may commit an offence.

ATTEMPTED OFFENCES

Attempting to commit a forbidden act is also an offence, if the person not only intends the act, but does something substantial in furtherance of the intention, even if the act is incomplete.[13]

> Jim plans to break into Jonathan's house to steal his stereo equipment. He breaks in and begins to disconnect the stereo, but is interrupted by Jonathan's large dog. He panics and leaves. He is stopped by the police, who charge him with breaking and entering and attempted theft. Jim has committed attempted theft, although he took nothing, because he did something substantial to further his intentions.

PARTIES TO AN OFFENCE

Persons who contribute in some way to the commission of an illegal act may also be guilty of the offence. This can occur in several ways.

1. Aiding and Abetting — if one person assists and encourages another to commit a forbidden act, both may be equally guilty.[14]
2. Common Intention — if two or more people form a common intention to commit an illegal act, and in the course of that act one of them commits a second offence which was reasonably foreseeable, all have committed the second offence.[15]
3. Counselling — a person who counsels another to commit an offence becomes a party to that offence and to any further offences which result from the counselling.[16]
4. Accessory after the Fact — anyone except a spouse who assists a person who has committed a criminal act to escape, becomes a party to the offence.[17]
5. Conspiracy — when two or more persons form a common intention to commit an illegal act or a legal act by illegal means, the very fact of making the illegal agreement is a criminal offence, whether or not it is carried out.

IGNORANCE OF THE LAW

It is quite true in criminal law that ignorance of the law by the person who commits the offence is no excuse,[18] even in circumstances where the person made reasonable inquiries of officials before committing the criminal act.[19] However, if the person had no means of knowing the act was an offence since that fact was never published, ignorance may be a defence to the charge.[20]

PRESUMPTION OF INNOCENCE

The very essence of the criminal law revolves around a central concept, that a person is innocent until proven guilty in a public trial before a fair and impartial tribunal.[21] This concept runs like a golden thread throughout the web of English Criminal Law.[22] The concept is important for another reason. There is both "subjective guilt", or the reality that a person committed a criminal act, and "legal guilt" which flows from the adjudication of the evidence in a trial, where the reality is tested in the adversarial system. They are not the same thing. A person may be guilty of something, but not the offence charged. Until the elements of an offence are tested against the legal standard, a person is presumed innocent. Where liberty of the person is at stake, mere probability is not enough; there must be certainty.

BURDEN OF PROOF

In criminal trials as in human existence, the absolute truth is elusive, if not impossible to determine. However, there must be a substantial degree of certainty in the mind of the judge or jury that the person intentionally committed the illegal act before he can be convicted. Therefore, the Crown prosecutor has the burden of proving guilt and he must prove the offence beyond a reasonable doubt. There is usually no requirement upon an accused to prove anything. He has an absolute right not to testify against himself and his silence is not to be taken as an admission of guilt.

STANDARD OF PROOF

"Reasonable doubt" means different things to different people. Many judges have struggled with the meaning. A definition which has met with judicial approval,[23] but is likely not the last word on the subject is:

> [A] reasonable doubt is "an honest doubt", a "real doubt", not "an imaginary doubt" conjured up by a juror in an attempt to escape his responsibility. It

> must be a doubt which prevents a juror from saying "I am morally certain that the accused committed the offence with which he is charged."[24]

The Crown prosecutor must prove the evil intention and the criminal act against the legal standard, or the accused person is entitled to be acquitted.

PRESUMPTIONS

In some cases, where the elements of the offence are hard to prove, the accused is presumed to have knowledge of the criminal circumstances or to have the requisite illegal intention. Among these offences are arson against the holder of insurance in the building,[25] breaking and entering[26] and care and control of a motor vehicle while under the influence of alcohol.[27] Perhaps the most positive presumption is that a person is presumed to be and to have been sane when he committed a criminal act.[28]

Presumptions are legal fictions, but they do have a common sense basis. They speak to the obvious. For example, if a person is charged with breaking and entering, and actually entered a building, he is presumed to have intended to do so. Without presumptions, convictions for criminal acts might be much more difficult to obtain. In some circumstances, they have been enunciated in legislation to remove the uncertainty of judicial interpretation.

PRESUMPTION AT BAIL HEARINGS

In bail hearings, properly called "judicial interim release", there is a presumption in favour of releasing a person from custody until trial, unless the Crown prosecutor shows cause why the accused should be detained in custody until trial. In a certain class of offences or circumstances, the onus is on the accused to "show cause" why he should be released. Included in this class of offences are murder, offences committed while out on bail, narcotics offences, and failure to appear on the date set for hearing.[29]

RETHINKING THE STRUCTURE OF CRIMINAL LAW

There is always more than one way of characterizing human behaviour and criminal law is no exception. Louk Holsman, the world-renowned Dutch criminologist, writes that "criminal acts" (as defined by various states) are indistinguishable from "intentional or negligent torts" (private wrongs). Yet the method of achieving redress for the wrong may be very different. For example, if one person assaults another, he may be charged with the criminal offence of assault. A criminal prosecution by the state may follow. If a conviction (finding of guilt) is made, the standard of proof is that he committed the assault beyond a reasonable doubt. He will be punished by the state by being fined or imprisoned.

If the same assault occurs, the victim always has the option of suing the assailant for assault (and possibly battery) in a civil action, which is a private prosecution, for damages (money) to compensate the victim for the attack. If the assailant is found to be liable (responsible) for the attack, the judge will have made the finding on the ordinary civil standard, on a balance of probabilities. The penalty is quantified in monetary terms.

The differences are four: the way in which the assault is defined, the method of prosecuting the assailant, the standard of proof required to find that the assailant committed the act, and the form of the penalty. Yet the two different procedures are responses to precisely the same act. Is there any sound reason why this should be so? What would happen if actions now defined as "crimes" with the exception of serious offences against the person, were prosecuted as civil actions, with financial penalties, instead of criminal trials and incarceration? Would that reduce the present court congestion in criminal matters?

It is also instructive to re-examine criminal and penal sanctions for crimes, with the objective of rehabilitation. We know that the origins of the modern penal system reside in the 18th century Quaker belief that, if people who offended against the laws of the state were isolated from the community in prisons and "penitentiaries", they would "repent" and mend their ways. Presumably, they would return to society as "reformed" individuals. Hence also the word "reformatory".

Dr. Ruth Morris has written extensively to the contrary. The research indicates that the longer a person is separated from society, the less likely is he or she to make a successful readjustment to society on release. In a particular study, prisoners who had served only part of their sentences, but were released to considerable community consternation, were more successful upon their release than prisoners who served their full sentence.[30] Why then are our politicians, the press and the media proposing ever-longer and harsher sentences, if they do not achieve the desired result?

Finally, it is common knowledge that minorities, people of colour and native Canadians are vastly over-represented in our prison population. It is interesting to speculate why this is so. One might conclude that criminal law can be used as a means of social control for the disadvantaged in our society.

Endnotes

1. See G. Parker, *An Introduction to Criminal Law* (Toronto: Methuen, 1977) at 20; and A. M. Kirkpatrick, and W. T. McGrath, *Crime and You* (Toronto: Macmillan, 1976) at 1.
2. Constitution Act, 1982, s. 91(27), being Schedule B of the Canada Act 1982 (U.K.), 1982, c. 11.
3. R.S.C. 1985, c. C-46.
4. R.S.C. 1985, c. N-1.
5. R.S.C. 1985, c. F-27.
6. R.S.C. 1985, c. Y-1.
7. See, for example, R.S.O. 1990, c. H.8, c. T.21, and c. L.7.
8. See *R. v. Sault Ste. Marie*, [1978] 2 S.C.R. 1299, 3 C.R. (3d) 30, 40 C.C.C. (2d) 353, 85 D.L.R. (3d) 161, 21 N.R. 295, 7 C.E.L.R. 53.
9. See *Tremblay v. R.*, [1969] S.C.R. 431, [1970] 4 C.C.C. (2d) 120, 10 D.L.R. (3d) 346.
10. Criminal Code, note 3 above, ss. 219-221.
11. *Ibid.*, s. 215.
12. *Ibid.*, s. 218.
13. *Ibid.*, s. 24.
14. *Ibid.*, s. 21(1).
15. *Ibid.*, s. 21(2). See *Chow Bew v. R.*, [1956] S.C.R. 124, 22 C.R. 253, 113 C.C.C. 337, 2 D.L.R. (2d) 294.
16. Criminal Code, note 3 above, s. 22.
17. *Ibid.*, s. 23.
18. *Ibid.*, s. 19.
19. *R. v. Potter* (1978), 3 C.R. (3d) 154, 39 C.C.C. (2d) 538 (P.E.I. S.C.).
20. *R. v. Molis*, [1980] 2 S.C.R. 356, 55 C.C.C. (2d) 558, 116 D.L.R. (3d) 291, 33 N.R. 411.
21. Now incorporated in the Canadian Charter of Rights and Freedoms, Pt. 1 of the Constitution Act, 1982 being Schedule B of the Canada Act 1982 (U.K.), 1982, c. 11, s. 11(*d*).
22. *Woolmington v. D.P.P.*, [1935] A.C. 462 at 481 (H.L.), per Sankey L.C.
23. See *R. v. Bell* (1973), 6 N.S.R. (2d) 351, 28 C.R.N.S. 55, 14 C.C.C. (2d) 225 (C.A.).
24. J. de N. Kennedy, *Aids to Jury Charges* (Toronto: Canada Law Book, 1965) at 21.
25. Criminal Code, note 3 above, s. 435.
26. *Ibid.*, ss. 348(2) and 349(2).
27. *Ibid.*, ss. 478.1(3) and 481(1)(*a*).
28. *Ibid.*, s. 16(4).

29. *Ibid.*, ss. 522 and 515(6).
30. Morris, Ruth. "Penal Abolition: The Practical Choice", Canadian Scholars Press 1996. See in particular "Gideon's Trumpet".

Bibliography

Armstrong-Esther, Dawn and Christopher Armstrong-Esther. "No Mandatory Retirement for Crime: Problems of Elderly Offenders (Nov., 1993) 18 *Law Now*, No. 3, 18-20.

Bennett, Elizabeth. "Disclosure of Complainant's Medical and Therapeutic Records" (1996) 1 *Canadian Criminal Law Review* 17-30.

Bourque, Paul C. "Mental Disorders: Amendments to the Criminal Code" (1994) 14 *Health Law in Canada* 108-114.

Brockman, Joan and V. Gordon Rose. *An Introduction to Canadian Criminal Procedure and Evidence for the Social Sciences* (Scarborough, Ont.: Nelson Canada, 1995).

Goff, Colin. *Criminal Justice in Canada: An Introduction* (Toronto: ITP Nelson, 1997).

Lockyer, James E. "The Roles and Responsibilities of the Legal Profession in Furthering Access to Justice" (1992) *Windsor Yearbook Access to Justice* 356-374.

Renaud, Gilles. "The Reformed Code of Criminal Restitution: Some Observations" (Sept. 1996) 54 Advocate (Van.), 725-732.

Shiner, Roger A. "Citizens' Rights and Police Powers", in *Police Powers in Canada: the Evolution and Practice of Authority*, ed. R.C. MacLeod and David Schneiderman (Toronto: University of Toronto Press, 1994), pp. 59-74.

Tanovich, David M. "The Right to Counsel and Police Lineups" (Dec. 1993) 24 *Criminal Reports* (4th) 125-136.

23

A Field Guide to the Criminal Code and Related Statutes

THE CRIMINAL CODE

The Criminal Code[1] is the major criminal statute, which has expanded greatly since its first enactment in 1892. Particularly astonishing has been the growth in the number of minor offences as society attempts to regulate an ever-broader range of activities, including the use of that twentieth century phenomenon, the automobile. But 98% of the increase[2] is attributable to summary (less serious) offences, punishable by a maximum six month sentence, $1,000 fine, or both. Of these, 90% are for traffic violations.[3] The present Code, which had its last major revision in 1995,[4] is divided into 28 Parts. The offences themselves and their classification present an interesting commentary on the behavioural targets for social control. The Parts can be grouped according to subject matter. The following sub- headings are intended to provide a conceptual framework.

Principles[5]

Included are a definition section and such concepts as age of criminal responsibility, persons to whom the law applies, parties to an offence and and defences to a criminal charge. A separate Part[6] defines attempts, conspiracies and accessories.

Jurisdiction

Two Parts define the power of superior and inferior courts to hear particular offences.[7] For example, murder may only be tried in a supreme court by a judge and jury,[8] while a provincial court judge has absolute power to try offences such as theft under $1,000 and betting and gaming offences. Also included are special powers respecting search warrants, seizure of goods and forfeiture of weapons connected with an offence.

Offences Against the Public at Large

This grouping defines and prescribes penalties for a mixed array of crimes, beginning with offences against public order, which include such acts as treason, breach of the public peace, sabotage, mutiny, passport offences, riots, piracy, forcible entry of a building, explosives offences and illegal prizefights.[9] Firearms and weapons offences have a separate Part.[10] Extensive amendments to this Part, enacted in 1995, have not yet been proclaimed in force. Offences against the administration of law and justice[11] and invasion of privacy, which is the Part dealing with illegal wiretaps and interception of communications,[12] are also separately codified.

Sexual Assault

Until recently, sexual assault was grouped with morals offences such as distribution of obscene materials, disorderly conduct, causing a disturbance, night prowling, and causing a common nuisance. January 4, 1983 ushered in a new era in the law of sexual assault. The offence is now included in the Part of the Criminal Code which addresses offences against the person and reputation.[13] Both husband and wife may now be charged with committing a sexual assault upon each other whether or not they are living together. The old term "rape" is deleted, as are the archaic evidentiary requirements which made a conviction for rape very difficult to obtain. Sexual assaults short of forced sexual intercourse are specific criminal offences which carry criminal penalties, and are applicable equally to both men and women.

There are three kinds of sexual assault, of increasing severity, which carry increasingly severe penalties upon conviction. The least serious, sexual assault, is committed when a person intentionally molests, threatens, or applies force of a sexual nature to another person. It has been found to include such acts as uninvited fondling of breasts or genitalia, bottom-pinching or threatened sexual acts which the assaulter appears able to carry out. The penalty on conviction is up to 10 years on indictment or six months upon summary conviction.[14] The second type, actual or threatened sexual assault with a weapon, or where a third party is threatened, or which causes bodily injury, is an indictable offence which may result in a 14-year sentence.[15] The most serious form, aggravated sexual assault, is committed when the victim of a sexual assault is wounded, maimed or disfigured, or whose life is endangered. The assaulter who seriously injures the victim or actually exposes him or her to possible death commits an indictable offence which may result in a life sentence.[16]

The evidentiary rules are radically changed. Proof of sexual intercourse, including penetration, is not necessary. Gone is the requirement that a sexual assault be corroborated by other evidence, or that the victim must have complained about the assault at the first reasonable opportunity.[17] Evidence of the complainant's sexual activity with others, or his or her sexual reputation is not relevant or admissible as a defence except in very restricted circumstances. The complainant cannot be compelled to testify about his or her usual sexual activity.[18] There are specific provisions to protect the identity of the complainant and to prevent publication of his or her name[19] and the presiding judge must so advise the complainant at the first reasonable opportunity.[20] The spouse of the person charged with sexual assault can be both a competent and compellable witness against the accused spouse.[21] This last amendment makes it possible for one spouse to testify against the other when he or she is the victim and only witness to a sexual assault, or when their child is the victim of incest.

Offences Against the Person and Reputation[22]

Only one Part is devoted exclusively to offences against people. These include murder, manslaughter and infanticide, criminal negligence, abandonment of children, kidnapping and assaults (including sexual assault), but also all federal motor vehicle offences, being a carrier of venereal disease, bigamy, criminal libel and disseminating hate propaganda. There appears to be little conceptual logic in this Part. Offences seem to have been added in response to public outcry about specific acts which, thrust into public consciousness, created a demand for criminal sanctions. One might speculate whether being a carrier of the AIDS virus will become a criminal offence, which is not the case at present.

It is also a criminal offence to detain or overhold a child, contrary to a custody order, or even without a custody order,[23] with the consent of the Crown Attorney.[24] However, police are usually most reluctant to enforce such orders, and will first ensure that a custody order continues in force before charges are laid. The practical effect of this provision is therefore limited.

Offences Against Property and Commerce[25]

Prohibited acts concerning property comprise a much larger group of offences. This group addresses not only such offences as breaking and entering and theft, but special kinds of theft such as stealing oysters from their beds, fish from hatcheries, money from a trust account, and owner-marked driftwood from a shoreline. These Parts also include robbery with a weapon, extortion, arson, possession of property obtained by crime, mail robbery, charging criminal interest rates, possession of tools under suspicious circumstances, forgery and counterfeiting, fraudulent contracts and transactions, trademark offences, wilful destruction of property, currency offences and even a trade union offence. This list is a hodge-podge catalogue of perceived wrongs, both regional and national.

Criminal Procedure[26]

The largest number of Parts are devoted to criminal procedure, from arrest and release or detention, laying of the charge and bail proceedings, through the trial process, conviction or acquittal, sentencing and punishments, and appeal provisions. Separate Parts deal with summary trials and accused with mental disorders, and another Part with the prescribed Forms for almost every eventuality.

A major substantive change in 1985 was the requirement for a pre-hearing conference in every case to be tried by a jury, and as an option in non-jury proceedings.[27] Pre-hearing conferences are now almost universal for all offences, in order to narrow issues and expedite criminal proceedings.

DRUG STATUTES

Drug offences are contained in the Narcotic Control Act[28] and Food and Drugs Act,[29] now amended by the Controlled Drugs and Substances Act,[30] which has not yet been proclaimed in force. Each statute contains a Schedule of drugs,[31] whose possession is prohibited entirely, such as heroin or marijuana in the Narcotic Control Act, referred to as "narcotics", or L.S.D. in the Food and Drugs Act, called "restricted drugs". In addition, the Food and Drugs Act identifies a number of substances whose use is "controlled" and may only be used as prescribed by a qualified physician. These include amphetamines and barbiturates.

The significant feature of both statutes is that a narcotic or restricted drug is any substance which the Acts include in the prohibiting Schedules. Marijuana is not generally considered a narcotic, but is included in the

Schedule under the Narcotic Control Act and is therefore treated like a narcotic. Similarly, L.S.D. is a restricted drug under the Food and Drugs Act and is therefore a forbidden substance in all circumstances. Amphetamines and barbiturates, however, are controlled under the Food and Drugs Act. Different consequences flow from their possession. Simple possession of a controlled drug is *not* a criminal offence, whereas simple possession of either a narcotic or a restricted drug *is*.

If any drug is possessed for the purpose of "trafficking", it is a crime. Remember that the definitions of "possession" and "trafficking" are both very broad. "Possession" means to actually possess the forbidden substance or to have it anywhere for one's own or another's use or possession. If one or more persons possess anything with the knowledge and consent of the rest, they are all considered to be in possession.[32] "Traffic" means to manufacture, sell, transport, deliver or distribute, or to offer to do any of those things, unless the Acts permit their manufacture and sale for pharmaceutical use.[33] The Narcotic Control Act adds giving or administering a forbidden substance to the definition of "traffic".

Both statutes have a number of common features. Simple possession of a narcotic or restricted drug is a criminal offence, and its possession for the purpose of trafficking is a more serious offence. Where a person has been found by the court to be in possession, the burden of proof at one time was *on the accused* to show that he was not in possession for the purpose of trafficking. This provision, however, conflicted with the presumption of innocence guaranteed by the Charter of Rights,[34] and the courts ruled that the reverse onus in trafficking prosecutions is contrary to the Charter.[35] Importing or exporting of a forbidden substance is a very serious offence. Where a narcotic is involved, a conviction carries a mandatory seven-year minimum sentence or a maximum of life imprisonment.[36] However, the seven year minimum has been held to offend the Charter proscription against cruel and unusual punishment and is no longer binding on the court.[37] In the case of a controlled or restricted drug, the maximum penalties are three and ten years respectively, but there is no mandatory minimum. Police have special search and seizure powers under both Acts.

Legal advice is necessary where a client is charged with a drug offence because of the consequences which may flow from a conviction. Unless an absolute discharge is granted, the person is left with a criminal record and possibly a substantial term of imprisonment.

CRIMINAL LAW REFORM

The Criminal Law Amendment Act, 1985[38] introduced revisions which identify very contemporary concerns, such as computer theft, dishonest use of credit cards, contempt of court, pornography, and prostitution. The nature of the foregoing offences is defined in explicit language and within a modern context. For example, theft of computer data or use of a computer to commit an offence are separate offences.[39] Credit card crime is now clearly defined to encompass forgery, illegal use of a card or use of invalid cards.[40] The powers of a judge to find a witness in contempt of court and to impose penalties are more narrowly defined, thus removing the almost unlimited discretion possessed by the judiciary in contempt matters. The accompanying duty of witnesses to testify is equally clearly articulated. The definition of prostitution includes obtaining the services of a prostitute in any public place. Consequently, both the prostitute and client can be charged with the offence, communication for the purpose of prostitution.[41]

In most other respects, criminal offences remain unchanged. Motor vehicle offences are a notable exception, for which the Act provides much harsher sanctions, undoubtedly reflecting the rising concern about alcohol-related injuries and fatalities. Where a person is injured or killed, the offence is redefined as causing death or bodily harm by dangerous driving or impaired driving. Minimum fines for all motor vehicle offences are raised substantially, as are the maximum sentences which may be imposed.[42] A further contemporary feature of the motor vehicle provisions are "telewarrants", or warrants issued by a judge or justice over the telephone, authorizing blood samples of an accused where impairment is suspected. The accused is later served a facsimile of the verbal warrant. This provision has created great consternation because of the potential violation of a person's Charter right to security of the person. The opposing argument supports the necessity for blood samples at the scene to prevent continuing death and injury on the highways.

The significant amendments to the Narcotic Control Act were two. The definition of "trafficking" was expanded to include prescribing of a narcotic by a physician for non-medical reasons, and the special search powers, called "writs of assistance", were abolished.[43] Recently, in two American states, California and Arizona, physicians can prescribe marijuana for medical purposes. Similar legal use is expected to be sought in Canada.[44]

The greatest impact of the Criminal Law Amendment Act occurred in the sentencing of offenders. The law of sentencing was restated to incorporate the principles and purposes enunciated by the courts. A broad range of alternatives to imprisonment are codified, including increased opportunity for restitution and reparation. Automatic imprisonment for non-payment of fines was replaced by alternative means of payment, but intentional non-payment may still result in imprisonment. A new and significant aspect was recognition of the victim in the criminal process. The effect of the crime on the victim may be considered, the victim may be called as a witness, and may have greater opportunity to recover his or her property concerned with the crime. This was a significant shift from the prevailing notion that all crimes are offences against the sovereign and the state. The Act now acknowledges that they are also affronts to the victim. A practice has developed whereby the Crown Attorney introduces a Victim Impact Statement as part of the submissions to sentence.

The question raised by these changes, however, is whether "criminal" law is being used to redress "civil" wrongs against the individual, and if so, where does the distinction lie. Victim statements are emotional appeals built on profound and personal hurt, but it is difficult to determine the weight to be given to such statements. In our system of law, crimes against the person are seen as crimes against the state, which then prosecutes the perpetrator on behalf of both the victim and society. It may be that this attempt to recognize the victim will interfere with the objectivity of the criminal process which purports to provide justice and fairness to all parties.

DEFENCES TO A CRIMINAL CHARGE

There are a number of defences open to anyone charged with a criminal offence. They may be raised alone or in combination, and are presented here in lay person's terms, but it is always advisable to have legal assistance to defend a criminal charge. The following are some, though not all of the possible defences.

Mistaken Identity

The person who says "I didn't do it" has a complete defence if he or she can raise a reasonable doubt. For example, his presence elsewhere, corroborated by one or more disinterested witnesses, would be a defence.

> Linda was charged with theft from a store. At trial, several classmates testified that at the time of the offence she was writing a college examination in English. She also produced her mark from that examination.

Another sort of mistaken identity occurs where the accused person resembles another person. In this instance he must raise a reasonable doubt that it was he who committed the offence, perhaps by cross-examination of the Crown's witness.

> Louise is charged with theft from a store. The security man testifies that he saw her enter, take some sweaters to try on and later leave the

store. Immediately afterwards, a cashmere sweater was missing. When she entered the store the next day, she was charged. She might question where he was located, who else was in the store, how many young women were trying on sweaters and what she was wearing that day in order to raise a reasonable doubt. It is then up to the judge to establish whether or not he has a reasonable doubt about the identity of the accused.

No Evil Intention

When a person claims he didn't *mean* to do it, it may be a complete defence, or may result in conviction for a lesser offence, depending on whether or not he was reckless in the circumstances.

Jim was cleaning his rifle in an isolated cabin in the hills. The rifle discharged accidentally, killing a solitary hiker who was looking in the window. If the circumstances showed that no one lived near, hikers were a rarity and the rifle had never discharged accidentally before, Jim may have a defence to the charge.

But if he was cleaning the rifle in a home on a suburban street and accidentally shot an inquisitive child, he would likely be found to be reckless and guilty of a lesser offence. In order to establish the absence of the necessary intent, the action must be blameless, or the possibility of harm to be so remote as to be unlikely to occur.

Mistake of Fact

An honest and reasonable mistake about the facts may be a defence to a criminal charge. It would be unfair to convict in these circumstances, since there was no evil intention, although the act was committed.

After a vigorous tennis match, Arnold picked up a tennis racquet which he thought was his and took it home. On closer inspection, he found that the grip size was different but otherwise it was exactly like his. In these circumstances, mistake of fact may be a complete defence. But if the racquet he took was a new oversized one, completely different from his own, he would have a problem claiming a mistake of fact.

Mistake of Law

A mistake about what the law says is *not* a defence, even if it is an honest and reasonable mistake. Ignorance of the law is almost never a defence.[45]

Justification

In very limited circumstances, the defence of justification may be available to an accused. For example, an assault upon an intruder who enters a person's home is justified, if the force used is no greater than necessary to prevent entry.[46] But shooting a gun at a mere trespasser is not justified, since the force used is greater than necessary.[47]

A parent or teacher is justified in using force to correct a child, as long as the force is reasonable in the circumstances.[48] But the harm caused must never be greater than the harm being prevented. The issue of permissible physical force against children is viewed by many interested in child welfare as a bar to comprehensive protection of children against physical abuse. The critical question is whether this section is used as a justification for physical punishment by parents or teachers.

Self-Defence

Self-defence to an unprovoked assault may be a complete defence, if the person assaulted uses no more than necessary force to repel the assault.[49] But, if the person who is assaulted expects to be killed, or to be seriously injured as a result, he may be justified in using greater force, even if it causes death or serious harm to his assailant. Excessive force is difficult to define and is decided by the court in all the circumstances of the case. Factors which may be considered are the respective ages of the assailant and the accused self-defender, the threats made, the perceived danger, the nature of the self-defence and any other surrounding facts.[50]

Where death to the assailant results from self-defence, it may have the effect of reducing the charge from murder to manslaughter, if the force used to defend was excessive.[510] Where the court decides it was not excessive in the circumstances, it may be a complete defence. Certainly, the law provides some leeway, since the person being assaulted cannot be expected to measure precisely the exact amount of force necessary in self-defence.[52]

Duress

The defence of duress is *only* available to persons who have committed an offence under threat of death or serious harm which they believed was imminent and would be carried out.[53] The defence is not available where the accused is charged with a serious offence such as murder or attempted murder, assisting in sexual assault, robbery, arson or causing bodily harm. A married woman cannot rely on a defence of duress merely because she committed an offence in her husband's presence.[54] She would have to raise the full defence, that she feared imminent death or serious harm if she did not commit the crime, and that her husband was in a position to carry out the threat. In any case, the harm done by the accused cannot be greater than the harm threatened. For example:

> Mark and Margaret are at a party. Mark spots a bracelet and tells Margaret to pick it up and pocket it or he will break every bone in her hand. She believes him because he recently beat up her brother so severely that he is still in hospital and she fears for her life. On their way home she is charged with theft. Margaret may be successful in pleading duress because the harm of her theft was probably less than her husband's threatened harm.

Provocation

The defence of provocation is only available to a charge of murder. Even if provocation is proved, it is not a complete defence, but has the effect of lessening the conviction from murder to manslaughter and thereby reducing the penalty.[55]

Mental Disorder

Insanity, now referred to as mental disorder, is a complete defence to a criminal charge. The criminal law has developed and codified its own definition of mental illness, which is more restrictive than any definition commonly understood by psychiatry and social work. A common working definition, which is in accord with many psychiatric theories, describes insanity as a state of emotional, mental and behavioural functioning which is outside the broad range of ordinarily acceptable speech and behaviour.

The Criminal Code defines mental disorder simply as "a disease of the mind", and creates a defence of mental disorder in the commission of a criminal offence,[56] but only if the mental illness renders the person incapable of appreciating the nature and quality of the act or omission or knowing that the act or omission is wrong.

The first question to be answered when the issue of mental disorder is raised is whether the accused is fit to stand trial. The test for unfit to stand trial means the accused is unable to conduct a defence to a charge, or to instruct his lawyer to do so because of a mental disorder, and in particular, to understand the nature or object of the proceedings; to understand the possible consequences of the proceeding; or to communicate with his lawyer.[57] The issue of fitness to stand trial can be raised by the accused person at any stage of the proceedings, or by the prosecutor, but only if the accused has first raised the issue of fitness during the preliminary stages, before commencement of the trial. The judge can also raise the issue of his or her own volition, at any time, and must ensure that an unrepresented accused person is represented by a lawyer.

The determination of fitness to stand trial is made by a Review Board established under the Criminal Code, but operating under provincial authority.[58] If an accused person is found to be unfit to stand trial, he will be remanded to a psychiatric facility and reviewed regularly and frequently until he is fit to stand trial. Even if forced to be fit to stand trial, he may still be forced not to be responsible by reason of mental disorder. If he is not found to be fit, there may never be a trial, and the accused may be found not guilty because of a mental disorder. On the other hand, if the person is found guilty before the issue of mental disorder is raised and then found to be suffering from a mental disorder which meets the lack of fitness test, he will be remanded to a psychiatric facility until he is found to be fit to be released to the community, instead of being sentenced to imprisonment.[59]

Two important aspects should be noted. The first is that insanity, or mental disorder, is a complete defence to a charge. That does not mean, however, that the accused person goes free. The second is that, once there has been a finding of not guilty by reason of a mental disorder, the accused cannot be tried later on the same charge. The policy consideration seems to be that if the accused is unable to appreciate the nature and quality of his acts, he cannot be required to suffer the usual consequences of his acts. Since the accused is deprived of his liberty because he is mentally disordered, he should not face the double risk of further deprivation of liberty.

The Criminal Code provides for an elaborate procedure for review of psychiatric detention orders, whereby the mentally disordered person is entitled to have the need for continued detention re-assessed at regular intervals, together with the right to a lawyer and full procedural safeguards. If the person is no longer a substantial risk to the community, he must be released. If the mental disorder continues, he may be detained for a long period of time, perhaps longer than the maximum sentence for the offence with which he is charged. For this reason, the insanity, or mental disorder defence is only pleaded in the most serious cases, or where the person's mental disorder is so extreme and obvious that it is raised by the judge.

A further legal anomaly is that the law does not recognize diminished responsibility, even though the person is ill at the time of the offence. He is technically sane if he meets the test of fitness as defined by the Criminal Code.[60] Similarly, psychopathy has not been accepted by the criminal law as insanity because a psychopath is capable of conducting a defence, instructing a lawyer and understanding the procedure and its possible consequences. He therefore meets the test of fitness.

DO YOU PLEAD GUILTY?

The two pleas which are available in criminal law are "guilty" or "not guilty". There is no such thing as "guilty with an explanation."[61] Only if a person actually committed the offence, intended to do so and all of the necessary elements are present should a person plead guilty. Even then, one of the legal defences may be available to the person charged. In any event, everyone charged with an offence is entitled to plead "not guilty" and to raise a defence at trial. The explanation for the offence may be a defence to the charge, or may mitigate the penalty if the accused person is found guilty at trial. Children and the public at large may find it confusing to hear a plea of not guilty when a person is known to have committed the criminal act. Legal guilt has a precise meaning which may distinguish it from subjective guilt. Legal advice should be sought before entering a plea of guilty.

Young persons charged with offences face special difficulties because of their physical size and lack of maturity. They are taught to tell the truth and to respect authority and are often urged to confess to the police and to plead guilty at trial by parents who are equally unaware of the legal meaning of a plea. Parents should therefore be advised to consult a lawyer before advising their children how to plead. The following case illustrates the problem. A 15-year-old youth was charged under the former Juvenile Delinquents Act with break, enter and theft after he and four others broke into a house and stole money and other items. He was charged with theft of a portable television set and camera. He agreed he had participated in the offences and was urged by his mother to tell the police everything and to plead guilty at trial. His evidence disclosed that he had participated under threat of a severe beating by one of the participants who had a well-known reputation in the neighbourhood for acts of violence so serious that several victims were hospitalized. Neither did the youth have an opportunity to leave and feared serious harm if he did. The stolen television was given to the threatener, who sold it. The youth obtained no benefit from the offence. The guilty plea was ordered struck by the trial judge and the youth was required to obtain counsel. At trial, the full defence of duress was led in evidence, corroborated by witnesses. The judge found that he had a doubt about the youth's intent to commit the offence and he was acquitted of the charge.[62]

CONSEQUENCE OF CONVICTION

If an accused person pleads guilty or is found guilty by the court, a conviction may be registered and the resulting penalties may range from an absolute discharge to life imprisonment, depending on the penalty prescribed by law and the seriousness of the offence in all the circumstances. Where the statute permits, the court may impose two sentences for the same offence. In the case of a person convicted of theft of property under $1,000, the resulting sentence might be a fine, imprisonment for up to two years, probation, or any two of the foregoing.[63]

ABSOLUTE AND CONDITIONAL DISCHARGE

The court may discharge the person absolutely or conditionally, unless the offence is very serious and is punishable by imprisonment of 14 years or for life, or where a minimum sentence must be imposed.[64] The discharge must be in the best interests of the accused and must not be contrary to the public interest, which usually requires that the person be of reasonably good character and that a deterrent sentence is not required. The importance of an absolute discharge is that it is *not* a conviction. A person can therefore say truthfully that he was not convicted of an offence, although the court record of guilt remains. An absolute discharge has no conditions attached, whereas a conditional discharge requires the conditions to be fulfilled before it becomes final. These conditions may include probation, restrictions on movement, or other provisions as ordered by the court.

FINE

A fine may be levied by the court upon conviction for an offence carrying less than five years' imprisonment, where no minimum sentence is prescribed. If the offence is indictable, the fine may be for any amount, but if the offence is prosecuted by summary conviction, the maximum is usually $2,000 for an individual or $25,000 for a corporation.[65]

Effect of Imprisonment for Fines

Dickensian debtors prisions have survived to the end of the twentieth century. Close to 50,000 admissions to provincial jails in 1992-1993 were for failure to pay fines. The offences were generally too minor to deserve jail in the first place, which is made even worse by the fact that a disproportionate number of those who go to jail for fines are aboriginal people.

The Manitoba Aboriginal Justice Inquiry blamed three factors for this problem.[66] The first is out-of-court processes for minor provincial offences. Most of them are violations of the Highway Traffic Act (including parking tickets) and the Liquor Control Act. In some provinces, failure to contest the fine and pay it leads automatically to jail. A person's ability to pay is never considered. To solve this, the Inquiry recommended that upon failure to pay a fine on time, an agency responsible for fine collections would contact the person to offer financial counselling or advise that their properties or salaries would be seized in payment. Failing this, delays would be offered or community service work suggested to settle the debt in kind. Only if nothing else worked would the person go to jail.

The second problem is under the Criminal Code, in that many judges who impose fines do not consider the accused's ability to pay. Instead, they impose fines without inquiring into this and impose default orders (to imprison in case of failure to pay) at the same time. The Inquiry recommended that the Criminal Code be amended to prevent judges from ordering automatic jail orders in cases of non-payment of finds.

Thirdly, problems exist with fine option programs, which arrange community work in place of imprisonment. Many offenders are not aware that the program exists or only learn about it after arrest. Aboriginal women have additional difficulties. Many cannot participate because they must take care of their children, cannot pay for transportation, or are afraid to participate. Ways need to be found to support and encourage these women, or find viable options for them. If these issues were addressed, Canadians would be less likely to go to jail for being poor and taxpayers could save on unnecessary prison costs.

COMMUNITY SENTENCES AND RELEASE

Suspended Sentence and Probation

Probation is, in effect, a community sentence.[67] Unless the offence provides for a minimum sentence, the judge may suspend sentence and release the accused on a probation order. Apart from the statutory requirement for good behaviour, the judge may prescribe a number of other conditions, which may include supervision by a probation officer, an order to provide support for dependants, abstention from alcohol, drugs or possession of a weapon, an obligation to seek and maintain employment, a treatment order, an order for restitution, compensation or community service, or an order to remain within the jurisdiction of the court. The term of a probation order is for any term up to three years and may be imposed either alone or in combination with another sentence, such as a fine or custodial sentence. Since a probation order is a court order, it is self-evident that the terms must be complied with. Otherwise, the person may be brought back and sentenced on the original offence.

Parole

Parole[68] and probation are often confused but occur under separate and distinct circumstances. Parole is not a sentence *per se*, but is a supervised community release. It is a portion of a custodial sentence which the person is permitted to serve in the community, at the discretion of the Parole Board. Generally, a person becomes eligible for parole after serving one third of a custodial sentence. If released, the person must serve the balance of the sentence in the community, under the supervison of a parole officer, and must comply with the conditions of the parole certificate. If the person violates the conditions, he or she may be returned to prison to serve the remainder of the sentence.

Mandatory Supervision

Mandatory supervision[69] is also a supervised community release which is required when a person has received a sentence of over two years, has earned time off the sentence for good behaviour, and is released before expiry of the full sentence. The underlying policy is to assist people who are released after lengthy sentences so that they will not commit further offences, a goal not always attained. As in the case of parole, a violator may be required to serve the full sentence.

Temporary Absence

A person who is serving a custodial sentence may be authorized to be absent from the institution for compassionate reasons or to pursue education or employment.[70] Temporary absence is not a right, but is granted at the discretion of the institution for rehabilitative purposes.

COMMUNITY RELEASE FACILITIES

Half-way houses, group homes, and similar residential facilities have been established across the country to assist in the reintegration of persons who have received and served custodial sentences. Unfortunately, the community has vacillated in their acceptance. When a violent incident occurs, an outcry against such homes is raised, quite understandably. The truth which tends to be overlooked is that offenders will be released on expiry of their sentences and that the community is better served by assisting than by rejecting the offender.

Social workers are aware that communities selected to contain such group homes have been exceedingly vocal in their opposition. Critics point to the danger to residents of the community with proof that innocent persons have been murdered by parolees living in half-way houses. Advocates have stressed the need for better trained staff and improved screening by the parole board, but have strongly supported the continuation of such homes.

CUSTODIAL SENTENCES

Federal

All sentences of two years or more are served in federally-operated custodial facilities,[71] which include all of the federal penitentiaries, facilities and work camps. Mandatory supervision applies to all federal sentences.

Provincial

Sentences under two years come under provincial jurisdiction and are served in jails and correctional centres operated by the province.[72] Mandatory supervision does not apply to provincial sentences, but parole does.

Intermittent sentences

Where the sentence imposed is not more than 90 days, the court may order that it be served intermittently,[73] for example, on weekends from Friday night till Monday morning. While the person is out of custody, he is subject to a probation order. The purpose of such a sentence is to allow the convicted person to continue his employment or carry out his community responsibilities. However, once the sentence has been ordered, it cannot be varied except on appeal. This situation often creates serious problems and may defeat the purpose of the sentence. For example, if the prisoner is required to change working hours or work weekends, which conflicts with the order, he may end up losing the very job which the sentence was designed to preserve.

Earned remission

Everyone who is sentenced to imprisonment is eligible to earn a reduction of up to one third of a total sentence for good behaviour.[74] The effect of this provision is to reduce a sentence to less than that imposed by the court. While earned remission is undoubtedly an inducement to good behaviour, it has been argued that a sentence should be for a stated period, which is not reducible.

Pardons

Many citizens are not aware that the federal government has enacted legislation which allows pardons for those who have been convicted of criminal offences.[75] Where the conviction was for a summary offence, the waiting period before application can be made is two years after completing the sentence; for an indictable offence, it is five years, and for a discharge, one year after all conditions are met.

To obtain a pardon, a person must apply to the Solicitor General of Canada through the local National Parole Board Office. The Royal Canadian Mounted Police investigate the applicant's behaviour since the date of conviction and forward a report to the Parole Board, which recommends to the Solicitor General whether or not a pardon should be granted. The procedure takes about six months and is a discretionary remedy.

The effect of a pardon is equivocal. The criminal record is removed from the file, sealed and kept separate, but there is no requirement that it be removed from police files. The criminal record cannot be used against a pardoned person by a federal government agency, such as the armed forces, but this may not apply to provincial or municipal institutions. Therefore, it is uncertain whether a person with a criminal record can claim never to have been convicted, for example, on an employment application. The best advice is to admit to the criminal record, but indicate that a pardon has been granted.

CONSEQUENCE OF ACQUITTAL

If an accused person is found not guilty, he or she is discharged by the court and is free to go. No further proceedings may be taken against that person concerning *that* particular offence except on appeal, where a new trial is ordered on the same offence. The underlying principle is that no person should be tried more than once for the same offence.[76] In some circumstances, the person who as been acquitted may subsequently be charged with another offence committed at the same time, which is a different offence.[77] In a highly publicized case[78] the accused was acquitted of murder which had been committed during a robbery. After acquittal, he confessed to the killing, was charged with robbery and perjury and was convicted. The court decided that, since a finding by the jury about his commission of the robbery was not essential to acquittal on the murder charge, he could be tried for robbery.

An acquittal is, of course, not a bar to prosecution for the same offence, committed at a different time.

Endnotes

1. R.S.C. 1985, c. C-46.
2. To illustrate, in 1901 there were 42,148 convictions for all offences, while the 1965 figure was 4,066,957, and the 1995 figure exceeded 5 million.
3. G. Parker, *An Introduction to Criminal Law* (Toronto: Methuen, 1977), pp. 41-42.
4. The Criminal Code Revision Committee completed its 1984 revision of the Criminal Code in 1988. Further amendments were made by S.C. 1995, c. 22 (Bill C-41) but many have not been proclaimed into force.
5. Criminal Code, note 1 above, Part I.
6. *Ibid.*, Part XIII.
7. *Ibid.*, Parts XIV and XV.
8. Except in Alberta; see Code, s. 471.
9. Criminal Code, note 1 above, Parts II-VII.
10. *Ibid.*, Part III.
11. *Ibid.*, Part IV.
12. *Ibid.*, Part VI.
13. Criminal Code, s. 265.
14. *Ibid.*, s. 271.
15. *Ibid.*, s. 272.
16. *Ibid.*, s. 273.
17. *Ibid.*, ss. 274 and 275.
18. *Ibid.*, ss. 276(1), (2), (3) and 277.
19. *Ibid.*, ss. 276(4) and 486(3).
20. *Ibid.*, s. 486(4).
21. Canada Evidence Act, R.S.C. 1985, c. C-15, s. 4(2).
22. Criminal Code, note 1 above, Part VIII.
23. Criminal Code, s. 282.
24. *Ibid.*, s. 283.
25. Criminal Code, note 1 above, Parts IX-XII.

26. *Ibid.*, Parts XVI-XXVIII.
27. R.S.C. 1985, c. 27 (1st Supp.), s. 127.
28. R.S.C. 1985, c. N-1.
29. R.S.C. 1985, c. F-27.
30. Bill C-8.
31. Narcotic Control Act, note 28 above, Schedule: Food and Drugs Act, note 29 above.
32. Criminal Code, R.S.C. 1985, c. C-46, s. 4(3), as incorporated by the Narcotic Control Act, note 28 above, s. 2 and the Food and Drugs Act, note 29 above, ss. 38 and 46.
33. Narcotic Control Act, note 28 above, s. 2; Food and Drugs Act, note 29 above, ss. 38 and 46.
34. Canadian Charter of Rights and Freedoms, Part 1 of the Constitution Act, 1982, being Schedule B of the Canada Act 1982 (U.K.), 1982, c. 11, s. 11(d).
35. *R. v. Oakes*, [1986] 1 S.C.R. 103, 53 O.R. (2d) 719 (headnote), 50 C.R. (3d) 1, 24 C.C.C. (3d) 321, 19 C.R.R. 308, 26 D.L.R. (4th) 200, 65 N.R. 87, 14 O.A.C. 335.
36. Narcotic Control Act, note 28 above, s. 5.
37. *Smith v. T.Q.*, [1987] 1 S.C.R. 1045, 15 B.C.L.R. (2d) 273, 58 C.R. (3d) 193, [1987] 5 W.W.R. 1, 34 C.C.C. (3d) 97, 31 C.R.R. 193, 40 D.L.R. (4th) 435, 75 N.R. 321.
38. R.S.C. 1985, c. 27 (1st Supp.).
39. Criminal Code, note 32 above, s. 342.1.
40. *Ibid.*, s. 342.
41. *Ibid.*, s. 213.
42. *Ibid.*, ss. 249-261, ss. 662(5), 665 and 667(1), (2), (2.1) and s. 700.
43. Narcotic Control Act, note 28 above, ss. 2 and 10.
44. Zimmer, Lynn and John Morgan. "*Marijuana Myths, Marijuana Facts*" (Chicago, Ill.: University of Chicago Press, 1986).
45. Criminal Code, note 32 above, s. 19.
46. *Ibid.*, s. 41(1).
47. *R. v. Baxter* (1975), 33 C.R.N.S. 22, 27 C.C.C. (2d) 96 (Ont. C.A.).
48. Criminal Code, note 32 above, s. 43.
49. *Ibid.*, s. 34(1).
50. *R. v. Trecroce* (1980), 55 C.C.C. (2d) 202 (Ont. C. A.).
51. *R. v. Fraser* (1980), 15 Alta. L.R. (2d) 25, 19 C.R. (3d) 193, 26 A.R. 33, 55 C.C.C. (2d) 503 (C.A.); *Gee v. R.* (1980), 19 C.R. (3d) 222, 26 A.R. 212, 55 C.C.C. (2d) 525 (C.A.).
52. See *R. v. Baxter*, note 47 above.
53. Criminal Code, note 32 above, s. 17. See *R. v. Morrison* (1980), 54 C.C.C. (2d) 447 (Ont. Dist. Ct.).

54. Criminal Code, note 32 above, s. 18.
55. Criminal Code, note 32 above, s. 36. See also *D.P.P. v. Beard*, [1920] A.C. 479 (H.C.).
56. Criminal Code, s. 16.
57. Criminal Code, ss. 2 and 672.23.
58. Criminal Code, s. 672.38.
59. Criminal Code, ss. 672.22 to 672.35.
60. *Chartrand v. R.*, [1977] 1 S.C.R. 314, 26 C.C.C. (2d) 417, 64 D.L.R. (3d) 145, 8 N.R. 503.
61. Except in relation to some provincial offences, which are not truly criminal.
62. *R. v. Kovack*, Ont. Fam. Ct., October 14, 1983 (unreported).
63. Criminal Code, R.S.C. 1985, c. C-46, ss. 334, 718 and 737.
64. *Ibid.*, s. 736.
65. *Ibid.*, s. 718.
66. "Legal Aid and the Poor", National Council on Welfare, Ottawa, 1995.
67. Criminal Code, s. 737.
68. Parole Act, R.S.C. 1985, c. P-2.
69. *Ibid.*, s. 21.
70. Prisons and Reformatories Act, R.S.C. 1985, c. P-20, s. 7; Ministry of Correctional Services Act, R.S.O. 1980, c. 275, s. 27; Parole Act, note 69 above.
71. Criminal Code, s. 731(1).
72. *Ibid.*, s. 731(3).
73. *Ibid.*, s. 737(1)(*c*).
74. Prisons and Reformatories Act, s. 6.
75. Criminal Records Act, R.S.C. 1985, c. C-47.
76. The principle is referred to as *res judicata*, or "matter adjudicated", popularly referred to as the prohibition against "double jeopardy".
77. *Kienapple v. R.*, [1975] 1 S.C.R. 729, 26 C.R.N.S. 1, 15 C.C.C. (2d) 524, 44 D.L.R. (2d) 351, 1 N.R. 322.
78. *Gushue v. R.*, [1980] 1 S.C.R. 798, 16 C.R. (3d) 39, 50 C.C.C. (2d) 417, 106 D.L.R. (3d) 152, 30 N.R. 204.

Bibliography

Gaudreault, Arlene. "Restitution Measures: A Promising Aspect of the Recent Sentencing Reform" (1997) 12, 2 *Justice Report*, 9-10.

Gemmell, Jack. "The New Conditional Sentencing Regime" (Feb., 1997) 39 Crim. L.Q. 334-61.

Hogarth, John. *Sentencing as a Human Process* (Toronto: Centre of Criminology, University of Toronto, 1971).

LeBlanc, Dianne. "The Time to Share Secrets: [Notifying Society of Potentially Dangerous Offenders]" (1997) 12, 2 *Justice Report*, 1(2).

Lewis, Tomas J. "Recent Proposals in the Criminal Law of Rape: Significant Reform or Semantic Change?" (1979) 17 Osgoode Hall L.J. 445.

McLeod, R.M., J.D. Takach, H.F. Morton and M.D. Segal. *The Canadian Charter of Rights: The Prosecution and Defence of Criminal and Other Statutory Offences* (Toronto: Carswell Co., 1983).

Ruby, Clayton. *Sentencing*, 2nd ed. (Toronto: Butterworths, 1983).

24

Finding and Using Legal Services

FINDING A LAWYER

How does anyone find the right person for the job? Most lawyers specialize in one or two fields. A criminal lawyer would not likely be the preferred expert to draft a will. How does one find an appropriate lawyer? Word of mouth and a recommendation from friends and neighbors is still the best referral source in most cases. Other lawyers who do not practise in the relevant field are also good referral sources. The local Law Society will certainly provide the names of several lawyers in the area. This referral will not guarantee that the lawyer will act for you, only that the person is qualified to practise law. Another source is the Yellow Pages in the local telephone directory. Most directories include the areas of specialization in which the listed lawyers practise. Until recently, lawyers in Canada were not permitted to advertise.

FEES

Legal fees vary widely from city to rural areas and from one part of Canada to another. Most lawyers charge an hourly rate depending on the locality and the lawyer's level of expertise. For some matters, such as wills, contracts or home sales, the lawyer usually charges a "block" or set fee.

USING LEGAL SERVICES

In general, the following are some useful guides to selecting and making the best use of a lawyer.

1. Know your area of concern and try to find a lawyer who possesses some special expertise in that area. Family law, immigration, landlord and tenant, criminal law, or real estate are some areas of specialization. Lawyers in rural areas are more likely to be generalists and may need to consult with or refer you to a specialist after discussing your problem.
2. Have your facts and questions prepared in advance. Collect any relevant documents that relate to your concern.
3. Discuss fees and expenses. Do not be afraid to ask about fees and about the amount of time that may be required to prepare and present your case. Most legal matters are brief but situations such as a full blown lawsuit may extend over several years.
4. Do not hesitate to shop for a lawyer if the first person you see does not give you a sense of confidence. You are purchasing knowledge and expertise as well as a sense of security and trust in that person to take charge.
5. Communication and mutual understanding are essential. Do not hesitate to say you do not understand and to ask for further explanation or elaboration.

LEGAL ASSISTANCE ON A LIMITED INCOME

Legal services are undisputably costly and beyond the means of many persons requiring legal assistance. There is no universal insurance guaranteeing legal services in the same manner as health services are underwritten in Canada. While some legal processes may be considered frivolous, there are many situations which require legal counsel to protect a person's rights, regardless of his capacity to buy legal service.

PROVINCIAL LEGAL AID SERVICES

Each of the Canadian provinces provides some form of legal aid. In the last decade, all ten provinces have developed some combinations of judicare and community legal service delivery models. Nova Scotia, Saskatchewan and Prince Edward Island have staff lawyers in community legal centres; Alberta, New Brunswick and Newfoundland have established judicare systems similar to that in Ontario; and British Columbia, Manitoba and Quebec have mixed systems. Both Ontario and Alberta have established clinics in remote areas of the provinces.

Legal aid was established in 1951 in Ontario on a voluntary basis. Since 1967, it has been administered and controlled by the Law Society of

Upper Canada using the English judicare model, and employs private lawyers on a fee for service basis.[1]

Legal aid plans are in serious jeopardy in every province. Funding is inadequate as costs and demand for services multiply. Services have been curtailed because of financial crises resulting in low income persons being denied representation. The entire system is in disarray. A report prepared by the National Council of Welfare, stated that low income wage earners have almost no access to legal assistance and that delivery of legal services is frequently "inefficient, wasteful and even harmful to their clients, especially in the area of criminal law".[2] Without legal aid, the poor and low income people have little chance of protecting themselves against exploitation or persecution in both civil and criminal matters. Police and courts are intimidating to most people, but especially confusing to people with limited education or from other cultures, or who suffer a disability. An adversarial system requires a level field to ensure justice.

The Supreme Court of Canada has been silent on whether the Charter gives low income people the right to government funded legal representation in criminal trials. Section 7 and 11(d) of the Charter give the right to be presumed innocent, the right not to be deprived of life, liberty, and security of person, except as a result of a fair trial.[3] The Supreme Court ruled that Section 10(b) of the Charter does not mean that arrest for a criminal offence requires mandatory provision of counsel, but rather that the accused be informed about the availability of legal services in the area and be given an opportunity to contact them.[4]

As for civil matters, it has been said that the poor are more dependent on law, regulations, and bureaucratic decisions for their daily needs. In addition, as consumers they are more often preyed upon by unscrupulous persons who take advantage of their vulnerability. Housing violations involving inadequate enforcement of building and housing codes, and discrimination against prospective tenants directed toward welfare recipients, visible minorities, and single parents are examples of civil concerns.

Whether criminal or civil, poor people are often ignorant of their legal rights and options and more reluctant to seek legal advice than are those with higher incomes who are more likely to seek legal assistance as soon as a problem arises. Collective legal challenges are another option frequently employed by community legal centres. These collected cases have more power than a single case and can result in a remedy for joint relief and justice that may become the impetus for more progressive legislation. A test case where an individual legal action can have a cumulative effect is another option that has been successful in bringing relief.

Funding of Legal Aid Programs

Responsibility for legal aid is shared between the federal and provincial governments, while the plans are administered solely by the provincial governments. The three main models of legal aid services are: the judicare model, where applicants who are eligible for legal aid are referred to a private lawyer who is in the judicare registry; the staff model, where services are provided by a staff lawyer employed by the plan; and the community clinic model, which uses staff lawyers who work for neighbourhood offices. Ontario refers all criminal and most family law cases to private lawyers, eligible civil cases are handled by staff lawyers in 72 community clinics.

It has been demonstrated that people who are marginalized to the periphery of society are often fearful and hesitant about seeking a legal solution. In particular, low income native people and first time offenders may refuse to seek representation by a lawyer because they feel there is no point or they may as well get it over with and plead guilty. A Toronto study found that accused people who were not represented by a lawyer were more likely to be found guilty[5] and more likely if charged with several related offences to be found guilty of the most serious charge.

The problems of cost-effectiveness and quality of service are under scrutiny but remain unresolved. Ontario has a large judicare system of referral to private lawyers and is administered by the Law Society. It may be that a mixed system which uses staff lawyers as well as private lawyers willing to take legal aid work may be most the equitable route. In addition, it has been noted that paralegal workers can also be used to represent clients before certain courts and many administrative tribunals.[6]

Mediation where appropriate can also provide resolution for many civil problems, with legal proceedings available should mediation fail. Family law matters for women who qualify for legal aid could be better dealt with by a social worker and lawyer working together in a family law clinic, such as the Manitoba legal aid plan has developed.[7]

The area director of the Legal Aid Plan has responsibility for the issuing of certificates on the basis of need, for determining the amount the client will contribute toward the fee, what work shall be undertaken by the lawyer, and the ongoing monitoring of that work. The area director's office is divided into a criminal unit and a civil unit.[8] The duty counsel service in the provincial courts (criminal and family divisions) is also the responsibility of the area director.

CERTIFICATES IN CRIMINAL MATTERS

A certificate is required to be issued to any applicant who qualifies where that applicant is charged with an indictable offence.[9] A certificate *may* be issued to an applicant charged with a summary conviction offence if, upon conviction, there is a likelihood of imprisonment or loss of the means of earning a livelihood. In civil matters, the issuance of a certificate is discretionary and is dependent upon the seriousness of the matter. Certificates may be issued for child custody, access, and maintenance matters, and divorce petitions. The director bases his decision on the dual criteria of the applicant's need and capacity to pay for the legal service requested. Capacity to pay is assessed by a legal aid officer who will consider employment, income, family resources, indebtedness, and ownership of property. Successful applicants may be required to pay back some or all of the costs incurred either directly or through a lien on property or assets. In the case of juveniles, certificates may be issued for disposition hearings. Where a family refuses to be financially responsible for a juvenile's legal services, it is necessary to make a rapid determination of the juvenile's need for immediate service. If such service is refused and no certificate is issued, service may be obtained from a Community Legal Clinic.

A study of legal aid in Ontario undertaken by the Social Planning Council of Metropolitan Toronto concluded that eligibility standards introduced in 1980 were "detailed and unnecessarily rigid, replacing the principle of ability to pay with a gross income test" and that "such restrictive access to legal aid recasts the concept of guaranteeing rights to legal services into one of providing charity to the destitute."[10] This observation is still true, and the application of the standard continues to be very restrictive, depriving many applicants of legal assistance. The result is that many persons now appear in court on their own behalf thereby clogging the courts.

Escalating total costs of legal services, due in part to new rights to legal representation under the Charter and the Young Offenders Act, raises the issue of community willingness to bear the cost of legal services to all who are entitled to them, despite their inability to pay.

CHILD WELFARE AND DOMESTIC CERTIFICATES

The issuing of these certificates is at the discretion of the area director. Where an applicant who wishes to press for support is receiving welfare or Family Benefits, a certificate for legal aid will not usually be issued. The decision has been justified on the basis that the Family Law Act enables an agency to make its own petition for support and to receive the benefit of any order that is issued. When welfare is not involved, the grounds for issuance of a certificate are less clear. A complex situation is more likely to be regarded as meriting a certificate.

DUTY COUNSEL

A permanent duty counsel project was established in Metropolitan Toronto in 1977 to provide salaried duty counsel for all criminal courts. Since that time there has been expansion of the provision of duty counsel to all suburban courts for juvenile cases and in child welfare courts. Duty counsel are located in offices in the provincial court buildings. An active panel of lawyers is maintained. The basic duties of duty counsel include advising persons who are accused of offences of their rights and taking steps to protect those rights, including representation on applications for remand or adjournment, or for bail, or on the entering of a plea of guilty, and making representations in regard to sentencing.[11] In general, duty counsel does not represent a client at trial.

APPEALS

An area committee deals with appeals where a certificate is refused. There are two types of appeals: an appeal to obtain a certificate for legal representation where a lower court decision is appealed to a higher court;[12] and an appeal from the area director's refusal to grant a certificate or the cancellation of a certificate.[13] The appeal procedure permits the applicant to appear before the committee with or without a representative, who need not be a lawyer, to present the situation. If the area committee refuses the certificate, a further appeal may be taken to the provincial director, whose decision is final.

COMMUNITY LEGAL CENTRES

Legal aid, though certainly providing broader access to legal representation, is inadequate and not always appropriate to meet the need for legal assistance of socially and economically disadvantaged people. This concern gave rise to community and neighbourhood clinics which opened toward the end of the 1960s. The Injured Workers Consultants was the first community legal service in Ontario and Parkdale Community Legal Services was the first clinic to hire staff lawyers through a federal grant. In 1976, the Ontario Legal Aid Plan (OLAP) was amended to provide for regular funding to approved community legal clinics. Similar plans are in effect in all Canadian provinces. Examples of Ontario community legal centres which serve a specific group include a legal clinic for African-

Canadians, which deals only with test cases and advocacy issues, children and youth, the elderly, persons with disabilities, Spanish speaking people, persons with HIV and AIDS, an industrial accident victims group, injured workers covered by Workers' Compensation, a landlord self-help clinic, a clinic for Chinese and Southeast Asians, and pay equity advocacy, as well as Aboriginal legal services. Other community legal centres serve a geographic catchment area.

An option for community clinics is that of collective action advocacy. For example, in a clinic in London, Ontario, it became apparent that 50 low-income families were being evicted from their homes weekly because no other recourse seemed to be possible. In response, the clinic looked into the feasibility of setting up a mediation service for landlords and tenants.[14]

Native persons have been involved in setting up special programmes. British Columbia funds 10 native communities to operate legal aid offices with their own boards of directors; Manitoba hired native paralegals to deliver services in northern Cree-speaking communities. The Ontario Legal Aid Plan formed the Nishnabe-Aski Legal Services Corporation which has an aboriginal board of directors and provides legal services through private lawyers in northern Ontario.[15]

The names, addresses and a description of the services provided by community legal clinics are available to the public through each provincial Law Society.

Endnotes

1. F. H. Zemans, "Community Legal Clinics in Ontario, 1980: A Data Survey" (1981), 1 Windsor Yearb. Access Justice 230.
2. "Legal Aid and the Poor", A Report by the National Council of Welfare, Winter, 1995.
3. *Ibid.*, p. 5.
4. *Prosper v. R.*, [1994] 3 S.C.R. 236, 33 C.R. (4th) 85; *R. v. Matheson*, [1994] 3 S.C.R. 328, 33 C.R. (4th) 136; *R. v. Cobham* (1993), 80 C.C.C. (3d) 449, 135 AR. 249; *R. v. Barthe*, [1994] 3 S.C.R. 173, 92 C.C.C. (3d) 289.
5. "Legal Aid and the Poor", *op. cit.*, p. 9. Information from Ab & Associates of Canada, Comprehensive Review and Evaluation of the Certificate Component of the Ontario Legal Aid Plan (Ottawa, 1991), Wilkins, James, L. *Legal Aid in the Criminal Courts* (Toronto: University of Toronto Press, 1975).
6. Zemans, Frederick, "The Non-Lawyer as a Means of Providing Legal Services in Canada" in *Lawyers and the Consumer Interest:*

Regulating the Market for Legal Services, Robert G. Evans and Michael S. Trebilcock, eds. (Toronto: Butterworths, 1982), p. 293.

7. *Legal Aid and the Poor, op. cit.*, p. 64.
8. J. Waterman, "Provincial Court (Family Division) and the Ontario Legal Aid Plan." Paper presented at Family Law in the Provincial Courts (Family Division) Workshop sponsored by the Young Lawyer's Division of the Canadian Bar Association — Ontario, 30 November 1982.
9. Legal Aid Act, R.S.O. 1990, c. L.9.
10. "Legal Aid in Ontario: From Rights to Charity?" Social Infopack, Vol. II, No. 2, June 1983.
11. Legal Aid Regulation, R.R.O. 1990.
12. Legal Aid Act, note 9 above, s. 14(1).
13. *Ibid.*, s. 16(10).
14. "Legal Aid and the Poor", *op. cit.*, p. 15.
15. *Ibid.*

Bibliography

Bacon, Stephen W., and Timothy F. Hartnagel. "Lock'em up: Attitudes Toward Punishing Juvenile Offenders" (April, 1996) 38 *Canadian Journal of Criminology* 191-212.

Gathercole, R. J. "Legal Services and the Poor." In Robert G. Evans, and Michael J. Trebilcock, eds. *Lawyers and the Consumer Interest: Regulating the Market for Legal Services*. Studies in Law and Economics, Vol. 2 (Toronto: Butterworths, 1982).

Legal Aid and the Poor: A Report by the National Council of Welfare. Ottawa: The Council, 1995.

Noone, Anne. "Paralegals and Legal Aid Organisations" (Fall, 1988) 4 J. of Law and Social Policy 146-163.

McIntyre, David H. *Delivery of Criminal Legal Aid Services in New Brunswick* (Fredericton: Law Society of New Brunswick, 1993).

Mossman, Mary Jane. "Toward a Comprehensive Legal Aid Program in Canada: Exploring the Issues" (May, 1993) 4 *Windsor Review of Legal and Social Issues* 1-89.

Reid, Gayla. *Family Problems? Where to Get Legal Help*, 2nd ed. (Vancouver: Legal Services Society of British Columbia, 1994). Co-published by Ministry of the Attorney General and Ministry of Social Services.

Timms, H. Grant. "Social Welfare Programs under Pressure: The Rise of Legal Clinics as Facilitators of Poverty Law Reform Activities" (Fall, 1993) 9 *Journal of Law and Social Policy* 126-172.

25

Legal Accountability of Social Workers

Social workers, regardless of their level of training, hold themselves out to the public as having particular knowledge and skill, or the fact of their employment implies it. Private practitioners and some agencies charge a fee for service, which implies a contractual relationship between worker or agency and client for service according to a particular standard. Other social workers practise under statutory authority, notably those employed by Children's Aid Societies, correctional systems, mental health and educational facilities. As a consequence, social workers may at some point in their careers be at risk of civil liability for acts or omissions in their dealings with clients. Workers may also face criminal prosecution if they are charged with intentional or negligent disregard of a statutory duty. Perhaps most distressing are the circumstances where a child who is under social work supervision is injured or dies and an inquiry is held. Professional reputations are destroyed and lives seriously affected, whether or not workers are sued civilly or charged criminally as a result of the inquiry. A recent inquiry into the death of a child who died through injuries inflicted by her mother while the family was under the supervision of a Children's Aid Society unquestionably will have a profound effect upon the reputations and professional careers of the social workers involved.[1] At the date of writing, criminal charges have also been laid against the worker, the supervisor and the Society in another baby death while the infant was under the care of a Society.[2]

Social workers are accountable to their employers to carry out the duties required by their agency or in accordance with a statute. This raises the obvious issue of where the worker's accountability lies for the consequences if the duties are not carried out in conformity with the employer's interpretation of agency policy or statutory duty. The danger of retaliation against a social worker who reports irregularities or maltreatment of clients which occur within their own agencies is always present. It may be difficult to prove that dismissal of a worker is directly related to that worker's advocacy action rather than for some other reason which may be claimed by the agency. In one jurisdiction in the United States, it has been established that there is a rebuttable presumption that action taken against a worker within 90 days of receiving a report from that worker claiming client mistreatment would be deemed to be retaliatory.[3]

A case heard in the Newfoundland Supreme Court tested the question of whether the government has the right to fire an employee carrying out his lawful duty because it does not like his decisions. Peter Brown, a social worker, was fired because he disagreed with the Social Service Minister's interpretation of a departmental regulation which would reduce welfare payments to people who have boarders living with them. Mr. Brown argued that the regulation did not apply to the Innu Indians because the concept of board and lodging is foreign to their culture. He asked the court to quash his dismissal, but the dismissal was upheld by the court.[4]

COMMON AREAS OF POTENTIAL LIABILITY

Any social work setting, either public or private, provides a potential for liability resulting from a claim of malpractice or negligence. There is an even greater liability risk, however, for the growing number of social workers in private practice. The National Association of Social Workers has listed the most common types of malpractice claims against social workers occurring between 1969 and 1990.[5] These are claims against NASW members who were covered by insurance available through NASW and, therefore, represent the experience of only one insurer. For the individual social worker, the largest number of claims were for charges of sexual impropriety, and other claims included allegations of incorrect treatment, improper child placement, and breach of confidentiality. Claims were also made alleging improper removal of a child in child custody dispute, failure to make a diagnosis, or making an improper diagnosis.

Once a suit has been initiated, the tendency is to sue everyone, worker, supervisor, director, agency board members, whoever may be considered to share accountability. Social workers may find that they are considered liable, not only for their own acts, but also for the acts of those they supervise, both workers and volunteers. Liability may arise from acts of omission as well as commission. In the last decade only a relatively small number of social workers, both American and Canadian, have been sued either in a criminal prosecution or a civil action. Criminal prosecutions have rarely succeeded and civil claims usually are settled without ever coming to court.

In general, volunteers and students in training will not be held to the standard of care expected of fully trained professionals but rather to what can be reasonably expected of a student or volunteer. They are, however, expected to be competent for their assigned position and to possess more skills than a lay person. They are also expected to know their limitations and to seek help from staff or supervisors, or, where appropriate, to refer the situation to qualified persons.

Vicarious liability equates with organizational liability, in which an aggrieved party may chose to sue not only the person directly providing a service but supervisors, administrators, and members of the board of directors. Even when the direct practitioner assumes that the agency liability insurance will cover civil matters, the employer may still sue that practitioner through the insurance provider taking control of the litigation and suing the practitioner directly. The legal principle involved is that of fiduciary responsibility, which means that a person involved in the agency or service has a duty to use professional expertise in the best interests of the client, based on the trust that client has placed on her or him. Though a professional person is seen to be competent to make decisions, other persons are involved because the master/servant aspect of employment implies that employers set work conditions and expectations and so are ultimately responsible for an employee's actions.

STANDARD OF PRACTICE

The absence of a uniform standard of social work practice, which is widely accepted by the profession and the community, makes it difficult to determine what constitutes competent practice. It is therefore not possible to state the particular standard of care which is owed to clients, nor when liability, either civil or criminal, arises. The Canadian Association of Social Workers has established a Code of Ethics for its member associations, but adherence to these codes is voluntary and not legally enforceable. In 1995 the Canadian Association of Social Workers published Standards of Practice in Social Work in order to define more precisely the standard of care ordinarily expected of a competent social worker, in accordance with a stated value base, ethical standards, and the scope of professional confidentiality.[6]

Nor is there clear legal recourse when reputations are attacked. Ontario is the only province which gives no legal recognition to social work at all.[7] One writer suggests that even where the worker is not a member of an association of social workers and has not subscribed to a formal code of ethics, the principles of that code may still be seen as the standard required of a person professing to be a social worker.[8] In general, provincial statutes provide only for registration or other legal acknowledgment of social workers who are eligible for membership. Until standards of practice are adopted as applying to all social workers, the standard of practice will remain unclear.

CIVIL RESPONSIBILITY AND LIABILITY

One can speak only in broad concepts in defining civil responsibility and liability. In general terms, when persons hold themselves out to have professional knowledge or skill, and have academic credentials or some experience to support their professional status, they are assumed to have the requisite knowledge and skill. They are responsible for work in accordance with a generally accepted standard of performance for that profession. If the person fails or neglects to do what a reasonable professional in similar circumstances would have done, or fails or neglects to carry out a statutory duty, and harm results to a client, he or she may become liable for civil damages. An English case establishes an important principle.

> [I]t should now be regarded as settled that if someone possessed of a special skill undertakes, quite irrespective of contract, to apply that skill for the assistance of another person who relies on such skill, a duty of care will arise. The fact that the service is to be given by means of . . . words can make no difference. Furthermore, if . . . others could reasonably rely on his judgment or his skill or on his ability to make careful inquiry . . . to give information or advice to . . . another person who, as he knows or should know, will place reliance on it, then a duty of care will arise.[9]

The following fictitious situations illustrate some circumstances in which civil liability may arise.

> Jason, a social worker, lives with and is responsible for the care and supervision of four mentally handicapped adults in a community apartment. Peter, one of the residents, has not returned home from the sheltered workshop by dinner time, nor by bed time. Jason is tired and does nothing, expecting Peter will come home. Peter is lost and wanders the streets. He is hit by a car and severely injured. Peter's family sues Jason for negligence in his care of Peter. In these circumstances, Jason has failed to exercise the reasonable care for Peter's safety that another social worker in similar circumstances would have exercised. As a result of Jason's neglect, Peter suffered injury, which may be directly attributable to Jason's failure to provide the necessary supervision. Damages could be awarded to Peter's family.

Marcia, a Children's Aid worker, supervises the Brownstone children, who are in their mother's care, under the authority of a court order. Marcia suspects that Jonathan, the 5-year-old boy, is being abused by his mother, since he always has an unusual number of bruises on his arms and face. She does not take him to a doctor for examination, as she is required by law to do if abuse is suspected. Jonathan is admitted to hospital after a beating by his mother and is found to have severe internal injuries and a broken arm. Jonathan's father sues Marcia and the Children's Aid Society for negligence in their supervision of Jonathan. Marcia failed in her statutory duty to inquire about Jonathan's health and safety where a reasonable social worker in similar circumstances would have made those inquiries. Both she and the Society might well be found to be negligent, and damages could be awarded to Jonathan and his father.

By any objective standard, the above situations are ones that could occur in the course of social work practice. All the elements are present: there is a duty of care, and neglect of the duty, resulting in harm to the client, which was reasonably foreseeable. In any law suit, the court would look to the prevailing community standard of practice to determine whether or not the conduct was negligent. The standard of proof would be the civil standard — whether, on a balance of probabilities, the worker was negligent. Workers also have a duty to conduct an objective inquiry before making allegations against person who are involved with children in their care. In an Ontario case, a child protection worker concluded that a father had abused his child, and initiated an action against the father. The father claimed that the social worker had believed the mother's story and so had not conducted an objective investigation because of bias. After three years of attempting to clear his name, a court found in the father's favour and awarded damages to the father.[10]

DUTY AND LIABILITY UNDER THE CRIMINAL CODE

The Criminal Code contains several sections which may pertain to social workers. It imposes a positive duty to provide the necessities of life upon anyone who has legal guardianship of a child, or has charge of any person who is detained in custody, is aged, ill, or insane, and cannot withdraw from that charge and cannot provide for himself.[11] There is also a positive duty to care for and protect a child under 10 years of age from harm.[12] Failure to do so may result in a penalty of up to two years' imprisonment.[13] However, there are several specific requirements. The worker must be under a legal duty to provide care for the person and the failure to provide care, or abandonment or exposure to harm must have occurred intentionally. The standard of proof must meet the criminal standard, that the act was committed intentionally and beyond a reasonable doubt.

An Ontario case arose from allegations that the caseworker, supervisor and agency director of the Brockville, Ontario Children's Aid Society exposed a child under 10 years of age to danger to its life or health, contrary to the Criminal Code.[14] The facts disclosed that the child had been returned to his mother's care after a period of Society wardship, with an order for close supervision. The mother, a borderline mental defective, was capable of distorting the truth, was unco-operative and difficult to work with. The father was at work and left care and control of the child to the mother. The assigned social worker maintained close and regular contact, obtained medical and social work assistance and kept close collateral contact with mental retardation and psychological services, while carrying a heavy additional caseload. Nevertheless, the placement was not successful, a court review was planned and the baby's mother notified. The day before the hearing, the child was seriously abused by his mother. The judge held:

> The Crown must prove in this case, as it is a criminal trial, . . . not only the *actus reus*, but also the *mens rea* . . . or to put it another way, "an intention to bring about the forbidden result or forbidden state of affairs". . . . The conduct must be "wilful" . . . by deliberate or purposeful conduct with full knowledge of or reckless of or indifferent to the consequences of his act or omission; a callous disregard, a complete and utter disregard for the safety of children.
>
> The Crown must, therefore, prove that the conduct of [the worker] was so negligent as to constitute a reckless or callous disregard for the safety of [the child]. The same onus is on the Crown with respect to the other two accused.
>
> The court found no evidence whatever against the other two accused, the Director of the C.A.S. and a supervisor. This leaves me with [the social worker] the remaining accused, and on the whole of the evidence . . . I cannot find any acts of commission or omission on her part that even approach the requirement of *mens rea* in this case. It is true, from the evidence, that some visits were missed, but these are easily explained by the mother's non co-operation, holidays on the part of [the worker] and, no doubt, her heavy caseload. She was on the firing line, to put it bluntly, she had to make her own decisions with whatever assistance she could get and hope that her decisions were correct, and, to my mind, she did the best she could under the circumstances, and I so find. I also find that she followed the guidelines set down by the Ministry of Community and Social Services to the best of her ability. Certainly there is no evidence that any omissions on her part amounted to wilful conduct amounting to a reckless or callous disregard for the child's safety.

> In summary, I find that the Crown's evidence has fallen far short of proving beyond a reasonable doubt that any of the three accused are guilty of the offence charged. Therefore, all three accused are acquitted.[15]

However, this case provides no assurance that similar charges will not be laid in similar circumstances. Indeed, such charges have recently been laid in another Ontario case.[16]

Record Keeping

Keeping proper records is a legal as well as a professional responsibility. The records of a practitioner can be subpoenaed, may be admissible in legal proceedings, and may be used to refresh memory while giving testimony regarding direct contacts with clients. There are federal criminal laws and a range of provincial laws that set out statutory obligations for specified records. In addition, failure to keep adequate records is a specific ground for professional misconduct for some health care professionals. A civil suit for negligence may arise where failing to keep records is thought to contribute to injury of a client or patient.[17]

Records must be objective and relevant to the focus of the intervention or treatment. They should be chronological, dated, and signed, with any subsequent alterations, additions or corrections dated and signed as well, leaving the original entry intact and legible. Records which are to be used in a legal proceeding cannot be altered or tampered with, as this is considered to be an obstrution of justice.[18] Private notes which are not part of an official record may be maintained, but they can also be subpoenaed and should be consistent with the official record. Opinions, impressions and other subjective entries are permissible if they are based on direct observation or the worker's own interpretation.

The length of time that records must be retained is difficult to ascertain. The limitation period is normally six years.[19] The courts, however, have decided that the clock only begins to run when the person discovers the harm, rather than when the event which caused the harm actually occurred. This finding flows from the recognition that persons, especially children who have suffered harm, may not be able to appreciate the harmful event until some years later. Therefore, there is no clear destruction date for records which are not specifically governed by statute. As a practical matter, records can now be kept for longer periods by computer storage or microfiche, as long as alteration or disclosure is safeguarded.

CONFIDENTIALITY AND PRIVILEGED COMMUNICATION

Privilege

In an important decision, the Supreme Court of Canada found that, while an individual may have a constitutional right to privacy in regard to information in the possession of a third party, counselling records may have relevance in a criminal prosecution. The court must balance the victim's constitutional right to privacy against the right of the accused to a full defence. Therefore, counselling records can be subpoenaed where they are properly applied for by the defence on behalf of the accused. The judge will then make a determination of relevance in whole or part of that record to the defence. Where the judge finds the information to have relevance, it can be disclosed to the court.[20]

Subsequently, the federal government introduced amendments to the Criminal Code permitting access to a complainant's records, but under restricted conditions. These records include medical, therapeutic, counselling, psychiatric, Children's Aid Society, school and employment records, personal diaries and journals. In order to access desired records, the accused must establish a potential relevance of the record to the issue in dispute before a judge. The judge will then review the record and must consider both the privacy and equality rights of the complainant as well as the right of the accused to a full and fair trial. These amendments have not yet been proclaimed in force.

Early in 1997, the Supreme Court of Canada ruled that a charge of gross indecency could not proceed because a rape crisis centre had shredded notes concerning an interview with the woman who had brought the complaint. The defence requested the counselling notes, which had been destroyed prior to the request being made. The majority found that the unavailability of these notes was a violation of the constitutional rights of the accused to a fair trial because, had the notes revealed inconsistencies upon which the complainant could be cross-examined, it is possible that this might have affected the outcome of the case in favour of the accused or appellant. Therefore, the case against the accused was stayed.[21]

In the United States, the thinking on this issue has gone in the opposite direction. In a civil rights case which involved a charge of wrongful death against a police officer, a social worker who counselled the officer refused to turn over her case records when they were requested by a federal court judge. An appeal court held in favour of privilege with the qualification that it is not absolute privilege and must be balanced by consideration of competing interests. The case was heard in the Supreme Court of the United States, which upheld an absolute right to refuse to disclose confidential counselling information to any court in the United States.[22]

Confidentiality

It is inherent in most professional and ethical codes that confidentiality is an important component of a professional relationship. Confidentiality imposes an obligation upon the worker not to disclose information obtained through that relationship with the consent of the client which should be in writing. Social workers, therefore, should define what will constitute confidentiality at the outset of the relationship. This will include limitations imposed by statute in the case of child protection workers, those conducting a court ordered assessment, or probation workers. It will also apply to those situations in which clients attempt to disclose information in exchange for a promise to keep it confidential. There can be legal consequences of breaching confidential obligations through civil action or, in some cases, criminal prosecution. Social workers should also be aware that where unsolicited inquiries for information about a client from third parties such as police, probation officers, employers, lawyers, reporters, outside health or government agencies occur, no information should be given without consultation with and written consent of the party involved. Never release such information over the telephone. As well, no promise of confidentiality should be given to third party sources regarding information about a client.

A privileged communication is one that cannot be used as evidence. The only privilege recognized by the law at this time are: the solicitor/client privilege, the privilege against self-incrimination, the marital communication privilege, but only during cohabitation, the Crown privilege on the grounds of specific public interests, and the police/informer privilege.[23] Social workers do not have privilege in Canada, nor is there doctor/patient or psychotherapist/patient privilege. Records can be ordered to be produced in court, which can create conflict of obligations because the issues involved are both legal and ethical arising from the value placed on confidentiality. Factors to be weighed are the public good to be served by disclosure against the client's right to privacy as well as the importance of a trust relationship for the client's well being. Clinical records of a psychiatric facility may be subpoenaed, but the attending doctor may state in writing that production of the records will likely result in harm to the treatment or eventual recovery of the patient or injury to a third party. In such a situation, the court has the discretion to grant privilege.[24]

In a case illustrating this point, a couple were involved in custody proceedings, in which the husband wanted the wife's psychiatric records to be disclosed in order to support his claim for custody of their two children, which he based on his wife's inability to care for them. Though the psychiatrist felt that to disclose would likely be harmful to the wife, the judge placed a higher value on potential harm to the children if all the facts were not known than on any resultant harm to the wife. Privilege was denied.[25]

The notion of a holder of a privilege, such as a patient or a client implies a one-to-one relationship between client and worker. Once the communication goes beyond them, for example, when other persons, such as a supervisor in an agency is involved, the privilege ceases to exist. When others are involved, such as participants in group therapy, a member of the group could be subpoenaed to give testimony about a communication heard from someone in the group. It could be said that all members of a therapy group are therapeutic agents of the others, but it is uncertain how a court would decide.

In regard to negotiations, settlement offers, and mediation, privilege may be extended to oral and written communications made for the purpose of settlement. Privilege may also extend to mediation when the agreement to mediate specifies that the mediation will be closed and is being conducted for the purpose of settlement. In this event, only the resulting agreement is reported, but the proceedings are protected, unless all parties give consent to disclose the discussions during mediation.

Social workers should bear in mind that, since privilege does not apply in relationships with clients, clients should be made aware of this fact. When giving testimony in court, moreover, questions should be answered honestly but economically and the same caution should be applied when preparing records. Workers should be aware that there is sometimes a legal obligation to disclose information. The two most significant situations are where there are reasonable grounds to believe that sexual harm to a child has occurred[26] and under the common law, where there is risk of imminent harm to a third party.

The landmark case in liability for failure to inform which is often cited in the United States and, to some degree, in Canada is *Tarasoff v. The Regents of the University of California* which was heard in 1976. A psychotherapist employed by the University Counselling Service was informed by a student client that he, the client, intended to kill his girlfriend. The therapist did not warn the parents of the girl who was murdered by the client. The parents brought a suit against the therapist and the University which succeeded in establishing that a duty to warn is paramount over therapist/client confidentiality.[27]

It is important that social work practitioners carry insurance that will provide protection against legal charges of malpractice, especially for those in private practice. While many social workers are protected through insurance carried by their agencies or institutions, personal liability insurance protection is advisable. The greatest protection, however, is prevention through informed and thoughtful practice and continuing professional education. Threshold guidelines include: knowing and following agency procedures, seeking supervision or consultation, respecting clients' rights to be informed and involved throughout the course of their engagement with the worker, and recognizing and respecting professional boundaries between worker and client in regard to relationship, intimacy and sexuality as legitimate protection for both client and worker. In addition, keeping accurate and timely records can also ensure some protection. In the final analysis, it is personal judgment that determines and governs professional competence and culpability.

Endnotes

1. Shanay Johnson Inquiry, April, 1997.
2. *R. v. C.C.A.S. of Metro Toronto et al — Globe & Mail*, July 8, 1997.
3. D. Besharov, *The Vulnerable Social Worker: Liability for Serving Children and Families* (Silverspring, Md.: National Assoc. of Social Workers, 1985).
4. *Globe & Mail* (April 28, 1984).
5. Frederic Reamer, "Malpractice Claims against Social Workers: First Facts", *Social Work*, Sept. 1995, Vol. 40, No. 5, 597.
6. See Table of Concordance.
7. Canadian Association of Social Workers, Ottawa, March 1995. See discussion in Chapter 26.
8. T.T. Daley, "Negligent Statements and the Social Worker" (1979), 10 R.F.L. (2d) 1 at 5.
9. *Hedley Byrne & Co. v. Heller & Partners*, [1964] A.C. 465, [1963] 2 All E.R. 575 at 594 (H.L.).
10. *B. (D.) v. Children's Aid Society of Durham Region* (1996), 30 C.C.L.T. (2d) 310 (Ont. C.A.)
11. Criminal Code, R.S.C. 1985, c. C-46, s. 215.
12. *Ibid.*, s. 218.
13. *Ibid.*, ss. 215(3) and 218.
14. *R. v. Leslie, Simpson and Fenemore*, Ont. Co. Ct., April 20, 1982.
15. *Ibid.*
16. See note 2, Heikamp C.C.A.S.
17. Robert Solomon Seminar material, Legal Survival for Counsellors and Therapists, Whitby, May 2, 1997.
18. *Ibid.*
19. Limitations Act, R.S.O. 1990, c. L.15.

20. *R. v. O'Connor*, [1995] 3 S.C.R. 263.
21. *R. v. Carosella*, [1997] S.C.J. No. 12.
22. *Jaffee v. Redmond*, 51 F.3d 1346 (7 Cir. 1995), S.C.T., U.S. Lexis 3879 (1996).
23. Canada Evidence Act, R.S.C. 1985, c. C-15, s. 4(3).
24. Mental Health Act, R.S.O. 1990, c. 262, s. 29.
25. *Gibbs v. Gibbs* (1985), 1 W.D.C.P. 6 (Ont. S.C.).
26. Child and Family Services Act, R.S.O. 1990, c. C-11.
27. *Tarasoff v. Regents of the University of California*, 17 Cal. 3d 425 (1976).

Bibliography

Alderson, Bill. "*R. v. O'Connor* and Bill C-76: Two Wrongs Do Not Make a Right", (Nov., 1996) 39 *Criminal Law Quarterly* 181-226.

Alexander, Rudolph Jr. "Social Workers and Immunity from Civil Lawsuits", *Social Work*, Vol. 40, No. 5, September, 1995, 648-54.

Barker, Robert L. and Douglas M. Bramson. *Forensic Social Work: Legal Aspects of Professional Practice* (New York: Haworth Press, 1993).

Besherov, Douglas. *The Vulnerable Social Worker* (Silverspring, Md.: NASW, 1985).

Besherov, Douglas and Susan Besherov. "Teaching about Liability", (1987/Nov./Dec.) *Social Work.*

Coughlan, Steven G. "Patients' Secrets and Threats to Third Parties: Where to Draw the Line" (1995) 15 *Health Law in Canada* 91-96.

Dickens, Bernard. "Implications of Health Professionals Legal Liability" (1993) 1 *Health Law Journal* 1-12.

Epp, John A. "Production of Confidential Records Held by a Third Party in Sexual Assault Cases: R. v. O'Connor", [1995] 4 S.C.R. 411, (1996-97) 28 *Ottawa Law Review* 191-202.

Hall-Finley, Elizabeth. *The Final Report of the Committee on Sexual Exploitation in Professional Relationships*, Edmonton: College of Physicians and Surgeons.

Mactavish, Anne L. "Mandatory Reporting of Sexual Abuse under the Regulated Professions Act" (1994) 14 *Health Law in Canada* 89-95.

Madelena v. Kuun (1987), 1 B.C.L.R. (2d) 90, 39 C.C.L.T. 81, 35 D.L.R. (4th) 222 (S.C.). One of only two cases reported in the Canadian high courts alleging social work negligence. In August, 1997, a social worker with the Catholic Children's Aid Society in Toronto was charged with criminal negligence in the death of an infant.

Poirer, Donald. "Social Worker Enforcement of Child Welfare Legislation: An Increasing Potential for Abuse of Power" (1986) 5 *Canadian Journal of Family Law* 16.

Reamer, Frederic. *Social Work Malpractice and Liability: Strategies for Prevention* (New York: Columbia University Press, 1994).

Watkins, S. "Confidentiality and Privileged Communication: Legal Dilemma for Family Therapists" (1989) 34:2 *Social Work* 113-36.

26

Self Regulation of Social Workers

The hallmarks of an autonomous profession include public accountability and the provision of protection through the establishment of minimum professional standards and mechanisms for review and discipline. Four essential aspects of provincial legislation are: a profession is regulated in the public interest; appropriate standards of practice are established; individuals have access to services; and, individuals are treated with sensitivity. Regulation can establish standards of service, which the public can expect to receive.[1] Ontario remains the only province in Canada that has not enacted legislation providing for some regulation of social workers.

Each of the other provincial jurisdictions, through legislation, has restricted the use of specific titles, such as Registered Social Worker (in Quebec, Travailleur Social Professionnel; in New Brunswick, Travailleur Social Immatricule) to persons who meet the specified criteria and has made it an offence to use the title without authorization. In Quebec, social workers are included among other professionals regulated by a common Professional Code. Other provinces have enacted legislation specific to professional social workers and protection of title.

STATUS OF SOCIAL WORK LEGISLATION IN CANADA: A SUMMARY

Alberta

Title

Social Work Profession Act (1991)

Type of Regulation

The Act provides for the restricted use of the title registered social worker or the abbreviation of such title.

Penalty

(a) for a first offence a fine of not more than $2,000.00;
(b) for a second offence a fine of not more than $4,000.00;
(c) for a third and every subsequent offence, a fine of not more than $6,000.00 or imprisonment for not more than six months or both that fine and imprisonment.

Governing Body

The Council of the AASW consists of:

(a) not fewer than six members elected in accordance with the bylaws;
(b) when the number of persons elected is not more than ten, two members of the public or when this number is more than ten, three members of the public appointed by the Lieutenant Governor in Council.

The Universities Co-ordinating Council grants or withdraws the designation "approved social work program" subject to approval of the Lieutenant Governor in Council. This Council also sets the term of practical experience to be completed, approves the examination, sets the requirements for a specialty, and assesses the academic qualifications and practical experience of persons who have not obtained their degree or diploma from an approved social work program.

Alberta Association of Social Workers

The Associations makes regulations and bylaws.

Qualifications

(a) (i) An undergraduate degree or diploma in social work from an approved social work program, or
(ii) A combination of academic qualifications and practical experience considered by the Universities Co-ordinating Council as substantially equivalent to the qualifications required for an undergraduate degree or diploma from an approved social work program.

(b) Completed any term of practical experience set by the Council;
(c) Passed the examination approved by the Council.

Discipline

A Discipline Committee composed of no fewer than four members of the Association appointed by the Council, and one member of the public appointed by the Lieutenant Governor in Council.

A Practice Review Board composed of not fewer than four members of the Association appointed by the Council.

Disciplinary measures by the Board include, but are not limited to, reprimand, suspension or cancellation of registration, and limitation of right to practice social work.

In addition, the payment of the costs of the hearing, a fine not exceeding $5,000.00 for each finding and $10,000.00 in aggregate for all findings.

Minister Responsible

The Minister of Labour

British Columbia

Title

Social Workers Act, R.S B.C. 1979, c. 389

Type of Regulation

The Act provides for the control of the use of the title registered social worker and limited control of the title social worker.

Penalty

A person who is not registered under the provision of this Act or who is not employed by Canada, the Province or other employers as provided under this Act, shall not represent himself or herself as a social worker or a registered social worker and whoever contravenes these provisions commits an offence and is liable to a fine of not more than $1,000.00.

Governing Body

The Board of Registration for social workers is composed of not more than 12 or less than 10 members appointed by the Lieutenant Governor in Council

(a) two persons who are not social workers and
(b) remainder to be R.S.W.s.

Qualifications

1) A bachelor's or master's degree in social work; or
2) a degree or certificate deemed by the Board to be equivalent to a master's degree in social work or the postgraduate degree in social work; or
3) to be a "registered social worker" or "professional social worker" in another province where the standards are not less than the minimum standards prescribed under this Act and regulations.

Discipline

A Practice Review Committee composed of four Registered Social Workers appointed by the Board.

Disciplinary measures by the Board include, but are not limited to, an educative warning, reprimand, limitation of right to practice social work, suspension or cancellation of membership.

Minister Responsible

The Minister of Social Services.

Manitoba

Title

The Manitoba Institute of Registered Social Workers Incorporation Act (1966)

Type of Regulation

The Act provides for voluntary registration and control of the designation "Registered Social Worker" or the initials corresponding to that designation or abbreviations.

Penalty

A fine of not less than $100.00 and not more than $200.00 and costs.

Governing Body

The Board of the Manitoba Institute of Registered Social Workers.

Manitoba Association of Social Workers

No relationship to this act.

Qualifications

BSW or MSW or an equivalent degree issued by a university or college accredited by the Council on Social Work Education, or which in the opinion of the head of the Faculty of the School of Social Work of the University of Manitoba is an accredited university or college.

Discipline

The Board may reprimand, suspend or cancel registration.

Minister Responsible

No Minister responsible.

New Brunswick

Title

New Brunswick Association of Social Workers Act (1988)

Type of Regulation

The Act provides for the regulation of practice and the control of the use of title social worker or registered social worker, or abbreviations.

Penalty

For a first offence a fine of not less than $500.00 and not more than $2,000.00 and costs, and for any subsequent offence a fine of not less than $1,000.00 and not more than $5,000.00 and costs or imprisonment for not more than six months, or both, and upon failure to pay a fine, imprisonment for not more than six months.

Governing Body

The Board of the NBASW consists of the president, vice-president, immediate past president, secretary and treasurer, and other members as established by the bylaws, and one other person, not a member of the association, appointed by the Minister of Health and Community Services from a list of three names submitted by the Association.

The Committee of Examiners consists of seven members of whom six are appointed by the Association and one by the Minister from a list of three names submitted by the Association.

New Brunswick Association of Social Workers

1) The Association regulates the practice of social work and governs its members.
2) The Association determines standards of professional conduct.
3) The Association appoints six members of the Committee of Examiners and submits names to the Minister for appointment of the seventh member.

Qualifications

A bachelor's, master's or doctoral degree in social work or the equivalent from a School of Social Work approved by the Committee;

— a person who has passed the examination prescribed by the Committee and has sufficient experience; or
— a person who is a registered member of an association of social workers approved by the Committee.

Discipline

A Complaints Committee composed of a member of the Board, who is chairperson, and two other members of the Association appointed by the Board.

A Discipline Committee composed of five persons, four members appointed by the Board and a non-member appointed by the Minister.

Disciplinary measures include, but are not limited to, revocation, suspension and limitation of right to practice social work, and a fine to a maximum of $5,000.00.

Minister Responsible

The Minister of Health and Community Services.

Newfoundland and Labrador

Title

Social Workers Act (1993)

Type of Regulation

The Act provides for the control of practice of social work and the use of the title social worker or registered social worker, or abbreviations of such titles.

Penalty

Section 54 provides for penalties for "holding out as a social worker". For a first offence a fine of not less than $500.00 and not more than $2,000.00 and costs and for subsequent offences a fine of not less than $1,000.00 and a term of imprisonment of not more than six months, or both a fine and imprisonment.

Governing Body

The Board of the Newfoundland and Labrador Association of Social Workers is composed of the president, a president elect, a secretary, a treasurer, a member who is a member of the Board of CASW, the immediate past president and other members as provided by the bylaws and a member appointed by the Minister. The Board of Directors is empowered to be the regulatory body and the professional association for social workers.

The committee of examiners consisting of six persons appointed by the Board and a seventh person appointed by the Minister.

Qualifications

A bachelor's, master's or doctoral degree or other equivalent education in social work from an educational institution approved by the committee of examiners and completion of the examination prescribed.

Temporary registration is provided for up to seven years to persons without social work degrees who are asked to work in areas of the province where a duly qualified social worker is not available. To remain registered a temporary registrant must agree to acquire a social work degree within seven years of the initial registration.

Discipline

A Discipline Committee composed of five members of the association appointed by the Board.

Disciplinary measures by the Board include, but are not limited to, reprimand, revocation, suspension and limitation of right to practice social work.

Minister Responsible

The Minister of Social Services.

Nova Scotia

Title

Social Workers Act (1993)

Type of Regulation

The Act provides for the control of practice and of the use of title social worker or registered social worker, or abbreviations.

Penalty

For a first offence a fine of not less than $500.00 and costs, and for any subsequent offence a fine of not less than $1,000.00 and costs and a term of imprisonment of not more than six months, or both.

Governing Body

The Council of the NSASW consists of the president, vice-president, secretary, treasurer, immediate past president and other members as provided by the bylaws and the chair of the Board of Examiners.

The Board of Examiners consists of:

(a) seven social workers appointed by the Council who represent the diversity of various fields of social work practice and who reflect the sex, racial, and ethnic composition of the Association, one of whom is teaching at an approved school of social work;
(b) three persons appointed by the Governor in Council who are neither social workers nor social worker candidates.

Nova Scotia Association of Social Workers

— The Association regulates the practice of social work and governs the profession.
— The Association makes bylaws and regulations.
— The Association appoints seven members of the Board of Examiners.

Qualifications

A doctoral or master's degree or a graduate-level diploma in social work from an approved faculty of social work and

(i) has completed two years of experience,
(ii) has passed the examination required by the Board.

A bachelor's degree in social work from an approved faculty of social work and

(i) has completed a least three years of experience;
(ii) has passed the examination required by the Board.

Is a registered member in good standing of an association of social workers approved by the Council.

Discipline

A Complaints Committee composed of three members of the Board, one of whom shall be a person appointed to the Board by the Governor in Council.

A Discipline Committee composed of five persons appointed by the Board, three of whom are members of the Board, one a member of the Association, and one who is appointed to the Board by the Governor in Council.

Disciplinary measures include, but are not limited to, revocation, suspension and limitation of right to practice social work.

Minister Responsible

No minister responsible.

Ontario

Title

No Act. The Ontario College of Certified Social Workers was established under the OASW Bylaws (The Ontario Government has committed itself to introduce an Act to regulate the social work profession).

Type of Regulation

Voluntary registration. Only members of the College can use the title Certified Social Worker.

Penalty

No legal sanction.

Governing Body

The Council of the OCCSW is composed of a chairperson, secretary-treasurer, a registrar, and 18 councillors of whom four are members of the public.

Ontario Association of Social Workers

No legal relationship.

Qualifications

— A university degree in social work from an accredited School of Social Work in Canada or the U.S.A. or a degree deemed equivalent by the Canadian Association of Social Workers;
— two professional references;
— successful completion of a three-hour multiple choice examination which tests general social work knowledge in the areas of human growth and development; social welfare policy; social work practice with individuals, families, small groups and communities; social work research; and ethics and values;
— successful completion of an oral examination which tests practice

knowledge. A panel of three examiners tests each candidate in the areas of problem identification and strategy formulation, strategy implementation, openness to consultation and other perspectives, evidence of self-awareness, sensitivity to social issues and application of social work values and ethics.

Requirements for ongoing membership include demonstration of continuing competence through professional development and recertification every five years.

Discipline

A Complaints Committee composed of not less than nine persons, of whom six are college members. The chairperson is a member of the council. This committee investigates complaints.

A Discipline Committee composed of not less than nine persons, of whom six are college members. The chairperson is a member of the council. This committee conducts hearings and imposes sanctions.

Minister Responsible

No Minister responsible.

Prince Edward Island

Title

Social Work Act (1988)

Type of Regulation

The Act provides for the control of the practice of social work and the use of the title social worker or registered social worker, or abbreviations of such titles.

Penalty

A fine not exceeding $500.00.

Governing Body

The P.E.I. Social Work Registration Board is composed of five members nominated by the P.E.I. Association of Social Workers and appointed by the Minister:

a) four are registered social workers and members of the Association; and
b) one person to represent the perspective of the general public.

Prince Edward Island Association of Social Workers

The Executive of the Association consists of a president, vice- president, secretary, treasurer and other members as prescribed by the bylaws.

— Nominates members to the Board.

Qualifications

a) a degree from a School of Social Work recognized by the Board;
b) practical training as prescribed;
c) professional competency demonstrated by examination;
d) good standing under any existing legislation;
e) currency of professional knowledge and skills.

Discipline

The Board serves as a complaints and discipline committee. (The role of the Board in this respect is under review and changes are anticipated within the next year.)

Disciplinary measures by the Board include, but are not limited to, reprimand, suspension, cancellation and limitation of right to practice social work.

Minister Responsible

The Minister of Health and Social Services.

Quebec

Title

Code des professions (1973, Amended 1974, 1975, 1994)

Type of Regulation

The Act provides for control of the use of the title social worker or other title which suggests this designation or an equivalent one, or the use of the initials P.S.W., T.S.P., S.W., T.S.

Penalty

A fine of at least $600.00.

Governing Body

Ordre Professionnel des travailleurs sociaux du Québec:

— Board of 20 directors elected on a regional basis;
— Four directors appointed by the Office des professions du Quebec.

Ordre Professionnel des travailleurs sociaux

— The main function of the Order is to ensure the protection of the public and to supervise the practice of its members.
— The Order stipulates the skills and conditions required to practice.
— It appoints the Inspection and Discipline Committees.

Qualifications

BSW or MSW or equivalent diploma if obtained outside the province.

Discipline

A Professional Inspection Committee composed of not less than three members appointed by the Bureau.

A Discipline Committee composed of at least two members appointed by the Bureau and one member appointed by the Government, who shall be a lawyer of ten years experience and who is the chairperson.

The Discipline Committee may impose the following penalties but is not limited to: reprimand, temporary or permanent striking off the roll, a fine of not less than $600.00 and not more than $6,000.00 for each offence, the revocation of the permit, the revocation of the specialist certificate, restriction or suspension of the right to engage in professional activities.

Minister Responsible

The Minister of Justice.

Saskatchewan

Title

The Social Workers Act (1993)

Type of Regulation

The Act provides for the control of the use of the title social worker.

Penalty

For a first offence a fine of not more than $2,000.00; for a second offence, not more than $4,000.00; for each subsequent offence, not more than $6,000.00 or imprisonment for not more than six months or both that fine and imprisonment.

Governing Body

The Council of SASW consists of:

a) the number of members prescribed in the bylaws, but not less than five, elected by the members; and
b) a person appointed by the Lieutenant Governor in Council.

According to the bylaws, the officers are the past president, the president, the president-elect, the secretary, and the treasurer. The Council consists of seven persons including two members at large and the officers of the association.

The Board of Examiners consists of eight persons appointed by the council:

a) six appointed from among the members of the association who are practising social workers; and
b) two who are representative of the cultural or professional interests in the community.

Saskatchewan Association of Social Workers

— The Assocation establishes, maintains and develops standards of

knowledge, skills and competence for the purpose of serving and protecting the public interest.
— The Association makes bylaws.
— The Association appoints eight members of the Board of Examiners.

Qualifications

A certificate or a bachelor's, master's or doctoral degree in social work from a university approved in the bylaws.

A person who applies prior to the expiration of three years after the coming of this section, and on the date of the application has been employed in the practice of social work for at least five years, two years of which were within the five years preceding the date of application.

Discipline

A Discipline Committee composed of five members of the association appointed by the Board.

Disciplinary measures by the discipline committee include, but are not limited to, expulsion, suspension and limitation of the right to practice social work, or reprimand. In addition, the discipline committee may order that the member pay:

(i) a fine not exceeding $2,000.00 for each finding and $6,000.00 in the aggregate for all findings; and
(ii) the costs of the investigation and hearing and other related costs.

Minister Responsible

The Minister of Social Services.[2]

It is notable that Newfoundland and Labrador has built into their legislation a way to provide temorary registration to those persons practising social work without the requisite degree qualifications. This legislation specifically refers to areas where duly qualified social workers might not be available, but the concept can be applied to other situations. The Act grants permission to those persons to use the title and gives them seven years in which to obtain a degree in order to remain registered. Given such inclusion, it might be that some agencies or services would provide incentives to these persons to facilitate their completion of the educational requisites in the form of financial aid or release time and that educational institutions would provide part time study programs.

CODE OF ETHICS

The Ontario Association of Social Workers has set educational standards for membership[3] and requires members to abide by a code of ethics and to pass an examination, but membership in the association is voluntary.

Each provincial social work association has a Code of Ethics which forms the basis for the standard of professional conduct and practice for social workers. Many social workers while wishing to comply with the Code of Ethics, may fail to appreciate their significance. In the event of a complaint against a social worker which concerns their professional conduct, the Complaint or Discipline Committee or Board of the respective provincial professional body will refer to the Code of Ethics as the primary standard against which the act complained of will be measured. Social workers are urged to read their Code and to ensure that their professional behaviour falls within its boundaries.

The Canadian Association of Social Workers Code of Ethics incorporates the basic concepts contained in most Canadian professional associations' codes. In its preamble, it states that the profession of social work is founded on humanitarian and egalitarian ideals. Social workers believe in the intrinsic worth and dignity of every human being and are committed to the values of acceptance, self-determination and respect of individuality. They believe in the obligation of all people, individually and collectively, to provide resources, services, and opportunities for the overall benefit of humanity. The culture of individuals, families, groups, communities and nations has to be respected without prejudice.[4]

The Social Work Code of Ethics declares the first obligation of social workers is to maintain the best interest of the client. Under the heading of Professional Practice Conflicts, the Code states that "if a conflict arises in professional practice, the standards declared in this Code take precedence. Conflicts of interest may occur because of demands from the general public, workplace, organizations or clients. In all cases, if the ethical duties and obligations or ethical responsibilities of this Code would be compromised, the social worker must act in a manner consistent with this Code."[5]

We have observed that some lawyers believe that social workers are not truly free professionals because they may be employed by public, private or sectarian agencies and so may confront a conflict between client best interest and employer concerns. Social workers, like lawyers and other professionals may be influenced by factors which can compromise strict adherence to ethical behaviour, but it is clear that social workers, like lawyers, are held accountable to keep the best interests of clients as a primary responsibility.

Social Work Code of Ethics

Ethical Duties and Obligations

1. A social worker shall maintain the best interest of the client as the primary professional obligation.
2. A social worker shall carry out her or his professional duties and obligations with integrity and objectivity.
3. A social worker shall have and maintain competence in the provision of a social work service to a client.
4. A social worker shall not exploit the relationship with a client for personal benefit, gain or gratification.
5. A social worker shall protect the confidentiality of all information acquired from the client or others regarding the client and the client's family during the professional relationship unless

   (a) the client authorizes in writing the release of specified information,
   (b) the information is released under the authority of a statute or an order of a court of competent jurisdiction, or
   (c) otherwise authorized by this Code.

6. A social worker who engages in another profession, occupation, affiliation or calling shall not allow these outside interests to affect the social work relationship with the client.
7. A social worker in private practice shall not conduct the business of provision of social work services for a fee in a manner that discredits the profession or diminishes the public's trust in the profession.

Ethical Responsibilities

8. A social worker shall advocate for workplace conditions and policies consistent with the Code.
9. A social worker shall promote excellence in the social work profession.
10. A social worker shall advocate change

    (a) in the best interest of the client, and
    (b) for the overall benefit of society, the environment and the global community.[6]

Ontario has no statutory provision requiring that social workers be registered or certified as a condition of practice. Impetus to the development of a statutory regulatory body was provided by a report written as an outcome of the inquest into the death of an abused child.[7] A significant recommendation was that social workers be made legally accountable for their actions in regard to clients through the enactment of legislation which would then establish and regulate standards of practice.

There is some concern that the establishment of an Ontario statutory regulatory body would exclude many persons who provide some direct social services or who are involved in policy or programme formulation and implementation. Since the educational entry level requirement of the College is a B.S.W., those persons who perform social work functions but hold no social work degree could be excluded and the public would not be protected by legislation that applied only to members of the College. It would seem reasonable that statutory title protection for professional social workers be established and that the province seek ways to extend coverage and accountability to certain specified persons who are performing social work functions but who are not members of the College.

ONTARIO COLLEGE OF CERTIFIED SOCIAL WORKERS

In 1982, the Ontario College of Certified Social Workers was created, which, though still a voluntary membership body, serves as a professional regulatory body on a non-statutory basis. It certifies social workers as competent to practise at a defined level if they meet the requirements prescribed by the College in regard to education, experience, examination and peer review. The College then publishes the names of registered persons and acts to protect the public by investigating allegations of misconduct and recommending disciplinary action where it has been determined that ethical or practice standards have been breached.[8]

In the next decade, social workers will move toward innovative models of service delivery and create new settings which will be needed to provide comprehensive service both at the neighbourhood level and in agencies and institutions. The planners and providers of these programmes will represent many professions and diverse belief systems which will require high levels of interministerial and interdisciplinary cooperation. Alternate forms of litigation for the resolution of many social/legal issues will proliferate. It is essential that social workers protect their professional identity and expertise in order to collaborate with other professionals and service providers as well as to provide the public with assurance of accountability through the establishment of rigorous and accessible statutory regulation.

Endnotes

1. Dr. Robert Kyle, Commissioner and Medical Officer of Health for the Regional Municipality of Durham.
2. Canadian Association of Social Workers, June, 1996.
3. The baseline degree of entry is a B.S.W.
4. *Teaching and Learning about Human Rights: A Manual for Schools of Social Work and the Social Work Profession*, U.N. Centre for Human Rights, Co-operation with International Federation of Social Workers and International Association of Schools of Social Workers, United Nations, New York, 1992.
5. *Social Work Code of Ethics*, Canadian Association of Social Workers, January 1, 1994, 7.
6. *Ibid.*, 9.
7. *Kim Anne Popen Report.* Ontario Government Publications, October, 1982.
8. For a comprehensive review of legislation relevant to social work practice across Canada, see "Provincial Reports", (1984) 52:1 The Social Worker 22-38.

Bibliography

Andrae, Dan. "President's Message: Questions Regarding Social Work Regulatory Legislation", OASW Newsmagazine, Summer, 1996, pp. 4-5.

TABLES OF CONCORDANCE

Topic	Alberta	British Columbia	Manitoba	New Brunswick	Newfoundland	Nova Scotia	Ontario	Prince Edward Is.	Quebec	Saskatchewan	N.W.T. Yukon
Adoption	Adult Adoption Act, S.A. 1994, c. A-2.3 Child Welfare Act, R.S.A. 1984, c. C-8.1, Part 6	Adoption Act, R.S.B.C. 1996, c. 5	Child Welfare Act, S.M. 1974, c. 30 Child and Family Services Act, S.M. 1985-86, c. 8	Family Services Act, S.N.B. 1980, c. F-2.2, Part V	Adoption of Children Act, R.S.N. 1990, c. A-3	Children and Family Services Act, S.N.S. 1990, c. 5	Child and Family Services Act, R.S.O. 1990, c. C.11, Part VII	Adoption Act, S.P.E.I. 1992, c. 1	Art. 543-584 C.C.Q.	Adoption Act, S.S. 1989-90, c. A-5.1	Children's Act, R.S.Y. 1986, c. 22 Child Wewlfare Act, R.S.N.W.T. 1988, c. C-6
Children Who Break the Law	Child Welfare Act, R.S.A. 1980, c. C-8.1, Part 4 Child Welfare Amendment Act, 1988, S.A. 1988, c. 15	Correction Act, R.S.B.C. 1996, c. 74 Young Offenders (British Columbia) R.S.B.C. 1996, c. 494	Child and Family Services Act, S.M. 1985-86, c. 8	Training School Act, R.S.N.B. 1973, c. T-11 Custody & Detention of Young Persons Act, S.N.B. 1985, c. C-40	Young Offenders Act (applicable to all provinces)	Children and Family Services Act, S.N.S. 1990, c. 5	Children and Family Services Act, S.N.S. 1990, c. C.11, Part IV	Child Status Act, R.S.P.E.I. 1988, c. C-6	Youth Protection Act, R.S.Q. c. P-34.1	Age of Majority Act, R.S.S. 1978, c. A-6 Private Vocational Schools Regulation Act, S.S. 1995, c. P.26.2	Young Offenders Act, R.S.N.W.T. 1988, c. Y-1
Form of Marriage	Marriage Act, R.S.A. 1980, c. M-6 Marriage Amendment Act, S.A. 1988, c. 30	Marriage Act, R.S.B.C. 1996, c. 282	Marriage Act, R.S.M. 1987, c. M50	Marriage Act, R.S.N.B. 1973, c. M-3	Solemnization of Marriage Act, R.S.N. 1990, c. S-19	Solemnization of Marriage Act, R.S.N.S. 1989, c. 436	Marriage Act, R.S.O. 1990, c. M.3	Marriage Act, R.S.P.E.I. 1988, c. M-3	Art. 356-377 C.C.Q.	Marriage Act, S.S. 1995, c. M-4.1	Marriage Act, R.S.Y. 1986, c. 110 Marriage Act, R.S.N.W.T. 1988, c. M-4
Education	Department of Education Act, R.S.A. 1980, c. D-17 School Act, S.A. 1988, c. S-3.1	School Act, R.S.B.C. 1996, c. 412	Public Schools Act, R.S.M. 1987, c. P250	Schools Act, S.N.B. 1990, c. S-5.1	Schools Act, R.S.N. 1990, c. S-12		Education Act, R.S.O. 1990, c. E-2	School Act, S.P.E.I. 1993, c. 35	Education Act, R.S.Q. c. I-13.3	Education Act, S.S. 1995, c. E-0.2	Education Act, R.S.N.W.T. 1980, c. E-1

Topic	Alberta	British Columbia	Manitoba	New Brunswick	Newfoundland	Nova Scotia	Ontario	Prince Edward Is.	Quebec	Saskatchewan	N.W.T. Yukon
Human Rights Canadian Human Rights Act, R.S.C. 1985, c. H-6	Alberta Bill of Rights, R.S.A. 1980, c. A-16 Individual's Rights Protection Act, R.S.A. 1980, c. I-2	Human Rights Code, R.S.B.C. 1996, c. 210 Civil Rights Protection Act, R.S.B.C. 1996, c. 49	Human Rights Act, R.S.M. 1987, c. H175	Human Rights Act, R.S.N.B. 1973, c. H-11	Human Rights Code, R.S.N. 1990, c. H-14	Human Rights Act, R.S.N.S. 1989, c. 24 Blind Persons' Rights Act, R.S.N.S. 1989, c. 40	Human Rights Code, R.S.O. 1990, c. H.19	Human Rights Act, R.S.P.E.I. 1988, c. H-12	Charter of Human Rights and Freedoms, R.S.Q. c. C-12	Saskatchewan Human Rights Code, S.S. 1979, c. S-24.1	Fair Practices Act, R.S.Y. 1986, c. 62 Fair Practices Act, R.S.N.W.T. 1988, c. F-2 Human Rights Act, R.S.Y. 1986, c. 11
Evidence Canada Evidence Act, R.S.C. 1985, c. C-5	Alberta Evidence Act, R.S.A. 1980, c. A-21	Evidence Act, R.S.B.C. 1996, c. 124	Manitoba Evidence Act, R.S.M. 1987, c. E-150	Evidence Act, R.S.N.B. 1973, c. E-11	Evidence Act, R.S.N. 1990, c. E-16	Evidence Act, R.S.N.S. 1989, c. 154	Evidence Act, R.S.O. 1990, c. E.23	Evidence Act, R.S.P.E.I. 1988, c. E-11	Art. 2803-2810 C.C.Q.	Saskatchewan Evidence Act, R.S.S. 1978, c. S-16	Evidence Act, R.S.Y. 1986, c. 57 Evidence Act, R.S.N.W.T. 1988, c. E-8
Child Welfare (Child Protection, Children Born Outside Marriage)	Child Welfare Act, S.A. 1984, c. C-8.1 Parentage and Maintenance Act, S.A. 1990, c. P-0.7	Infants Act, R.S.B.C. 1996, c. 223 Family Maintenance Enforcement Act, R.S.B.C. 1996, c. 127 Child, Family and Community Service Act, R.S.B.C. 1996, c. 46 Child, Youth and Family Advocacy Act, R.S.B.C. 1996, c. 47	Child and Family Services Act, S.M. 1985-86, c. 8 Family Maintenance Act, R.S.M. 1987, c. F20	Child and Family Services and Family Relations Act, S.N.B. 1980, c. C-2.1	Child Welfare Act, R.S.N. 1990, c. C-12 Children's Law Act, R.S.N. 1990, c. C-13	Children and Family Services Act, S.N.S. 1990, c. C.5	Children's Law Reform Act, R.S.O. 1990, c. C.12, Part II Child and Family Services Act, R.S.O. 1990, c. C.11, Part III	Family and Child Services Act, R.S.P.E.I. 1988, c. F-2 Child Status Act, R.S.P.E.I. 1988, c. C-6	Youth Protection Act, R.S.Q. c. P-34.1 Art. 523-542 C.C.Q.	Child and Family Services Act, S.S. 1989-90, c. C-7.2 Children's Law Act, S.S. 1990-91, c. C-8.1, Part VI	Children's Act, R.S.Y. 1986, c. 22 Child Welfare Act, R.S.N.W.T. 1988, c. C-16

Topic	Alberta	British Columbia	Manitoba	New Brunswick	Newfoundland	Nova Scotia	Ontario	Prince Edward Is.	Quebec	Saskatchewan	N.W.T. Yukon
Family Law Matters (Maintenance, Property Division, Custody, Enforcement)	Domestic Relations Act, R.S.A. 1980, c. D-37 Matrimonial Property Act, R.S.A. 1980, c. M-9 Extra-provincial Enforcement of Custody Orders Act, R.S.A. 1980, c. E-17 Maintenance Enforcement Act, S.A. 1985, c. M-0.5 Maintenance Order Act, R.S.A. 1980, c. M-1 Reciprocal Enforcement of Maintenance Orders Act, R.S.A. 1980, c. R-7.1 International Child Abduction Act, S.A. 1986, c. I-6.5	Family Relations Act, R.S.B.C. 1996, c. 128 FamilyMaintenance Enforcement Act, R.S.B.C. 1996, c. 127	Family Maintenance Act, R.S.M. 1987, c. F20 Parents' Maintenance Act, R.S.M. 1987, c. P10 Child Custody Enforcement Act, R.S.M. 1987, c. C360 Reciprocal Enforcement of Maintenance Orders Act, R.S.M.. 1987, c. M-20 Dower Act, R.S.M. 1988, c. D-100 Marital Property Act, R.S.M. 1987, c. M45 Married Women's Property Act, R.S.M. 1987, c. M70	Child and Family Services and Family Relations Act, S.N.B. 1980, c. C-2.1 Reciprocal Enforcement of Maintenance Orders Act, S.N.B. 1985, c. R-4.01 Extra-Provincial Custody Orders Enforcement Act, S.N.B. 1977, c. E-15 Marital Property Act, S.N.B. 1980, c. M-1.1	Family Relief Act, R.S.N. 1990, c. F-3 Family Law Act, R.S.N. 1990, c. F-2 Support Orders Enforcement Act, R.S.N. 1990, c. S-31 Children's Law Act, R.S.N. 1990, c. C-13	Family Maintenance Act, R.S.N.S. 1989, c. 160 Matrimonial Property Act, R.S.N.S. 1989, c. 275 Maintenance Orders Enforcement Act, R.S.N.S. 1989, c. 268 Reciprocal Enforcement of Custody Orders Act, R.S.N.S. 1989, c. 387	Children's Law Reform Act, R.S.O. 1990, c. C.12 Family Law Act, R.S.O. 1990, c. F.3 Reciprocal Enforcement of Support Orders Act, R.S.O. 1990, c. R.7 Family Responsibility and Support Arrears Enforcement Act, S.O. 1996, c. 31	Family Law Act, S.P.E.I. 1995, c. 12 Family and Child Services Act, R.S.P.E.I. 1988, c. F-2 Maintenance Enforcement Act, R.S.P.E.I. 1988, c. M-1 Reciprocal Enforcement of Maintenance Orders Act, R.S.P.E.I. 1988, c. R-7	Act Respecting Reciprocal Enforcement of Maintenance Orders, R.S.Q. c. E-19 Art. 597-612 C.C.Q. Art. 431-492 C.C.Q. Art. 401-430 C.C.Q. Art. 585-596 C.C.Q. An Act to Facilitate the Payment of Support, R.S.Q. c. P-2.2 Act Respecting the Civil Aspects of International and Interprovincial Child Abduction, R.S.Q. c. A-23.01	Children's Law Act, S.S. 1990-91, c. C-8.1 Family Maintenance Act, S.S. 1990-91, c. F-6.1 Parents' Maintenance Act, R.S.S. 1978, c. P-1 International Child Abduction Act, S.S. 1986, c. I-10.1 Matrimonial Property Act, S.S. 1979, c. M-6.1 Enforcement of Maintenance Orders Act, S.S. 1984-85-86, c. E-9.2 Reciprocal Enforcement of Maintenance Orders Act, S.S. 1996, c. R-4.2	Family Property and Support Act, R.S.Y. 1986, c. 63 Maintenance and Custody Orders Enforcement Act, R.S.Y. 1986, c. 108 Reciprocal Enforcement of Maintenance Orders Act, R.S.Y. 1986, c. 148 Maintenance Act, R.S.N.W.T. 1988, c. M-1 Maintenance Orders Enforcement Act, R.S.N.W.T. 1988, c. M-2 Extra-Territorial Custody Orders Enforcement Act, R.S.N.W.T. 1988, c. E-12

Topic	Alberta	British Columbia	Manitoba	New Brunswick	Newfoundland	Nova Scotia	Ontario	Prince Edward Is.	Quebec	Saskatchewan	N.W.T. Yukon
Family Law Matters (*continued*)											Matrimonial Property Act, R.S.N.W.T. 1988, c. M-6
											Domestic Relations Act, R.S.N.W.T. 1988, c. D-8
											Children's Act, R.S.Y. 1986, c. 22
											Maintenance and Custody Orders Enforcement Act R.S.Y. 1986, c. 108
											Family Property and Support Act, R.S.Y. 1986, c. 63
											Reciprocal Enforcement of Maintenance Orders Act, R.S.Y. 1986, c.148

Topic	Alberta	British Columbia	Manitoba	New Brunswick	Newfoundland	Nova Scotia	Ontario	Prince Edward Is.	Quebec	Saskatchewan	N.W.T. Yukon
Landlord and Tenant	Landlord and Tenant Act, R.S.A. 1980, c. L-6	Residential Tenancy Act, R.S.B.C. 1996, c. 406 Rent Distress Act, R.S.B.C. 1996, c. 403	Landlord and Tenant Act, R.S.M. 1987, c. L70 Reenacted Statutes of Manitoba Act, S.M. 1987, c. 9, Sched. A. Pt. II Residential Rent Regulation Act, R.S.M. 1987, c. R118	Landlord and Tenant Act, R.S.N.B. 1973, c. L-1 Residential Rent Review Act, 1983, S.N.B. 1983, c. R-10.11	Residential Tenancxies Act, R.S.N. 1990, c. R-14	Residential Tenancies Act, R.S.N.S. 1989, c. 401 Overholding Tenants Act, R.S.N.S. 1989, c. 329 Rental Property Conversion Act, R.S.N.S. 1989, c. 399 Rent Review Act, R.S.N.S. 1989, c. 398 Tenancies and Distress for Rent Act, R.S.N.S. 1989, c. 464	Residential Rent Regulations Act, R.S.O. 1990, c. R.29 Landlord and Tenant Act, R.S.O. 1990, c. L.7	Landlord and Tenant Act, R.S.P.E.I. 198, c. L-4 Rent Review Act, R.S.P.E.I. 1988, c. R-13	Art. 1851-2000 C.C.Q.	Landlord and Tenant Act, R.S.S. 1978, c. L-6 Residential Tenancies Act, R.S.S. 1978, c. R-22 Distress Act, R.S.S. 1978, c. D-31	Landlord and Tenant Act, R.S.Y. 1986, c. 98 Residential Tenancies Act, R.S.N.W.T. 1988, c. R-5
Legal Aid		Legal Services Society Act, R.S.B.C. 1996, c. 256	Legal Aid Services Society of Manitoba Act, R.S.M. 1987, c. L105	Legal Aid Act, R.S.N.B. 1973, c. L-2	Legal Aid Act, R.S.N. 1990, c L-11	Legal Aid Act, R.S.N.S. 1989, c. 252	Legal Aid Act, R.S.O. 1990, c. L.9		Legal Aid Act, R.S.Q. c. A-14	Legal Aid Act, S.S. 1983, c. L-9.1	Legal Services Act, R.S.N.W.T. 1988, c. L-4 Legal Services Society Act, R.S.Y. 1986, c. 101

Topic	Alberta	British Columbia	Manitoba	New Brunswick	Newfoundland	Nova Scotia	Ontario	Prince Edward Is.	Quebec	Saskatchewan	N.W.T. Yukon
Social Work	Social Workers Act, R.S.A. 1980, c. S-17	Social Workers Act, R.S.B.C. 1996, c. 432	An Act to Incorporate the Manitoba Institute of Registered Social Workers, S.M. 1996, c. 104	An Act to Incorporate the New Brunswick Association of Social Workers, S.N.B. 1988, c. 78	Social Workers Registration Act, R.S.N. 1990, c. S-8	Social Workers Act, R.S.N.S. 1989, c. 434		Social Work Act, R.S.P.E.I. 1988, c. S-5	Act Respecting Health Services and Social Services, R.S.Q. c. S-4.2 Professioal Code, R.S.Q. c. C-26	Social Workers Act, S.S. 1993, c. S-52.1	
Mental Health	Mental Health Act, R.S.A. 1980, c. M-13	Mental Health Act, R.S.B.C. 1996, c. 288	Mental Health Act, R.S.M. 1987, c. M110 Mental Health Amendment Act, S.M. 1988-89, c. 24	Mental Health Act, R.S.N.B. 1973, c. M-10	Mental Health Act, R.S.N. 1990, c. M-9	Hospitals Act, R.S.N.S. 1989, c. C.208 Nova Scotia Hospital Act, R.S.N.S. 1989, c. 313 Incompetent Persons Act, R.S.N.S. 1989, c. 218 Adult Protection Amendment Act, R.S.N.S. 1989, c. 2	Mental Health Act, R.S.O. 1990, c. M.7	Mental Health Act, R.S.P.E.I. 1988, c. M-6 Adult Protection Act, R.S.P.E.I. 1988, c. A-5	Mental Patients Protection Act, R.S.Q. c. P-41 Art. 11-15 C.C.Q.	Mentally Disordered Persons Act, R.S.S. 1978, c. M-14 Mental Health Services Act, S.S. 1984-85-86, c. M-13.1	Mental Health Act, R.S.Y. 1986, c. 115 Mental Health Act, R.S.N.W.T. 1988, c. M-10

COURTS (BY NAME, AUTHORITY AND APPOINTMENT OF JUDGES)

Name of Court	Enabling Statutes	Judges Appointed Under	Alberta	British Columbia	Manitoba	New Brunswick	Newfoundland	Nova Scotia	Ontario	Prince Edward Island	Quebec	Saskatchewan	Yukon & N.W.T.
A. FEDERAL COURTS													
Supreme Court of Canada	s. 101, B.N.A. Act Supreme Court Act	Minister of Justice (Fed.)											
Federal Court —Appeal Division —Trial Division	s. 101, B.N.A. Act Federal Court Act	Minister of Justice (Fed.)											
B. PROVINCIAL SUPERIOR COURTS													
Appeal Court	s. 91(14) B.N.A. Act Judicature Act (Prov.)	s. 96 B.N.A. Act	Appellate Division of the Supreme Court (Court of Appeal)	Court of Appeal	Court of Appeal	Court of Appeal	Court of Appeal	Appeal Division of the Supreme Court	Court of Appeal	Supreme Court	Court of Appeal	Court of Appeal	Court of Appeal
Superior Trial Court			Court of Queen's Bench	Supreme Court	Court of Queen's Bench	Court of Queen's Bench	Supreme Court (Trial Division)	Supreme Court (Trial Division)	General Division	Supreme Court	Superior Court	Court of Queen's Bench	Supreme Court
Divisions of the Superior Court			↓	↓	Matrimonial Causes	Divorce & Matrimonial Causes	↓	Divorce & Matrimonial Causes	Divisional Court Small Claims Court	↓	↓	↓	↓
			▼	▼	▼		▼		Provincial Division	▼	▼	▼	▼

C. PROVINCIAL, COUNTY, OR DISTRICT AND SURROGATE COURTS

County or District Courts	s. 92(14) B.N.A. Act County or District Courts Act (Prov.)	s. 96 B.N.A. Act (Except Quebec)	District Court	County Court	County Court	County Court	District Court Unified Family Court	County Court	County or District Court	Division of the Supreme Court	Court of the Sessions of the Peace (Similar to District Courts)	District Court	
Surrogate Court	Surrogate Courts Act (Prov.)	s. 96 B.N.A. Act	Surrogate Court Division of Court of Queen's Bench		Division of County Courts				Surrogate Court	Division of Supreme Court			

D. PROVINCIAL COURTS

Criminal	Provincial Statute	Provincial Statute	Criminal Division		Provincial Judges Court (Criminal) Division	Juvenile Court	Juvenile Court	Provincial Magistrates Court			Youth Court Provincial Court		
Family			Family & Juvenile Division	Provincial Court	Provincial Judges Court (Family Division)	Provincial Court	Provincial Court	Family Court	Provincial Court (Family Division)	Provincial Courts	Social Welfare Court Youth Court	Provincial Courts	Courts of Justices of the Peace
Civil			Small Claims Court						Provincial Court (Civil Division)		Small Claims Court		
Provincial and Municipal Offences			Criminal Division		Provincial Judges Court (Traffic Division)		Traffic Court (St. John's)	Provincial Magistrates Court	Provincial Offences Court		Municipal Court and Court of Justices of the Peace		

SOURCES

Gall, G.L., *The Canadian Legal System*, 2d ed. Toronto: Carswell Co., 1983, Chapters 5 and 7.

Bracken, Susan, ed. *Canadian Almanac and Director, 1984*, Toronto: Copp Clark Pitman Ltd., 1984.

Index